THE PREPPER'S ULTIMATE FOOD STORAGE GUIDE

Your Complete Resource to Create a Long-Term, Lifesaving Supply of Nutritious, Shelf-Stable Meals, Snacks, and More

Julie Languille • Daisy Luther • Tess Pennington • Shelle Wells

Part 1 adapted from *Prepper's Food Storage* by Julie Languille
Part 2 adapted from *The Prepper's Cookbook* by Tess Pennington
Part 3 adapted from *The Prepper's Canning Guide* by Daisy Luther
Part 4 adapted from *Prepper's Dehydrator Handbook* by Shelle Wells

Published in the U.S. by
Ulysses Press
P.O. Box 3440
Berkeley, CA 94703
www.ulyssespress.com

ISBN: 978-1-64604-154-1
Library of Congress Control Number: 2020946739

Printed in China through Regent Publishing Ltd.

10 9 8 7 6 5 4 3 2 1

Front cover design: what!design @ whatweb.com
Cover artwork: © Madlen/shutterstock.com

IMPORTANT NOTE TO READERS: This book is independently authored and published and no sponsorship or endorsement of this book by, and no affiliation with, any trademarked brands or other products mentioned within is claimed or suggested. All trademarks that appear in ingredient lists and elsewhere in this book belong to their respective owners and are used here for informational purposes only. The authors and publisher encourage readers to patronize the quality brands mentioned in this book.

Contents

Part 4: Dehydrating 419

PART 1

Food Storage

Introduction

Congratulations on beginning (or continuing) your journey in food storage. Part 1 of this book is intended to be a helpful resource for everyone, from those just beginning to consider their food storage to those who are already well underway. Preparing your family for a variety of challenging circumstances is a really good idea and I congratulate you for having the wisdom and foresight to be prepared for whatever may come.

It could be that your family will never need its long-term food storage, and I hope that is the case. But if you do find yourself in trying circumstances, your preparedness may mean the difference between life and death; and even if no hardship befalls your family, you will at the very least sleep better knowing you are prepared.

Organization

Part 1 is organized into 101 steps. The intent of this is to reduce what can seem like a very daunting task into a series of reasonable steps. Each step includes an item or items to store, an indicator of costs, where you might buy the item, how to store it, how long it will last, what equipment you might need to use it (such as a can opener or a grain mill), and a recipe to get you started. Most recipes are for meals to eat right away, but there are also some meal-in-a-jar recipes that enable you to prepare meals in advance and have them ready to go at a moment's notice. You'll also find a host of other recipes later in the book.

In my family, when presented with a big or challenging task, we ask each other the rhetorical question, "How do you eat an elephant?" The answer is, of course, "One bite at a time!" Our hope with Part 1 is to divide the work of creating your family food storage into easily manageable steps. Plan to complete a couple of steps per week and you will build your storage in about a year. If you are an overachiever, you can double that and have it done in half the time! Depending on your budget and the size of your family, you may choose to divide some higher-cost items into two or three steps. That's perfectly okay. Just work on each step and mark it done when it is complete.

The goal here is to figure out what you need, plan your approach, get started (sometimes the hardest step), and then just keep going. Be very intentional about your efforts. After some time of being diligent and intentional, you'll find you have the vast majority of what you need.

How to Use

The steps are organized here in rough order of importance, from very high priority to high, medium, and low. Within each priority level, items are divided into categories to make them easier to find. Those categories are:

- Canned Goods
- Dairy (and Dairy Substitutes)
- Drinks (and Drink Mixes)
- Fats
- Pantry Staples
- Produce (Fresh and Dried)
- Sundries and Household Items
- Sweets and Sweeteners

Of course, you should adjust the plan to fit your budget, priorities, and schedule. If a trip to town finds you at Costco, we hope you'll have this book close at hand. Flip through and look for items best bought at Costco, and knock out as many as your budget and time allow.

Mark your progress as you go. It might be your plan to store 2,000 lbs. of wheat, but you might choose to do that 100 lbs. at a time. Keep track of your progress as you go and mark each step as done when you have purchased as much as planned.

COST INDICATORS *(1-year supply)*

$	Under $100 for family of 4
$$	Under $500 for family of 4
$$$	Under $1,000 for family of 4
$$$$	Over $2,000 for family of 4

Select Your Target

Planning your food storage starts with determining what your goal is. Start with the number of people in your family, including any likely guests or visitors. In my house, I have an immediate family of four. I also have an elderly relative and extended family of four who are my neighbors, as well as an adult grown son who would arrive at my door with at least one friend in tow. It adds up fast, doesn't it? You also need to think about having a portion to share if your budget allows.

What about children? They require fewer calories than adults, except when they become teens; then their caloric needs are about the same as, or even greater than, an adult's (depending on activity level). I count children as adults, knowing that a near-term emergency would leave me with some extra capacity (always a good thing) and that in the long run I'll still have enough food. Children do require extra milk, so plan accordingly.

Next, determine how long a period of time you'd like to store for. What would be the maximum time to plan for? Count the people you need to feed, consider your budget, and pick a starting target. You can always do the 101 steps again to increase your stores. So from one person for six months up to 12 people for a year—pick your starting target.

What to Store

On the following pages you will find a sample menu and a table to use as the basis for planning. This will need to be adjusted for individual families' tastes. If your family eats gluten-free or vegetarian, for example, adjustments will need to be made to store more non-gluten grains or vegetables than specified in the guidelines suggested here. If your family doesn't eat wheat, eliminate that line, but increase the amount of beans, corn, oats, or other tolerable foods to account for the same number of pounds as the wheat you are replacing. If your family won't eat beans, increase the beef, chicken, pork, and/or pasta to replace the beans you would have stored. Food storage is most successful when you store what your family truly likes to eat.

Note on "Your Storage Essentials for One Year" chart: If you choose to store less than a year's worth of food, simply adjust your target by reducing the number of people you count for food storage. For example, if you choose to store for four people for six months, use the column for two people for a year. If you have an odd number of people to store for, round up and have enough to share.

YOUR STORAGE ESSENTIALS FOR ONE YEAR

	For 1	For 2	For 4	For 6	For 8	For 12
Beef (3 servings/week)	39 lbs.	78 lbs.	156 lbs.	234 lbs.	312 lbs.	468 lbs.
Chicken (4 servings/week)	52 lbs.	104 lbs.	208 lbs.	312 lbs.	416 lbs.	624 lbs.
Pork (5 servings/week)	65 lbs.	130 lbs.	260 lbs.	390 lbs.	520 lbs.	780 lbs.
Beans (5 servings/week)	65 lbs.	130 lbs.	260 lbs.	390 lbs.	520 lbs.	780 lbs.
Eggs (3 servings/week)	2 cans	4 cans	8 cans	12 cans	16 cans	24 cans
Wheat (14 servings/week)	182 lbs.	364 lbs.	728 lbs.	1092 lbs.	1456 lbs.	2184 lbs.
Pasta (7 servings/week)	91 lbs.	182 lbs.	364 lbs.	546 lbs.	728 lbs.	1092 lbs.
Rice (6 servings/week)	78 lbs.	156 lbs.	312 lbs.	468 lbs.	624 lbs.	936 lbs.
Oats (2 servings/week)	10 lbs.	20 lbs.	40 lbs.	60 lbs.	80 lbs.	120 lbs.
Corn (6 servings/week)	78 lbs.	156 lbs.	312 lbs.	468 lbs.	624 lbs.	936 lbs.
Vegetables (14 servings/week)	1.4 cans	2.8 cans	5.6 cans	8.4 cans	11.2 cans	16.8 cans
Fruit (10 servings/week)	1 can	2 cans	4 cans	6 cans	8 cans	12 cans
Sugar (16 servings/week)	26 lbs.	52 lbs.	104 lbs.	156 lbs.	208 lbs.	312 lbs.
Butter (8 servings/week)	13 lbs.	26 lbs.	52 lbs.	78 lbs.	104 lbs.	156 lbs.
Oil	2.5 gal.	5 gal.	10 gal.	15 gal.	20 gal.	30 gal.
Salt	10 lbs.	20 lbs.	40 lbs.	60 lbs.	80 lbs.	120 lbs.
Milk	75 gal.	150 gal.	300 gal.	450 gal.	600 gal.	900 gal.
Cheese (2 servings/week)	6.5 lbs.	13 lbs.	26 lbs.	39 lbs.	52 lbs.	104 lbs.

SAMPLE OF A WEEKLY MENU

Sunday	Breakfast	Scrambled eggs with sausage gravy and toast
	Lunch	Chili with cornbread and honey
	Dinner	Chicken pot pie
	Dessert	Apple pie
	Snacks	Trail mix
Monday	Breakfast	Granola with toasted almonds, dried apples, dried cranberries, and milk
	Lunch	Spaghetti with mushroom marinara sauce
	Dinner	Beef shepherd's pie
	Dessert	Banana walnut muffins
	Snacks	Popcorn
Tuesday	Breakfast	Pancakes with butter and brown sugar syrup
	Lunch	Chicken noodle soup
	Dinner	Pulled pork sandwiches
	Dessert	Jam tarts
	Snacks	Applesauce
Wednesday	Breakfast	Ham and cheese omelets with hash brown potatoes
	Lunch	Black bean soup with quesadilla wedges
	Dinner	Beef, vegetable, and pasta skillet dinner with garlic bread
	Dessert	No-bake chocolate cookies
	Snacks	Granola with dried cranberries
Thursday	Breakfast	Oatmeal with raisins, brown sugar, and butter
	Lunch	Pasta with broccoli, brown butter, and Parmesan cheese
	Dinner	Chicken stew with biscuits
	Dessert	Apple cobbler
	Snacks	Apple slices with peanut butter
Friday	Breakfast	French toast with sausage
	Lunch	Chicken salad sandwiches and peanut butter cookies
	Dinner	Chili con carne with cornbread
	Dessert	Peanut butter cookies
	Snacks	Dried apples
Saturday	Breakfast	Crispy cornmeal pancakes with fruit jam
	Lunch	Southwest vegetable and bean stew
	Dinner	Teriyaki beef stir-fry with steamed rice
	Dessert	Chocolate cupcakes
	Snacks	Popcorn with butter and Parmesan cheese

Food Type Totals for a Sample Week of Menus

BREAKFASTS

4 DAYS A WEEK: Wheat/grains (cereal, oatmeal, granola, pancakes, French toast, biscuits and sausage gravy, grits) with fruit, butter/oil/shortening, and sugar

3 DAYS A WEEK: Eggs and pork (ham, sausage, or bacon) with wheat or corn (toast, grits)

LUNCHES

3 DAYS A WEEK: Beans and grains (rice and beans, burritos, chili and cornbread, minestrone, beef barley soup, lentil soup, split pea soup) with vegetables and fruit

2 DAYS A WEEK: Chicken, vegetables, and wheat or rice (chicken noodle soup, chicken rice soup, chicken and gravy on a biscuit, chicken pot pie, chicken noodle casserole, arroz con pollo, chicken tacos, chicken fettuccine Alfredo)

2 DAYS A WEEK: Pasta and vegetables (macaroni and cheese, pasta with butter and vegetables, spaghetti with marinara sauce, pasta with peas and bacon or ham, pasta with olive oil, vegetables, and breadcrumbs)

DINNERS

3 DAYS A WEEK: Beef with vegetables and rice, pasta, or grains (beef teriyaki over rice, beef stir-fry and rice, spaghetti Bolognese (meat sauce), beef stew with crusty bread, braised beef over polenta, shepherd's pie, beef and potato casserole, tacos, burritos, enchiladas, etc.)

2 DAYS A WEEK: Chicken and vegetables with rice, wheat, or corn (chicken stew, chicken pot pie, chicken and noodle casserole, chicken fettuccine Alfredo, chicken and dumplings, chicken enchiladas, etc.)

1 DAY A WEEK: Pork, vegetables, and grains (braised pork over polenta, pulled pork sandwiches, pork ribs, carnitas, pork tacos, burritos)

1 DAY A WEEK: Beans, vegetables, and grains (chili and cornbread, vegetable stew, black bean soup, barley stew, beans and rice, beans and ham, baked beans, posole, lentil stew, fried rice)

DAILY BREAD

Loaf of bread, rolls, tortillas, flatbread

SNACKS

Fruit, granola, popcorn

SWEETS

Honey, jelly, sugared tea or coffee

Plan for Abundant Calories

The recommendations in this section are intended to give you a few extra servings per week, because you don't want anyone to go hungry. Commercially sold meal kits start as low as 1,100 to 1,800 calories per day. My husband is 6'4" and would need almost 4,000 calories to maintain his current weight if he were exercising 60 minutes per day. Only 1,100 calories would be slow starvation for him. I choose to have abundant calories and also have some extra that could be shared.

Where to Store

The next key step in planning your food storage is to determine where you will store your food. A cool, dry, dark place is best. Plan to set up at least two main pantries, one for items packaged to last 20 to 30 years, and another with food which should be rotated because it will only last about two years (such as canned goods and home-pressure-canned meats). I call my shorter-term pantry my "rotation pantry" because the idea is to constantly use and refill all the items contained therein. You might choose another location for meal-in-a-jar-type readymade meals.

Scout your home and surroundings for the best possible sites. Cooler is better, so basement spaces are better than attics. Consider your climate as well. An outdoor storage shed might work in temperate climates, but not in areas that get very hot in summer.

Root cellars are prevalent in some parts of the country where homes predate refrigeration. They are wonderful places to store your food and in fact they were intended for that very purpose. If your home is without a basement, or on a cement slab, you might find an under-the-stairs storage area, shelves in the garage, an unused bedroom closet, or under beds. You might need or choose to break up your storage into several locations, so you would be unlikely to lose it all if a single location were compromised by flood, fire, earthquake, or other damage. Also, if you own a summer cabin, you might choose to locate some storage there for safety's sake. In urban locations where storage is limited, a climate-controlled storage facility might be a good secure choice.

The volume of food stored for a single person for a year is roughly the volume of a loaded pallet. Keep that in mind when you consider locations for your larder. The volume will vary, but 40 cubic feet per person per year is a good estimate of how much room food storage will require.

Supplies and Equipment

You can buy food in ready-to-store containers such as #10 cans and vacuum-sealed pouches, but depending on the amount of food you choose to store, it may be preferable to prepare and package the food yourself. Unfortunately, you can't just store food; you have to dry it and wet- or dry-pack can it or vacuum-seal it. It won't stay safe to consume unless you prepare it carefully.

If you plan to prepare and package some or all of your food yourself, you will need some of the equipment and supplies listed on the next pages.

If you are only storing a small amount of food, it might be cheaper to buy it ready to store. If you are storing for a large group for months or more, you might choose to prepare and store it yourself. The decision might come down to whether you have more time or money to spare. If you've got more time than money and are storing a large amount of food, plan to prepare and store it yourself. If you've got more money than time, you might consider simply buying your food from retailers. In either case this section will help you determine what to store.

GRAIN MILL—A grain mill is a must-have if you are going to store wheat or corn. Grains mills are either manual (hand crank) or electric. I have both and we periodically practice grinding wheat into flour and corn into cornmeal. Please plan to have at least one grain mill. If for some reason you get caught without one, you could soak wheat berries in water overnight to make a wheat berry cereal.

FOOD DEHYDRATOR—A food dehydrator is used to dry fresh foods for storage. Dehydrated foods can be vacuum-sealed and dry-pack canned in #10 cans. Food dehydrators can often be found at thrift stores. (People start raw food diets, and then change their minds about that.)

VACUUM SEALER AND VACUUM-SEALER BAGS—Vacuum sealers are used to seal bags of food. You can usually pick one up at a thrift store. Over time you might choose to spend the money to get a more robust model to reduce food-processing time. Look for a model that has a small round port for sealing mason jars; you may also need a special attachment.

OXYGEN ABSORBERS—Oxygen absorbers are small moisture-absorbing packets like the silica packets you find in some products you buy. Toss an oxygen absorber into a vacuum-seal bag to absorb any residual oxygen, which shortens the storage time of foods. They can also be used in mason jars to seal a meal in a jar.

MASON JARS, CANNING LIDS, AND RINGS—Mason jars or canning jars are used to store water-bath canned high-acid foods such as fruits and to pressure-can low-acid foods such as meats, poultry, and vegetables.

#10 CANS AND #10 CAN SEALER—#10 cans store 10 to 12 cups of food and have the advantage of being rodent-, water-, puncture-, and sunlight-proof. They are also pretty inexpensive at about 85 cents per can. The LDS (Church of Jesus Christ of Latter-day Saints) sells #10 cans at its cannery (page 9).

FOOD-GRADE BUCKETS OR BARRELS—Many people choose to store food in food-grade buckets, sometimes with a large mylar bag (or many smaller bags) inside. Buckets are slightly less rodent-proof and lightproof than cans. When considering what containers to store in, consider how much of a given food you want to have open at one time. (It might not be preferable to have five gallons of wheat or salt open all at once.) Gamma lids (a type of screw-on resealable bucket lid) will reseal buckets, but new oxygen absorbers may be needed each time a bucket is opened, for maximum food shelf life. You may choose to store food first in vacuum or mylar bags of a smaller size and then group them in buckets. Buckets cost about $5–$10 dollars and gamma lids are about $10 each. Food-grade barrels are also great for storing water.

MYLAR BAGS – Mylar bags are used like vacuum-sealer bags, but have the advantage of being more puncture-proof and light resistant than vacuum bags, more durable than glass jars, and also light and portable. Mylar bags can be purchased online.

PRESSURE CANNER – Pressure canners are used to wet-pack pressure-can low-acid foods such as meats, fish, and vegetables. Dry-pack canning is putting dry ingredients in a can and sealing it. Wet canning is raw-food canning. A high-acid fruit can be stored with water-bath canning, while low-acid foods are wet-pack canned in a pressure canner.

Where to Shop

The LDS operates a national, not-for-profit distribution center for a limited number of foods and storage-related supplies. These LDS canneries also have #10 can sealers, which they loan out to members, or you may be able to use the can sealer on site at the cannery. To find your local LDS Home Storage Center Locations, go to providentliving.org.

Club stores such as Sam's Club and Costco are great sources of food to store, letting you take advantage of the large quantities and economy of scale. Restaurant supply stores also sell large volumes of food at great prices. Big box stores such as Walmart are great places to get items at good prices. They also sometimes carry freeze-dried items and other items intended for long-term prepper storage.

Dehydrating and Canning Food

Food can be prepared at home for long-term storage in two ways: It can be dehydrated or canned. Dehydrating food is really easy and very satisfying. Most foods can just be washed, sliced, and dried. Beef jerky is made by dehydrating, and almost every fruit or vegetable can be dehydrated easily. See Part 4: Dehydrating for detailed information on dehydrating food.

There are two methods of canning: water-bath canning, which is used for high-acid foods such as fruits, tomatoes, and jams, and pressure-canning. Pressure-canning is required for low-acid foods such as meats and vegetables, but can also be used for some high-acid foods (such as fruits). Pressure-canning requires the ability to read and follow directions well. Failure to do so could threaten your family's health. Please follow all directions carefully and adhere to current USDA guidelines for proper timing and procedures. See Part 3: Canning for detailed information on canning food.

***

Here are 101 easy steps to building your food storage. Mark your progress as you go along and remember the tortoise and the hare—steady progress wins the race. Are you ready? Let's get started!

1

WATER, FILTERS, & POOL SHOCK

PRIORITY: *Very high* | **CATEGORY:** *Drinks*

The number-one priority in a survival scenario is a source of water. A typical person needs two quarts (eight cups or one-half gallon) of water per day for drinking. You will also need water for cooking, washing, and hygiene. I plan on at least a gallon per person per day.

If you live in a rainy climate, you can catch water from the roof and filter it for drinking. A water filter such as a Katadyn or a Berkey is very important to have on hand.

"Pool shock" (calcium hypochlorite) is a chemical used to purify swimming pool water. It is a powdered form of bleach and can be also used to purify water for drinking. Pool shock can be bought at Walmart and Home Depot, is inexpensive, and has a two-year shelf life. It is stronger than bleach, so care should be used to keep it away from children and pets, out of eyes, etc. Do not breathe the fumes from pool shock and keep it away from heat. Store at cool room temperatures.

The amount of pool shock needed to purify a gallon of water varies according to the concentration of each brand. If the recipe is not printed on the package, consult a reliable source and write it on the package for future reference. For the most common concentration, ½ teaspoon is added to a gallon of water and this makes a cleaning solution similar to liquid bleach and appropriate for disinfecting surfaces. Add 2½ tablespoons of this liquid to a gallon of water and let sit 30 minutes. It should smell slightly of chlorine.

A pound of pool shock will purify about 10,000 gallons of drinking water. Again: Please use caution when handling, keep away from children and pets, and verify the recipe to make drinking water for your concentration.

Water purification tablets are easily portable and perfect for purifying small amounts of water. Typically a single tablet will purify 1 pint (16 oz.) of water.

2

SALT

PRIORITY: *Very high* | **CATEGORY:** *Pantry staples*

Salt can be used to make every meal taste better and is also important for preserving food. It lasts forever, but needs to be kept dry.

SHELF LIFE: Forever

COST: $ (about $32 for a year's supply for a family of 4)

WHERE TO BUY: Although salt is inexpensive, it's heavy, so shipping adds up. Buy it locally at the grocery store or grab it at Costco or Walmart if you happen to be there.

HOW TO STORE: In #10 cans with an oxygen absorber, or vacuum-sealed in bags with an oxygen absorber, and then stored in buckets

If you can't buy it all at once, track your progress below.

SERVING SIZE: a pinch | **SEASON:** anytime

Persons	Quantity for 1 year	Mark Off What You Have
1	10 lbs.	
2	20 lbs.	
4	40 lbs.	
6	60 lbs.	
8	80 lbs.	
12	120 lbs.	

What to do with salt

- Make your own seasoning mixture of salt, pepper, garlic powder, onion powder, and paprika. Season all your food deliciously.

❑ **Done**

3

CANNED BEANS

PRIORITY: *High* | **CATEGORY:** *Canned goods*

Canned beans are a great convenience food. Add them to soups, stews, and salads for protein, or whirl them in the blender with olive oil and garlic for a great vegetable or cracker dip. Canned beans don't require soaking overnight or a long cook time. Good choices are chili beans, baked beans, and plain canned beans (pintos, kidney beans, etc.).

> **SHELF LIFE:** 2–5 years
>
> **COST:** $ (about $100 for a year's supply for a family of 4)
>
> **WHERE TO BUY:** Sam's Club, Costco, or online
>
> **HOW TO STORE:** In your rotation pantry

If you can't buy it all at once, track your progress below.

SERVING SIZE: ½ can; see note | **SEASON:** anytime

Persons 1 serving/week	Quantity for 1 year	Mark Off What You Have
1	26 (14.5-oz.) cans	
2	52 (14.5-oz.) cans	
4	104 (14.5-oz.) cans	
6	156 (14.5-oz.) cans	
8	208 (14.5-oz.) cans	
12	312 (14.5-oz.) cans	

A note on serving size: 1 (14.5-oz.) can will create 2 servings of an entree-type bean dish or 4 servings as an ingredient in a recipe.

Prerequisite: Can opener(s)

What to do with canned beans

- **Make a bean salad:** Combine cans of pintos, kidney beans, and garbanzos with vinaigrette for a bean salad. Add onion and feta cheese if desired.
- **Make a bean spread:** Mix drained canned beans in the blender with olive oil and garlic to make a bean dip. Serve with crackers or vegetables.
- **Make refried beans:** Fry drained pinto beans in lard or vegetable shortening and mash them to make refried beans. Spread on a fried tortilla and make a tostada or bean burritos.
- **Make a taco salad:** Combine drained canned black beans with lettuce, grated cheese, and salsa to make a taco salad.

❑ **Done**

CANNED MEALS

PRIORITY: *High* | **CATEGORY:** *Canned goods*

Canned meals that you can just heat and eat are critical for your food storage, because they may be the first things you reach for in an emergency. I generally assume that one can will provide two servings.

We have separate items for canned soups, meats, fruits, and vegetables, so for this item we will just focus on the complete canned meals your family will eat.

SHELF LIFE: About 2 years

COST: $$ ($1–$1.50 per can, about $260 per year for a family of 4)

WHERE TO BUY: Walmart, Sam's Club, Costco, any grocery store

HOW TO STORE: In your rotation pantry, in cans or cases of cans

If you can't buy it all at once, track your progress on page 14.

CHILI AND PASTA

SERVING SIZE: ½ can; see note | **SEASON:** anytime

Persons 4 servings/week	Quantity for 1 year	Mark Off What You Have
1	52 (14.5-oz.) cans	Chili: Pasta:
2	104 (14.5-oz.) cans	Chili: Pasta:
4	208 (14.5-oz.) cans	Chili: Pasta:
6	312 (14.5-oz.) cans	Chili: Pasta:
8	416 (14.5-oz.) cans	Chili: Pasta:
12	624 (14.5-oz.) cans	Chili: Pasta:

A note on serving size: 1 (14.5-oz.) can will create 2 servings of an entree.

STEW

SERVING SIZE: ½ can; see note | **SEASON:** anytime

Persons 4 servings/week	Quantity for 1 year	Mark Off What You Have
1	52 (14.5-oz.) cans	Stew: Other:
2	104 (14.5-oz.) cans	Stew: Other:
4	208 (14.5-oz.) cans	Stew: Other:
6	312 (14.5-oz.) cans	Stew: Other:
8	416 (14.5-oz.) cans	Stew: Other:
12	624 (14.5-oz.) cans	Stew: Other:

A note on serving size: 1 (14.5-oz.) can will create 2 servings of an entree.

Prerequisite: Can opener(s)

What to do with canned meals

- Just heat and eat, or serve them over rice, noodles, mashed potatoes, grits, or polenta. Mix small amounts with leftover mashed potatoes or rice, form into patties, and pan-fry into cakes.

❑ **Done**

5

CANNED SOUPS

PRIORITY: *High* | **CATEGORY:** *Canned goods*

Canned soups are both a great go-to meal when you don't have time to cook and a useful ingredient for other recipes such as casseroles. I like to keep a supply of many varieties of soups around, but you can fill in your family's favorites on the chart below and keep track of what you have. Good options are chicken noodle soup, chicken rice, vegetable beef, cream of mushroom, tomato/tomato rice, and clam chowder.

    SHELF LIFE: About 2 years

    COST: $$ (about $150–$200 a year for a family of 4)

    WHERE TO BUY: Walmart, Sam's Club, Costco, any grocery store

    HOW TO STORE: In your rotation pantry, in cans or cases of cans

If you can't buy it all at once, track your progress below.

SERVING SIZE: ½ can; see note | **SEASON:** anytime

Persons 2 servings/week	Quantity for 1 year	Mark Off What You Have
1	26 (14.5-oz.) cans	
2	52 (14.5-oz.) cans	
4	104 (14.5-oz.) cans	
6	156 (14.5-oz.) cans	
8	208 (14.5-oz.) cans	
12	312 (14.5-oz.) cans	

A note on serving size: 1 (14.5-oz.) can will create 2 servings of an entree

Prerequisite: Can opener(s)

What to do with canned soups

- Just heat and eat, or serve them over rice, noodles, mashed potatoes, grits, or polenta.
- Combine a broth-based soup with a bit of butter and flour cooked together to thicken it into a gravy-style stew.
- Top soup with a slice of bread topped with cheese and broil briefly (and well watched) until cheese is melted.
- Dilute a can of cream soup with 1 can of water, add tuna or chicken and cooked pasta, and put in a baking dish. Top with grated cheese and/or buttered breadcrumbs. Bake until bubbly.

❑ **Done**

SPAGHETTI SAUCE, TOMATOES, & TOMATO SAUCE

PRIORITY: *High* | **CATEGORY:** *Canned goods*

We plan to serve either pizza or spaghetti once a week, and we also find a use for canned tomatoes about once a week. Store cans of spaghetti sauce that you enjoy and that come in a size correct for your family. Alternately, buy in-season tomatoes and water-bath can or pressure-can them or dehydrate them yourself.

    COST: $$ (varies)

    WHERE TO BUY: Costco, Sam's Club, Walmart, any grocery store, Amazon.com

    HOW TO STORE: In cans or cases of cans in your rotation pantry

If you can't buy it all at once, track your progress below.

TOMATOES

SERVING SIZE: about ¼ can | **SEASON:** see note

Persons 1 serving/week	Quantity for 1 year	Mark Off What You Have
1	13 lbs.	
2	26 lbs.	
4	52 lbs.	
6	78 lbs.	
8	104 lbs.	
12	156 lbs.	

SPAGHETTI SAUCE

SERVING SIZE: about ¼ can | **SEASON:** see note

Persons 1 serving/week	Quantity for 1 year	Mark Off What You Have
1	13 cans	
2	26 cans	
4	52 cans	
6	78 cans	
8	104 cans	
12	156 cans	

A note on season: Any season will work if buying canned. You can also can your own. End of summer is a great time to buy local tomatoes inexpensively to can your own sauce.

How to dehydrate tomatoes

- Wash tomatoes. To remove skin, blanch tomatoes in boiling water for about 2 minutes until skins split. Plunge into ice water to stop the cooking and peel the tomatoes once they are cool enough to handle. Core the tomatoes and slice them. (Cherry tomatoes can just be washed, halved, and dried.) Dehydrate at 120°F for 12 to 16 hours until perfectly dry. You can whirl fully dried tomatoes in the blender to create tomato powder, or you can store them in a vacuum-sealed bag with an oxygen absorber. Alternately you can dry them about halfway, and then put them in a clean jar and cover them with olive oil. Fully dried tomatoes will need to be soaked in very hot water for 15 minutes before using. Half-dried tomatoes can be stored in oil and be used without reconstituting.

What to do with tomatoes

- **Make a skillet supper:** Add ½ pound cooked and drained pasta, 1 pint canned ground beef, 1 can of tomatoes, and rehydrated onion, peppers, and garlic to a skillet and bring to a simmer. Season to taste with salt, pepper, and red pepper flakes. Optionally add olives and/or cheese.

What to do with spaghetti sauce

- Use to top cooked pasta or pizza.

❏ **Done**

7

EGGS

PRIORITY: *High* | CATEGORY: *Dairy*

Dried eggs come as whole eggs and egg whites. Buy whole eggs, which can be used to make scrambled eggs, omelets, and French toast or in baking in place of eggs.

SHELF LIFE: 5–10 years

COST: $$ (about $264 for a year's supply for a family of 4)

WHERE TO BUY: Sam's Club or online

SAMPLE PRICING: Sam's Club $32.98 for 142 servings (2 cans), Honeyville $58.99 for 144 servings (2 cans)

HOW TO STORE: Purchase already sealed in #10 cans. Store cans in a cool, dark place.

If you can't buy it all at once, track your progress below.

SERVING SIZE: 2 eggs; see note | **SEASON:** anytime

Persons 3 servings/week	Quantity for 1 year	Mark Off What You Have
1	2 (#10) cans	
2	4 (#10) cans	
4	8 (#10) cans	
6	12 (#10) cans	
8	16 (#10) cans	
12	24 (#10) cans	

A note on serving size: 2 eggs (2 tablespoons powder + 4 tablespoons water = 1 egg; if for baking, no need to reconstitute)

What to do with eggs

- **Make French toast:** Reconstitute 2 eggs per person in water, add an equivalent amount of milk, ½ teaspoon of vanilla, and a sprinkle of cinnamon. Drench bread in the egg mixture and pan-fry in butter over medium-high heat until golden on both sides.

- **Make scrambled eggs:** Reconstitute 2 eggs per person. Add salt. Cook in a skillet over low/medium heat in butter. If desired add grated cheese, ham, onions, vegetables, or just about anything. You can also finish in the broiler to brown the top and you have a frittata. If you add cubed bread to the mix, you have strata. Eggs are a great vehicle for whatever leftovers you have on hand.

❏ **Done**

8

MILK

PRIORITY: *High* | **CATEGORY:** *Dairy*

There are two main types of storable milk available: powdered and instant. Powdered milk may contain both dairy and soy, while instant milk is completely dairy. Powdered milk has a shelf life of five years, while instant milk's shelf life is much shorter, about six months. For this reason I prefer powdered milk over instant. Powdered milk is also more concentrated, requiring less powder to reconstitute into milk. Milk is important for children to drink and also great for cooking. Thicken milk with a roux (butter and flour) and you've got a white sauce. Add cheese and you have the basis for macaroni and cheese, and a million casseroles.

SHELF LIFE: 5+ years

COST: $$$ (about $570 for a year's supply for a family of 4)

SAMPLE PRICING: LDS $47.20 for 25 lbs., Sam's Club $109.98 for 37 lbs., Costco $99.99 for 27 lbs., Honeyville $70.99 for 25 lbs.

WHERE TO BUY: LDS, Sam's Club, Costco, or online

HOW TO STORE: In #10 cans with oxygen absorbers

If you can't buy it all at once, track your progress below.

SERVING SIZE: 1 cup | **SEASON:** anytime

Persons 7 servings/week	Quantity for 1 year	Mark Off What You Have
1	75 lbs.	
2	150 lbs.	
4	300 lbs.	
6	450 lbs.	
8	600 lbs.	
12	900 lbs.	

What to do with powdered milk

- **Make milk, chocolate milk, or cocoa:** For each cup of milk desired, start with a cup of water and add ⅓ cup of powdered milk. Add cocoa powder and sugar to make chocolate milk. Heat it to make cocoa.

- **Make yogurt:** In a quart canning jar or other clean container, stir together 3¾ cups of water and 1¾ cups of powdered milk. Whisk in ¼ cup of commercial yogurt with active cultures (read the label to be sure the yogurt has active cultures). Store the milk in a warm spot, between 80°F and 110°F. Allow it to sit undisturbed for 6 to 8 hours. It will become thick and creamy.

- **Make macaroni and cheese:** Cook 1 pound of macaroni or other pasta until al dente, drain and set aside. In a sauce pan, mix together ¼ cup of flour and ¼ cup of butter, oil, or shortening and cook, stirring for about 3 minutes. In a separate container, make 3 cups of milk from 2⅔ cups of water mixed with ⅔ cup of powdered milk. Add the milk to the butter and flour mixture and cook over medium-high heat, stirring constantly until thickened. Season with salt, and add about 3 to 4 cups of grated cheddar cheese. Combine the sauce and macaroni in a baking dish and if desired, bake until bubbly and crusty around the edges. Optionally, add diced ham or cooked broccoli or top with breadcrumbs before baking.

❏ **Done**

COCONUT OIL

PRIORITY: *High* | **CATEGORY:** *Fats*

Coconut oil is delicious and has a long shelf life. You can toss it with vegetables, use it to cook steak, or spread it on toast.

SHELF LIFE: 2+ years

COST: $$ (about $200 for a year's supply for a family of 4)

WHERE TO BUY: Sam's Club, Costco, or online

SAMPLE PRICING: Amazon.com $15 for 30 oz.

HOW TO STORE: In original packaging

If you can't buy it all at once, track your progress below.

SERVING SIZE: ½ tablespoon | **SEASON:** anytime

Persons 5 servings/week	Quantity for 1 year	Mark Off What You Have
1	.5 gal.	
2	1 gal.	
4	2 gal.	
6	3 gal.	
8	4 gal.	
12	6 gal.	

What to do with coconut oil

- Toss with hot, freshly cooked vegetables.
- Spread on toast.
- Use to pan-fry meat.
- Cook pancakes (page 31).

❑ **Done**

10

OLIVE OIL

PRIORITY: *High* | **CATEGORY:** *Fats*

Olive oil is the healthiest of the oils you can store, with lots of monounsaturated fatty acids.

SHELF LIFE: Up to 4 years

COST: $ (about $100 for a year's supply for a family of 4)

WHERE TO BUY: Sam's Club or Costco

SAMPLE PRICING: Costco $13 for 2 liters (about half a gallon)

HOW TO STORE: In original packaging in the freezer

If you can't buy it all at once, track your progress below.

SERVING SIZE: ½ tablespoon | **SEASON:** anytime

Persons 12 servings/ week	Quantity for 1 year	Mark Off What You Have
1	1 gal.	
2	2 gal.	
4	4 gal.	
6	6 gal.	
8	8 gal.	
12	12 gal.	

What to do with olive oil

- Make hummus (page 81).
- Make vinaigrette: Mix 2 parts oil with 1 part vinegar or lemon juice, then add a smidge of Dijon mustard, salt, and pepper. Whisk together and use to dress vegetables.

❑ **Done**

11

VEGETABLE OIL

PRIORITY: *High* | **CATEGORY:** *Fats*

Another important oil for your food storage, vegetable oil has the highest smoke point of the oils covered in this section and is best for frying.

SHELF LIFE: 30 years

COST: $ (about $75 for a year's supply for a family of 4)

WHERE TO BUY: LDS, Sam's Club, Costco, or online

SAMPLE PRICING: Costco $25 for 35 lbs., which is 4.375 gallons (16 ounces per lb.)

HOW TO STORE: In #10 cans with an oxygen absorber

If you can't buy it all at once, track your progress below.

SERVING SIZE: ½ tablespoon | **SEASON:** anytime

Persons 12 servings/ week	Quantity for 1 year	Mark Off What You Have
1	1 gal.	
2	2 gal.	
4	4 gal.	
6	6 gal.	
8	8 gal.	
12	12 gal.	

What to do with vegetable oil

- Make pancakes (page 31).

❏ **Done**

12

CORN

PRIORITY: *High* | **CATEGORY:** *Pantry staples*

Corn comes in two main varieties: flint and dent. Dent corn is distinguishable by a dent in the fully ripened kernel and is used for animal feed. Flint corn does not have the dented appearance and is used for popcorn and also ground into cornmeal—this is the variety to purchase for your food storage. Cornmeal can be used to make cornbread, polenta, grits, and tortillas.

SHELF LIFE: 30 years

COST: $$$ (about $530 for a year's supply for a family of 4)

WHERE TO BUY: Sam's Club, Costco, or online

SAMPLE PRICING: Costco for $75 for 240 servings

HOW TO STORE: In #10 cans with an oxygen absorber, or vacuum-sealed in bags with an oxygen absorber, then stored in buckets. Can be bought ready to store.

If you can't buy it all at once, track your progress below.

SERVING SIZE: ½ cup | **SEASON:** anytime; see note

Persons 3 servings/week	Quantity for 1 year	Mark Off What You Have
1	78 lbs.	
2	156 lbs.	
4	312 lbs.	
6	468 lbs.	
8	624 lbs.	
12	936 lbs.	

A note on season: Late summer is best if you are dehydrating your own corn.

Prerequisite: A grain mill

What to do with corn

- Grind corn to make cornmeal, grits, and polenta.
- Make popcorn.
- Make cornbread (page 29).

❑ **Done**

13

CORNMEAL, GRITS, & POLENTA

PRIORITY: *High* | **CATEGORY:** *Pantry staples*

Cornmeal, grits (white coarse-ground corn), and polenta (yellow coarse-ground corn) make amazing accompaniments to any meal. Pair cornbread with beans; serve braised beef or pork over polenta. For breakfast, stir up some cheesy grits.

SHELF LIFE: 30 years

COST: $ (about $80 for a year's supply for a family of 4)

WHERE TO BUY: Sam's Club, Costco, or online

SAMPLE PRICING: Sam's Club $41 for 38 lbs.

HOW TO STORE: In #10 cans with an oxygen absorber

If you can't buy it all at once, track your progress below.

CORNMEAL

SERVING SIZE: ½ cup; see note | **SEASON:** anytime

Persons 3 servings/week	Quantity for 1 year	Mark Off What You Have
1	13 lbs.	
2	26 lbs.	
4	52 lbs.	
6	78 lbs.	
8	104 lbs.	
12	156 lbs.	

GRITS

SERVING SIZE: ½ cup; see note | **SEASON:** anytime

Persons 1 serving/week	Quantity for 1 year	Mark Off What You Have
1	4 lbs.	
2	8 lbs.	
4	16 lbs.	
6	24 lbs.	
8	32 lbs.	
12	48 lbs.	

POLENTA

SERVING SIZE: ½ cup; see note | **SEASON:** anytime

Persons 1 serving/week	Quantity for 1 year	Mark Off What You Have
1	4 lbs.	
2	8 lbs.	
4	16 lbs.	
6	24 lbs.	
8	32 lbs.	
12	48 lbs.	

A note on serving size: ½ cup of cooked cornmeal, grits, or polenta is a serving. ½ cup of uncooked cornmeal, grits, or polenta will yield 4 cups of cooked grains.

What to do with cornmeal, polenta, and grits

- **Make cornbread:** Combine 1 cup flour, 1 cup cornmeal, 1 cup sugar, 1 tablespoon baking powder, ⅓ cup vegetable oil, 1 egg, 1 cup milk, and 1 teaspoon salt. Bake at 350°F for 30 minutes.
- **Make grits:** Combine 2 cups of milk and 2 cups of water and bring to a boil. Add 1 cup of grits, 1½ teaspoons of salt, and ½ teaspoon of ground black pepper and stir well. Cook, stirring frequently for about 20 minutes. Finish with cheese and butter if desired.
- **Make polenta:** Add ½ cup of polenta to 3 cups of boiling, salted water. Cook and stir until cooked through and creamy, about 15 minutes. Add butter and cheese as desired.

❏ **Done**

14

DRIED BEANS, PEAS, & LENTILS

PRIORITY: *High* | **CATEGORY:** *Pantry staples*

Beans and legumes are a very important component of your food storage. They are very inexpensive and have a 30-year shelf life. Beans can be bought dry in bulk bags or #10 cans, cooked and commercially canned, as well as par-cooked. The legume family also includes lentils, garbanzo beans (also called chickpeas), and split peas.

Pinto, kidney, black, garbanzo, and cannellini beans all require soaking overnight and cooking for 1½ to 2 hours. Be sure to change the water after soaking and before cooking to minimize flatulence. In lieu of soaking overnight, beans can be cooked for 2 to 3 hours. Lentils and split peas do not require soaking overnight and cook in 30 to 40 minutes.

Par-cooked (partially cooked or "quick cook") beans can be purchased commercially or prepared at home. To prepare your own quick cook beans, pressure cook them in abundant water and seasonings for about 9 minutes, and then dry in a dehydrator until completely dry, about 12 hours at 120°F. Par-cooked beans are wonderful for creating meals in a jar.

Beans significantly increase the nutritional value of a vegetable soup, and chili is a hearty and filling meal, especially when paired with cornbread. Beans and rice are an international staple meal. Beans should be paired with a grain-based food such as rice or wheat to make a complete protein.

When planning beans for your food storage, it is worth taste-testing them with your family and deciding which beans you'd like to include. In my planning, I plan to have beans in 5 out of 21 meals per week. Adjust the quantity of beans to fit your family and also consider the proportion of each type of bean. For the purposes of this section, the breakdown of types of beans is as follows:

% of beans supply	Type of bean	Quantity for 1 year	Number of Servings
30%	pinto	20 lbs./person	80
15%	black	10 lbs./person	40
15%	kidney	10 lbs./person	40
15%	white	10 lbs./person	40
15%	lentil	10 lbs./person	40
5%	garbanzo	4 lbs./person	16
5%	split pea	4 lbs./person	16

A note on serving size: ½ cup of uncooked beans yields 1 cup cooked beans, which is traditionally 2 entree-sized servings, but I prefer to plan more plentiful servings than the ½-cup standard serving. ½ pound of beans is about 1 cup of uncooked beans and yields 3 cups of cooked beans, which is 3 servings for the purposes of this section.

Eating beans 5 times per week, a person would consume 260 servings per year, which is 65 pounds per person, per year. This is a plentiful allotment and allows for sharing.

If you can't buy it all at once, track your progress below.

ALL BEANS

SERVING SIZE: 1 cup; see note | **SEASON:** anytime

Persons 5 servings/week	Quantity for 1 year	Mark Off What You Have
1	65 lbs.	
2	130 lbs.	
4	260 lbs.	
6	390 lbs.	
8	520 lbs.	
12	780 lbs.	

❑ **Done**

15

FLOUR

PRIORITY: *High* | **CATEGORY:** *Pantry staples*

Flour is a part of your wheat allotment, but should not be the majority, because it doesn't last as long as wheat berries. Consider it a convenience food and plan to have 10 pounds per person to get you started, knowing that you can always grind more wheat into flour.

SHELF LIFE: 10 years

COST: $ (about $20 for a year's supply for a family of 4)

SAMPLE PRICING: LDS $8.85 for 25 lbs., Sam's Club $69.99 for 41 lbs., Costco $72.99 for 42 lbs., Honeyville $78.99 for 50 lbs.

WHERE TO BUY: LDS (preferably) or at Sam's Club, Costco, or online

HOW TO STORE: Vacuum-sealed in bags or in #10 cans with an oxygen absorber

If you can't buy it all at once, track your progress below.

SERVING SIZE: varies by recipe | **SEASON:** anytime

Persons	Quantity for 1 year	Mark Off What You Have
1	10 lbs.	
2	20 lbs.	
4	40 lbs.	
6	60 lbs.	
8	80 lbs.	
12	120 lbs.	

What to do with flour

- **Make pancakes:** Whisk together 2 cups of flour with 2 tablespoons of sugar, 2 teaspoons of baking powder, ½ teaspoon of salt, 1 cup milk, 2 tablespoons of butter or oil, and 1 egg. Oil a skillet and heat over medium-high heat. Pour the mix into 4-inch puddles and cook until the batter is bubbly. Flip and cook on the other side until golden and cooked through.

- **Make biscuits:** Mix 2 cups of flour with 1 tablespoon of baking powder, 1 tablespoon of sugar, a teaspoon of salt, and ⅓ cup of shortening until the mixture looks like coarse crumbs. Add 1 cup of milk. Roll and cut into rounds or drop by big spoonfuls onto a baking sheet and bake at 425°F for 12 to 15 minutes.
- **Make tortillas:** Mix 2 cups of flour with 1 teaspoon of salt, ¼ teaspoon of baking powder, ¼ cup oil, and ⅔ cup of water. Knead and roll into a ball. Divide into 8 pieces. Roll each piece until ⅛ inch thick and cook one by one on a lightly greased hot griddle until spotted and cooked through.
- **Make bread (page 45).**

❏ **Done**

16

JIFFY MIXES

PRIORITY: *High* | **CATEGORY:** *Pantry staples*

Jiffy mixes are fabulous for food storage, because they cost about 50 cents per box and come in lots of varieties from white, yellow, and chocolate cake to frostings, pie crust, corn muffins, and brownies. Each variety is about $6 for a case of 12. If your local store doesn't carry them, you can order them directly from Jiffy at jiffymix.com.

SHELF LIFE: About 2 years

COST: $ (about $50 for a year's supply for a family of 4—includes cake, frosting, corn muffins, muffins, pie crusts, and brownies)

WHERE TO BUY: Sam's Club, Costco, or online

SAMPLE PRICING: $.50 per box, $6 for a case of 12

HOW TO STORE: In #10 cans with an oxygen absorber

If you can't buy it all at once, track your progress below.

MUFFINS AND CORN MUFFINS

SERVING SIZE: ⅙ of a package | **SEASON:** anytime

Persons 1 serving/week	Quantity for 1 year	Mark Off What You Have
1	13 boxes	
2	26 boxes	
4	52 boxes	
6	78 boxes	
8	104 boxes	
12	156 boxes	

CAKES, FROSTINGS, BROWNIES

SERVING SIZE: ⅙ of a package | **SEASON:** anytime

Persons ½ serving/week	Quantity for 1 year	Mark Off What You Have
1	7 boxes	Cake: Frosting: Brownies:
2	13 boxes	Cake: Frosting: Brownies:
4	26 boxes	Cake: Frosting: Brownies:
6	26 boxes	Cake: Frosting: Brownies:
8	52 boxes	Cake: Frosting: Brownies:
12	52 boxes	Cake: Frosting: Brownies:

PIE CRUST

SERVING SIZE: ⅙ of a package | **SEASON:** anytime

Persons ½ serving/week	Quantity for 1 year	Mark Off What You Have
1	7 boxes	
2	13 boxes	
4	26 boxes	
6	26 boxes	
8	52 boxes	
12	52 boxes	

What to do with Jiffy mixes

- **Make corn muffins:** Add grated cheese and/or green chiles.
- **Make brownies:** Add chocolate chips, chopped caramels, or nuts.
- Make pie, pot pie (page 245), or rustic pie (page 50).

❑ **Done**

17

KIDNEY BEANS

PRIORITY: *High* | **CATEGORY:** *Pantry staples*

Kidney beans are slightly lower in calories and slightly higher in protein than pinto beans. They are perfect for chili, because they don't fall apart and take well to spices.

SHELF LIFE: 30 years

COST: $ (about $66 for a year's supply for a family of 4)

WHERE TO BUY: Sam's Club, Costco, or online

HOW TO STORE: In #10 cans with an oxygen absorber

If you can't buy it all at once, track your progress below.

SERVING SIZE: 1 cup; see note | **SEASON:** anytime

Persons ¾ serving/week	Quantity for 1 year	Mark Off What You Have
1	10 lbs.	
2	20 lbs.	
4	40 lbs.	
6	60 lbs.	
8	80 lbs.	
12	120 lbs.	

A note on serving size: 1 cup cooked beans is 1 serving as an entree; ½ cup cooked beans is 1 serving as a side. 1 cup of uncooked beans weighs ½ pound and yields 3 cups of cooked beans.

What to do with kidney beans

- Combine cooked kidney beans with other beans and vinaigrette to make a bean salad.
- Add cooked kidney beans to vegetables with Italian herbs and small cooked pasta to make a minestrone soup.
- Soak kidney beans overnight, drain, and add new water. Bring to a boil, reduce to a simmer, and cook 1½ to 2 hours until tender. Season and serve.

❏ **Done**

18

PASTA

PRIORITY: *High* | **CATEGORY:** *Pantry staples*

Pasta is counted as part of your wheat allotment. I plan on two parts wheat to one part pasta, because pasta is a great starting place for a meal. You can purchase spaghetti and also different shapes such as rigatoni, penne, etc.

   SHELF LIFE: 30 years

COST: $$ (about $350 a year for a family of 4)

SAMPLE PRICING: LDS $23.85 for 25 lbs., Costco $49.99 for 25 lbs.

WHERE TO BUY: LDS, at Costco, or online

HOW TO STORE: In #10 cans with an oxygen absorber, or vacuum-sealed in bags with an oxygen absorber, then stored in buckets. Can be bought ready to store.

If you can't buy it all at once, track your progress below.

SERVING SIZE: ¼ pound | **SEASON:** anytime

Persons 7 servings/ week	Quantity for 1 year	Mark Off What You Have
1	91 lbs.	
2	182 lbs.	
4	364 lbs.	
6	546 lbs.	
8	728 lbs.	
12	7092 lbs.	

What to do with pasta

- Bring a pot of abundantly salted water to a boil, add pasta and cook until just tender, about 5 minutes.

Meal ideas

- Top with spaghetti sauce, with or without meat (or textured vegetable protein) and Parmesan cheese.
- Add to soup.
- Top with olive oil, garlic, salt, and red pepper flakes.
- Top with a can of chili.
- Toss with canned chopped tomatoes, olives, garlic, and red pepper flakes.
- Top with canned clams, olive oil, and garlic.
- Add dehydrated vegetables to the cooking water, cook until very tender, smash together with butter/ghee and Parmesan, and toss with pasta.

- Toss pasta with peas, diced ham, cream, and Parmesan cheese.
- Toss cooled pasta with vinaigrette, chopped salami, peas, and feta or Parmesan cheese.
- Toss with jarred Alfredo sauce, chicken, and Parmesan cheese.
- Toss very hot pasta with an egg yolk and add crumbled cooked bacon.
- Mix pasta with chopped, cooked chicken and mushroom soup, top with bread crumbs and bake.

❑ **Done**

19

PINTO BEANS

PRIORITY: *High* | **CATEGORY:** *Pantry staples*

Pinto beans are very common, easy to cook, and wonderfully nutritious, packed with protein and healthy carbohydrates. In this section we'll plan for pinto beans to be 30 percent of the supply of beans, with kidney beans, white beans (Great Northern), black beans, and garbanzo beans making up the remainder of the bean supply.

SHELF LIFE: 30 years

COST: $ (about $60 a year for a family of 4, plus $25 for cans)

SAMPLE PRICING: LDS $18.55 for 25 lbs., Sam's Club $69.99 for 41 lbs., Costco $72.99 for 42 lbs., Honeyville $78.99 for 50 lbs.

WHERE TO BUY: LDS (preferably) or at Sam's Club, Costco, or online

HOW TO STORE: Package in #10 cans with oxygen absorbers, or vacuum-seal in bags with oxygen absorbers and store in buckets

If you can't buy it all at once, track your progress below.

SERVING SIZE: 1 cup; see note | **SEASON:** anytime

Persons 1 ½ servings/ week	Quantity for 1 year	Mark Off What You Have
1	20 lbs.	
2	40 lbs.	
4	80 lbs.	
6	120 lbs.	
8	160 lbs.	
12	240 lbs.	

A note on serving size: 1 cup cooked beans is 1 serving as an entree; ½ cup cooked beans is 1 serving as a side. 1 cup of uncooked beans weighs ½ pound and yields 3 cups of cooked beans.

What to do with pinto beans

- Cover beans with water and allow them to sit overnight if time allows. The next day, drain the beans and cover with water again. Bring to a boil and simmer 1 to 2 hours. Season with salt, pepper, and garlic if desired. Simmer 30 minutes more or until tender and cooked through. Serve with cornbread.
- To make refried beans, in a frying pan add lard, Crisco, or oil. Add fully cooked beans and mash slightly until warmed through. Taste for seasoning and add salt and pepper as needed. Serve with tortillas.
- **Make rice and beans:** Add nearly cooked beans to a pot with 1 part rice and 2 parts water. Bring to a boil, turn heat to low, cover, and simmer 20 minutes.

❏ **Done**

20

RICE

PRIORITY: *High* | **CATEGORY:** *Pantry staples*

Rice comes in two main varieties: brown rice and white rice. Brown rice is more nutritious but takes longer to cook and has a very short shelf life, so it is preferable to store all or mostly white rice. Store brown rice in your rotation pantry and plan to use and replace it within a year. Properly stored, white rice will last 30 years or more.

SHELF LIFE: White rice, 30 years; brown rice, about a year

COST: $$ (About $150 a year for a family of 4 if purchased from the LDS, plus $55 for cans)

WHERE TO BUY: LDS or at Sam's Club, Costco, or online

HOW TO STORE: In #10 cans with an oxygen absorber, or vacuum-sealed in bags with an oxygen absorber, then stored in buckets. Can be bought ready to store.

If you can't buy it all at once, track your progress below.

SERVING SIZE: 1 cup; see note | **SEASON:** anytime

Persons 6 servings/week	Quantity for 1 Year	Mark Off What You Have
1	78 lbs.	
2	156 lbs.	
4	312 lbs.	
6	468 lbs.	
8	624 lbs.	
12	936 lbs.	

A note on serving size: 1 pound of rice is about 2⅓ cups, and each cup of uncooked rice yields 3 cups of cooked rice. So 1 pound of rice yields 8 cups of cooked rice. For the purposes of meal planning for this section, plan about 1 cup of rice per person, even though the official serving size for rice is ½ cup.

What to do with white rice

- Combine 1 part white rice with 2 parts water in a pot with lid. Bring to a boil, then reduce to a low simmer, cover, and cook 20 minutes. Optionally, add salt, butter, and/or powdered soup base at the start of cooking. Stir in cooked chopped meat or vegetables. Stir-fry with oil, vegetables, and an egg for fried rice.

What to do with brown rice

- Combine 1 part brown rice with 2 parts water in a pot with lid. Bring to a boil, reduce to a low simmer, cover, and cook about 50 minutes until tender. Optionally add salt, butter, and/ or powdered soup base at the start of cooking.

- **Make Northwest pilaf meals in a jar:** Vacuum-seal together 1 cup of rice, 1 tablespoon of powdered chicken bouillon, and a separate baggie containing ¼ cup each of sweetened dried cranberries and slivered almonds. To prepare, add rice, bouillon, and 2 cups of water to a pan, stir, and bring to a boil. Reduce heat to low, cover, and cook 20 minutes. Stir in fruit and nuts. Let sit 5 minutes covered and serve.

❏ **Done**

21

SEEDS

PRIORITY: *High* | CATEGORY: *Pantry staples*

For $55 at Sam's Club you can buy two #10 cans filled with 13 varieties of seeds that can grow up to 4600 pounds of fresh vegetables (such as green beans, carrots, corn, and squash) and provide seeds for the next year if necessary.

SHELF LIFE: 30 years

COST: $$$

WHERE TO BUY: LDS, Sam's Club, Costco, or online

HOW TO STORE: In #10 cans with an oxygen absorber

If you can't buy it all at once, track your progress below.

Persons	Quantity for 1 year	Mark Off What You Have
1		
2		
4		
6		
8		
12		

❑ **Done**

22

SPROUTING SEEDS

PRIORITY: *High* | **CATEGORY:** *Pantry staples*

Sprouting seeds are great for food storage. In a few days you can have a supply of fresh food and great nutrition. Try making sprouted grain bread or just eating wheatgrass. The sprouting kits from Sam's Club come with an assortment of seeds, including alfalfa, mung bean, and lentils.

> **SHELF LIFE:** 30 years
>
> **COST:** $ (about $80 for a year's supply for a family of 4)
>
> **WHERE TO BUY:** Sam's Club
>
> **SAMPLE PRICING:** Sam's Club $70 for 12 lbs.
>
> **HOW TO STORE:** In #10 cans with an oxygen absorber

If you can't buy it all at once, track your progress below.

SERVING SIZE: 1 cup | **SEASON:** anytime

Persons 3 servings/week	Quantity for 1 year	Mark Off What You Have
1	2 (#10) cans	
2	4 (#10) cans	
4	8 (#10) cans	
6	12 (#10) cans	
8	16 (#10) cans	
12	24 (#10) cans	

What to do with sprouts

- Add to salads and sandwiches.
- Puree wheatgrass and drink.
- **Sprout wheat berries:** In a jar, add 1 part seeds to 2 parts water and soak overnight. The next day, drain off the liquid and place the jar in a dark place. Rinse the berries with water at least twice a day, draining each time, and shake occasionally to prevent clumping. When the sprout tails are about twice as long as the berries, they are ready, 3 to 4 days. Don't rinse the berries the day you plan to grind them for bread.
- **Make sprouted wheat bread:** Grind the sprouts in a grain mill; they will be sticky. With wet hands, form into a loaf shape. You may also add soaked, dried fruit. Bake at 250°F until the outside of the loaf is firm but not hard and the bottom springs back when gently pressed.

❑ **Done**

23

WHEAT

PRIORITY: *High* | **CATEGORY:** *Pantry staples*

Wheat comes in three main varieties: hard red and hard or soft white. Hard wheat is best for bread, while soft white wheat is best for pastry. Hard red wheat makes a dense, dark loaf of bread. For the most palatable bread, choose hard white or a mixture of red and white. Wheat can be ground into flour, served as wheat berries, or sprouted into wheat grass. If your family enjoys quinoa or barley, or other grains, you can substitute these for some amount of wheat.

SHELF LIFE: 30 years

COST: $$ ($333 a year for a family of 4 if purchased at the LDS, plus about $125 for cans)

WHERE TO BUY: LDS, Sam's Club, Costco, or online

SAMPLE PRICING: LDS $11.45 for 25 lbs., Sam's Club $33.98 for 40 lbs., Costco $44.99 for 40 lbs., Honeyville $49.99 for 50 lbs.

HOW TO STORE: In #10 cans with an oxygen absorber, or vacuum-sealed in bags with an oxygen absorber, then stored in buckets. Can be bought ready to store.

If you can't buy it all at once, track your progress below.

SERVING SIZE: ½ cup; see note | **SEASON:** anytime

Persons 14 servings/ week	Quantity for 1 year	Mark Off What You Have
1	182 lbs.	
2	364 lbs.	
4	728 lbs.	
6	1092 lbs.	
8	1456 lbs.	
12	2184 lbs.	

A note on serving size: 1 serving is ½ cup cooked wheat; 1 cup raw wheat berries will yield 2½ cups cooked.

Prerequisite: A grain mill

What to do with wheat berries

- Grind them to make wheat flour for bread, flatbread, hardtack, or tortillas. Use as a thickener.

- Soak them overnight in 3 parts water to 1 part wheat, and then simmer them for about 50 minutes until chewy, nutty, and delicious. Add fruit and eat like you would oatmeal, or add to soups or stews as you would barley.

- Wheat berries can also be sprouted. Soak the berries in water, rinsing them and changing the water every 8 hours. They should begin to sprout in 2 days and can be eaten right away or grown into wheat grass.

❑ **Done**

24

YEAST

PRIORITY: *High* | **CATEGORY:** *Pantry staples*

Yeast is needed to make bread, which makes it critically important. A pound of yeast will make about 75 loaves of bread. To calculate the amount of yeast needed, I figure one loaf of bread for four people per day. Store yeast in the freezer or refrigerator for maximum shelf life and try to use and replace it yearly.

SHELF LIFE: 1 year (keep it in the freezer to extend it indefinitely)

COST: $ (about $15 for a year's supply for a family of 4)

SAMPLE PRICING: Costco $2.85 for 1 lb.

WHERE TO BUY: Costco or the grocery store

HOW TO STORE: In the freezer or a cool, dark place

If you can't buy it all at once, track your progress below.

YEAST

SERVING SIZE: about 2 teaspoons | **SEASON:** anytime

Persons	Quantity for 1 year	Mark Off What You Have
1	2 lbs.	
2	3 lbs.	
4	5 lbs.	
6	8 lbs.	
8	10 lbs.	
12	15 lbs.	

BREAD

SERVING SIZE: ¼ loaf | **SEASON:** anytime

Persons 7 servings/week	Quantity for 1 year	Mark Off What You Have
1	62 loaves	
2	124 loaves	
4	248 loaves	
6	372 loaves	
8	496 loaves	
12	744 loaves	

What to do with yeast

- **Bake bread/rolls:** Mix 3 cups of flour with 2 teaspoons of salt and 2 teaspoons of yeast. Add 1⅛ cups of water and mix to form a dough. If it is too wet and sticks to the bowl or keeps sticking to your hands, add a little more flour. If it is too dry and won't form into a ball, add a bit of water. Knead for 10 minutes. Cover it and set it aside to rise until it doubles in size, about 90 minutes. Punch it down and let it rise again. Shape it, either by putting it in a greased loaf pan or by rolling it out into a long loaf and putting it on the back of a cookie sheet. Bake at 375°F for 40 to 50 minutes depending on the shape. Long, narrow loaves bake faster. You can also form the dough into individual sandwich rolls and use them for sloppy joes or pulled pork sandwiches.

- **Make pizza crust:** Add 2 tablespoons of sugar, 1 tablespoon of yeast, 1 egg, and 1 tablespoon of oil to 1¼ cups of warm water. Stir to combine and let stand until foamy. Add 1½ teaspoons of salt and stir into 3 cups of flour. Stir until a soft dough forms. Knead about 10 minutes, then let rise 1 hour. Roll into 4 crusts. Top with sauce, cheese, and toppings, and bake at 450°F until golden.

❑ **Done**

25

CARROTS

PRIORITY: *High* | **CATEGORY:** *Produce*

Carrots are part of the holy trinity of onions, carrots, and celery. They are also great as a side dish.

SHELF LIFE: 30 years

COST: $ (about $65 for a year's supply for a family of 4)

WHERE TO BUY: LDS, Sam's Club, Costco, or online

SAMPLE PRICING: LDS $66 for 25 lbs.

HOW TO STORE: In #10 cans with an oxygen absorber

If you can't buy it all at once, track your progress below.

SERVING SIZE: ⅛ to ½ cup; see note | **SEASON:** anytime

Persons 6 servings/week	Quantity for 1 year	Mark Off What You Have
1	1 (#10) can	
2	2 (#10) cans	
4	4 (#10) cans	
6	6 (#10) cans	
8	8 (#10) cans	
12	12 (#10) cans	

A note on serving size: Most recipes for 4 call for ½ to 1 cup.

What to do with carrots

- Make chicken noodle soup (page 53).
- Make lentil soup (page 84).
- Make split pea soup (page 86).

❑ **Done**

26

CELERY

PRIORITY: *High* | **CATEGORY:** *Produce*

Also part of the trifecta of vegetable flavor, celery is not only great in soups and stew, but also adds crunch to chicken salad.

> **SHELF LIFE:** 30 years
>
> **COST:** $ (about $64 for a year's supply for a family of 4)
>
> **WHERE TO BUY:** Online
>
> **SAMPLE PRICING:** Online $16 per can

HOW TO STORE: In #10 cans with an oxygen absorber

If you can't buy it all at once, track your progress below.

SERVING SIZE: ½ cup; see note | **SEASON:** anytime

Persons 6 servings/week	Quantity for 1 year	Mark Off What You Have
1	1 (#10) can	
2	1 (#10) can	
4	2 (#10) cans	
6	3 (#10) cans	
8	4 (#10) cans	
12	6 (#10) cans	

A note on serving size: The ½ cup serving is reconstituted. ¼ cup dehydrated celery yields about ½ cup reconstituted.

What to do with celery

- Make minestrone in a jar (page 90).
- Make chili mac in a jar (page 90).

❏ **Done**

27

FALL FRUITS: APPLES AND PEARS

PRIORITY: *High* | **CATEGORY:** *Produce*

Apples are great for snacks, pies, crisps, and other delicious things. You can either buy them already dried from the LDS and dry-pack can them or vacuum-seal them, or you can make your own dried apples and pears.

> **SHELF LIFE:** 30 years
>
> **COST:** $ (about $100 for a year's supply for a family of 4)
>
> **WHERE TO BUY:** LDS, Sam's Club, Costco, or online

SAMPLE PRICING: LDS $5.70 per can

HOW TO STORE: In #10 cans with an oxygen absorber

Adjust the proportions and varieties of fruit according to your family's tastes.

SERVING SIZE: ½ cup; see note | **SEASON:** fall; see note

Persons 5 servings/week	Quantity for 1 year	Mark Off What You Have
1	6 (#10) cans	
2	12 (#10) cans	
4	24 (#10) cans	
6	36 (#10) cans	
8	48 (#10) cans	
12	72 (#10) cans	

A note on serving size: The ½ cup serving is rehydrated. ¼ cup dehydrated fruit yields about ½ cup rehydrated fruit.

A note on season: Fall offers the most apple varieties at their peak flavor.

How to dehydrate apples and pears

- Use an apple peeler, corer, or slicer to prepare the apples. Layer on dehydrator trays and dry at 120°F for about 8 to 12 hours. Vacuum-seal in bags or jars.

What to do with fall fruits

- Snack on them.
- **Make applesauce or pear sauce:** Rehydrate dried apples or pears in water and cook in a pot, with some sugar and cinnamon if desired.
- **Make an apple or pear crisp:** Rehydrate apples or pears in water and drain. Place in a baking dish. Mix together butter (or ghee) with sugar, brown sugar, cinnamon, and oats and crumble on top of apples. Bake at 350°F until golden and bubbly.
- **Make apple or pear butter:** Quarter 4 to 5 pounds of apples or pears. Season with cinnamon, 3 cups of sugar, and the zest and juice of 1 lemon. Cook on low heat in a pot or slow cooker until completely soft. Strain through a food mill or strainer, pressing to keep as much puree as possible while removing the peel and seeds. Return the puree to the pot or slow cooker

and cook uncovered for another hour over low heat, stirring very often to prevent sticking, until smooth, brown, and thickened. Serve like jam with toast, biscuits, or pancakes. Also pairs well with pork.

- **Make a rustic pie:** Rehydrate about 4 cups of apples (or fruit of choice) in water, cover for about 30 minutes, and then drain off any excess water. Preheat the oven to 350°F. Make a pie crust using a Jiffy pie crust kit (see page 32). Roll it out and transfer to a rimmed baking sheet. Toss the fruit with 1 teaspoon of cinnamon, 1 tablespoon of flour, and 3 tablespoons of sugar. Mound the fruit in the center of the pie crust, dot with pieces of butter, and fold the edges of the crust up and over the apples. Bake for about 45 minutes or until the crust is golden brown and the fruit filling is bubbling. (For a quick-and-easy version, mound canned pie filling in the center of your pie crust and bake as directed.)

❏ **Done**

28

ONIONS

PRIORITY: *High* | **CATEGORY:** *Produce*

Onions are a staple that goes into many recipes, often along with carrots and celery, so plan to store lots.

SHELF LIFE: 30 years

COST: $ (about $35 for a year's supply for a family of 4)

WHERE TO BUY: LDS, Sam's Club, Costco, or online

SAMPLE PRICING: LDS $88 for 25 lbs.

HOW TO STORE: In #10 cans with an oxygen absorber

If you can't buy it all at once, track your progress below.

SERVING SIZE: 1 tablespoon; see note | **SEASON:** anytime

Persons 6 servings/week	Quantity for 1 year	Mark Off What You Have
1	1 (#10) can	
2	1 (#10) can	
4	2 (#10) cans	
6	3 (#10) cans	
8	4 (#10) cans	
12	6 (#10) cans	

A note on serving size: Most recipes for 4 call for ¼ cup.

What to do with onions

- Make chili con carne (page 104).
- Make cowboy stew (page 105).
- Make tuna casserole (page 52).

❏ **Done**

29

CANNED TUNA

PRIORITY: *High* | **CATEGORY:** *Protein*

Canned tuna is a great source of protein and a sandwich and casserole classic.

SHELF LIFE: At least 3 years

COST: $ (about $91 for a year's supply for a family of 4)

WHERE TO BUY: Sam's Club, Costco, or online

SAMPLE PRICING: Sam's Club $8.78 for 10, Costco $18.27 for 12

HOW TO STORE: In your rotation pantry

If you can't buy it all at once, track your progress below.

SERVING SIZE: 3 oz. | **SEASON:** anytime

Persons 1 serving/week	Quantity for 1 year	Mark Off What You Have
1	26 (6-oz.) cans	
2	52 (6-oz.) cans	
4	104 (6-oz.) cans	
6	156 (6-oz.) cans	
8	208 (6-oz.) cans	
12	312 (6-oz.) cans	

What to do with tuna

- **Make tuna melts:** Add a slice of cheese to a tuna sandwich and grill it.
- **Make a tuna casserole:** Combine 1 (14.5-oz.) can of cream of mushroom soup with 2 cans of tuna, drained, 12 oz. cooked pasta, and 1 cup grated cheese (optionally: add minced onion, sliced mushrooms, or peas). Mix together and pour into a baking dish. Top with crushed potato chips or buttered breadcrumbs and bake in a 350°F oven until bubbly.

❑ **Done**

30

CHICKEN (PRESSURE-CANNED AND FREEZE-DRIED)

PRIORITY: *High* | **CATEGORY:** *Protein*

So many things "taste like chicken," it must be the most flexible ingredient in your food storage. It can be purchased raw and home-canned or purchased freeze-dried in cans. Consider storing both.

SHELF LIFE: 30 years for freeze-dried, about 2 years for home-canned

COST: $$ (about $330 for a year's supply for a family of 4 of fresh, home-canned chicken, about $400 for a year's supply of freeze-dried chicken for a family of 4)

WHERE TO BUY: Sam's Club, Costco, or online

SAMPLE PRICING: Sam's Club $46 for 1 can of freeze-dried chicken, Costco $1.59 per lb. of boneless, skinless thighs or $400 for 544 servings of freeze-dried chicken (12 cans)

HOW TO STORE: In #10 cans with an oxygen absorber

If you can't buy it all at once, track your progress below.

SERVING SIZE: ¼ pound | **SEASON:** anytime

Persons 4 servings/week	Quantity for 1 year	Mark Off What You Have
1	52 lbs.	
2	104 lbs.	
4	208 lbs.	
6	312 lbs.	
8	416 lbs.	
12	624 lbs.	

What to do with home-canned chicken

- **Make chicken noodle soup:** Add carrots, onion, celery, chicken soup base, and noodles.
- **Make chicken salad:** Chop and mix with mayonnaise, minced onion, and celery and serve on lettuce or in a sandwich.
- **Make chicken and gravy on biscuits:** Thicken the juice with a roux made of half butter/oil/shortening and half flour cooked together and add the juices from the jar and chicken stock (soup base and water) or milk. Add chopped chicken and heat through. Ladle over hot biscuits.

How to pressure-can chicken

- Place raw chicken into sterile pint or quart jars. Cover with water to within 1 inch of the rim, add a pinch of salt, and pressure-can for 70 minutes for pints or 90 minutes for quarts.

What to do with freeze-dried chicken

- **Make chicken soup meals in a jar:** In a quart jar add 1 cup chicken, 2 cups noodles, 3 tablespoons chicken soup base, ¼ cup dehydrated onion, ¼ cup dehydrated celery, 1 cup dehydrated carrots, and 2 dehydrated lemon slices. To serve add to 8 cups of water, simmer for 20 minutes, and serve, adding more water if needed. Remove lemon before serving.

- **Make chicken and rice meals in a jar:** In a quart jar add 3 tablespoons powdered milk, ½ teaspoon celery seed, ½ teaspoon herbs de Provence, ½ teaspoon dried rosemary, ½ teaspoon garlic powder, ¼ teaspoon ground black pepper, 1 tablespoon chicken bouillon, ¼ cup dehydrated carrots, ¼ cup dehydrated peas, ¼ cup dehydrated onion, ¼ cup dehydrated celery, 1½ cups minute rice, 1 cup freeze-dried chicken, and 1 cup dehydrated sliced mushrooms. Add an oxygen absorber or vacuum-seal. To serve, add 3 cups of water and simmer until rice is tender, about 15 minutes.

❏ **Done**

31

HAMBURGER

PRIORITY: *High* | **CATEGORY:** *Protein*

Hamburger is a very useful ingredient to have on hand. You can use it in a variety of recipes. Purchase it in bulk when it goes on sale, brown it lightly, and then pressure-can it in pint jars.

The food plan in this section calls for serving beef three times a week and there are several choices for which type of beef to store. Hamburger is fabulous for pasta and casseroles. Freeze-dried beef is more costly but lasts longer and is perfect for dried meals in a jar. Textured vegetable protein (TVP) is a beef stretcher, costing about a third as much as beef, but is fairly indistinguishable in something like spaghetti sauce, especially when combined with real beef. Braised beef is stringy beef roast perfect for burritos and tacos, or you can thicken the broth into gravy and serve it over polenta or biscuits. Beef chunks are perfect for stew or shepherd's pie. Meatballs are awesome with spaghetti, or course, and also make wonderful sandwiches.

SHELF LIFE: About 2 years

COST: $$ (about $115 for a year's supply for a family of 4)

WHERE TO BUY: Costco, Sam's Club, or grocery store specials

SAMPLE PRICING: Costco $2.21 per lb., Sam's Club $2.98 per lb.

Decide what type(s) of beef to store depending on your preferences.

BEEF

SERVING SIZE: ¼ pound | SEASON: anytime

Persons 3 servings/week	Quantity for 1 year	Mark Off What You Have
1	39 lbs.	
2	78 lbs.	
4	156 lbs.	
6	234 lbs.	
8	312 lbs.	
12	468 lbs.	

HAMBURGER

SERVING SIZE: ¼ pound | SEASON: anytime

Persons 1 serving/week	Quantity for 1 year	Mark Off What You Have
1	13 lbs.	
2	26 lbs.	
4	52 lbs.	
6	78 lbs.	
8	104 lbs.	
12	156 lbs.	

What to do with hamburger

- Add it to spaghetti sauce and serve over pasta. Optionally mix it half-and-half with TVP (see page 114).
- Mix it with macaroni and cheese.
- Toss it with cooked pasta, olive oil, garlic, Parmesan cheese, and peas.

- **Pressure-can it:** Buy a 10 lb. chub pack from Sam's Club or Costco, and in a large skillet with sides or an electric roaster, cook it in about 2 cups of water (so it poaches gently instead of getting a brown crust), breaking it up as it cooks. Cook it until well crumbled, but only about half cooked, and then ladle into sterile pint jars. Wipe the rims of the jars with a paper towel moistened with a bit of vinegar to cut the fat. Add about ¼ teaspoon of salt to each jar and then fill to within 1 inch of the rim with hot water. Pressure-can 75 minutes for pints, 90 minutes for quarts.

- **Make "Bleep on a Shingle" (creamed beef on toast):** This is a meal my father loves from his days in the military, although it had a more colorful, if less appetizing name. It is pure comfort food. Cook ground beef in a skillet until cooked through (reserving any canning liquid if using canned ground beef). Some fat should accumulate in the bottom of the pan, and if not add about 2 tablespoons of oil, shortening, butter, or ghee to the pan. Sprinkle in about 3 tablespoons of flour and stir it into the beef and fat. Cook for 3 or 4 minutes until bubbly. Add back any reserved liquid from the can, plus milk to make about 2 cups total. Stir well and let simmer until thickened. Season generously with salt and pepper, and serve spooned over toast or biscuits.

❑ **Done**

32

LAUNDRY DETERGENT, DISH SOAP, SPRAY CLEANER, BLEACH (UNSCENTED), & CLEANSER

PRIORITY: *High* | **CATEGORY:** *Sundries & household*

Being able to keep clean and to disinfect surfaces is important in emergencies; it can prevent the spread of illness.

SHELF LIFE: 30 years

COST: $$$

WHERE TO BUY: LDS, Sam's Club, Costco, or online

HOW TO STORE: Store as packaged

If you can't buy it all at once, track your progress below.

Persons	Quantity for 1 year	Mark Off What You Have
1		Detergent: Dish soap: Bleach: Spray cleaner: Cleanser:
2		Detergent: Dish soap: Bleach: Spray cleaner: Cleanser:
4		Detergent: Dish soap: Bleach: Spray cleaner: Cleanser:
6		Detergent: Dish soap: Bleach: Spray cleaner: Cleanser:
8		Detergent: Dish soap: Bleach: Spray cleaner: Cleanser:
12		Detergent: Dish soap: Bleach: Spray cleaner: Cleanser:

❑ Done

33

LIGHTING & COOKING SUPPLIES

PRIORITY: *High* | **CATEGORY:** *Sundries & household*

Determine how you will light your home and cook if the power is out, and what you would need to do that. Consider what you would do in winter and in summer, and plan to have a backup method (or three). Think about flashlights, batteries, candles, matches, lighters, firewood, kindling, matches, briquettes, extra propane, camp stoves, grills, and Dutch ovens, etc.

> **SHELF LIFE:** Varies
>
> **COST:** Varies
>
> **WHERE TO BUY:** LDS, Sam's Club, Costco, or online
>
> **HOW TO STORE:** Varies

34

PET FOOD

PRIORITY: *High (for pet lovers)* | **CATEGORY:** *Sundries & household*

Pets are family too. Be sure to lay in a large supply of pet food. The oils in dog food can go rancid over time, so store it in your rotation pantry and keep it fresh. Canned dog and cat food will last very well.

> **SHELF LIFE:** 30 years
>
> **COST:** $$ (varies)
>
> **WHERE TO BUY:** Sam's Club, Costco, or Walmart
>
> **SAMPLE PRICING:** Varies
>
> **HOW TO STORE:** In 5-gallon buckets with an oxygen absorber

If you can't buy it all at once, track your progress below.

Animals	Quantity for 1 year	Mark Off What You Have
1		Dog food: Cat food: Bird food:
2		Dog food: Cat food: Bird food:
4		Dog food: Cat food: Bird food:
6		Dog food: Cat food: Bird food:
8		Dog food: Cat food: Bird food:
12		Dog food: Cat food: Bird food:

Animals	Quantity for 1 year	Mark Off What You Have
1		Other: Other:
2		Other: Other:
4		Other: Other:
6		Other: Other:
8		Other: Other:
12		Other: Other:

❏ **Done**

SHAMPOO, SOAP, TOOTHPASTE, RAZORS, DEODORANT, & MOUTHWASH

PRIORITY: *High* | **CATEGORY:** *Sundries & household*

Hygiene is important in emergencies; it can prevent the spread of illness.

SHELF LIFE: 30 years

COST: $$$

SAMPLE PRICING: N/A

WHERE TO BUY: LDS, Sam's Club, Costco, or online

HOW TO STORE: In #10 cans with an oxygen absorber

If you can't buy it all at once, track your progress below.

Persons	Quantity for 1 year	Mark Off What You Have
1		Shampoo: Soap: Toothpaste:
2		Shampoo: Soap: Toothpaste:
4		Shampoo: Soap: Toothpaste:
6		Shampoo: Soap: Toothpaste:
8		Shampoo: Soap: Toothpaste:
12		Shampoo: Soap: Toothpaste:

Persons	Quantity for 1 year	Mark Off What You Have
1		Razors:
		Deodorant:
		Mouthwash:
		Other:
		Other:
2		Razors:
		Deodorant:
		Mouthwash:
		Other:
		Other:
4		Razors:
		Deodorant:
		Mouthwash:
		Other:
		Other:
6		Razors:
		Deodorant:
		Mouthwash:
		Other:
		Other:
8		Razors:
		Deodorant:
		Mouthwash:
		Other:
		Other:
12		Razors:
		Deodorant:
		Mouthwash:
		Other:
		Other:

❏ **Done**

36

VITAMINS, ASPIRIN, ANTACIDS, COLD MEDS, BAND-AIDS, HAND SANITIZER, & ALCOHOL

PRIORITY: *High* | **CATEGORY:** *Sundries & household*

Store a year's worth of vitamins in your rotation pantry and replace them as they are used. Other good first aid items to store include Band-Aids, rubbing alcohol, hand sanitizer, cold medication, antacids, and Bactine.

SHELF LIFE: A year or more

COST: Varies

WHERE TO BUY: Sam's Club, Costco, or online

SAMPLE PRICING: Costco $20 for 200 vitamins

HOW TO STORE: Store as packaged

If you can't buy it all at once, track your progress below.

Persons	Quantity for 1 year	Mark Off What You Have
1		Vitamins:
		Aspirin:
		Cold meds:
2		Vitamins:
		Aspirin:
		Cold meds:
4		Vitamins:
		Aspirin:
		Cold meds:
6		Vitamins:
		Aspirin:
		Cold meds:
8		Vitamins:
		Aspirin:
		Cold meds:
12		Vitamins:
		Aspirin:
		Cold meds:

Persons	Quantity for 1 year	Mark Off What You Have
1		Band-Aids: Rubbing alcohol: Hand sanitizer: Other:
2		Band-Aids: Rubbing alcohol: Hand sanitizer: Other:
4		Band-Aids: Rubbing alcohol: Hand sanitizer: Other:
6		Band-Aids: Rubbing alcohol: Hand sanitizer: Other:
8		Band-Aids: Rubbing alcohol: Hand sanitizer: Other:
12		Band-Aids: Rubbing alcohol: Hand sanitizer: Other:

What to do with vitamins and first aid

• Take vitamins daily.

❏ **Done**

37

HONEY

PRIORITY: *High* | **CATEGORY:** *Sweets & sweeteners*

Honey has an indefinite shelf life. It can be used to treat coughs as well as wounds and burns. Honey is a natural antibacterial and is also a humectant and can be used in lotions to treat dry skin. It is also fabulous on biscuits and cornbread.

> **SHELF LIFE:** Forever
>
> **COST:** $
>
> **SAMPLE PRICING:** LDS $15.05 for 25 lbs., Sam's Club $11.19 for 25 lbs., Costco $15.25 for 25 lbs., Honeyville $71.99 for 50 lbs.
>
> **WHERE TO BUY:** LDS, Sam's Club, or Costco
>
> **HOW TO STORE:** Store honey in its original packaging

If you can't buy it all at once, track your progress below.

SERVING SIZE: 1 teaspoon | **SEASON:** anytime

Persons 2–3 servings/ week	Quantity for 1 year	Mark Off What You Have
1	2 lbs.	
2	4 lbs.	
4	8 lbs.	
6	12 lbs.	
8	16 lbs.	
12	24 lbs.	

What to do with honey

- Top biscuits (page 32) or cornbread (page 29).
- Sweeten tea.

❏ **Done**

38

SUGAR (WHITE, BROWN, & POWDERED)

PRIORITY: *High* | **CATEGORY:** *Sweets & sweeteners*

Sugar, honey, and jam are the main types of sweeteners planned for storage. Fortunately, sugar lasts forever. Feel free to adjust the proportions among the various sweeteners according to your family's preferences.

> **SHELF LIFE:** Forever
>
> **COST:** $
>
> **WHERE TO BUY:** LDS, Sam's Club, or Costco
>
> **SAMPLE PRICING:** LDS $15.05 for 25 lbs., Sam's Club $11.19 for 25 lbs., Costco $15.25 for 25 lbs., Honeyville $71.99 for 50 lbs.
>
> **HOW TO STORE:** In #10 cans with an oxygen absorber, or vacuum-sealed in bags with an oxygen absorber, then stored in buckets. Can be bought ready to store.

If you can't buy it all at once, track your progress below.

ALL SUGAR

SERVING SIZE: 1 teaspoon | **SEASON:** anytime

Persons	Quantity for 1 year	Mark Off What You Have
1	24 lbs.	
2	48 lbs.	
4	96 lbs.	
6	144 lbs.	
8	192 lbs.	
12	288 lbs.	

WHITE SUGAR

SERVING SIZE: 1 teaspoon | **SEASON:** anytime

Persons 25 servings/ week	Quantity for 1 year	Mark Off What You Have
1	14 lbs.	
2	28 lbs.	
4	56 lbs.	
6	84 lbs.	
8	112 lbs.	
12	168 lbs.	

BROWN SUGAR

SERVING SIZE: 1 teaspoon | **SEASON:** anytime

Persons 15 servings/ week	Quantity for 1 year	Mark Off What You Have
1	8 lbs.	
2	16 lbs.	
4	32 lbs.	
6	48 lbs.	
8	64 lbs.	
12	96 lbs.	

POWDERED SUGAR

SERVING SIZE: 1 teaspoon | **SEASON:** anytime

Persons 4 servings/week	Quantity for 1 year	Mark Off What You Have
1	2 lbs.	
2	4 lbs.	
4	8 lbs.	
6	12 lbs.	
8	16 lbs.	
12	24 lbs.	

What to do with sugar

- **Bake sugar cookies:** In a bowl, mix together 1 cup butter flavor shortening and 1½ cups white sugar. Beat well. Add 1 egg and 1 teaspoon vanilla extract. Add 2¾ cups all-purpose flour, 1 teaspoon baking soda, and ½ teaspoon baking powder, and mix well. Preheat oven to 350°F. Roll heaping teaspoons of dough and place on a baking sheet 2 inches apart. Bake 8 to 10 minutes or until golden.

- **Bake a cake:** Beat together 1 cup white sugar and ½ cup butter flavor shortening. Add 2 eggs and 2 teaspoons vanilla extract. Mix well. Add 1½ cups all-purpose flour and 1¾ teaspoons baking powder and mix well. Stir in ½ cup milk. Pour into a greased 9 x 9 pan and bake at 350°F for 30 to 40 minutes.

- **Make frosting:** Mix together 1 cup of powdered sugar, ¼ cup of butter, and 1 tablespoon of milk. If desired, add 1 tablespoon of cocoa powder.

❑ **Done**

39

CANNED VEGETABLES

PRIORITY: *Medium* | **CATEGORY:** *Canned goods*

For your rotation pantry, make a list of any vegetables your family routinely enjoys canned and calculate about a two-year supply, and then keep your stock in rotation. This is an item you can work on little by little by buying a few extra cans each time you go to the grocery store. Good staple canned vegetables to keep on hand include green beans, corn, mushrooms, and peas.

SHELF LIFE: 2 years

COST: $ (about $100 for a year's supply for a family of 4)

WHERE TO BUY: Sam's Club, Costco, or the grocery store

SAMPLE PRICING: About $1.00–$1.50 per can

HOW TO STORE: In cans in your rotation pantry

Choose the types and quantities your family will enjoy.

SERVING SIZE: ½ can | **SEASON:** anytime

Persons	Quantity for 1 year	Mark Off What You Have
1		Green beans: Corn:
2		Green beans: Corn:
4		Green beans: Corn:
6		Green beans: Corn:
8		Green beans: Corn:
12		Green beans: Corn:

Persons	Quantity for 1 year	Mark Off What You Have
1		Mushrooms: Peas: Other: Other:
2		Mushrooms: Peas: Other: Other:
4		Mushrooms: Peas: Other: Other:
6		Mushrooms: Peas: Other: Other:
8		Mushrooms: Peas: Other: Other:
12		Mushrooms: Peas: Other: Other:

What to do with canned vegetables

• Add to soups, stews, salads, or casseroles.

❑ **Done**

40

CHEESE

PRIORITY: *Medium* | **CATEGORY:** *Dairy*

Cheese can be bought commercially as cheese powder, freeze-dried cheese, or canned cheese, or you can purchase cheese and either vacuum-seal it or wax it to maximize the shelf life.

SHELF LIFE: 2–5 years properly stored

COST: $$ (about $260 for a year's supply for a family of 4)

WHERE TO BUY: Washington State University sells canned cheese (cougarcheese.wsu.edu); online for powdered or freeze-dried cheese; Costco or Sam's Club for fresh cheese to wax or vacuum-seal

SAMPLE PRICING: Washington State University $22 for about 2 lbs. (30 oz.)

HOW TO STORE: In the refrigerator in cans, or in a cool location such as a root cellar

If you can't buy it all at once, track your progress below.

SERVING SIZE: 1 oz. | **SEASON:** anytime

Persons 2 servings/week	Quantity for 1 year	Mark Off What You Have
1	6.5 lbs.	Powder: Freeze-dried: Canned:
2	13 lbs.	Powder: Freeze-dried: Canned:
4	26 lbs.	Powder: Freeze-dried: Canned:
6	39 lbs.	Powder: Freeze-dried: Canned:
8	52 lbs.	Powder: Freeze-dried: Canned:
12	104 lbs.	Powder: Freeze-dried: Canned:

What to do with cheese

- Make grilled cheese sandwiches.
- **Make macaroni and cheese:** Combine ¼ cup butter, shortening, or ghee with ¼ cup flour, stir and cook together for 4 minutes. Add 2½ cups of milk, and stir constantly until thickened. Add 4 cups of grated cheese. Combine with 1 pound of cooked macaroni and bake at 375°F until bubbly and golden.
- **Make a mock soufflé:** Butter 8 slices of bread and cut into cubes. Butter the sides and bottom of a straight-sided baking dish. Add half the bread and top with a cup of grated cheese and 2 tablespoons of Parmesan cheese. Repeat the layers and press down. In a bowl, combine 5 eggs, 2 cups of milk, 1 teaspoon of Worcestershire sauce, ½ teaspoon dry mustard and ½ teaspoon of salt and beat well. Pour over bread and cheese. Cover tightly and refrigerate at least 2 hours or overnight. Bake at 350°F for 45 to 50 minutes.

❏ **Done**

BUTTER & MARGARINE

PRIORITY: *Medium* | **CATEGORY:** *Dairy*

Butter and margarine are luxury items in long-term food storage, but there are a few options. For baking I prefer butter-flavored Crisco and for making a roux to thicken a sauce, shortening or oil works equally well, but there is nothing like butter to spread on toast, pancakes, or biscuits. For real butter there are two main choices: Red Feather makes a canned butter that tastes exactly like fresh, creamy butter. Another option is ghee, a form of clarified butter that can be canned, requires no refrigeration, and lasts about a year. It is also possible to make ghee at home. I store both butter and ghee. For the purposes of this exercise, I am basing my calculations on ½ pound of butter/ghee for a family of 4 per week.

SHELF LIFE: About a year for ghee and at least 2 years for canned butter

COST: $–$$ (ghee, about $100 for a year's supply for a family of 4; butter, about $295 for a year's supply for a family of 4)

WHERE TO BUY: Costco or Amazon.com

SAMPLE PRICING: Costco $2 per lb.

HOW TO STORE: Purchase already sealed. Store cans/jars in a cool dark place.

If you can't buy it all at once, track your progress below.

SERVING SIZE: 1 teaspoon | **SEASON:** anytime

Persons 3 servings/week	Quantity for 1 year	Mark Off What You Have
1	6.5 lbs.	Butter: Margarine: Ghee:
2	13 lbs.	Butter: Margarine: Ghee:
4	26 lbs.	Butter: Margarine: Ghee:
6	39 lbs.	Butter: Margarine: Ghee:
8	52 lbs.	Butter: Margarine: Ghee:
12	78 lbs.	Butter: Margarine: Ghee:

What to do with butter

• Put it on toast, biscuits, pancakes, cornbread, bread, rice, noodles, popcorn, etc.

❑ **Done**

42

COCOA

PRIORITY: *Medium* | CATEGORY: *Drinks*

Powdered cocoa mix is an excellent addition to your food storage.

SHELF LIFE: 2 years

COST: $ (about $72 for a year's supply for a family of 4)

WHERE TO BUY: LDS, Sam's Club, or Costco

SAMPLE PRICING: LDS $36 for 25 lbs., Costco $5.83 for 70 servings

HOW TO STORE: In #10 cans with an oxygen absorber

If you can't buy it all at once, track your progress below.

SERVING SIZE: 1 oz. | SEASON: anytime

Persons 2 servings/week	Quantity for 1 year	Mark Off What You Have
1	6.5 lbs.	
2	13 lbs.	
4	26 lbs.	
6	39 lbs.	
8	52 lbs.	
12	78 lbs.	

What to do with cocoa

• Make hot chocolate. Optionally add marshmallows, whipped cream, or cinnamon.

❑ **Done**

43

POWDERED DRINKS

PRIORITY: *Medium* | **CATEGORY:** *Drinks*

Powdered drinks are a convenient way to add taste and variety to your family's food storage. Kool-Aid, Tang, instant lemonade, and powdered fruit punch are enjoyed by all ages.

SHELF LIFE: 30 years

COST: $ (about $72 for a year's supply for a family of 4)

WHERE TO BUY: LDS, Sam's Club, Costco, or online

SAMPLE PRICING: Sam's Club—Kool-Aid $6 for a 34-quart canister, Costco—Tang $6 for 22 quarts

HOW TO STORE: As packaged

If you can't buy it all at once, track your progress below.

SERVING SIZE: 8 oz. | **SEASON:** anytime

Persons 7 servings/week	Quantity for 1 year	Mark Off What You Have
1	3 canisters	Kool-Aid: Other:
2	6 canisters	Kool-Aid: Other:
4	12 canisters	Kool-Aid: Other:
6	18 canisters	Kool-Aid: Other:
8	24 canisters	Kool-Aid: Other:
12	36 canisters	Kool-Aid: Other:

What to do with instant drink mixes

- Blend with fruit juice for a fruit punch.

❏ **Done**

44

VEGETABLE SHORTENING

PRIORITY: *Medium* | **CATEGORY:** *Fats*

Ideally vegetable shortening should be used within two years, but depending on storage conditions, it can last much longer. Cool, dark places are best. Shortening is great for cooking and baking. I like to store regular shortening as well as butter-flavored shortening to use in baking.

SHELF LIFE: 2 years

COST: $ (Costco $9.13 for 6 lbs.)

WHERE TO BUY: Costco, Walmart, or the local grocery store

HOW TO STORE: Unopened in original packaging in your rotation pantry

If you can't buy it all at once, track your progress below.

SERVING SIZE: varies by recipe | **SEASON:** anytime

Persons 3 servings/week	Quantity for 1 year	Mark Off What You Have
1	6 lbs.	
2	12 lbs.	
4	24 lbs.	
6	36 lbs.	
8	48 lbs.	
12	52 lbs.	

What to do with shortening

- Make biscuits (page 32).
- Make chocolate chip cookies (page 152).
- **Thicken a sauce:** Cook together equal parts shortening and flour (2 to 4 tablespoons of each) and stir into brothy soups to thicken into a gravy-like texture.

❏ **Done**

45

BAKING SODA & BAKING POWDER

PRIORITY: *Medium* | **CATEGORY:** *Pantry staples*

Baking soda and baking powder are key ingredients for baking. Use in muffins, cakes, biscuits, and much more.

> **SHELF LIFE:** About 2 years
>
> **COST:** $ (about $13 for a year's supply of both for a family of 4)
>
> **WHERE TO BUY:** Sam's Club, Costco, or the grocery store
>
> **SAMPLE PRICING:** Costco $4.33 for 5 lbs. baking soda, $9 for 5 lbs. baking powder
>
> **HOW TO STORE:** In original packaging in your rotation pantry

If you can't buy it all at once, track your progress below.

SERVING SIZE: N/A | **SEASON:** anytime

Persons	Quantity for 1 year	Mark Off What You Have
1	1 lb.	
2	2 lbs.	
4	4 lbs.	
6	6 lbs.	
8	8 lbs.	
12	12 lbs.	

What to do with baking soda

- **Make biscuit mix:** In a large bowl, mix together 9 cups flour, 1½ cups nonfat dry milk, ½ cup granulated sugar, 3 teaspoons baking powder, 1 teaspoon baking soda, 3 teaspoons salt, and 2¼ cups vegetable shortening. Portion out into 2¼-cup portions. To prepare, preheat oven to 450°F. Combine mix with ⅔ cup of milk. Pat into 1½-inch-thick round. Cut into 2-inch rounds and place on a baking sheet. Bake 7 to 10 minutes or until lightly golden.

❏ **Done**

46

BARLEY

PRIORITY: *Medium* | **CATEGORY:** *Grains*

Barley works well in soups and stew. Pearled barley (barley which has had the hull removed) requires about 35 to 40 minutes of simmering to cook but doesn't have to be pre-soaked.

SHELF LIFE: 2 years

COST: $ (about $30 for a year's supply for a family of 4)

WHERE TO BUY: LDS, Sam's Club, Costco, or online

SAMPLE PRICING: Honeyville $55 for 50 lbs.

HOW TO STORE: In #10 cans with an oxygen absorber

If you can't buy it all at once, track your progress below.

SERVING SIZE: ½ cup | **SEASON:** anytime

Persons 1 serving/week	Quantity for 1 year	Mark Off What You Have
1	4 lbs.	
2	8 lbs.	
4	16 lbs.	
6	24 lbs.	
8	32 lbs.	
12	48 lbs.	

What to do with barley

- Add to soups.
- Add to stews, such as cowboy stew (page 105).
- **Make beef barley meals in a jar:** In a quart jar add ¾ cup dehydrated carrots, ⅓ cup beef bouillon granules, ¼ cup dried onion flakes, 1 cup small pasta (orzo, ditilini), 1 cup pearled barley, and 1 cup freeze-dried ground beef. Add an oxygen absorber or vacuum-seal. When ready to serve, add 12 cups of water and simmer 30 to 45 minutes.

❑ **Done**

47

BISQUICK

PRIORITY: *Medium* | **CATEGORY:** *Pantry staples*

Bisquick can be used to make biscuits, pancakes, or waffles, plus impossible pies (pies that form their own crusts while baking). Don't forget biscuits and gravy, chicken and gravy on a biscuit, and biscuit-topped pot pies. For a fabulous biscuit à la Red Lobster, add grated cheddar to the mix and brush with garlic butter when fresh out of the oven.

>   **SHELF LIFE:** About 2 years
>
>   **COST:** $ (about $48 for a year's supply for a family of 4)
>
>   **WHERE TO BUY:** Sam's Club, Costco, or online
>
>   **SAMPLE PRICING:** Costco $6 for 96 oz. (67 servings), Sam's Club $4.83 for 80 oz. (56 servings)
>
>   **HOW TO STORE:** In #10 cans with an oxygen absorber

If you can't buy it all at once, track your progress below.

SERVING SIZE: ⅓ cup | **SEASON:** anytime

Persons 2 servings/week	Quantity for 1 year	Mark Off What You Have
1	4 (40-oz.) boxes	
2	8 (40-oz.) boxes	
4	16 (40-oz.) boxes	
6	24 (40-oz.) boxes	
8	32 (40-oz.) boxes	
12	48 (40-oz.) boxes	

What to do with Bisquick

- Make pancakes, biscuits, waffles, or scones for breakfast.
- Make chicken and gravy (page 53) or creamed beef (page 56) over biscuits.
- Make shortcakes (add sugar to the biscuit recipe, page 32) and serve with fruit.

❑ **Done**

48

BLACK BEANS

PRIORITY: *Medium* | **CATEGORY:** *Pantry staples*

Black beans are commonly used in Latin food. They are a delicious addition to soups and salads and can also be prepared as refried beans.

SHELF LIFE: 30 years

COST: $ (about $40 for a year's supply for a family of 4)

SAMPLE PRICING: LDS $18.55 for 25 lbs., Sam's Club $69 for 42 lbs., Costco $17.88 for 25 lbs.

WHERE TO BUY: LDS, Sam's Club, Costco, or online

HOW TO STORE: In #10 cans with an oxygen absorber

If you can't buy it all at once, track your progress below.

SERVING SIZE: 1 cup; see note | **SEASON:** anytime

Persons ¾ serving/week	Quantity for 1 year	Mark Off What You Have
1	10 lbs.	
2	20 lbs.	
4	40 lbs.	
6	60 lbs.	
8	80 lbs.	
12	120 lbs.	

A note on serving size: 1 cup cooked beans is 1 serving as an entree; ½ cup cooked beans is 1 serving as a side. 1 cup of uncooked beans weighs ½ pound and yields 3 cups of cooked beans.

What to do with black beans

- **Make nachos:** Spread grated cheese and black beans over corn chips or fried tortilla triangles. Bake or broil briefly until cheese melts.

❏ **Done**

49

CANNELLINI BEANS

PRIORITY: *Medium* | **CATEGORY:** *Pantry staples*

Cannellini (white beans) are commonly used in Italian cuisine. They are a great addition to soups and salads and are delicious when pureed with garlic and olive oil and used as a dip or spread.

SHELF LIFE: 30 years

COST: $ (about $32 for a year's supply for a family of 4)

WHERE TO BUY: LDS, Costco, or online

SAMPLE PRICING: LDS $16 for 25 lbs., Honeyville $47 for 25 lbs.

HOW TO STORE: In #10 cans with an oxygen absorber

If you can't buy it all at once, track your progress below.

SERVING SIZE: 1 cup; see note | **SEASON:** anytime

Persons ¾ serving/week	Quantity for 1 year	Mark Off What You Have
1	10 lbs.	
2	20 lbs.	
4	40 lbs.	
6	60 lbs.	
8	80 lbs.	
12	120 lbs.	

A note on serving size: 1 cup cooked beans is 1 serving as an entree; ½ cup cooked beans is 1 serving as a side. 1 cup of uncooked beans weighs ½ pound and yields 3 cups of cooked beans.

What to do with white beans

- **Make an awesome dip or spread:** Puree the beans with olive oil, salt, garlic, and a splash of lemon juice.

❏ **Done**

50

GARBANZO BEANS (CHICKPEAS)

PRIORITY: *Medium* | **CATEGORY:** *Pantry staples*

Chickpeas can be used in soups and stew to add protein and fiber, or pureed with garlic, tahini, and lemon to make hummus, a fabulous Middle Eastern dip and spread.

    SHELF LIFE: 30 years

    COST: $ (about $20 for a year's supply for a family of 4)

    WHERE TO BUY: Costco or online

    SAMPLE PRICING: Costco $22.73 for 25 lbs., Honeyville $46.99 for 25 lbs.

    HOW TO STORE: In #10 cans with an oxygen absorber

If you can't buy it all at once, track your progress below.

SERVING SIZE: 1 cup; see note | **SEASON:** anytime

Persons 3 servings/week	Quantity for 1 year	Mark Off What You Have
1	8 lbs.	
2	16 lbs.	
4	32 lbs.	
6	48 lbs.	
8	64 lbs.	
12	96 lbs.	

A note on serving size: 1 cup cooked beans is 1 serving as an entree; ½ cup cooked beans is 1 serving as a side. 1 cup of uncooked beans weighs ½ pound and yields 3 cups of cooked beans.

What to do with garbanzo beans

- **Make hummus:** Puree with garlic, olive oil, tahini, and lemon.
- Soak overnight, drain, replace the water, bring to a boil, reduce to a simmer, and cook 2 to 3 hours.
- Toss cooked garbanzos in oil and season abundantly with seasoning salt. Place on a rimmed baking sheet and roast at 400°F for 30 to 40 minutes until golden and crunchy. Delicious!

❑ **Done**

51

HERBS & SPICES

PRIORITY: *Medium* | **CATEGORY:** *Pantry staples*

According to your family's taste, you may want to store garlic, thyme, sage, rosemary, parsley, pepper, garlic powder, onion powder, Italian seasoning, seasoned salt, Montreal steak seasoning, curry powder, paprika, red pepper flakes, taco seasoning, and chili powder, etc.

> **SHELF LIFE:** About 1 year for herbs and many years for seasoning salt
>
> **COST:** $ (about $100 for a year's supply for a family of 4)
>
> **WHERE TO BUY:** Sam's Club or Costco
>
> **SAMPLE PRICING:** Sam's Club $4.38 for 32 oz. of seasoning salt
>
> **HOW TO STORE:** As packaged in your rotation pantry

If you can't buy it all at once, track your progress below.

SERVING SIZE: 1 teaspoon | **SEASON:** anytime

Persons	Quantity for 1 year	Mark Off What You Have
1	1 jar per spice	
2	2 jars per spice	
4	4 jars per spice	

What to do with seasoning salt, garlic, and onion powder

- Season meat, fish, or vegetables.

❏ **Done**

52

LENTILS

PRIORITY: *Medium* | **CATEGORY:** *Pantry staples*

Lentils count as part of your supply of beans and, like beans, are filled with healthy proteins and carbohydrates. Lentils are among the quickest-cooking members of the bean and legume family; they require no pre-soaking and cook in 20 to 40 minutes, unlike beans, which must be soaked and/or cooked for hours. This makes them a great choice for lunch.

SHELF LIFE: 30 years

COST: $$ (about $250 for a year's supply for a family of 4)

WHERE TO BUY: Sam's Club, Costco, online, or at the grocery store

SAMPLE PRICING: Sam's Club $64.98 for 40 lbs., Costco $74.99 for 44 lbs., Honeyville $38.99 for 25 lbs.

HOW TO STORE: Package in #10 cans with oxygen absorbers, or vacuum-seal in bags with oxygen absorbers and store in buckets

If you can't buy it all at once, track your progress below.

SERVING SIZE: 1 cup; see note | **SEASON:** anytime

Persons ¾ serving/week	Quantity for 1 year	Mark Off What You Have
1	10 lbs.	
2	20 lbs.	
4	40 lbs.	
6	60 lbs.	
8	80 lbs.	
12	120 lbs.	

A note on serving size: 1 cup cooked lentils is 1 serving as an entree; ½ cup cooked lentils is 1 serving as a side. 1 cup of uncooked lentils weighs about ½ pound and yields 2½ to 3 cups of cooked lentils.

What to do with lentils

- **Cook the lentils:** Bring 5½ cups water to a boil with 1 teaspoon salt. Add 1 pound lentils, reduce heat to low, cover, and cook 20 minutes or until water is absorbed and lentils are tender.
- **Make tacos:** Substitute cooked lentils for meat in tacos.
- **Make lentil hummus:** Puree 2 cups cooked lentils with 2 teaspoons chopped garlic, ⅓ cup olive oil, 3 tablespoons tahini, and ¼ cup lemon juice. Serve as a dip with crackers or vegetables.
- **Make lentil soup:** In a soup pot, sauté 1 cup chopped onion, 1 cup chopped carrots, and 1 cup chopped celery in 1 tablespoon olive oil until softened. Add 1 can of chicken stock, 1 cup cooked lentils, and 1 teaspoon chopped garlic. Add 2 teaspoons of red wine vinegar and season to taste with salt and pepper.

❑ **Done**

53

MACARONI & CHEESE

PRIORITY: *Medium* | **CATEGORY:** *Pantry staples*

Macaroni and cheese is an easy, family-pleasing meal. You can serve it as is for non-picky palates or add diced ham or broccoli for more discriminating tastes. You can also dress it up with grated cheese. Only buy this if your family will eat it.

SHELF LIFE: 30 years

COST: $ (about $80 for a year's supply for a family of 4)

WHERE TO BUY: Sam's Club, Costco, or any grocery store

SAMPLE PRICING: Sam's Club $10 for 12

HOW TO STORE: In original packaging in your rotation pantry

Persons 1 serving/week	Quantity for 1 year	Mark Off What You Have
1	26 boxes	
2	52 boxes	
4	104 boxes	
6	156 boxes	
8	208 boxes	
12	312 boxes	

What to do with macaroni and cheese

• Prepare as directed. Optionally, add ham, broccoli, peas, or grated cheese.

❏ **Done**

54

SPLIT PEAS

PRIORITY: *Medium* | CATEGORY: *Pantry staples*

Split peas are famous for soup and also used in Indian cuisine for a dish called dahl.

SHELF LIFE: 30 years

COST: $ (about $12 for a year's supply for a family of 4)

WHERE TO BUY: LDS, Sam's Club, Costco, or online

SAMPLE PRICING: Costco $11.57 for 25 lbs., Amazon.com $32 for 25 lbs.

HOW TO STORE: In #10 cans with an oxygen absorber

If you can't buy it all at once, track your progress below.

SERVING SIZE: ½ cup; see note | **SEASON:** anytime

Persons 3 servings/week	Quantity for 1 year	Mark Off What You Have
1	4 lbs.	
2	8 lbs.	
4	16 lbs.	
6	24 lbs.	
8	32 lbs.	
12	48 lbs.	

A note on serving size: ½ cup cooked is 1 serving; ¼ cup dry split peas yields 2½ cups cooked.

What to do with split peas

- **Make split pea soup:** Sauté a cup of chopped onions and some garlic in oil until softened. Add 2 cups of carrots, 1 cup of diced potatoes, 1½ teaspoons of salt, and a teaspoon of pepper. Add 8 cups of chicken stock (or 8 cups of water plus 3 tablespoons of chicken soup base or bouillon). Add ½ pound of split peas (1¼ cups) and simmer 40 minutes. And an additional ½ pound of split peas and simmer another 40 minutes.

❑ **Done**

55

OATS

PRIORITY: *Medium* | **CATEGORY:** *Pantry staples*

Oats are delicious for breakfast—very comforting and filling. They also make fabulous cookies and wonderful granola.

SHELF LIFE: 30 years

COST: $ (about $40 for a year's supply for a family of 4)

SAMPLE PRICING: LDS $15.35 for 25 lbs., Sam's Club $69.99 for 41 lbs., Costco $72.99 for 42 lbs., Honeyville $78.99 for 50 lbs.)

WHERE TO BUY: LDS (preferably) or at Sam's Club, Costco, or online

HOW TO STORE: In #10 cans with oxygen absorbers, or vacuum-seal in bags with oxygen absorbers and store in buckets

If you can't buy it all at once, track your progress below.

SERVING SIZE: ½ cup oats; see note | **SEASON:** anytime

Persons 2 servings/week	Quantity for 1 year	Mark Off What You Have
1	10 lbs.	
2	20 lbs.	
4	40 lbs.	
6	60 lbs.	
8	80 lbs.	
12	120 lbs.	

A note on serving size: ½ cup uncooked oats yields 1 cup oatmeal.

What to do with oats

- **Make oatmeal:** Add 1 part rolled oats to 2 parts water, milk, or a mixture in a pot and add a pinch of salt. Bring to a boil, reduce to a simmer, and cook 5–6 minutes (until tender and creamy). If desired, add sugar and cinnamon.

- **Bake oatmeal cookies:** In a large bowl, cream together 1 cup shortening, 1 cup sugar, and 1 cup brown sugar. Add 2 eggs and 1 teaspoon vanilla extract. Stir in 2 cups flour, 1 teaspoon baking soda, 1 teaspoon salt, 1½ teaspoons ground cinnamon, and then 3 cups of oats. Spray a cookie sheet with cooking spray and drop spoonfuls 2 inches apart. Bake at 375°F for 8 to 10 minutes.

- **Make granola:** In a large bowl, stir together 3 cups rolled oats, 3 tablespoons packed light brown sugar, ½ teaspoon ground cinnamon, ¼ teaspoon salt, ⅓ cup honey, ¼ cup vegetable oil, and 1 teaspoon vanilla extract. Spread on a baking sheet and toast at 300°F for 20 minutes. Remove from oven and stir in ½ cup small-dice dried fruit and ½ cup coarsely chopped raw or toasted nuts or seeds.

- **Make your own instant oatmeal packets:** Using 12 cups of rolled oats (about 2½ lbs.), preheat the oven to 325°F and using a rimmed baking sheet toast the oatmeal in about 3 batches of 4 cups each for 20 minutes. For the last batch, let cool slightly and, working in batches, puree in a blender or food processor until powdery. Transfer both powdered and unpowdered oatmeal to a large bowl, add 2 tablespoons of ground cinnamon, 1 teaspoon of salt, and 1 cup of brown sugar. Stir the mixture well and then divide the mixture into about 25 vacuum bags and vacuum-seal (or store in zip-top baggies). Optionally, add 1 tablespoon of chopped dried fruit such as apples, raisins, cranberries, or toasted chopped nuts. (Adding nuts will shorten the shelf life so eat those first, or toss them in the freezer for a longer shelf life.) To prepare, add about ¾ cup of very hot water to the contents of one packet, let sit for a minute, and stir.

❏ **Done**

56

PANCAKE MIX

PRIORITY: *Medium* | **CATEGORY:** *Pantry staples*

Pancakes make an easy and crowd-pleasing breakfast. You can always grind flour and make them from scratch, but why not keep a reasonable supply of pancake mix on hand for convenience?

SHELF LIFE: About 10 years

COST: $ (about $45 for a year's supply for a family of 4)

WHERE TO BUY: Sam's Club

SAMPLE PRICING: Sam's Club $45 for 31 lbs. (206 servings) in an emergency food storage bucket

HOW TO STORE: Sam's Club sells it in a bucket, ready for food storage

If you can't buy it all at once, track your progress below.

SERVING SIZE: ½ cup | **SEASON:** anytime

Persons 1 serving/week	Quantity for 1 year	Mark Off What You Have
1	1 bucket	
2	1 bucket	
4	1 bucket	
6	2 buckets	
8	2 buckets	
12	3 buckets	

What to do with pancake mix

• Make pancakes, adding fruits, nuts, and/or cocoa powder for variety

....

❏ **Done**

57

QUICK COOK BEANS

PRIORITY: *Medium* | **CATEGORY:** *Pantry staples*

Quick cook or par-cooked beans have been cooked until they are almost done and then dehydrated. In the 10 to 15 minutes of simmering it takes to rehydrate them, they will be fully cooked. You can either purchase par-cooked beans or make them yourself.

> **SHELF LIFE:** 20 years
>
> **COST:** $ (about $60 for a year's supply for a family of 4)
>
> **WHERE TO BUY:** Costco or make your own
>
> **SAMPLE PRICING:** Costco 17 lbs. 10oz. for $70 for red beans or $65 for pintos, or LDS $18.55 for 25 lbs. of uncooked dry beans

HOW TO STORE: In #10 cans with an oxygen absorber or vacuum-sealed in bags

If you can't buy it all at once, track your progress below.

SERVING SIZE: ½ cup rehydrated | **SEASON:** anytime

Persons 1 serving/week	Quantity for 1 year	Mark Off What You Have
1	15 lbs.	
2	30 lbs.	
4	60 lbs.	
6	90 lbs.	
8	120 lbs.	
12	180 lbs.	

How to make quick cook beans

- Soak beans overnight in water. Drain, cover with new water, season with salt, pepper, and cumin, and simmer until tender, about 2 hours (or pressure cook for 6 minutes). Remove from the cooking liquid with a slotted spoon. Let cool slightly and place on dehydrator trays. Dehydrate until completely dry, about 12 hours. 2 lbs. of beans will make 3 quarts of quick cook beans.

What to do with quick cook beans

- Add to soups or stews.
- **Make minestrone in a jar:** In a quart jar combine ⅔ cup of tomato powder, ⅓ cup of dehydrated onion, 1½ tablespoons of Italian seasoning, 1 teaspoon of garlic powder, and 1 tablespoon of beef bouillon or soup base. Add 1 cup of quick cook beans, ¼ cup dehydrated onion, ¼ cup dehydrated celery, ¾ cup dehydrated carrots, and ¾ cup dehydrated mushrooms. Add an oxygen absorber and close the jar or seal with a vacuum-sealer. To prepare, add ingredients to about 8 cups of water and simmer 20 minutes.
- **Make chili mac in a jar:** In a quart jar combine ⅔ cup tomato powder, 1 cup quick cook beans, 1 cup of macaroni, ⅓ cup dehydrated onion, ⅓ cup dehydrated celery, ⅓ cup dehydrated bell peppers, 1 teaspoon garlic powder, 1 teaspoon black pepper, 1 tablespoon chili powder, and 1 tablespoon beef bouillon or soup base. To prepare, add 8 cups of water and simmer 20 minutes.

❑ **Done**

58

QUINOA

PRIORITY: *Medium* | **CATEGORY:** *Pantry staples*

Quinoa is a delicious whole grain. It's got whole grain goodness, and is very satisfying and nutritious.

> **SHELF LIFE:** 30 years
>
> **COST:** $ (about $100 for a year's supply for a family of 4)
>
> **WHERE TO BUY:** Online
>
> **SAMPLE PRICING:** Bobsredmill.com about $7 per lb.
>
> **HOW TO STORE:** In #10 cans with an oxygen absorber

If you can't buy it all at once, track your progress below.

SERVING SIZE: ½ cup | **SEASON:** anytime

Persons 1 serving/week	Quantity for 1 year	Mark Off What You Have
1	4 lbs.	
2	8 lbs.	
4	16 lbs.	
6	24 lbs.	
8	32 lbs.	
12	48 lbs.	

What to do with quinoa

- Add it to soups and stews.
- Cook it like rice (2 parts water to 1 part quinoa, simmer 20 minutes) and serve as a side dish.
- **Make quinoa and vinaigrette salad:** Cook quinoa in 2 parts water to 1 part quinoa; simmer 20 minutes. Add vinaigrette, feta, cubed yams, and crispy kale.

❑ **Done**

VANILLA, CINNAMON, NUTMEG, & SYRUP

PRIORITY: *Medium* | **CATEGORY:** *Pantry staples*

Vanilla, cinnamon, nutmeg, and maple syrup are important ingredients for baking. It would be sad to have a year's supply of pancakes and no syrup, like a day without sunshine.

> **SHELF LIFE:** Varies
>
> **COST:** $$ (about $100 for a year's supply for a family of 4)
>
> **WHERE TO BUY:** Sam's Club or Costco
>
> **SAMPLE PRICING:** Sam's Club $7 for vanilla, $5 for cinnamon, $14 for syrup (pure), $10 for nutmeg
>
> **HOW TO STORE:** In original packaging in a cool, dark place

If you can't buy it all at once, track your progress below.

VANILLA

SERVING SIZE: varies | **SEASON:** anytime

Persons 2 servings/week	Quantity for 1 year	Mark Off What You Have
1	1 (16-oz.) bottle	
2	2 (16-oz.) bottles	
4	4 (16-oz.) bottles	
6	6 (16-oz.) bottles	
8	8 (16-oz.) bottles	
12	12 (16-oz.) bottles	

CINNAMON, NUTMEG

SERVING SIZE: varies | **SEASON:** anytime

Persons 2 servings/week	Quantity for 1 year	Mark Off What You Have	
1	1 (18-oz.) container	Cinnamon:	
	1 (2 to 3-oz.) jar	Nutmeg:	
2	1 (18-oz.) container	Cinnamon:	
	1 (2 to 3-oz.) jar	Nutmeg:	
4	2 (18-oz.) containers	Cinnamon:	
	1 (2 to 3-oz.) jar	Nutmeg:	
6	3 (18-oz.) containers	Cinnamon:	
	2 (2 to 3-oz.) jars	Nutmeg:	
8	4 (18-oz.) containers	Cinnamon:	
	2 (2 to 3-oz.) jars	Nutmeg:	
12	6 (18-oz.) containers	Cinnamon:	
	3 (2 to 3-oz.) jars	Nutmeg:	

SYRUP

SERVING SIZE: varies | **SEASON:** anytime

Persons 2 servings/week	Quantity for 1 year	Mark Off What You Have
1	1 (32-oz.) bottle	
2	2 (32-oz.) bottles	
4	4 (32-oz.) bottles	
6	6 (32-oz.) bottles	
8	8 (32-oz.) bottles	
12	12 (32-oz.) bottles	

What to do with vanilla, cinnamon, nutmeg, and syrup

- Add to oatmeal.
- Top French toast or pancakes; make cinnamon toast; or make pumpkin pie.

❑ **Done**

BROCCOLI & CAULIFLOWER

PRIORITY: *Medium* | **CATEGORY:** *Produce*

Broccoli and cauliflower are great vegetables to have in food storage. They can be bought commercially but are also very easy to dehydrate on your own.

SHELF LIFE: 30 years

COST: $$ (about $200 for a year's supply for a family of 4)

WHERE TO BUY: Costco or online

SAMPLE PRICING: Costco $140 for 12 cans

HOW TO STORE: In #10 cans with an oxygen absorber

If you can't buy it all at once, track your progress below.

SERVING SIZE: ½ cup | **SEASON:** anytime

Persons 3 servings/week	Quantity for 1 year	Mark Off What You Have
1	4 (#10) cans	
2	8 (#10) cans	
4	16 (#10) cans	
6	24 (#10) cans	
8	32 (#10) cans	
12	48 (#10) cans	

What to do with broccoli and cauliflower

- **Make cream of broccoli (or cauliflower) soup meals in a jar:** In a quart jar combine 1 cup dried onion and 4 cups dried broccoli (or cauliflower). In a baggie combine ⅔ cup dry powdered milk, ⅓ cup sour cream powder, ¼ cup flour, 2 tablespoons chicken soup base, and ¼ teaspoon ground nutmeg. Add the baggie on top of the ingredients in the jar. To make soup, combine broccoli and onion with 6 cups of water and simmer 30 minutes. Then stir in baggie contents. Simmer 10 minutes, stirring often, and serve.

- **Make broccoli cheddar soup:** In a quart jar combine ½ cup dried onion and 3 cups dried broccoli. In a baggie combine ⅔ cup dry powdered milk, ⅓ cup sour cream powder, ¼ cup flour, 2 tablespoons chicken soup base, ¼ teaspoon ground nutmeg, and 1 cup freeze-dried cheddar cheese. To make soup, combine broccoli and onion with 6 cups of water and simmer 30 minutes. Then stir in baggie contents. Simmer 10 minutes, stirring often, and serve.

How to dehydrate your own broccoli and cauliflower

- Blanch florets for 2 minutes in boiling water. Let cool. Layer onto dehydrator tray and dehydrate about 12 hours or until completely dry.

❏ **Done**

KALE

PRIORITY: *Medium* | **CATEGORY:** *Produce*

Ounce for ounce, kale is one of the most nutritious foods on the planet. You can grow it in your garden and dehydrate it yourself. Tossed with olive oil and salt and then dehydrated, kale is so delicious it's almost addictive.

SHELF LIFE: 6 months to a year

COST: $ (about $48 for a year's supply for a family of 4)

WHERE TO BUY: Costco, the farmer's market, or grow your own

SAMPLE PRICING: Amazon.com fresh (frozen) $1.89 per lb.

HOW TO STORE: Dehydrate and store in #10 cans with an oxygen absorber

If you can't buy it all at once, track your progress below.

SERVING SIZE: ½ oz. dehydrated | **SEASON:** summer

Persons ½ serving/week	Quantity for 1 year	Mark Off What You Have
1	2 (#10) cans	
2	4 (#10) cans	
4	8 (#10) cans	
6	12 (#10) cans	
8	16 (#10) cans	
12	24 (#10) cans	

What to do with kale

- Toss with olive oil and sea salt and dehydrate at 120°F for 8 to 12 hours until crispy.
- Snack on kale any time or use it as a crispy topper for salads.

❑ **Done**

62

POTATO SHREDS, FLAKES, & CUBES

PRIORITY: *Medium* | **CATEGORY:** *Produce*

Potato is an inexpensive ingredient to store that adds stick-to-your-ribs substance to meals. You can add it to soups and stews, and just about anything tastes good served over mashed potatoes. Potato flakes reconstitute into mashed potatoes. Shreds are used to make hash browns or potato pancakes. Cubes are perfect for stews and soups.

SHELF LIFE: 30 years

COST: $$ (about $200 for a year's supply for a family of 4)

WHERE TO BUY: LDS, Sam's Club, Costco, or online

SAMPLE PRICING: LDS $33 for 25 lbs., Sam's Club $10 per can, Costco $15 per can

HOW TO STORE: In #10 cans with an oxygen absorber

If you can't buy it all at once, track your progress below.

SERVING SIZE: ½ cup; see note | SEASON: anytime

Persons 4 servings/week	Quantity for 1 year	Mark Off What You Have
1	5 (#10) cans	
2	10 (#10) cans	
4	20 (#10) cans	
6	30 (#10) cans	
8	40 (#10) cans	
12	60 (#10) cans	

A note on serving size: One serving is ½ cup reconstituted potatoes. ¼ cup dehydrated yields ½ cup reconstituted.

What to do with potatoes

- **Make hash browned potatoes:** Rehydrate potato shreds in water and drain. Cook in a skillet in oil over medium-high heat.
- Make cowboy stew meals in a jar (page 105).
- **Make scalloped potatoes meals in a jar:** In a quart jar add 3 cups dehydrated potatoes, ¼ cup dehydrated bell peppers, ½ cup nonfat dry milk, 3 tablespoons dry butter powder, 2 tablespoons dehydrated onions, 2 tablespoons corn starch, 3 tablespoons finely grated Parmesan cheese, and 1 tablespoon chicken bouillon or soup base. Add an oxygen absorber or vacuum-seal the jar. When ready to eat, mix contents with 2¾ cups of water. Place in a baking dish and bake at 350°F for about 45 minutes.

❏ **Done**

RAISINS, DATES, DRIED CRANBERRIES, & DRIED CHERRIES

PRIORITY: *Medium* | **CATEGORY:** *Produce*

Commercially available dried fruits are a great addition to your food storage. They come ready to vacuum-seal and store and last a long time. They are great for snacking, in baked goods, or in salads.

> **SHELF LIFE:** 2–5 years
>
> **COST:** $$ (about $120 for a year's supply for a family of 4)
>
> **WHERE TO BUY:** LDS, Sam's Club, Costco, or online
>
> **SAMPLE PRICING:** Sam's Club $1.50 per lb.
>
> **HOW TO STORE:** Vacuum-seal in bags

Adjust the proportions and varieties of fruit according to your family's tastes.

RAISINS AND DATES

SERVING SIZE: ½ cup | **SEASON:** anytime

Persons 1 serving/week	Quantity for 1 year	Mark Off What You Have
1	6.5 lbs.	Raisins: Dates:
2	13 lbs.	Raisins: Dates:
4	26 lbs.	Raisins: Dates:
6	39 lbs.	Raisins: Dates:
8	52 lbs.	Raisins: Dates:
12	78 lbs.	Raisins: Dates:

DRIED CRANBERRIES AND DRIED CHERRIES

SERVING SIZE: ½ cup | **SEASON:** anytime

Persons 1 serving/week	Quantity for 1 year	Mark Off What You Have
1	6.5 lbs.	Cranberries: Cherries:
2	13 lbs.	Cranberries: Cherries:
4	26 lbs.	Cranberries: Cherries:
6	39 lbs.	Cranberries: Cherries:
8	52 lbs.	Cranberries: Cherries:
12	78 lbs.	Cranberries: Cherries:

What to do with raisins, dates, dried cranberries, and dried cherries

- Add to salads.
- Add to quinoa and vinaigrette salad (page 91).
- Add to Northwest pilaf (page 40).
- Add to oatmeal or wheat berry cereal.

❏ **Done**

BRAISED BEEF

PRIORITY: *Medium* | **CATEGORY:** *Protein*

Braised beef is simply delicious. You can thicken the juices to form a sauce and serve over potatoes, rice, or polenta. Or shred the beef and make BBQ beef sandwiches, tacos, or burritos.

SHELF LIFE: About 2 years

COST: $ (about $100 for a year's supply for a family of 4)

WHERE TO BUY: Costco

SAMPLE PRICING: Costco, about $2.25 per lb.

HOW TO STORE: Pressure-canned in pint jars

Decide the type(s) of beef to store depending on your preferences.

SERVING SIZE: ¼ lb. | **SEASON:** anytime

Persons ½ serving/week	Quantity for 1 year	Mark Off What You Have
1	7 lbs.	
2	13 lbs.	
4	26 lbs.	
6	39 lbs.	
8	52 lbs.	
12	78 lbs.	

What to do with braised beef

- **Make tacos:** Shred the beef, season it generously with seasoning salt or taco seasoning, and serve in tortillas.
- **Make sandwiches:** Shred the beef, mix it with BBQ sauce, and serve warm in buns.
- **Make braised beef over polenta:** Make a batch of polenta, thicken the beef juices with ½ tablespoon of butter/oil/ghee and ½ tablespoon of flour. Cook together until thickened. Serve warmed beef and sauce over polenta.

How to pressure-can braised beef

- Cut beef roast into large chunks and brown the outsides all around. Place into sterile pint (preferably) or quart jars. Cover with water to within 1 inch of the rim, add a pinch of salt, and pressure-can for 75 minutes for pints or 90 minutes for quarts.

❑ **Done**

65

BEEF CHUNKS

PRIORITY: *Medium* | **CATEGORY:** *Protein*

Beef chunks can be pressure-canned from raw meat at home or it can be purchased freeze-dried.

SHELF LIFE: 30 years for freeze-dried, 2 years for pressure-canned

COST: $-$$$ (about $688 for a year's supply of freeze-dried for a family of 4)

WHERE TO BUY: Sam's Club or online

SAMPLE PRICING: Sam's Club $43 per can (13 servings) or Costco $2.25 per lb. for brisket

HOW TO STORE: Freeze-dried, store as purchased, in #10 cans with an oxygen absorber; or pressure-can fresh beef in pint or quart jars.

Decide the type(s) of beef to store depending on your preferences.

SERVING SIZE: ¼ lb. | **SEASON:** anytime

Persons ½ serving/week	Quantity for 1 year	Mark Off What You Have
1	7 lbs.	
2	13 lbs.	
4	26 lbs.	
6	39 lbs.	
8	52 lbs.	
12	78 lbs.	

What to do with beef chunks

- **Make beef stew:** Add beef and juices (if using canned beef) to carrots, potatoes, peas, beef soup base, and water. Simmer and serve.
- **Make tacos:** Season beef with taco seasoning and serve in tortillas.
- **Make shepherd's pie:** Make a beef stew as above, top with mashed potatoes, and bake until heated through and lightly golden.
- **Make a skillet supper:** Mix beef with cooked pasta and canned tomatoes, season well, and top with Parmesan cheese.

How to pressure-can beef chunks

- Cut beef roast, such as brisket or any cut on sale, into small chunks and brown the outsides briefly. Place into a sterile pint (preferably) or quart jars. Cover with water to within 1 inch of the rim; add a pinch of salt and pressure-can for 75 minutes for pints or 90 minutes for quarts.

❏ **Done**

66

CANNED SALMON

PRIORITY: *Medium* | **CATEGORY:** *Protein*

Canned salmon is a nutritional powerhouse with healthy omega-3 fatty acids and abundant protein. Salmon can be substituted for tuna in any preparation.

SHELF LIFE: At least 5 years

COST: $$ (about $156 for a year's supply for a family of 4)

WHERE TO BUY: Grocery store, Costco

HOW TO STORE: In your rotation pantry

If you can't buy it all at once, track your progress below.

SERVING SIZE: 3 oz. | **SEASON:** anytime

Persons 1 serving/week	Quantity for 1 year	Mark Off What You Have
1	26 (6-oz.) cans	
2	52 (6-oz.) cans	
4	104 (6-oz.) cans	
6	156 (6-oz.) cans	
8	208 (6-oz.) cans	
12	312 (6-oz.) cans	

What to do with canned salmon

- **Make salmon cakes:** Sauté ¼ cup minced onion in oil until soft. Let cool. In a bowl mix together 2 (6-oz.) can salmon, flaked, the sautéed onion, 1 egg (beaten), and ¾ cup crushed saltines. Form into patties and pan-fry in oil. Mix together 3 parts mayonnaise with 1 part mustard and add a bit of lemon juice to serve as a dipping sauce. Optionally, add minced bell pepper in with the onions at the sauté step.
- **Make salmon frittata:** Beat together 6 eggs. Add ¼ cup minced onion, 1 cup grated cheese, and 1 (6-oz.) can of salmon, flaked. Add to a medium skillet and cook until set on the bottom. Either flip and cook on the other side or finish in a hot oven until set on top.
- **Make salmon pasta:** Toss together 12 oz. pasta, cooked, 2 tablespoons of ghee, 2 (6-oz.) cans of salmon, flaked, and ⅓ cup of peas. Season with salt to taste and top with Parmesan cheese.

❑ **Done**

67

FREEZE-DRIED BEEF

PRIORITY: *Medium* | **CATEGORY:** *Protein*

Freeze-dried beef is wonderful to have in your food storage. It has a very long shelf life and rehydrates well. Buy an extra can or two and make meals in a jar to have in your pantry.

> **SHELF LIFE:** 25 years
>
> **COST:** $ (about $85 for a year's supply for a family of 4)
>
> **WHERE TO BUY:** Costco
>
> **SAMPLE PRICING:** Sam's Club $87 for 2 cans (26 servings), Costco $216 for 266 servings
>
> **HOW TO STORE:** As purchased (cans or pouches)

Decide the type(s) of beef to store depending on your preferences.

SERVING SIZE: ¼ cup | **SEASON:** anytime

Persons ½ serving/week	Quantity for 1 year	Mark Off What You Have
1	7 lbs.	
2	13 lbs.	
4	26 lbs.	
6	39 lbs.	
8	52 lbs.	
12	78 lbs.	

What to do with freeze-dried beef

- Make chili mac meals in a jar (page 90).
- **Make chili con carne meals in a jar:** To a quart jar add 1 cup quick cook beans to ½ cup tomato powder and shake well. Add 1 cup ground beef, ¼ cup freeze-dried onion, ½ cup freeze-dried bell peppers, ½ cup freeze-dried tomatoes, ¼ cup freeze-dried celery, 1 tablespoon chili powder, 1 teaspoon garlic powder, and 1 tablespoon beef bouillon.

- **Make cowboy stew meals in a jar:** In a bowl, mix together 1 cup quick cook beans, 1 cup dried carrots, 1 cup freeze-dried ground beef or beef-flavored TVP (page 114), 1 cup dehydrated diced potatoes, ¼ cup dehydrated onion, ½ cup tomato powder, 1 teaspoon thyme, 1 teaspoon garlic powder, ¼ cup flour, and 1 tablespoon beef bouillon. Mix well and, using a canning funnel, pour into a quart jar. To serve, add contents to 6 cups of water, simmer 20 to 30 minutes, and serve.

❏ **Done**

68

HAM

PRIORITY: *Medium* | CATEGORY: *Protein*

Ham is a delicious and very versatile ingredient—it works for breakfast, lunch, or dinner. Ham can be pressure-canned at home or purchased freeze-dried in a small dice. It is also possible to make ham jerky. Ham tends to go on sale around Easter. Buy several on sale and pressure-can them.

SHELF LIFE: 30 years for freeze-dried, 2 years for canned

COST: $$$ (about $624 for a year's supply for a family of 4, or $477 for 9 cans of freeze-dried ham)

WHERE TO BUY: Costco or Sam's Club

SAMPLE PRICING: Costco about $3 per lb. for fresh ham or online, about $53 for 1 can (48 servings)

HOW TO STORE: Purchase and store in #10 cans with an oxygen absorber for freeze-dried ham, or store in pint or quart jars for pressure-canned.

If you can't buy it all at once, track your progress below.

SERVING SIZE: ¼ pound | **SEASON:** anytime

Persons 2 servings/week	Quantity for 1 year	Mark Off What You Have
1	26 lbs.	
2	52 lbs.	
4	104 lbs.	
6	156 lbs.	
8	208 lbs.	
12	312 lbs.	

What to do with ham

- Serve with eggs for breakfast.
- Pan-fry and serve for dinner.
- Add to quiche, frittata, or strata.
- Make a ham and cheese sandwich.
- Add to baked potatoes.
- Cook with cheese in tortillas for a ham quesadilla.

How to pressure-can ham

- Chop or slice and place in sterile pint or quart jars. Cover with water to within 1 inch of the rim, add a pinch of salt, and pressure-can for 75 minutes for pints or 90 minutes for quarts.

❑ **Done**

69

JERKY

PRIORITY: *Medium* | **CATEGORY:** *Protein*

Jerky is a wonderful snack and a great source of protein. Unfortunately, the shelf life is relatively short. Consider making your own and keeping it on hand in your rotation pantry. Another item to consider for your dried beef category is chipped beef, a commercially available dried beef product classically served in a cream sauce over toast. Unlike jerky, it has an indefinite shelf life.

SHELF LIFE: About a year (about 5 years for chipped beef)

COST: $$$

WHERE TO BUY: Sam's Club, Costco

SAMPLE PRICING: About $10 per lb., or make your own

HOW TO STORE: Vacuum-seal

Make a note of how much jerky your family eats, and decide how much you'd like to keep on hand.

SERVING SIZE: about 3–4 oz. | **SEASON:** anytime

Persons 1 serving/week	Quantity for 1 year	Mark Off What You Have
1	13 lbs.	
2	26 lbs.	
4	52 lbs.	
6	78 lbs.	
8	104 lbs.	
12	156 lbs.	

What to do with jerky

• Eat it straight from the bag, or chop it up and add to soup.

How to make jerky

- Ask your butcher to slice a large roast for you about ¼ inch thick. Make a mixture of half soy sauce and half Worcestershire sauce and add black pepper, onion powder, and, if desired, red pepper flakes and a bit of liquid smoke. Spread out in a single layer on a dehydrator rack (or oven rack) and dehydrate overnight at 120°F in a dehydrator or at the lowest oven setting.

❑ **Done**

70

MEATBALLS

PRIORITY: *Medium* | **CATEGORY:** *Protein*

Meatballs can be purchased frozen at club stores and pressure-canned into quart or pint jars.

SHELF LIFE: 2 years

COST: $ (about $65 for a year's supply for a family of 4)

WHERE TO BUY: Costco

SAMPLE PRICING: Costco $2.50 per lb.

HOW TO STORE: Pressure-canned in quart or pint jars

Decide the type(s) of meatballs to store depending on your preferences.

SERVING SIZE: 4 (1-oz.) meatballs | **SEASON:** anytime

Persons ½ serving/week	Quantity for 1 year	Mark Off What You Have
1	7 lbs.	
2	13 lbs.	
4	26 lbs.	
6	39 lbs.	
8	52 lbs.	
12	78 lbs.	

What to do with meatballs

- **Make meatball sandwiches:** Heat meatballs in spaghetti sauce and spoon into sandwich rolls.
- Add to spaghetti sauce and serve with pasta.
- Add to vegetable soup or minestrone.

To pressure-can meatballs

- Place meatballs into sterile pint or quart jars. Cover with water to within 1 inch of the rim, add a pinch of salt, and pressure-can for 75 minutes for pints or 90 minutes for quarts.

❏ **Done**

71

PEANUT BUTTER

PRIORITY: *Medium* | **CATEGORY:** *Protein*

Peanut butter is an important and tasty part of your fat quota and also an excellent source of protein. Unfortunately, most peanut butter has a shelf life of about a year. Powdered peanut butter, which is reconstituted with water into paste, may last either one year or up to five to ten years depending on the brand. Peanut butter is one of those foods where the amount used will vary according to your family's preferences. The baseline quantity here is one can per person per year. Please adjust accordingly to your family's eating style.

SHELF LIFE: 1–10 years depending on the variety and brand

COST: $ (about $60 for a year's supply for a family of 4)

WHERE TO BUY: Honeyville or Amazon.com

SAMPLE PRICING: About $15 per #10 can

HOW TO STORE: As packaged in a cool, dark place

If you can't buy it all at once, track your progress below.

SERVING SIZE: 1 tablespoon | **SEASON:** anytime

Persons 1.5 servings/ week	Quantity for 1 year	Mark Off What You Have
1	1 (#10) can	
2	2 (#10) cans	
4	4 (#10) cans	
6	6 (#10) cans	
8	8 (#10) cans	
12	12 (#10) cans	

What to do with peanut butter

- Make sandwiches with jelly, syrup, jam, or marshmallow fluff.
- **Make peanut butter cookies:** Preheat oven to 350°F (175°C). Grease cookie sheets. In a medium bowl, stir 2 cups of peanut butter and 2 cups of sugar together until smooth. Beat in 2 eggs, one at a time, then stir in 2 teaspoons of baking soda, a pinch of salt, and 1 teaspoon of vanilla. Roll dough into 1-inch balls and place the balls 2 inches apart onto the prepared cookie sheets. Press a criss-cross pattern into the top using the back of a fork. Bake at 350°F for 8 to 10 minutes.
- Eat on sliced apples or spread on crackers.

❑ **Done**

72

PORK SHOULDER

PRIORITY: *Medium* | **CATEGORY:** *Protein*

Everybody loves pulled pork, which is just pork shoulder that has been braised, seasoned, and mixed with BBQ sauce. It's also awesome in tacos and burritos, or over noodles or polenta. Pork shoulder typically goes on sale around the 4th of July. Watch for sales, buy several, and can them up.

    SHELF LIFE: 2 years

    COST: $ (about $86 for a year's supply for a family of 4)

    WHERE TO BUY: Costco or your local grocer

    SAMPLE PRICING: Costco $1.66 per lb.

    HOW TO STORE: Pressure-canned in pint or quart jars

If you can't buy it all at once, track your progress below.

PORK SHOULDER

SERVING SIZE: ¼ pound | **SEASON:** anytime

Persons 5 servings/week	Quantity for 1 year	Mark Off What You Have
1	65 lbs.	
2	130 lbs.	
4	260 lbs.	
6	390 lbs.	
8	520 lbs.	
12	780 lbs.	

PULLED PORK AND BACON

SERVING SIZE: ¼ pound | **SEASON:** anytime

Persons 1 serving/week	Quantity for 1 year	Mark Off What You Have
1	13 lbs.	Pulled pork: Bacon:
2	26 lbs.	Pulled pork: Bacon:
4	52 lbs.	Pulled pork: Bacon:
6	78 lbs.	Pulled pork: Bacon:
8	104 lbs.	Pulled pork: Bacon:
12	156 lbs.	Pulled pork: Bacon:

What to do with pork shoulder

- **Make pulled pork sandwiches:** Shred the pork and season it well with seasoning salt. Add BBQ sauce and serve in buns. Optionally add coleslaw.
- Serve pork chunks over polenta.
- Season the pork and serve in tacos or burritos.

How to pressure-can pork shoulder

- Cut pork into large chunks and brown lightly. Place in sterile pint or quart jars. Cover with water to within 1 inch of the rim, add a pinch of salt, and pressure-can for 75 minutes for pints or 90 minutes for quarts.

❏ **Done**

73

SAUSAGE

PRIORITY: *Medium* | **CATEGORY:** *Protein*

Sausage can be pressure-canned or purchased freeze-dried in cans. We plan on having sausage with breakfast weekly.

SHELF LIFE: 30 years for freeze-dried and 2 years pressure-canned

COST: $$ (about $104 for a year's supply for a family of 4)

WHERE TO BUY: Costco or Sam's Club

SAMPLE PRICING: Costco about $2 per lb.

HOW TO STORE: For freeze-dried, purchase and store in #10 cans with an oxygen absorber; or store pressure-canned sausage in pint or quart jars.

If you can't buy it all at once, track your progress below.

SERVING SIZE: ¼ pound | **SEASON:** anytime

Persons 1 serving/week	Quantity for 1 year	Mark Off What You Have
1	13 lbs.	
2	26 lbs.	
4	52 lbs.	
6	78 lbs.	
8	104 lbs.	
12	156 lbs.	

What to do with sausage

- Have it for breakfast with eggs.
- Add it to quiche, frittata, strata, or baked eggs.

How to pressure-can pork sausage

- Form pork into patties and brown lightly. Place in sterile pint or quart jars. Cover with water to within 1 inch of the rim, add a pinch of salt, and pressure-can for 75 minutes for pints or 90 minutes for quarts.

❑ **Done**

74

TEXTURED VEGETABLE PROTEIN (TVP)

PRIORITY: *Medium* | **CATEGORY:** *Protein*

TVP is less expensive than freeze-dried beef, but can substitute for all or part of the ground meat in recipes. TVP comes in beef, chicken, or sausage flavor.

> **SHELF LIFE:** 30 years
>
> **COST:** $ (about $100 for a year's supply for a family of 4)
>
> **WHERE TO BUY:** Online
>
> **SAMPLE PRICING:** Online about $4 per lb.
>
> **HOW TO STORE:** Buy and store in #10 cans with an oxygen absorber

SERVING SIZE: ¼ cup | **SEASON:** anytime

Persons ½ serving/week	Quantity for 1 year	Mark Off What You Have
1	7 lbs.	
2	13 lbs.	
4	26 lbs.	
6	39 lbs.	
8	52 lbs.	
12	78 lbs.	

What to do with TVP

- Put it in spaghetti sauce; add to casseroles; or serve it in gravy over biscuits.
- **Make sloppy joes:** Mix with hamburger, ketchup, and BBQ sauce; serve in sandwich buns.

❑ **Done**

75

TURKEY

PRIORITY: *Medium* | **CATEGORY:** *Protein*

Just as versatile an ingredient as chicken, turkey is great to have on hand for quick sandwiches, salads, and casseroles.

SHELF LIFE: 15 years for freeze-dried, 2 years for pressure-canned

COST: $$ (about $100 for a year's supply for a family of 4)

WHERE TO BUY: Costco or any grocery store

SAMPLE PRICING: Costco $199 for 266 servings of freeze-dried turkey and $1.97 per lb. for fresh

HOW TO STORE: Purchase and store freeze-dried turkey in #10 cans with an oxygen absorber or store pressure-canned turkey in pint or quart jars.

If you can't buy it all at once, track your progress below.

SERVING SIZE: ¼ pound | **SEASON:** anytime

Persons 1 serving/week	Quantity for 1 year	Mark Off What You Have
1	13 lbs.	
2	26 lbs.	
4	52 lbs.	
6	78 lbs.	
8	104 lbs.	
12	156 lbs.	

What to do with turkey

- Make Monte Cristo sandwiches (page 117).
- **Make a turkey noodle casserole:** Combine 12 oz. cooked noodles with 1 can cream soup, a pint chopped turkey with juice, 1 cup sliced mushrooms, ¼ cup minced onion, ¼ cup minced celery (rehydrate mushrooms, onions, and celery in hot water if using dehydrated vegetables). Place in a casserole dish and bake at 350°F until bubbly, about 25 minutes. Optionally top with buttered breadcrumbs for some crunch.

What to do with freeze-dried turkey

- Substitute for chicken in the chicken noodle soup meal in a jar or the chicken and rice meal in a jar (page 54).

How to pressure-can turkey

- Place raw turkey into sterile pint or quart jars. Cover with water to within 1 inch of the rim, add a pinch of salt, and pressure-can for 70 minutes for pints or 90 minutes for quarts.

❏ **Done**

76

JELLY & JAM

PRIORITY: *Medium* | **CATEGORY:** *Sweets & sweeteners*

Jelly and jam are delicious additions to your food storage. Spread them on hot biscuits or fresh bread. Make your own jam when fruit is abundant.

SHELF LIFE: 2–5 years or longer

COST: $ (about $30 for a year's supply for a family of 4)

WHERE TO BUY: LDS, Sam's Club, Costco, or online

SAMPLE PRICING: Costco $3.76 for 4 lbs.

HOW TO STORE: In #10 cans with an oxygen absorber

If you can't buy it all at once, track your progress below.

SERVING SIZE: 1 tablespoon | **SEASON:** anytime

Persons 3 servings/week	Quantity for 1 year	Mark Off What You Have
1	2 (32-oz.) cans	
2	4 (32-oz.) cans	
4	8 (32-oz.) cans	
6	12 (32-oz.) cans	
8	16 (32-oz.) cans	
12	24 (32-oz.) cans	

What to do with jelly or jam

- Put on toast or biscuits, or serve with Monte Cristo sandwiches.
- **Make a Monte Cristo sandwich:** Make 3 pieces of French toast by beating together 2 eggs and ⅓ cup of milk. Soak bread, and then cook in butter until golden on both sides. Top 2 of the slices with sliced turkey and Swiss cheese. Stack the 2 slices one on top of the other and top with the third piece of French toast. Toast on both sides until the cheese melts and the turkey is heated through. Serve with jelly or jam.
- Make sugar cookies (page 67).

❑ **Done**

77

FREEZE-DRIED YOGURT

PRIORITY: *Low* | **CATEGORY:** *Dairy*

Freeze-dried yogurt is a great snack. It can be reconstituted with water into a yogurt-like consistency, but it is really delicious in its freeze-dried state.

SHELF LIFE: 3–5 years

COST: $$ (about $320 for a year's supply for a family of 4)

WHERE TO BUY: Online

SAMPLE PRICING: Online about $40 per #10 can

HOW TO STORE: As purchased, in #10 cans with an oxygen absorber

If you can't buy it all at once, track your progress below.

SERVING SIZE: ¼ cup | **SEASON:** anytime

Persons 1 serving/week	Quantity for 1 year	Mark Off What You Have
1	2 (#10) cans	
2	4 (#10) cans	
4	8 (#10) cans	
6	12 (#10) cans	
8	16 (#10) cans	
12	24 (#10) cans	

What to do with freeze-dried yogurt

• Eat as a snack.

❏ **Done**

78

SOUR CREAM POWDER

PRIORITY: *Low* | **CATEGORY:** *Dairy*

Sour cream powder adds a creamy taste of dairy to your recipes.

    SHELF LIFE: 10 years

    COST: $ (about $100 for a year's supply for a family of 4)

    WHERE TO BUY: Online

    SAMPLE PRICING: Online about $25 per can (210 1-tablespoon servings)

    HOW TO STORE: In #10 cans with an oxygen absorber

If you can't buy it all at once, track your progress below.

SERVING SIZE: 1 tablespoon | **SEASON:** anytime

Persons 1 serving/week	Quantity for 1 year	Mark Off What You Have
1	1 (#10) can	
2	2 (#10) cans	
4	4 (#10) cans	
6	6 (#10) cans	
8	8 (#10) cans	
12	12 (#10) cans	

What to do with sour cream powder

- Add to macaroni and cheese (page 22).
- Dollop on top of chili mac in a jar (page 90) or chili con carne (page 104).

❏ **Done**

COFFEE, TEA, & CREAMER

PRIORITY: *Low* | **CATEGORY:** *Drinks*

We've already accounted for sugar and honey, but if creamer is needed, stock up.

SHELF LIFE: About 1 year for coffee. Powdered creamer will last for several years, as will tea.

COST: $$ (depending on your family's tastes)

WHERE TO BUY: Sam's Club, Costco, Walmart, or the grocery store

SAMPLE PRICING: Costco $6 for 1 lb. of coffee, $9 for 144 tea bags; Sam's Club $5 for 22 oz. of creamer

HOW TO STORE: In #10 cans with an oxygen absorber

If you can't buy it all at once, track your progress below.

Persons	Quantity for 1 year	Mark Off What You Have
1		Coffee: Tea: Creamer:
2		Coffee: Tea: Creamer:
4		Coffee: Tea: Creamer:
6		Coffee: Tea: Creamer:
8		Coffee: Tea: Creamer:
12		Coffee: Tea: Creamer:

❏ **Done**

80

JUICES: CANNED ORANGE, PINEAPPLE, APPLE, & GRAPE

PRIORITY: *Low* | **CATEGORY:** *Drinks*

If your family drinks fruit juices, plan to have about a year's supply on hand in your rotation pantry.

   SHELF LIFE: 2 years

   COST: $ (about $20 for a year's supply for a family of 4)

   WHERE TO BUY: Sam's Club, Costco, or any grocery store

   SAMPLE PRICING: Sam's Club about $.02 per ounce

   HOW TO STORE: In original packaging in your rotation pantry

If you can't buy it all at once, track your progress below.

SERVING SIZE: ½ cup | **SEASON:** anytime

Persons 1 serving/week	Quantity for 1 year	Mark Off What You Have
1	2 gal.	Orange juice: Apple juice:
2	4 gal.	Orange juice: Apple juice:
4	8 gal.	Orange juice: Apple juice:
6	12 gal.	Orange juice: Apple juice:
8	16 gal.	Orange juice: Apple juice:
12	24 gal.	Orange juice: Apple juice:

Persons 1 serving/week	Quantity for 1 year	Mark Off What You Have
1	2 gal.	Other: Other: Other: Other:
2	4 gal.	Other: Other: Other: Other:
4	8 gal.	Other: Other: Other: Other:
6	12 gal.	Other: Other: Other: Other:
8	16 gal.	Other: Other: Other: Other:
12	24 gal.	Other: Other: Other: Other:

What to do with fruit juice

- Drink it.
- Reduce it and use it as a sauce for meats, such as pork.

❑ **Done**

BOXED CEREALS

PRIORITY: *Low* | **CATEGORY:** *Pantry staples*

Keep a year's worth of cereal on hand; it lasts one to two years unopened.

SHELF LIFE: 1–2 years

COST: $$ (about $120 for a year's supply for a family of 4)

WHERE TO BUY: Sam's Club or Costco

SAMPLE PRICING: Sam's Club $6 for 40 oz., Costco $9 for 55 oz.

HOW TO STORE: In your rotation pantry

If you can't buy it all at once, track your progress below.

SERVING SIZE: ½ cup | **SEASON:** anytime

Persons 1 serving/week	Quantity for 1 year	Mark Off What You Have
1	10 (40-oz.) boxes	
2	20 (40-oz.) boxes	
4	40 (40-oz.) boxes	
6	60 (40-oz.) boxes	
8	80 (40-oz.) boxes	
12	120 (40-oz.) boxes	

What to do with cereal

• Eat it for breakfast. Optionally add berries, apples, or bananas.

❑ **Done**

CANNED PUMPKIN

PRIORITY: *Low* | **CATEGORY:** *Produce*

Pumpkin is nice to have on hand to make pies and quick breads. Canned pumpkin goes on sale around Thanksgiving. Stock up.

> **SHELF LIFE:** 30 years
>
> **COST:** $ (about $20 for a year's supply for a family of 4)
>
> **WHERE TO BUY:** LDS, Sam's Club, Costco, or the grocery store
>
> **HOW TO STORE:** In cans in your rotation pantry

If you can't buy it all at once, track your progress below.

SERVING SIZE: ¼ cup | **SEASON:** anytime

Persons	Quantity for 1 year	Mark Off What You Have
1	2 (28-oz.) cans	
2	4 (28-oz.) cans	
4	8 (28-oz.) cans	
6	12 (28-oz.) cans	
8	16 (28-oz.) cans	
12	24 (28-oz.) cans	

What to do with canned pumpkin

- **Make pie:** Follow directions on the can and use a Jiffy pie crust mix (see page 32).
- **Make pumpkin bread:** Preheat oven to 350°F. In a large bowl beat together 1 cup pumpkin puree, ½ cup olive oil, 2 eggs (beaten), and ¼ cup water. Stir in 1 cup of sugar. Add 1½ cups flour, ½ teaspoon salt, 1 teaspoon baking soda, ½ teaspoon nutmeg, ½ teaspoon cinnamon, and ½ teaspoon allspice, and stir until just combined. Add ½ cup of chopped walnuts, pour into a loaf pan, and bake for 50 to 55 minutes or until a toothpick inserted comes out clean.

❑ **Done**

83

CANNED PIE FILLING

PRIORITY: *Low* | **CATEGORY:** *Sweets & sweeteners*

Canned pie filling makes it easy to create a pie or crumble dessert.

SHELF LIFE: 2 years

COST: $ (about $48 for a year's supply for a family of 4)

WHERE TO BUY: LDS, Sam's Club, Costco, or online

SAMPLE PRICING: Costco or the grocery store about $3 per can

HOW TO STORE: In cans in your rotation pantry

Adjust this quantity to your family's tastes.

SERVING SIZE: ¼ can | **SEASON:** anytime

Persons	Quantity for 1 year	Mark Off What You Have
1	4 (21-oz.) cans	
2	8 (21-oz.) cans	
4	16 (21-oz.) cans	
6	24 (21-oz.) cans	
8	32 (21-oz.) cans	
12	48 (21-oz.) cans	

What to do with canned pie filling

- Bake a pie with Jiffy crust mix (see page 32).
- **Make a rustic pie:** Spread a pie crust on a rimmed baking sheet, mound the pie filling in the center, fold the edges over the top, and bake at 350°F for about 45 to 50 minutes or until golden.
- **Make a "dump cake":** In a baking dish add 2 cans of pie filling, or 1 can of pie filling and 1 can of fruit, chopped and drained. Top with 1 box of cake mix, and pour on 1 cube (½ cup) of melted butter or ghee. Bake at 350°F for about 50 minutes or until golden and bubbly.

❑ **Done**

CONDIMENTS

PRIORITY: *Low* | **CATEGORY:** *Pantry staples*

Condiments like mayonnaise, mustard, ketchup, salad dressing, BBQ sauce, soy sauce, Worcestershire sauce, teriyaki sauce, Tabasco, and salsa make everything taste better. Make a note of what and how much your family uses routinely and plan to stock a year's supply in your rotation pantry. You may not want to purchase condiments in large quantities, as they could go bad if you were without refrigeration in an emergency. Consider getting some single-serving packets to include in your food storage.

SHELF LIFE: 1–2 years

COST: $$ (about $100 for a year's supply for a family of 4)

WHERE TO BUY: Sam's Club, Costco, or Walmart

HOW TO STORE: In original packaging in your rotation pantry

If you can't buy it all at once, track your progress below.

MAYONNAISE

SERVING SIZE: 1 teaspoon | **SEASON:** anytime

Persons 4 servings/ week	Quantity for 1 year	Mark Off What You Have
1	3 jars	
2	6 jars	
4	12 jars	
6	18 jars	
8	24 jars	
12	36 jars	

MUSTARD, KETCHUP, SALAD DRESSING, AND BBQ SAUCE

SERVING SIZE: 1 teaspoon | **SEASON:** anytime

Persons	Quantity for 1 year	Mark Off What You Have
1	2 jars	Mustard: Ketchup: Salad dressing: BBQ sauce:
2	4 jars	Mustard: Ketchup: Salad dressing: BBQ sauce:
4	8 jars	Mustard: Ketchup: Salad dressing: BBQ sauce:
6	12 jars	Mustard: Ketchup: Salad dressing: BBQ sauce:
8	16 jars	Mustard: Ketchup: Salad dressing: BBQ sauce:
12	24 jars	Mustard: Ketchup: Salad dressing: BBQ sauce:

SOY SAUCE, TABASCO, AND SALSA

SERVING SIZE: 1 teaspoon | **SEASON:** anytime

Persons	Quantity for 1 year	Mark Off What You Have
1	2 jars	Soy sauce: Tabasco: Salsa: Other:
2	4 jars	Soy sauce: Tabasco: Salsa: Other:
4	8 jars	Soy sauce: Tabasco: Salsa: Other:
6	12 jars	Soy sauce: Tabasco: Salsa: Other:
8	16 jars	Soy sauce: Tabasco: Salsa: Other:
12	24 jars	Soy sauce: Tabasco: Salsa: Other:

What to do with condiments

- Mix BBQ sauce with canned beef or pork for BBQ sandwiches.
- Mix BBQ sauce, ketchup, and ground beef for sloppy joes.
- **Make deviled eggs:** Hard boil eggs, slice in half, and mash yolks with mayonnaise and mustard. Refill yolks into egg white halves.

❑ **Done**

CRACKERS

PRIORITY: *Low* | **CATEGORY:** *Pantry staples*

Keep a year's supply of saltines on hand and make sure to rotate your stock, because saltines do go stale. There are also crackers in #10 cans, called pilot bread crackers, commercially available from Mountain House.

> **SHELF LIFE:** 30 years
>
> **COST:** $$ (about $100 for a year's supply for a family of 4)
>
> **WHERE TO BUY:** LDS, Sam's Club, Costco, or online
>
> **HOW TO STORE:** In your rotation pantry

If you can't buy it all at once, track your progress below.

SALTINES

SERVING SIZE: ½ cup | **SEASON:** anytime

Persons 1 serving/week	Quantity for 1 year	Mark Off What You Have
1	4 boxes	
2	8 boxes	
4	16 boxes	
6	24 boxes	
8	32 boxes	
12	48 boxes	

PILOT BREAD CRACKERS

SERVING SIZE: ½ cup | **SEASON:** anytime

Persons 1 serving/week	Quantity for 1 year	Mark Off What You Have
1	4 cans	
2	8 cans	
4	16 cans	
6	24 cans	
8	32 cans	
12	48 cans	

What to do with crackers

- Serve them topped with tuna or salmon.
- Serve them with hummus for dipping.
- Serve them with soup.

❑ **Done**

86

GRANOLA BARS

PRIORITY: *Low* | **CATEGORY:** *Pantry staples*

Buy granola bars from Costco or Sam's Club and keep a year's worth on hand.

SHELF LIFE: About 18 months

COST: $ (about $48 for a year's supply for a family of 4)

WHERE TO BUY: LDS, Sam's Club, Costco, or online

SAMPLE PRICING: Costco $12 for 60, Sam's Club $8.78 for 30

HOW TO STORE: In your rotation pantry

If you can't buy it all at once, track your progress below.

SERVING SIZE: 1 bar | **SEASON:** anytime

Persons 1 serving/week	Quantity for 1 year	Mark Off What You Have
1	1 box	
2	2 boxes	
4	4 boxes	
6	6 boxes	
8	8 boxes	
12	12 boxes	

What to do with granola bars

- Eat as a snack.
- Crumble a bar on yogurt.

❑ **Done**

87

RICE MIXES

PRIORITY: *Low* | **CATEGORY:** *Pantry staples*

Rice mixes like Rice-A-Roni or Spanish rice make for a fast, easy, shelf-stable side dish.

SHELF LIFE: 5 years

COST: $ (about $67 for a year's supply for a family of 4)

WHERE TO BUY: Grocery store

SAMPLE PRICING: About $1.29 per box

HOW TO STORE: In #10 cans with an oxygen absorber

If you can't buy it all at once, track your progress below.

SERVING SIZE: ½ box | SEASON: anytime

Persons 1 serving/week	Quantity for 1 year	Mark Off What You Have
1	13 boxes	
2	26 boxes	
4	52 boxes	
6	78 boxes	
8	104 boxes	
12	156 boxes	

What to do with rice mixes

- Prepare as directed. Optionally, add chopped ham or vegetables, or add an egg as you would with fried rice.

❑ **Done**

88

RAMEN NOODLES & INSTANT NOODLE CUP

PRIORITY: *Low* | **CATEGORY:** *Pantry staples*

Ramen makes cheap, quick lunches, and kids love it. Add some meat or vegetables to ramen to make it more nutritious.

SHELF LIFE: 2 years

COST: $ (about $40 for a year's supply for a family of 4)

WHERE TO BUY: Sam's Club, Costco, or the grocery store

SAMPLE PRICING: Costco $9.70 for 48

HOW TO STORE: In #10 cans with an oxygen absorber

If you can't buy it all at once, track your progress below.

RAMEN

SERVING SIZE: ½–1 package; see note | **SEASON:** anytime

Persons 1 serving/week	Quantity for 1 year	Mark Off What You Have
1	52 packages	
2	104 packages	
4	208 packages	
6	312 packages	
8	416 packages	
12	624 packages	

A note on serving size: 1 package serves 1–2 people; 1 case contains 52 packages.

INSTANT NOODLE CUP

SERVING SIZE: ½–1 package; see note | **SEASON:** anytime

Persons ½ serving/week	Quantity for 1 year	Mark Off What You Have
1	26 packages	
2	52 packages	
4	104 packages	
6	156 packages	
8	208 packages	
12	312 packages	

A note on serving size: 1 package serves 1–2 people; 1 case contains 52 packages.

What to do with ramen

- Add egg, vegetables, or meat.
- Toast crushed raw noodles in oil and use as a snack or salad topping.

- **Make sesame noodles:** Cook noodles and drain. Add a tablespoon of soy sauce, a spoonful of peanut butter, 1 teaspoon sesame oil, and 1 teaspoon sesame seeds. Add shredded carrots and cabbage if desired.

❑ **Done**

89

SQUASH: BUTTERNUT, ACORN, & ZUCCHINI

PRIORITY: *Low* | **CATEGORY:** *Produce*

Squashes and zucchini will add variety and nutrition to your food storage vegetables. You can grow zucchini in your garden and dehydrate the excess, which is often plentiful. Acorn and butternut squash are fantastic side dishes and great in soups. Zucchini is great is soups too, but is also in quick breads and in zucchini patties.

SHELF LIFE: 10 years

COST: $ (about $100 for a year's supply for a family of 4)

WHERE TO BUY: LDS, Sam's Club, Costco, or grow your own

SAMPLE PRICING: About $1.50 per lb.

HOW TO STORE: In #10 cans with an oxygen absorber

If you can't buy it all at once, track your progress below.

SERVING SIZE: ½ cup | **SEASON:** late summer–early fall

Persons 1 serving/week	Quantity for 1 year	Mark Off What You Have
1	13 lbs.	
2	26 lbs.	
4	52 lbs.	
6	78 lbs.	
8	104 lbs.	
12	156 lbs.	

How to dehydrate squash and zucchini

- **For summer squash and zucchini:** Slice on a mandoline to about ³⁄₁₆ inch thick or grate. Salt lightly and layer on dehydrator trays. Dehydrate at 115°F for about 8 to 12 hours or until completely dry.

How to dehydrate acorn squash and butternut squash

- Peel, cut into chunks, and blanch for 2 minutes. Dry on trays at 120°F for 12–15 hours.

What to do with squash and zucchini

- Add to vegetable soup.
- Add to cowboy stew (page 105).
- **Snack on chips:** For snacking, you may toss the slices lightly in olive oil before dehydrating them per the instructions above. This shortens the shelf life but adds delicious flavor.
- **Make zucchini patties:** Rehydrate zucchini shreds in water, drain, and squeeze dry. Add 1 egg lightly beaten, some Parmesan cheese, and some flour, salt, and pepper. Pan-fry in hot oil until golden on the outsides and cooked through.
- **Make zucchini bread:** Preheat the oven to 350°F. In a large bowl mix together 2 eggs, beaten, 1⅓ cups sugar, 2 teaspoons vanilla, 3 cups grated, rehydrated, and drained zucchini, ⅔ cup oil, 2 teaspoons baking soda, a pinch salt, 3 cups flour, ½ teaspoon nutmeg, 2 teaspoons cinnamon, 1 cup chopped pecans or walnuts (optional), and 1 cup dried cranberries or raisins (optional). Pour into 2 loaf pans and bake for 50–55 minutes.

❑ **Done**

FRUIT LEATHER

PRIORITY: *Low* | **CATEGORY:** *Produce*

Fruit leather (dehydrated pureed fruit) is delicious for snacking and easy to make.

SHELF LIFE: 2 years

COST: $ (about $100 for a year's supply for a family of 4)

WHERE TO BUY: Sam's Club, Costco, or online

SAMPLE PRICING: Sam's Club $15 for 30

HOW TO STORE: Wrapped in plastic and vacuum-sealed

Adjust the proportions and varieties of fruit according to your family's tastes.

SERVING SIZE: 1 fruit roll-up | **SEASON:** anytime; see note

Persons 1 serving/week	Quantity for 1 year	Mark Off What You Have
1	52	
2	104	
4	208	
6	312	
8	416	
12	624	

Late summer is the best time for making your own.

How to make fruit leather

• See Part 4, Chapter 6: Fruit and Vegetable Leathers (page 451).

What to do with fruit leather

• Eat it as a snack.

❏ **Done**

91

SUMMER FRUITS: PEACHES, PLUMS, CHERRIES, & PINEAPPLE

PRIORITY: *Low* | **CATEGORY:** *Produce*

Preserve summer's bounty by dehydrating or canning summer fruits to enjoy all year long. These fruits also make delicious pies and crisps.

> **COST:** $ (about $100 for a year's supply for a family of 4)
>
> **WHERE TO BUY:** Sam's Club, Costco, or online
>
> **SAMPLE PRICING:** Costco about $1.50 per lb.
>
> **HOW TO STORE:** Dehydrate and vacuum-seal or store in #10 cans with an oxygen absorber.

Adjust the proportions and varieties of fruit according to your family's tastes.

PINEAPPLE

SERVING SIZE: ½ cup | **SEASON:** summer

Persons 1 serving/week	Quantity for 1 year	Mark Off What You Have
1	2 (#10) cans	
2	4 (#10) cans	
4	8 (#10) cans	
6	12 (#10) cans	
8	16 (#10) cans	
12	24 (#10) cans	

PEACHES/PLUMS/CHERRIES

SERVING SIZE: ½ cup | **SEASON:** summer

Persons 2 servings/week	Quantity for 1 year	Mark Off What You Have
1	1 (#10) can	Peaches: Plums: Cherries:
2	2 (#10) cans	Peaches: Plums: Cherries:
4	4 (#10) cans	Peaches: Plums: Cherries:
6	6 (#10) cans	Peaches: Plums: Cherries:
8	8 (#10) cans	Peaches: Plums: Cherries:
12	12 (#10) cans	Peaches: Plums: Cherries:

How to dehydrate summer fruits

- Pit them, peel them (if desired), and dehydrate for about 8 to 12 hours at 120°F.

What to do with summer fruits

- Eat as a snack.
- Make a crisp like apple crisp (page 49) but substitute other fruit.

❑ **Done**

92

SWEET POTATOES AND YAMS

PRIORITY: *Low* | **CATEGORY:** *Produce*

Sweet potatoes and yams make a delicious and nutritious side dish and add variety to a diet that could otherwise get very dull.

SHELF LIFE: 30 years

COST: $ (about $100 for a year's supply for a family of 4)

WHERE TO BUY: Sam's Club, Costco, or the grocery store

SAMPLE PRICING: About $2 per lb.

HOW TO STORE: In #10 cans with an oxygen absorber

If you can't buy it all at once, track your progress below.

SERVING SIZE: ½ cup | **SEASON:** anytime

Persons 1 serving/week	Quantity for 1 year	Mark Off What You Have
1	13 lbs.	
2	26 lbs.	
4	52 lbs.	
6	78 lbs.	
8	104 lbs.	
12	156 lbs.	

How to dehydrate sweet potatoes or yams

• Peel and slice or cube. Blanch in boiling water until about two-thirds cooked. Place on dehydrator trays and dehydrate at 120°F about 12 to 18 hours until completely dry.

What to do with sweet potatoes

• Add to soups and stews.
• Simmer in water, add butter, brown sugar, or maple syrup, and mash.

❏ **Done**

93

TRAIL MIX

PRIORITY: *Low* | **CATEGORY:** *Pantry staples*

Buy trail mix from Costco or Sam's Club and keep a year's worth on hand.

SHELF LIFE: About 18 months

COST: $$ (about $150 for a year's supply for a family of 4)

WHERE TO BUY: Sam's Club or Costco

SAMPLE PRICING: Sam's Club $9.78 for 48 oz., Costco $14.53 for 4 lbs.

HOW TO STORE: In your rotation pantry

If you can't buy it all at once, track your progress below.

SERVING SIZE: ½ cup | **SEASON:** anytime

Persons 1 serving/week	Quantity for 1 year	Mark Off What You Have
1	13 lbs.	
2	26 lbs.	
4	52 lbs.	
6	78 lbs.	
8	104 lbs.	
12	156 lbs.	

What to do with trail mix

- Eat it as a snack.
- Add it to muffins or cookies.
- Layer it with yogurt.

❑ **Done**

94

VINEGAR

PRIORITY: *Low* | **CATEGORY:** *Pantry staples*

Vinegar is great for making vinaigrette to dress up vegetables. It is also useful for cleaning.

 SHELF LIFE: Forever

 COST: $ (about $5 for a year's supply for a family of 4)

 WHERE TO BUY: Walmart or the grocery store

 SAMPLE PRICING: About $5 per gallon

 HOW TO STORE: In original packaging

If you can't buy it all at once, track your progress below.

SERVING SIZE: 1 teaspoon | **SEASON:** anytime

Persons 3 servings/week	Quantity for 1 year	Mark Off What You Have
1	1 gal.	
2	1 gal.	
4	1 gal.	
6	2 gal.	
8	2 gal.	
12	3 gal.	

What to do with vinegar

- Make vinaigrette.
- Use it to clean greasy counters.
- Make pickles.

❏ **Done**

WINTER FRUITS: CITRUS

PRIORITY: *Low* | **CATEGORY:** *Produce*

Citrus fruit dries beautifully, makes wonderful drinks, and adds a great flavor to dishes.

SHELF LIFE: 30 years

COST: $ (about $40 for a year's supply for a family of 4)

WHERE TO BUY: LDS, Sam's Club, Costco, or the grocery store

SAMPLE PRICING: Lemons are about $.26 each and oranges about $1

HOW TO STORE: In #10 cans with an oxygen absorber

If you can't buy it all at once, track your progress below.

SERVING SIZE: ½ fruit | **SEASON:** cheapest in winter

Persons 1 serving/week	Quantity for 1 year	Mark Off What You Have
1	10 lbs.	Lemons: Oranges: Other:
2	20 lbs.	Lemons: Oranges: Other:
4	40 lbs.	Lemons: Oranges: Other:
6	60 lbs.	Lemons: Oranges: Other:
8	80 lbs.	Lemons: Oranges: Other:
12	120 lbs.	Lemons: Oranges: Other:

How to dehydrate lemons and oranges

- Slice ⅛ inch thick using a mandoline. Layer on dehydrator trays and dehydrate at 120°F for 8 to 12 hours or until completely dry. Vacuum-seal in bags.

What to do with citrus

- Add a cup of lemon or orange slices to a large pitcher and fill with water. Add 1 cup of sugar and let stand in the refrigerator at least an hour to infuse the flavor.
- Add a slice of lemon to chicken soup.
- Soak orange slices in water, cut up, and add to beef and vegetable stir-fry.

❑ **Done**

96

DRIED CHILIES, CANNED CHILIES, PICKLES, PEPPERS, OLIVES, & ENCHILADA SAUCE

PRIORITY: *Low* | **CATEGORY:** *Produce*

Stock a years's supply of the extras your family loves.

SHELF LIFE: About 2 years

COST: Varies

WHERE TO BUY: LDS, Sam's Club, Costco, or the grocery store

HOW TO STORE: In #10 cans with an oxygen absorber

Persons 1 serving/ week	Quantity for 1 year	Mark Off What You Have
1		Dried chiles: Pickles: Olives: Enchilada sauce:
2		Dried chiles: Pickles: Olives: Enchilada sauce:
4		Dried chiles: Pickles: Olives: Enchilada sauce:
6		Dried chiles: Pickles: Olives: Enchilada sauce:
8		Dried chiles: Pickles: Olives: Enchilada sauce:
12		Dried chiles: Pickles: Olives: Enchilada sauce:

What to do with enchilada ingredients

- **Make enchiladas:** Roll corn tortillas stuffed with beef, pork, chicken, or cheese. Optionally add chiles to the degree of heat you like. Top with enchilada sauce and grated cheese.

❏ **Done**

CANNED MEATS: SPAM, VIENNA SAUSAGE, CANNED BEEF, CANNED HAM, & CANNED CHICKEN

PRIORITY: *Low* | **CATEGORY:** *Protein*

Spam, Vienna sausage, canned beef, canned ham, and canned chicken are commercially prepared canned meats and you should determine the amount you'd like to store according to your family's preferences.

SHELF LIFE: 2–5 years

COST: $ (about $100 for a year's supply for a family of 4)

WHERE TO BUY: Sam's Club or Costco

HOW TO STORE: In cans in your rotation pantry

If you can't buy it all at once, track your progress below.

SERVING SIZE: 1 can serves 2 | **SEASON:** anytime

Persons 1 serving/ week	Quantity for 1 year	Mark Off What You Have
1	26 lbs.	Spam: Vienna sausage:
2	52 lbs.	Spam: Vienna sausage:
4	104 lbs.	Spam: Vienna sausage:
6	176 lbs.	Spam: Vienna sausage:
8	208 lbs.	Spam: Vienna sausage:
12	312 lbs.	Spam: Vienna sausage:

Persons 1 serving/ week	Quantity for 1 year	Mark Off What You Have		
1	26 lbs.	Beef:	Ham:	Chicken: Other:
2	52 lbs.	Beef:	Ham:	Chicken: Other:
4	104 lbs.	Beef:	Ham:	Chicken: Other:
6	176 lbs.	Beef:	Ham:	Chicken: Other:
8	208 lbs.	Beef:	Ham:	Chicken: Other:
12	312 lbs.	Beef:	Ham:	Chicken: Other:

What to do with canned meats

• Pan-fry spam or canned ham and serve with eggs for breakfast or make into sandwiches.

• Season canned chicken, pan-fry, and serve in tacos.

• Crumble canned roast beef into a vegetable soup and serve over mashed potatoes.

❏ **Done**

TOILET PAPER, PAPER TOWELS, PAPER PLATES, PLASTIC CUPS, & SILVERWARE

PRIORITY: *Low* | **CATEGORY:** *Sundries & household*

In a storm or emergency, being prepared and having convenience items will make life easier. Keep a stock of paper and plastic goods on hand.

SHELF LIFE: Forever

COST: Varies

WHERE TO BUY: LDS, Sam's Club, or Costco

SAMPLE PRICING: Varies

HOW TO STORE: As packaged

If you can't buy it all at once, track your progress below.

Persons	Quantity for 1 year	Mark Off What You Have
1		Toilet paper: Paper towels: Paper plates:
2		Toilet paper: Paper towels: Paper plates:
4		Toilet paper: Paper towels: Paper plates:
6		Toilet paper: Paper towels: Paper plates:
8		Toilet paper: Paper towels: Paper plates:
12		Toilet paper: Paper towels: Paper plates:

Persons	Quantity for 1 year	Mark Off What You Have
1		Other:
		Other:
		Other:
		Other:
		Other:
2		Other:
		Other:
		Other:
		Other:
		Other:
4		Other:
		Other:
		Other:
		Other:
		Other:
6		Other:
		Other:
		Other:
		Other:
		Other:
8		Other:
		Other:
		Other:
		Other:
		Other:
12		Other:
		Other:
		Other:
		Other:
		Other:

❏ **Done**

CAKE MIX & FROSTING

....

PRIORITY: *Low* | **CATEGORY:** *Sweets & sweeteners*

I like to store one birthday cake per person in the flavor of their choosing. Be sure to keep a box of birthday candles on hand.

> **SHELF LIFE:** About 2 years
>
> **COST:** $ (about $20 for a year's supply for a family of 4)
>
> **WHERE TO BUY:** Sam's Club, Costco, or the grocery store
>
> **SAMPLE PRICING:** Grocery store about $2–$3 per box
>
> **HOW TO STORE:** In original packaging in your pantry
>
> If you can't buy it all at once, track your progress below.

CAKE AND FROSTING

SERVING SIZE: ⅛ cake | **SEASON:** anytime

Persons	Quantity for 1 year	Mark Off What You Have
1	1 box	Cake:
	1 can	Frosting:
2	2 boxes	Cake:
	2 cans	Frosting:
4	4 boxes	Cake:
	4 cans	Frosting:
6	6 boxes	Cake:
	6 cans	Frosting:
8	8 boxes	Cake:
	8 cans	Frosting:
12	12 boxes	Cake:
	12 cans	Frosting:

What to do with cake and frosting

- Make a cake to celebrate birthdays.

....

❏ **Done**

CANNED FRUIT

PRIORITY: *Low* | **CATEGORY:** *Produce*

Canned fruits are tasty, comforting, and a good source of liquid. Store some of the varieties your family enjoys. My secret favorite is fruit cocktail. It is certainly not gourmet, but I still find it comforting and like when I was a kid, I still covet the cherries.

SHELF LIFE: About 2 years

COST: $$ (about $150 for a year's supply for a family of 4)

WHERE TO BUY: Sam's Club, Costco, or the grocery store

SAMPLE PRICING: About $1.50 per can (Amazon.com)

HOW TO STORE: In #10 cans with an oxygen absorber

If you can't buy it all at once, track your progress below.

SERVING SIZE: ½ cup; see note | **SEASON:** anytime

Persons 1 serving/week	Quantity for 1 year	Mark Off What You Have
1	26 (14.5-oz.) cans	
2	52 (14.5-oz.) cans	
4	104 (14.5-oz.) cans	
6	156 (14.5-oz.) cans	
8	208 (14.5-oz.) cans	
12	312 (14.5-oz.) cans	

A note on serving size: 1 (14.5-oz.) can serves about 2.

What to do with canned fruit

- Eat it as a snack.
- Use it in quick bread.

❏ **Done**

101

SWEETS

PRIORITY: *Low* | **CATEGORY:** *Sweets & sweeteners*

Of sweets like candy, gum, mints, and Jolly Ranchers, hard candy lasts the longest. Also store chocolate chips for baking.

    SHELF LIFE: 30 years for hard candy, about 1 year for chocolate chips

    COST: $ (about $100 for a year's supply for a family of 4)

    WHERE TO BUY: Sam's Club, Costco, or the grocery store

    SAMPLE PRICING: Varies

    HOW TO STORE: In #10 cans with an oxygen absorber for best shelf life

If you can't buy it all at once, track your progress below.

SERVING SIZE: ¼ cup | **SEASON:** anytime

Persons ¼ serving/week	Quantity for 1 year	Mark Off What You Have
1		Chocolate chips: Candy: Gum:
2		Chocolate chips: Candy: Gum:
4		Chocolate chips: Candy: Gum:
6		Chocolate chips: Candy: Gum:
8		Chocolate chips: Candy: Gum:
12		Chocolate chips: Candy: Gum:

Persons ¼ serving/week	Quantity for 1 year	Mark Off What You Have
1		Mints: Other: Other:
2		Mints: Other: Other:
4		Mints: Other: Other:
6		Mints: Other: Other:
8		Mints: Other: Other:
12		Mints: Other: Other:

What to do with chocolate chips

- **Make chocolate chip cookies:** In a bowl, mix together 1 cup butter, ghee, or butter-flavored shortening, ¾ cup white sugar, and ¾ cup brown sugar. Add 2 eggs and 1 teaspoon vanilla and mix well. Add 2¼ cups flour, 1 teaspoon baking soda, and 1 teaspoon salt. Mix well and add 2 cups of chocolate chips. Bake 1-inch balls 2 inches apart on a baking sheet at 350°F for 8 to 10 minutes or until just golden at the edges.
- Add to muffins.
- Sprinkle in crepes and add strawberries.

❏ **Done**

PART 2

Recipes from the Pantry

CHAPTER 1

Introduction

Throughout my childhood, I heard stories of how my pioneering great-great-grandmother, Lillie May Busby, drove a covered wagon across Oklahoma to Texas with her 17 children. In these stories, she often set up camp and fed her family. The members of my family knew how to make do with very little, but they were able to generate enough food to feed a hungry family. As my grandmother once said, "We were very poor, but our love for each other made us rich."

I come from a generous, loving family, and they have passed down their recipes as gifts to be shared with the younger generations. My family is my inspiration for what I've written in this book, and it is my firm belief that they would enjoy sharing their gifts with you.

We Are Neo-Pioneers!

Homesteading, or self-reliance, and what many of us call "prepping" is really neo-pioneerism. When early Americans migrated westward, they had to adapt to a new environment, and their supplies had to become multifunctional. Their wherewithal to live on very little by using the available resources is something to marvel at. Pioneers lived on the food they produced, and a portion of their harvest was put aside for future use.

Don't wait for an emergency to venture back to our pioneering past and to live simply. Start practicing these skills now in order to have them in place—along with the necessary supplies—when a disaster or unexpected emergency does strike.

Every Family Should Prepare

With the increase of natural and man-made disasters, many people feel that it's time to get preparations together. Being prepared for emergencies that may directly affect you and your family is like purchasing an insurance policy. When you need those preparations the most, they'll be there for you.

This book will give you tips on how to preserve food just as your ancestors did. You'll find a list of foods to have in your food pantry, and I share many favorite recipes for using them.

We've witnessed first-hand how unprepared our society is to handle disasters, natural or man-made. Sadly, for the majority of us, we will watch as the disasters play out time and again on our televisions. Yet we fail to realize that this is not some distant phenomenon that can't happen in our neighborhoods and communities. We haven't yet learned the importance of being prepared. Good planning leads to a good response, and the more planning you've done, the more steadfast you'll be in your response to a disaster. Understanding what types of foods to keep in your pantry for the best overall health and nutrition, and having an array of recipes on hand for using them, will help keep you thriving.

The Economics of Prepping

Many believe that stocking preparedness items is too pricey for their family budgets. But let's be honest with ourselves—can we afford an extra $5 per grocery-shopping trip? By adding a few items to your cart each time, you can create a solid preparedness pantry. A benefit of this approach is that you won't have to buy everything at once. Prepping and stockpiling can actually be your economic salvation.

Beat the Grocery Stores at their Own Game

Grocery stores play a weekly shell game with customers. They advertise a loss-leader item, such as a jar of spaghetti sauce for $1. Consumers are excited, because that same jar of sauce is normally $3. They don't notice that the pasta they buy to go with the sauce has been marked up by 33 percent to allow for profit. Have you ever gone to the store and discovered that your child's favorite breakfast cereal has gone from $3.99 a box to $5.99 in a week? This is the grocery industry in action—getting the consumer to pay whatever's asked by adjusting prices constantly.

You can beat them at this game by starting a price book. If you have your grocery receipts from the last few weeks, that will give you a starting point; otherwise, scour the sales flyers. For each item you normally buy, write down the best price you can find. This is your baseline, which you can adjust up or down as time goes on. For example:

>Spaghetti sauce (can)—$.89
>Lean ground beef—$2.99 per pound
>Spaghetti—$1.19

The following week, check the flyers again. And look—now spaghetti is on sale! Compare these prices:

>Spaghetti sauce (can)—$1.29
>Lean ground beef—$2.99 per pound
>Spaghetti—$0.99

Notice that the price of sauce went up and the price of pasta went down. If you purchased the sauce when it was on sale and the pasta on sale this week, you've saved $.50 on your family's meal. If you could save $.50 on every supper over the course of a year, you'd save $182.50. If you could save that much for three meals a day, the number jumps to nearly $550 per year. You can buy a lot of extra food for $550!

I estimate that I save even more than that, because I now purchase only loss leaders. Look for words like these:

- Limited quantities
- Only six per family
- While supplies last

Of course, this doesn't always guarantee a good deal. Check your price book to be sure.

You Can Eat Your Preps

Purchase items your family normally enjoys for your stockpile. If you invest in a dozen #10 cans of freeze-dried whatchamacallits and then discover you really hate freeze-dried whatchamacallits, you've just wasted a lot of money, and valuable storage space.

Think about the menu you've served your family over the past weeks. Write down what you normally have for breakfast, pack in school lunches, and eat for dinner. These are what you should look for great deals on. In fact, many of your favorite perishable items can be dehydrated or canned for future use. And any of the recipes in this book can be made with dehydrated, canned, or freeze-dried foods.

If you buy a dozen cans of tuna on sale, whip up some tuna salad for school lunches. Make a tuna noodle casserole for supper!

You Can't Afford Not to Stock Up!

Take a look at your grocery budget. Whatever you normally spend, try to take at least 10 percent of that amount to start your stockpile. Make a commitment to your family to build your stockpile; this is the one investment guaranteed to yield a solid return. Here are some quick tips:

- **Buy at least one stockpile item every week**. A 1-pound bag of dried beans makes 10 to 12 adult servings. A 1-pound bag of rice also makes about 10 servings. For just a few dollars, these two ingredients could combine to make nearly a dozen meals.

- **Work cheap meals into your weekly menu.** Get out of the meat-and-potatoes mindset and add some inexpensive meals to your repertoire. If you can feed your family for $2 instead of $10, you've just saved $8 that can go toward your stockpile. Consider homemade soups, spaghetti with marinara sauce, beans and rice, or baked potatoes.

- **Use your leftovers.** If food that normally gets thrown away is combined into a new dish, in effect you've gotten a free meal. Save the last little bits of food and combine them in a pot pie, a soup, a stew, or a casserole.

- **Make meat an accent instead of the main course**. For example, instead of serving ham along with scalloped potatoes, dice up some ham into a ham and potato casserole.

- **Brew your own coffee.** Do you hit the drive-thru every morning to get coffee before work? Spend $5 per workday and you'll end up spending a whopping $1,825 per year! If you and your spouse both indulge in this habit, you're looking at $3,650 per year.

- **Take your lunch to work.** The average fast-food meal costs $7; at that rate, lunches out could cost you nearly $2,000 per year. Your wallet, waistline, and cholesterol level will all thank you.

CHAPTER 2

Don't Just Survive, Thrive!

After Hurricane Katrina stopped food supply lines dead in their tracks, many hurricane victims didn't have access to food or clean water for weeks. To prevent starvation, they were given Meals Ready to Eat (MREs), and in most cases these instant meals weren't well received. Rather than depending on government organizations and emergency responders to provide you with food, why not create a versatile emergency pantry that encompasses your family's dietary preferences and needs? Your emergency food pantry should include dry goods that you normally buy. Many favorite foods are available as "just add water" mixes, and having a supply of these will cut down on preparation time. For example, my family loves to eat pancakes for breakfast on weekends, so we keep a good supply of the "just add water" pancake mix on hand.

A healthy diet incorporates carbohydrates, proteins, fats, and vitamins. Your overall health will benefit from making the substitutions shown in the following chart.

Ingredients	Healthy Substitutes	Did You Know?
Table salt	Sea salt	Sea salt contains 84 minerals that are removed in the processing of table salt.
White sugar	Honey, molasses	Natural sugars don't cause the blood sugar crash that comes after eating refined sugar.
White flour	Whole wheat flour	Whole wheat flour still contains the bran, the most nutritious part of the wheat.
White rice	Brown rice, quinoa	As with wheat, the bran is removed to make white rice white.
Butter/oil	Herbs	Try seasoning dishes highly with herbs instead of added fats.
Whole eggs	1 tablespoon soy flour mixed with 1 tablespoon water	This is an easy low-cholesterol baking substitute (it's frugal, too!).
Oil/vegetable shortening	Applesauce	Substitute applesauce for half the oil in muffin and cake recipes to cut fat and cholesterol. It can be used as an egg substitute, too; add ¼ cup applesauce per egg in baked goods such as muffins, pancakes, or yeast-free quick breads.
White pasta	Whole wheat pasta	Much of the fiber is lost in the processing of white pasta.
Ground beef	Organic soy crumbles/TVP	For a dish with ground beef, replace half the beef with TVP (textured vegetable protein).
Craisins	Dried cranberries	Craisins are loaded with sulphites and added sugar.
Canned beef	Freeze-dried beef or dehydrated beef pieces	You'll get all of the protein without the added chemicals.

Water: Your Most Vital Prep

Water is more important than food. During a natural emergency, the water supply can be interrupted for days, even weeks. At the very least, you should have a three-day water supply consisting of 1 gallon per person per day, the amount recommended by national disaster organizations. Moreover, it would be wise to prepare for the event that the water supply isn't safe for longer periods and have a means to filter water. A normally active person needs to drink at least 2 quarts (8 cups) of water every day. Take into account that if you live in a hot environment, even more water is required especially by children, nursing mothers, and the ill. Besides drinking water, you'll need water for cleaning/sanitizing, food preparation, and pets.

What Foods Should I Store?

To be nutrition-ready for extended emergencies, you need to store the right types of foods. Keep carbohydrates, proteins, fats, and vitamins in mind when planning your food pantry to give you the best bang for your buck as far as nutrition goes.

- **Carbohydrates**. Carbohydrates provide the body with energy. They have a symbiotic relationship with proteins by protecting the protein stores in the body. The American College of Sports Medicine suggests that between 45 percent and 65 percent of your daily calories should come from carbs. The best carbs are complex and come from natural sources containing fiber, such as fresh vegetables, fruits, whole grains, and low-fat milk.

Which are most important?	Why do you need them?	Where can you find them naturally?
Vitamin A	Helps with vision, the immune system, major organ functioning, growth, and reproduction.	Dairy products, animal fat, carrots, and leafy green vegetables. Dandelions are full of vitamin A, and the green leaves are packed with other vitamins and nutrients, including calcium.
Vitamin B complex	Needed for the nervous system, healthy skin, healthy energy levels, cell production, digestion, respiration, and bone marrow production. Helps metabolism, regulates hormone production, and protects the body from free-radical damage.	All meats, green plants (vegetables), dairy products, grains, and cereals. Try dandelions, chicory, or banana leaf, pine nuts, walnuts, and perhaps even wild grains or rice.
Vitamin C	Builds healthy skin, bones, tissues, and tendons and assists in absorbing iron. Essential for healthy teeth and gums and for healing wounds or fractures. Protects the body from free-radical damage.	Fresh fruits and vegetables. Citrus fruits, tomatoes, and broccoli have high levels of vitamin C. Rosehips are extremely high in vitamin C. The needles on pine boughs can be brewed to make a tea—not that tasty, but it does provide vitamin C.

THE PREPPER'S ULTIMATE FOOD STORAGE GUIDE

Which are most important?	Why do you need them?	Where can you find them naturally?
Vitamin D	Helps maintain the immune system. Regulates the absorption of phosphorus and calcium in the body.	Eggs, dairy products, and fish with fatty flesh (tuna, salmon, sardines, and oysters).
Vitamin E	Protects the body from free-radical damage. Contributes to immune system functioning.	Rice and green leafy vegetables.
Vitamin K	Assists in blood clotting.	Produced naturally by our intestinal tract and present in soybean, olive, and canola oils, broccoli, watercress, spinach, egg yolks, leafy green plants, wild chicory, fish liver oils, and other foods.

- **Protein.** Protein will help your body repair cells and rebuild muscles. It is recommended that 15 percent of daily calories come from protein.
- **Beans**. An excellent storage food—they become a complete protein when accompanied by a grain such as rice or quinoa.
- **Fats**. As much as we might like to eliminate fats from our diets, they play a vital role in maintaining healthy skin and hair, insulating body organs against shock, maintaining body temperature, and promoting healthy cell function. Fats also serve as an energy store for the body. A 2,000-calorie-per-day diet should include 67 grams of fat per day.
- **Vitamins and minerals**. Vitamins protect against infection and disease, help the body grow, assist in metabolism, and facilitate the removal of waste. For a regular diet, it's recommended that we get our vitamins by eating fresh fruits and vegetables; however, it doesn't hurt to take a multivitamin daily.

Popular Emergency Pantry Foods

When you make a list of foods to stockpile, keep these basic principles in mind:

- Emergency food shouldn't need refrigeration, and it should require little electricity or fuel to prepare.
- The food should be versatile and have a long shelf life.
- It should provide nutrition and should contain little salt.

Here's a list of the most popular food staples to stock in emergency pantries:

1. Canned fruits, vegetables, meats, and soups
2. Dried legumes (beans, lentils, etc.)
3. Crackers
4. Nuts
5. Pasta sauce
6. Peanut butter
7. Pasta

8. Flour (white, whole wheat)

9. Seasonings (vanilla, salt, pepper, paprika, cinnamon, taco seasoning, etc.)

10. Sugar

11. Bouillon cubes or granules (chicken, vegetable, beef)

12. Kitchen staples (baking soda, baking powder, yeast, vinegar)

13. Honey

14. Unsweetened cocoa powder

15. Jell-O or pudding mixes

16. Whole grains (barley, bulgur, cornmeal, couscous, oats, quinoa, rice, wheat berries)

17. Nonfat dried milk

18. Plant-based oil (corn oil, vegetable oil, coconut oil, olive oil)

19. Cereals

20. Seeds for eating and sprouting

21. Popcorn (not the microwavable kind)

22. Instant potato flakes

23. Packaged meals (macaroni and cheese, hamburger helper, ramen noodles, etc.)

24. Purified drinking water

25. Fruit juices, teas, coffee, drink mixes

When you visit the grocery store, don't limit yourself to these items. You can create a personalized preparedness pantry to suit your family's unique dietary needs and preferences. For example, I have a friend who keeps a stock of protein powder because she subscribes to a high-protein diet. She's taught me that you can add protein powder to more than just drinks.

How Much Food Do I Need?

Figuring out how much food to store can seem overwhelming at first. The following charts can help you calculate how much of certain foods you need to weather a 30-day disaster. (Canned goods aren't included.) I've provided amounts that would meet the needs of 1) two adults for a month and 2) a family of two adults and three children would need for a month.

LEGUMES
(2 adults for 30 days)

Type of Food	Quantity
Lima beans	0.83 lbs.
Soy beans	1.67 lbs.
Split peas	0.83 lbs.
Lentils	0.83 lbs.
Dry beans (mix)	5.00 lbs.
Total Legumes	10.00 lbs.

LEGUMES
(2 adults and 3 children for 30 days)

Type of Food	Quantity
Lima beans	1.08 lbs.
Soy beans	2.92 lbs.
Split peas	1.08 lbs.
Lentils	1.08 lbs.
Dry beans (mix)	8.75 lbs.
Dry soup mix	1.08 lbs.
Total Legumes	16.00 lbs.

GRAINS
(2 adults for 30 days)

Type of Food	Quantity (2 adults for 30 days)
Wheat	25.00 lbs.
Flour	4.17 lbs.
Cornmeal	4.17 lbs.
Oats	4.17 lbs.
Rice	8.33 lbs.
Pasta	4.17 lbs.
Total Grains	50.01 lbs.

GRAINS
(2 adults and 3 children for 30 days)

Type of Food	Quantity (2 adults, 3 children)
Wheat	43.75 lbs.
Flour	7.17 lbs.
Cornmeal	7.17 lbs.
Oats	7.17 lbs.
Rice	14.58 lbs.
Pasta	7.17 lbs.
Total Grains	87.01 lbs.

FATS AND OILS
(2 adults for 30 days)

Type of Food	Quantity
Shortening	0.67 lbs.
Vegetable oil	0.33 gal
Mayonnaise	0.33 qts
Salad dressing	0.17 lbs.
Peanut butter	0.67 lbs.
Total Fats	2.17 lbs.

FATS AND OILS
(2 adults and 3 children for 30 days)

Type of Food	Quantity
Shortening	1.17 lbs.
Vegetable oil	0.58 gal
Mayonnaise	0.58 gal
Salad dressing	0.42 lbs.
Peanut butter	1.17 lbs.
Total Fats	3.92 lbs.

SUGARS
(2 adults for 30 days)

Type of Food	Quantity
Honey	0.50 lbs.
Sugar	6.67 lbs.
Brown sugar	0.50 lbs.
Molasses	0.17 lbs.
Corn syrup	0.50 lbs.
Jams	0.50 lbs.
Flavored gelatin	0.17 lbs.
Fruit drink mix	1.00 lbs.
Total Sugar	10.00 lbs.

SUGARS
(2 adults and 3 children for 30 days)

Type of Food	Quantity
Honey	0.75 lbs.
Sugar	11.67 lbs.
Brown sugar	0.75 lbs.
Molasses	0.42 lbs.
Corn syrup	0.75 lbs.
Jams	0.75 lbs.
Flavored gelatin	0.42 lbs.
Fruit drink mix	1.75 lbs.
Total Sugar	17.25 lbs.

KITCHEN ESSENTIALS
(2 adults for 30 days)

Type of Food	Quantity
Baking powder	0.17 lbs.
Baking soda	0.17 lbs.
Yeast	0.08 lbs.
Salt	0.83 lbs.
Vinegar	0.08 gal

KITCHEN ESSENTIALS
(2 adults and 3 children for 30 days)

Type of Food	Quantity
Baking powder	0.42 lbs.
Baking soda	0.42 lbs.
Yeast	0.21 lbs.
Salt	1.58 lbs.
Vinegar	0.21 gal

DAIRY
(2 adults for 30 days)

Type of Food	Quantity
Dry milk	10.00 lbs.
Evaporated milk	2 cans
Other	2.17 lbs.
Total Dairy	16.17 lbs.

DAIRY
(2 adults and 3 children for 30 days)

Type of Food	Quantity
Dry milk	17.50 lbs.
Evaporated milk	3.5 cans
Other	3.67 lbs.
Total Dairy	28.17 lbs.

To determine the quantities of other foods for your family, visit ReadyNutrition.com for a food storage calculator.

Be a Planner!

To make the most of your preparedness grocery list, preplan your emergency menus to ensure that you have everything you need for a varied diet. Having your meals planned out relieves a tremendous amount of stress and cuts down on food fatigue (the boredom of eating the same food repeatedly). Be sure to include special treat items for family members—and yourself. If you're having an emotional or rainy day, indulging in a treat or treating your children to something special will lift spirits and break up the monotony. Treats might be pudding, Jell-O, cheese crackers, applesauce, hot chocolate, popcorn, or dried fruit leathers, for example.

Spice of Life!

One way to avoid food fatigue when cooking from your storage pantry is to add herbs and spices. A trip to the bulk-foods store can get you some gourmet blends; all you'll need are a few jars in which to store them. Another option is to start your own herb garden. If you dehydrate your cut herbs, you'll have a constant supply to use in your own seasoning blends.

The following mixes can be made from dried herbs that you've purchased or that you've grown yourself and dehydrated. Some of the mixes call for salt, and although regular table salt can be used, kosher salt is recommended because its larger grains are more absorbent. That will keep your blends fresh longer. To test whether an herb or spice is still potent, rub or crush a small amount in your hand, then taste and smell it. If the aroma and flavor is weak, it should be discarded. In general, use the following guidelines to estimate the shelf lives of your spices:

- Herbs: 1 to 3 years
- Extracts: 4 years, except pure vanilla, which lasts indefinitely
- Ground Spices: 2 to 3 years
- Whole Spices: 3 to 4 years
- Seasoning Blends: 1 to 2 years

Use a spice mill or electric coffee grinder to grind these spice mixes into fine powders and then transfer them into glass jars. A pepper mill or mortar and pestle is a suitable off-grid alternative to grinding spices.

APPLE PIE SPICE MIX

¼ cup ground cinnamon

1 tablespoon ground allspice

2 teaspoons ground nutmeg

2 teaspoons ground ginger

½ teaspoon grated dried lemon zest

1 teaspoon ground cardamom (optional)

PUMPKIN PIE SPICE MIX

¼ cup ground cinnamon

2 tablespoons ground ginger

2 teaspoons ground cloves

1 teaspoon ground nutmeg

¼ teaspoon ground cardamom (optional)

CAJUN SEASONING

Add a taste of New Orleans to rice, beans, fish, or chicken with this zesty blend.

⅓ cup kosher salt

¼ cup chili powder

¼ cup Hungarian paprika

1 tablespoon onion powder

1 tablespoon garlic powder

1 tablespoon coarsely ground black pepper

1 tablespoon dried basil

1 tablespoon dried oregano

1 tablespoon ground coriander

½ teaspoon cayenne pepper

2 teaspoons dried thyme

¼ teaspoon ground cumin

¼ teaspoon white pepper

CHILI POWDER

2 tablespoons paprika

2 teaspoons dried oregano

1½ teaspoons ground cumin

1¼ teaspoons garlic powder

1¼ teaspoons cayenne pepper

1 teaspoon onion powder

FRENCH HERB MIX

Try adding this mixture to soups, meats, or vegetables.

3 tablespoons dried marjoram

3 tablespoons dried thyme

3 tablespoons dried summer savory

2 tablespoons minced dried garlic

1 teaspoon dried basil

1 teaspoon dried rosemary

1 teaspoon dried sage

½ teaspoon ground fennel seeds

CHINESE FIVE-SPICE MIX

Grind the whole spices together to make this blend perfect for sprinkling into stir-fries or onto meats.

- 2 tablespoons ground anise seed or 2 whole star anise, ground
- 2 tablespoons ground fennel seed
- 2 tablespoons ground cloves
- 2 tablespoons ground peppercorns

TEX-MEX SPICE BLEND

Turn dinner into a fiesta by adding this blend to chili, taco meat, beans, or rice.

- ½ cup chili powder (purchased or made from recipe)
- ¼ cup paprika
- 1 tablespoon ground cumin
- 1½ teaspoons garlic powder
- 1 teaspoon onion powder
- 2 teaspoons dried oregano
- 2 teaspoons dried parsley
- 1 teaspoon salt

FAJITA SEASONING MIX

- 2½ tablespoons chili powder (purchased or made from recipe)
- 1 tablespoon kosher salt
- 1 tablespoon lemon pepper seasoning
- 1 tablespoon sugar
- 2½ teaspoons crushed chicken bouillon cubes or granules
- 2 teaspoons onion powder
- ½ teaspoon garlic powder
- ½ teaspoon cayenne pepper
- ¼ teaspoon crushed red pepper flakes
- ½ teaspoon ground cumin

GREEK SEASONING MIX

Flavor shish kebobs, veggies, meat, and rice with this mixture.

- 2 tablespoons dried oregano
- 4 teaspoons dried mint
- 4 teaspoons dried thyme
- 1 tablespoon dried minced garlic
- 2 teaspoons dried basil
- 2 teaspoons dried marjoram
- 2 teaspoons dried minced onion

HOMEMADE VEGETABLE ALL-PURPOSE SEASONING

Makes 2 cups

- 3 medium onions, cut into 2-inch cubes
- 5 celery ribs, diced
- 3 medium russet potatoes, peeled and diced
- 3 medium red bell peppers, diced
- 3 large green bell peppers, diced
- 3 large carrots, peeled and diced
- 2 large parsnips, peeled and diced
- 8 to 10 garlic cloves
- 1 bunch fresh parsley
- chicken bouillon granules, to taste

In a saucepan over high heat, combine diced potatoes and carrots with enough water to cover them. Cook for 5 minutes until soft. Drain.

Combine all the ingredients except the bouillon in a blender or food processor and whirl until fully processed. Place on a jelly roll tray in food dehydrator at a setting of 135°F to 145°F for 5 hours or until dried and crumbly. Once the mixture is thoroughly dried, add 1 tablespoon bouillon granules at a time to taste. Store in a jar for up to one year.

Rotating Your Food Supply

Think of your preparedness pantry as your in-home convenience store, to be used whenever you need it. In fact, incorporating your stored foods into your regular menu-planning and replenishing them as they get used up will ensure that your preparedness foods are at optimal freshness. First In First Out (FIFO) is a restaurant-business term that can be incorporated into your food storage philosophy. To get the most out of your investment, use the FIFO approach by placing items with the earliest expiration dates in front so they'll be used first.

Keeping your pantry stocked with fresh food means doing inventory checks from time to time. My family takes inventory of our supplies every six months to make sure canned goods, preserves, and other items are within their expiration dates. We also check to make sure we're not running low on any essentials. If anything is close to expiring, it's taken to the kitchen pantry to be used. Follow the FIFO strategy for both store bought and home-canned goods.

Essential Tools

In an emergency, when you're likely to be without many modern conveniences, certain tools become essential. When selecting your tools, keep your lifestyle in mind. For example, if you have a baby, you'll probably need a baby food mill.

Food Dehydrator—This is probably the most used of all of my preparedness tools. I use meat or cut up older produce and dehydrate it for snacks or to use in cooking.

Outdoor Grill—Many meals can be prepared on a gas or charcoal grill. Keep extra fuel for whatever type of grill you have.

Sun Oven—A solar oven will cook your meals and bake tasty breads and desserts! The only drawback is that certain foods take longer to cook and you're dependent on full sun.

Non-Electric and Hand-Crank Appliances—Did you know that there are hand-crank blenders, popcorn poppers, baby food mills, and ice-cream makers? These "off-grid" appliances can add convenience at an otherwise chaotic moment.

Wheat Grinder—Wheat grinders grind wheat, as well as smaller grains and legumes, into flour so you can bake fresh bread. The higher-end models can be costly, but there are basic grinders that cost around $70 and work very well.

Sprouter—This will more than likely be the least expensive tool you'll purchase, but it will pay for itself many times over while helping to keep you healthy.

Water Purification Systems—Having a supply of fresh drinking water is essential for thriving during an emergency. One way to cut down on water storage space is to invest in a water purification system.

Making Meals Stretch

A wise home economist can put together a meal out of thin air when other people would say, "There's nothing to eat."

Making do with fewer ingredients while wanting meals to be as filling as ever is quite a conundrum. My grandmother once told me that her mother always had a soup on the stove. The ingredients were usually leftovers, and if she was told that company was coming, she'd add water and throw in some potatoes or beans to thicken the soup.

Making the most of your food pantry is all about your mindset. Learning how to stretch food supplies helps to create a frugal lifestyle and allows us to make the most of our food investments.

Inexpensive additions can go a long way to making the most of a meal. Here are six easy ways to make meals more filling:

1. Fiber: Fiber-rich food sources such as beans and lentils are ideal to have in your food supply. Beans are the quintessential prepper food—cheap, nutritious, easy to store, and extremely filling. Throwing a half-cup of beans into a soup or casserole, or cooking them as a side dish, definitely fills up those hungry bellies.

2. Whole grains: Grains are the basis of many pantries because of their fiber and protein content. Whole grains are popular sources of fiber, having much greater amounts of nutrients, soluble fiber, and protein than refined grains such as white bread. Whole grains can be ground into flour or used to add texture to dishes, such as if they are made into dumplings and added to a soup or stew. Wheat berries in particular are great for longer-term storage. If stored properly and in the right environment, wheat berries can last a lifetime.

3. Bread and pasta: The starches from some "white foods" will bring some sustenance and keep morale up during an extended emergency. Simply adding a slice of bread or sprinkling in breadcrumbs will instantly thicken a soup and make it more filling. Even the water used for cooking pasta can be re-used as a soup thickener, thanks to the starch in the water.

4. Nuts: Almonds especially are rich in monounsaturated fatty acids and protein. Just one handful of almonds will keep you full for a long time. Don't limit your nut selections to just almonds, though; any nut will do. Nuts can also be ground into flour or included in a main dish or salad to add flavor and crunch. I love adding almonds to my rice dishes.

5. Trimmings: Freeze vegetable and meat trimmings to use for making broths and stocks. Toss peeled veggies or leftover meat parts into labeled freezer bags. When you're ready to use them, cover these trimmings with water and simmer on low for an hour or two to make a delicious soup or stew.

"Leftover Stew or Chowder" is just what it sounds like—a marriage of leftovers that might normally be thrown out. Designate a large plastic freezer container and dump in all the tiny bits of leftovers you might previously have considered "not enough to keep." When the container is full, add water and a couple of bouillon cubes and see what you come up with. During lean times, my family has created some surprisingly tasty concoctions.

Another way of prolonging this type of meal is to dehydrate it; dehydrate the broth as you would fruit leather (see page 207) and dry the vegetables on a separate tray.

It All Starts with a List

I don't know about you, but I'm a "list person." I simply cannot operate without my lists. They keep me organized and on task, and they keep me from purchasing extraneous items.

If you're just starting out, I recommend developing a month's menu plan and purchasing the food to fulfill it. Once you've acquired a full month's food supply, you can add on and shoot for a three-month supply, a six-month supply, and so forth.

Determine how many people you'll be feeding. Creating a list of everything you need for your basic food pantry will help you keep your family's dietary needs in mind when you go shopping. A few things to consider:

- Keep things affordable. Keep a price book (see page 155) so that you'll know when to stock up on various foods.
- Look for foods that don't require electricity (refrigeration or freezing) for storage.
- Keep tabs on how much food you have in various nutrient groups: protein, fruits, vegetables, grains, and dairy.
- If there's a power outage, do you have an alternate way to cook food? Is there a way to at least boil water? If not, are you prepared with food that doesn't require heating?

The Basic Meal-by-Meal Pantry

The most basic way to stock your long-term pantry is with a meal-by-meal plan; it's utilitarian and will cover your family basic nutritional and caloric needs. It won't be gourmet, but it's a starting point to give you a month's worth of food. Many people like to start here and then expand to tastier meals offering greater variety.

Let's break this down meal by meal. Our sample family will consist of two adults and two children.

BREAKFASTS—For breakfasts, cold cereal is a quick, high-energy option that doesn't require cooking. Top your cereal with reconstituted nonfat milk and dried fruit for a well-balanced breakfast.

Based on a 1-cup serving for children and a 1½-cup serving for adults, we're looking at 5 cups of cereal per day for our family of four, or 150 cups for a 30-day month. A box of cornflakes (18 ounces) contains about 18 cups of cereal, so it would provide three days of breakfasts for all four family members, plus two additional adult servings. To feed our theoretical family for a month, we'd need eight boxes of cereal.

You can perform the same calculations for nonfat dry milk and dried fruit servings.

Tip: For the best flavor, stir reconstituted dry milk well and chill it in the refrigerator. When my kids are drinking it, they prefer it with chocolate drink mix powder added, but over cereal the taste isn't that noticeable.

LUNCHES—Depending on the time of year, a piping-hot cup of soup or pasta can make for a comforting lunch. Served with crackers and a drink, this inexpensive option is easy to stock for. Condensed soups take up little space, and they can be heated quickly. Canned pasta, such as ravioli, also requires nothing more than a way to heat it. In a pinch, it can be eaten at room temperature.

Two cans of condensed soup per lunch would keep the edge off hunger for our hypothetical family of four, especially if it's served with crackers or over leftover rice from the previous night's meal. That means that 60 cans of soup, plus crackers, would last for 30 days of lunch.

DINNERS—For dinner, most people like a sit-down meal that's a bit more elaborate than lunch and breakfast. An excellent way to prep for dinners for a basic one-month stockpile is to select seven recipes that you'll be able to prepare, and simply buy four times the ingredients needed for each recipe. Browse through the recipes in this book, try out some of them, and shop for what you need to make your favorites.

Meals for the Week

Use this chart to list meals you plan on preparing for the week.

	Breakfast	Lunch	Dinner
Monday			
Tuesday			

	Breakfast	Lunch	Dinner
Wednesday			
Thursday			
Friday			
Saturday			
Sunday			

Food Storage 101

Storing food for short- and long-term emergencies is not without its challenges. Over time, moisture, sunlight, oxygen, temperature fluctuations, and bug infestations can compromise your food supply. When this occurs, food may lose essential nutrients or be tainted and need to be thrown out—along with your monetary investment. One way to keep the enemies of food at bay is to repack your purchased dry goods in higher-quality packaging.

Most of the dry goods we buy have packaging designed for short-term use. Clear and flimsy plastic packaging can't stand up to long-term storage; it's easily punctured and is no match for the elements or hungry bugs. We need to repackage our food in higher-quality containers. Plastic 5-gallon pails, Mylar liner bags, oxygen absorbers, and desiccant pouches create additional layers of protection.

According to the United States Food and Drug Administration, certain "defects" in our food supply are unavoidable. Bugs and their eggs are on that list. But taking steps to destroy them before you repackage food can extend its shelf life. There are three methods you can use:

1. Freeze-dry goods for 72 hours.
2. Heat food in a 170°F oven for 15 to 20 minutes.
3. Add diatomaceous earth, the fossilized remains of a type of algae. Organic and safe to use on food, it kills bugs. Be sure to purchase food-grade diatomaceous earth, and add 1 cup to every 25 pounds of food. Sprinkle the bottom of the container with food-grade diatomaceous earth. Add 3 to 4 inches of dry food. Using a sifter or metal colander, sprinkle another layer of diatomaceous earth. Repeat until all the dry food is treated. Sprinkle a final light layer of diatomaceous earth on the top, then seal.

Many of the following food storage products can be purchased at preparedness stores geared toward long-term food storage such as www.PrepperPackaging.com. This website carries Mylar bags, oxygen absorbers, desiccant packets, and many other essential items.

Plastic Containers

Any food that you plan to keep indefinitely should be stored in food-grade plastic. Such containers won't transfer any non-food chemicals into the food, nor do they contain any chemicals that are hazardous to humans. Typically a food-grade container has a "#2" with the recycle symbol or the high-density polyethylene (HDPE) stamp on the bottom and is 75 milliliters thick. Clean containers with soapy water, rinse, and dry thoroughly. Five-gallon plastic containers are the most popular for storing food in bulk.

Make sure that your containers have airtight and spillproof lids. Lids with gaskets and gamma lids are great, as they can be opened with a simple twist of the wrist. These are typically a little more expensive than the traditional bucket lid, but they're easier to open and close—and worth every penny.

Food Liners

Research has shown that small amounts of oxygen seep through the walls of plastic containers. Consequently, natural elements and even insects can find a way in. Adding a food liner such as a 5-milliliter Mylar bag will provide extra protection. Thick Mylar bags have a middle layer of aluminum and two different plastic layers on the inside and outside, making them ideal for long-term food storage. Further, Mylar bags make for a good investment because they can last up to 20 years if properly cared for, are reusable, and make a big difference in the taste of stored food.

Oxygen Absorbers and Desiccants

Oxygen absorbers can greatly prolong the shelf life of stored food by inhibiting the growth of aerobic pathogens and molds. If you live in an area prone to high humidity, you may also want to consider adding desiccant packets to your food storage.

OXYGEN ABSORBERS—Oxygen absorbers come in vacuum-sealed packs and begin working the moment they're exposed to oxygen, so it's best to work as efficiently as possible.

To determine how many cubic centimeters your oxygen absorber should be, it's important to consider the type of food being packed. Requirements vary depending on the volume of the food, the "void space" (the space between food particles), and the "headspace" (the container space not filled with food). For example, if you fill a 5-gallon bucket all the way to the top with marbles, leaving no headspace, the void space is the amount of air between marbles. Because marbles don't pack as densely as, say, salt, your bucket will require a larger oxygen absorber than a 5-gallon bucket of salt.

This is the general formula for the cubic centimeters of oxygen absorption required:

Container volume
− Food volume
= Residual air volume

Residual air volume
x 0.21 (because air is 21 percent oxygen)
= Oxygen absorber size requirement

You want your oxygen absorber to meet or exceed the residual air volume in the packed container. Here's how it works. To pack 35 pounds of rice in a 5-gallon bucket, an online calculator tells us that 35 pounds of rice is equivalent to 15,875 grams (or cubic centimeters). Our 5-gallon bucket is equivalent to 18,942 cubic centimeters of air volume. Assuming the rice fills the bucket to the top, leaving no headspace, we can calculate the void space (oxygen absorber size requirement) as follows:

18,942 cc (container volume)
− 15,875 cc (food volume)
= 3,067 cc (residual air volume)

3,067 (residual air volume)

X 0.21 (oxygen)

= 644 cc (oxygen absorber size requirement)

Note: Use an online calculator, such as www.metric-conversions.org, to convert pounds to grams; 1 gram is equal to 1 cubic centimeter.

The following chart is a guide to the oxygen absorber sizes you're likely to need for some food you'll be packing. The chart assumes that containers are full and that as much air as possible has been removed. (Vacuum sealing is recommended when possible.) Oxygen absorbers are typically sold in 50, 100, 300, 500, 1,000, and 1,500-cc sizes. Since headspace and void space can't be calculated exactly, when in doubt it's best to err on the side of caution and use a larger size, as has been done for this chart.

OXYGEN ABSORBER SIZE REQUIREMENTS

Food type	1-quart pouch (8" x 8") 947 cc	#10 can (0.82 gallon) 3,910 cc	5-gallon bucket 18,942 cc	6-gallon bucket 22,730 cc
Flour, pancake mix, fine powders	50–100 cc	200–300 cc	750 cc	1,000 cc
Sugar, salt, dry milk	50–100 cc	200–300 cc	750 cc	1,000 cc
Rice, grains (wheat berries, oats, etc.)	50–100 cc	200–300 cc	750–1,000 cc	1,000–1,500 cc
Dried beans	100–150 cc	300–500 cc	1,000 cc	1,500 cc
Pasta	100–200 cc	300–600 cc	1,000–1,500 cc	1,500–2,000 cc

DESICCANTS—Desiccant packets only moderate the moisture levels in food containers; they don't completely absorb the moisture. Desiccants shouldn't be added to flour, sugar, and salt; these ingredients need a certain amount of moisture to stay activated, and if desiccant is added, they'll turn into hard bricks.

Desiccant manufactures recommend adding two 1-ounce packets per 5 or 6-gallon pail or large barrier bag. Make sure the desiccant packets aren't touching oxygen absorbers.

Desiccant is not edible—if the packet somehow breaks open and spills onto the stored food, the entire contents of the container must be thrown away.

The Sealing Process

1. Place a Mylar bag in the plastic container. The Mylar bag should be fitted for the size of container you are using. For example, if you are using a 5-gallon plastic bucket, you will want to use an 18 x 28-inch or a 20 x 30-inch Mylar bag.
2. Add oxygen absorbers and/or desiccant in the bottom of the bag. (You'll add another oxygen absorber at the top.)

3. Begin pouring food into the Mylar bag. When the bag is about half full, shake it to make sure the food gets into all the crevices of the bag.

4. Continue adding food into the Mylar bag until the bag is ¾ full. Add another oxygen absorber on the top of the contents.

5. Begin folding the Mylar down to let any trapped air escape.

6. Seal the Mylar, using a heat clamp or an iron on its highest setting. If you use an iron, work on a hard surface, moving slowly and gently to keep from damaging the bag. Seal across the bag in a straight line, leaving the last 2 or 3 inches unsealed.

7. Push out the last remaining trapped air, then finish sealing the bag.

8. Push the sealed Mylar bag into the plastic storage container. If you wish, add another oxygen absorber on top of the sealed bag. Place the lid securely on the container.

9. Place in a dark storage area where temperature, moisture level, and sunlight don't fluctuate.

DRY ICE ALTERNATIVE—This is another method used for food preservation. Many preppers use dry ice with Mylar bags and plastic containers, and some preppers only use the plastic food-grade containers. Dry ice can be purchased at many grocery stores, ice cream stores, and even welding stores. What makes this storage method popular is that it's very economical: a 5-pound bag of dry ice costs just $5. Dry ice is very cold, so if you use this method, use gloves when handling, and ensure that you work in a ventilated area. Also, if you're using oxygen absorbers, there is no need to use the dry ice method. Use 3 to 4 ounces of dry ice per 5-gallon bucket. This storage method can be done two different ways:

Ice on top:

1. Spread a single layer of nonconductive (insulating) material such as kraft paper or foil over the contents of a nearly filled 5-gallon container. Place 4 ounces of dry ice on top.

2. Leave part of the lid unsealed until the dry ice completely evaporates (sublimates).

3. Check every 30 minutes to see if the dry ice has completely evaporated. If not, keep checking every 5 minutes.

4. When the dry ice has evaporated, remove the insulating material and seal the container.

Tip: If the sealed lids begin to bulge up, then you have sealed them prematurely. If this happens, use a bucket lid remover to crack open the lid on one side to let the excess gas escape, then seal the lid back down.

Ice on bottom:

Place 4 ounces of dry ice in the bottom of a 5-gallon storage container. Cover with nonconductive (insulating) material, such as kraft paper or foil. Add the food. Press the lid down lightly, allowing air to escape. Continue as for the on-top method.

Building Your Pantry

Building your food pantry can seem overwhelming, but you might be surprised at how much you've already accomplished without even realizing it. An inventory of your cupboards can help you to realize how far you've already come.

The best way to see what you have is to bring it all out in the open and take inventory. (This might also be a great time to do some "spring cleaning" of your cabinets.) Use your countertops and kitchen table to organize, sort, and count what you have.

Sort things into groups. Your categories might include the following:

- Canned meats (tuna, chicken, Spam, dinner ham)
- Canned soups
- Canned dinners (beef stew, chili, Beefaroni)
- Canned beans
- Canned vegetables
- Canned fruit
- Jelly and jam
- Peanut butter
- Baking supplies (flour, yeast, baking soda, etc.)
- Desserts (gelatin, pudding mix)
- Boxed meals (Hamburger Helper, macaroni and cheese)
- Packaged side dishes (scalloped potatoes, flavored rice or pasta, sauce packets)
- Cereal (dry breakfast cereal, oatmeal, cream of wheat)
- Dried legumes (kidney beans, split peas, etc.)
- Dried fruit
- Sweeteners (honey, sugar, maple syrup, stevia)
- Pancake mix
- Baking mixes (cake mix, cookie mix)
- Crackers
- Canned tomato products (spaghetti sauce, tomato paste, diced tomatoes)
- Herbs and spices

Once you have everything out and organized, I bet you'll be surprised by how much you have. This, my friend, is the start of your survival pantry! Your next step is to identify how many servings of the different foods you have. Grab a pen, a notebook, and a calculator (unless you're a big fan of doing math in your head).

Use the following table to calculate the servings in some of your food packages.

Serving size	Food type	Servings per weight
1 cup	Beans, dried	10 per 1 pound
1 cup	Rice	12 per 1 pound
1 cup	Pasta	8 per 1-pound bag
1 cup	Condensed soup	2 per 10.7-ounce can
½ cup	Canned veggies	3 per 15-ounce can

Look for serving information on the packages of other items. Once you know how many servings of various items you have, plug the numbers into an online food storage calculator like the one found at the Ready Nutrition website (readynutrition.com/resources/category/preparedness/calculators).

You'll be able to see how long your family could sustain itself on the food you already have, and you'll be able to see where your weak points are. You may have enough pasta to last for six months because you recently hit a sale, but only enough canned fruit for a couple of weeks. Or you may have a month's supply of canned fish and meat but only a two-week supply of powdered milk. Now it's time to build on what you have.

Creating a Master List

The best way to keep track of your preps is with a master inventory list. My family has an alphabetized list that includes everything. Here are some suggestions for creating your own master list:

- Use a computer spreadsheet program to organize and categorize your preps.
- List everything! Nothing should be excluded from your inventory.
- Alphabetizing your food categories and listing where everything is stored can be helpful when you're in a pinch.
- Store your master list in a binder that also contains emergency procedures (including evacuation routes), pertinent phone numbers and other useful information.

Where to Store Food?

Ideal temperatures for food storage are between 60°F and 75°F. To ensure that the area where your food is stored is at the proper temperature and moisture level, install an indoor thermometer and hygrometer or humidity gauge. Food is best stored in relatively low humidity levels; 15 percent humidity or less is ideal, although ideal conditions are not always practical. Hygrometers and thermometers are available at most hardware or home-improvement stores and are relatively inexpensive.

Make sure that your food storage area is clean, free of trash, and protected from insects and the elements. Keep containers from touching walls to allow constant air circulation. Also, avoid storing food containers directly on concrete or dirt floors. Use shelving, pallets, boards, or blocks to raise the food storage above ground level.

Here are a few ideas of where you can safely store your emergency food supply:

KITCHEN PANTRY—Your kitchen pantry is the go-to place for your cooking needs, and it should continue to be so. When the food is used up here, it can be replenished with items from your emergency stores.

COLD CELLAR—Root cellars date back to prehistoric times, and cellaring remains one of the best ways to maintain the freshness and nutritional value of some foods. A root cellar is a simple way to preserve food without processing it or using any electricity or fuel. An underground storage space provides the right temperature and humidity level for many fruits (such as apples, oranges, or pears) and root vegetables (such as potatoes, turnips, carrots, beets, and onions). Winter squash and pumpkins also do well in a root cellar.

CLOSET—A closet can be a very useful food pantry. A closet has all the recommended essentials: it's dark, temperature-controlled, and easily accessible. It's ideal to have a shelving or storage system that keeps food 6 inches off the floor to protect it in case of flooding.

UNDER THE BED—Storing food under the bed is a great way to take advantage of unused space. This area is dark and typically in a controlled climate, and if food is in a plastic container, it should be well protected. Keep in mind that food kept under the bed needs to be in a container that can't be tampered with by pets. In our home, we have a plastic underbed container filled with vacuum-sealed beans and rice.

Get Organized

These steps will help keep your pantry easy to use and maintain:

- Label each container or package with the contents, packing date, and any necessary instructions.
- Assign locations within the storage area to keep items organized (medical, baking, sanitation, breakfast, canned goods, and so on). Group items typically used together; for example, keep baking supplies (flour, sugar, baking soda, salt) next to each another for easy access.
- Place goods with the farthest-away expiration dates in the back and work forward to the nearest expiration dates.
- Systematically rotate and organize your storage. Check your storage inventory every six months to make sure items are properly rotated and used within their expiration dates.

CHAPTER 3

Preserving Your Food

Preserving food is something of a lost art, in my opinion. What was once a necessary skill has now becoming a thing of the past. What if I told you that the typical contents of a refrigerator could all be canned or dehydrated to last up to 12 months longer? That's right, I'm talking about meats, vegetables and fruits, condiments, and juices. In this chapter, I'm going to provide you with information on how to properly preserve these foods using techniques that were familiar to our ancestors. Throughout this book, when a recipe calls for a fresh ingredient or meat, you can replace it with dehydrated or canned goods that you've preserved on your own.

Making Your Food Last

During the 1930s, my great-grandmother firmly believed in canning to make the most of the food they had. Canning was essentially her day's equivalent of the Tupperware that we have around today for leftovers. Back then, everything was canned to keep it for as long as possible. Nothing was wasted.

My Grandma Francis reminisces about her family's garden during the Depression: "Gardening was a family affair. The kids would pick the bugs off tomatoes and other vegetables so that Momma could put them up. She would put on her straw hat and get to working. When everything was picked, it was canning time. Momma could can anything, even fried chicken! She canned all of our leftovers so that they wouldn't go bad."

Preserving techniques can make most foods last on a pantry shelf for up to 12 months; preserved meats should be eaten within three to six months of processing. After a food's recommended shelf life has expired, natural chemical changes may affect its color, flavor, texture, or nutritional content.

Today those who preserve their own food may do so for economic reasons, as a way to embrace the past, or because they prefer knowing just where and how their food is grown. These are the principal methods of preserving food:

CANNING—By hermetically sealing food in a jar or can, the canning process destroys microorganisms and deactivates naturally occurring enzymes in food. Heating and then cooling the container forms a vacuum seal that keeps microorganisms from getting in. Acidic foods (such as tomatoes and certain fruits) can be processed or "canned" in boiling water—the "water bath method"—while low-acid vegetables and meats must be processed in a pressure canner at a higher temperature.

DEHYDRATING—Drying food is a very low-cost approach to use for long-term storage, and the dehydration process minimally affects the nutritional content. You can purchase a food dehydrator for as little as $40, or you can dehydrate foods in your oven at a very low setting. (Some people have even used their cars as a dehydrator during the hot summer months.) Dried foods will keep for 6 to 12 months.

FERMENTING AND PICKLING—This is a common way to preserve food, because the acidity level makes it difficult for bacteria to grow.

What's So Great about Preserving Foods?

Aside from providing you with a reliable food supply made to your own specifications, an added benefit of preserving food is that the vitamins and nutrients in most foods won't be destroyed during the process.

If you preserve berries, pears, apples, or apricots when they are almost ripe or at their peak, they are full of vitamins and antioxidants. A study at the University of Illinois Department of Food Science and Human Nutrition found that canned fruits and vegetables are nutritionally comparable to their fresh or frozen counterparts. The fermentation method of preserving food even adds vitamins.

Food Safety

Despite our best efforts, canned goods sometimes do go bad. Advises the National Center for Home Food Preservation, "Growth of spoilage bacteria and yeast produces gas, which pressurizes the food, swells lids, and breaks jar seals. As each stored jar is selected for use, examine its lid for tightness and a strong seal." In more cases than not, you will visibly notice or smell that spoilage has occurred.

Some clues that canned goods have spoiled:

- The jar or lid contains mold, and food has leaked out.
- The contents are discolored, cloudy, or slimy.
- The jar or can is swollen, and the contents may ooze out when you open it.
- The liquid in the jar looks as if it is bubbling.
- The contents have an "off" smell.

If you suspect that canned goods aren't safe, discard the jar and its contents.

Botulism

Clostridium botulinum—botulism—is a concern for anyone who cans their own food. Ingesting or even coming in contact with this contaminant can be fatal.

According to the Centers for Disease Control, on average there are 145 cases of botulism each year in the United States, of which approximately 15 percent are foodborne. Foodborne botulism most frequently comes from home-canned foods with low acid content (such as asparagus, green beans, beets, and corn), caused by failure to follow proper canning procedures.

The CDC advises that botulism can be destroyed by boiling home-canned food in the jar. Heating the canned food to an internal temperature of 185°F (85°C) for at least ten minutes will detoxify contaminated food or drink. However, it is best to err on the side of caution. If you suspect that food may be contaminated with botulism, discard the contents and can in its entirety.

Follow these safety tips to avoid contact with botulism:

- Wear rubber or heavy plastic gloves when handling suspect food or cleaning up contaminated surfaces and equipment.
- Using a solution of 1 part unscented liquid household chlorine bleach (5 percent to 6 percent sodium hypochlorite) to 5 parts clean water, treat work surfaces and anything else that may have been contaminated, including can openers, utensils, and clothing. Spray or wet contaminated surfaces with the solution and let stand for 30 minutes.
- Wearing gloves, wipe up the treated area with paper towels, being careful not to spread contamination. Seal the paper towels in a plastic bag before putting them in the trash.
- Apply the bleach solution again, let stand for another 30 minutes, and rinse off with paper towels and discard in a plastic bag.
- Discard your gloves when the cleaning process is complete. Thoroughly clean any contaminated clothing as well.

Truth be told, when I began reading about botulism and the serious health issues it causes, it made me not want to can food at all. Why take the risk? In the end, my desire to learn this skill and my need to provide healthy food for my family outweighed my fear. I educated myself and paid close attention to canning procedures and guidelines. I learned to trust my canning skills, and you can, too.

Water Bath Canning

If you have a way to boil water, you have a way to preserve food. There are two basic methods of canning: water bath canning and pressure canning. If you plan to preserve a great deal of food, you need to learn how to do both, since certain foods (low-acid vegetables and meats) require the higher temperatures of pressure canning to be safely canned. (See page 191 for details on pressure canning and Part 3 for even more information on canning.) However, jams and jellies, fruits, applesauce, pickles, and tomato products are all high-acid foods that can be safely preserved in a boiling water bath.

To prevent spoilage, the entire contents of your jar must be covered in liquid. You can preserve fruit in heavy, medium, or light sugar syrup, in a non-overpowering fruit juice such apple or white grape, or even in plain water.

Making Sugar Syrup

	2 cups sugar		3 cups sugar		4¾ cups sugar
+	4 cups water	+	4 cups water	+	4 cups water
=	5 cups light syrup	=	5½ cups medium syrup	=	6½ cups heavy syrup

Measure the sugar and water into a saucepan and cook over medium-high heat until the mixture comes to a boil. Then turn the heat down to low to keep the syrup warm. About 1 cup of syrup is needed for 1 quart of fruit.

Don't throw it out! Once you've used the contents of the jar, don't discard the syrup. Here are some ways to use it:

- Sweeten beverages (powdered drink mixes, juices, teas).
- Cook oatmeal.
- Make fruit smoothies.
- Make fruit drinks (mix 1 quart fruit syrup with 1 gallon water).
- Thicken with cornstarch to drizzle on cake, pancakes, or waffles (mix 1 cup fruit syrup with 1 tablespoon cornstarch).
- Marinate meats (acidic fruits in particular).
- Replace the water in Jell-O recipes.
- Sweeten a fruit salad.
- Replace the liquid in cakes, cookies, or brownies.
- Make a sweet rice dessert.

Step-by-Step Process

These are the basic tools you'll need in order to can properly and safely, using the water bath method:

- Jars
- Flats (snap lids)
- Rings
- A large pot that is both wide and deep. The height of the pot needs to be at least 3 to 4 inches taller than the height of your canning jars.
- Rack (or a towel folded in the bottom of the pot)
- Jar lifter
- Jar funnel
- Labels

There are all sorts of other gadgets out there—such as magnetized lid lifters and tools for measuring headspace—but if you have the things on the this list, you are ready to can! So imagine a big pot of fruity jam bubbling away on the stove, ready to be canned. Doesn't it smell great?

1. **Sanitize your jars, lids, and rings.** You can wash them in a dishwasher, which will get hot enough to sterilize everything. Otherwise, you need to submerge them in boiling water for at least 10 minutes, lifting them carefully in and out with the jar lifter. Leave the sterilized items in the dishwasher or hot water until you're ready to use them.

2. **Prepare your canner.** Place your rack or folded towel in the bottom of the canner and fill the canner with water to the line on the inside. (If your canner doesn't have a line, fill to within 3 to 5 inches of the top.) Bring to a boil.

3. **Fill your jars.** Line up your jars on the counter near the stove. If the surface isn't heatproof, set them on a towel, because they'll be very hot when filled. Using the funnel, ladle in the prepared food, leaving the headspace recommended in your recipe.

4. **Put on the lids.** With a clean, dry dish towel, carefully wipe the rims of the filled jars, making sure to remove any food residue. Place a flat on each jar, then twist on a ring—you don't have to really torque it.

5. **Place the jars in the canner.** Using your jar lifter, place the closed jars on the rack or towel in the canner. Be careful not to let them touch each other, because they could break if they bump together in the boiling water. Make sure the lids are completely submerged in the water.

6. **Process the jars.** Bring the water in the canner back to a boil. Don't start clocking your processing time until the water is at a full boil. Then process the jars in the water bath for the amount of time specified in your recipe (see Part 3 for canning recipes).

7. **Remove the jars from the canner.** Using your jar lifter, carefully remove the jars from the boiling water, one by one. Tip each jar to the side to allow the hot water to drip off the top, then place on your heatproof or towel-lined surface.

8. **Allow 12 to 24 hours for the jars to cool and seal.** Let the jars stand in a draft-free place where they won't be moved or bumped, usually for overnight. You'll hear a musical "pop" as a jar seals in the cool air—that's the lid being sucked down and forming a seal. When you are ready to store the jars, you can remove the rings and test the seals by pushing down with your finger. If a lid pops back and forth, it's not sealed; refrigerate to use right away. Store your sealed jars in a cool, dark place.

CANNING FRUIT: PROCESSING IN BOILING WATER BATH

Leave ½ inch headspace in each jar. Add 1 additional minute for each 1,000 feet of elevation above sea level for processing times of 20 minutes or less, 2 minutes for longer processing times.

Fruit	Preparation	Cold pack method	Hot pack method
Apples	Peel, core, and cut into halves, quarters, or smaller pieces.	Pack raw in hot, sterilized jars, cover with boiling-hot light sugar syrup (light). Process at once.	Boil in light syrup over medium-high heat until apples are heated through, about 6 minutes. Pack in sterilized jars. Process at once.
Applesauce	See page 266.	N/A	Pack in hot, sterilized jars and process.
Berries (raspberries, blackberries, blueberries, huckleberries)	Pick over and rinse thoroughly; remove hulls.	Pack raw in sterilized jars. Cover with hot syrup (medium) and process.	Cover in juice or hot sugar syrup (medium), just enough to cover; cook until softened. Process at once.
Strawberries	Pick over and rinse thoroughly; remove stems.	N/A	For each quart of berries, add 1 cup sugar; let sit at room temperature until the juices flow. Boil rapidly for 5 minutes, then let sit overnight. Pack in sterilized jars in hot light to medium sugar syrup.
Cherries	Wash and remove pits and stems.	Pack raw in sterilized jars; cover with boiling syrup (thick syrup for sour cherries, medium for sweet cherries). Process immediately.	Mix syrup (medium for sweet cherries, thick for sour cherries) in a saucepan. Add cherries and cook over medium heat. Stir occasionally until sugar dissolves and mixture is heated. Pack in sterilized jars.
Peaches, Apricots, Nectarines	Drop peaches into boiling water to loosen the skins; peel. Cut fruit in halves or slices and remove the pits.	Rack raw in sterilized jars. Cover with hot sugar syrup (medium). Process immediately.	In a saucepan, add peaches and pour hot light to medium syrup over fruit until sugar has dissolved and mixture is heated. Pack hot peaches cavity-side down and pour syrup over. Process immediately.

CANNING FRUIT: PROCESSING IN BOILING WATER BATH

Leave ½ inch headspace in each jar. Add 1 additional minute for each 1,000 feet of elevation above sea level for processing times of 20 minutes or less, 2 minutes for longer processing times.

Fruit	Preparation	Cold pack method	Hot pack method
Pears	Peel and remove the cores. Cut in halves or quarters; small pears can be left whole.	Pack raw in sterilized jars. Cover with sugar syrup (medium) and process immediately.	If pears are hard or whole, cook 4 to 8 minutes in boiling-hot syrup. For halved and quartered pears, over medium heat, warm pears in medium syrup for 5 minutes or until syrup is heated. Pack hot pears with their cavity down and process immediately.
Pineapple	Cut in thick slices, about ½ inch, then remove skin and core.	Pack raw in sterilized jars and cover with boiling light to medium sugar syrup. Process immediately.	Remove pits, add syrup, and boil over medium-low heat for 2 to 4 minutes, or until soft. Pack and process immediately.
Plums	Pit if desired by cutting plum in half (plums are usually processed with the skin on). If left whole, prick all over with a fork so syrup can penetrate.	Pack raw in hot jars. Cover with boiling sugar syrup (medium) and process immediately.	Bring sugar syrup to a boil and add the pitted plums. Bring to a rapid boil and then pack and process immediately.
Rhubarb	Cut in ½-inch pieces.	N/A	Place in a baking dish with ¼ the amount of sugar as rhubarb, by volume. Cover and bake at 350°F for 30 to 35 minutes, or until tender. Pack hot in sterilized jars and process immediately.
Tomatoes	Pour boiling water over to loosen the skins. Remove stems, cores, and skins. Leave whole, or halve or quarter.	Pack raw in sterilized jars and cover with boiling water. Add 1 teaspoon salt to each quart jar. Process immediately.	Over medium heat, add tomatoes to a saucepan and cover with water. Allow tomatoes to boil for 5 minutes and pack hot in sterilized jars. Add 1 teaspoon salt to each quart jar. Note: If canning whole tomatoes, do not layer them in saucepan.

Chart inspired by *The Settlement Cook Book*, originally published in 1903.

CANNING FRUIT: PROCESSING IN PRESSURE CANNER

Fruit	Cold Pack	Hot Pack	Pressure Canner
Apples	15 minutes	15 minutes	10 minutes at 5 pounds pressure
Applesauce	N/A	10 minutes	5 minutes at 5 pounds pressure
Berries (raspberries, blackberries, blueberries, huckleberries)	20 minutes	15 minutes	10 minutes at 5 pounds pressure
Strawberries	N/A	15 minutes	5 minutes at 5 pounds pressure
Cherries	25 minutes	20 minutes	10 minutes at 5 pounds pressure
Peaches, apricots, nectarines	25 minutes	25 minutes	10 minutes at 5 pounds pressure
Pears	20 minutes	20 minutes	10 minutes at 5 pounds pressure
Pineapple	20 minutes	20 minutes	10 minutes at 5 pounds pressure
Plums	25 minutes	15 minutes	10 minutes at 5 pounds pressure
Rhubarb	N/A	10 minutes	5 minutes at 5 pounds pressure
Tomatoes	25 minutes	10 minutes	15 minutes at 5 pounds pressure

Pectin or No Pectin?

Pectin is a thickening and jelling agent commonly used in jams and jellies. It's available in powdered, liquid, and low-sugar varieties. You can also make your own (see the directions for Homemade Apple Pectin, on page 185). Pectin is naturally found in fruits and vegetables.

Depending on the type of fruit you are preserving, you may need to use more pectin or citric acid in your recipes. Pectin can be added by means of acidic fruit juices (such as apple, plum, or quince), or by using homemade or purchased pectin.

Since most fruits do not contain enough natural pectin to make preserves, it is helpful to know which fruits do. The following chart shows the naturally occurring pectin content of some popular fruits.

High Pectin Content (Has enough natural pectin or acid for gel formation)	Medium Pectin Content (May need additional pectin or acid)	Low Pectin Content (Needs additional acid, pectin, or both)
Apples, tart (e.g., Granny Smith)	Apples, sweet	Apricots
Blackberries, sour	Blackberries	Blueberries
Crab apples	Cherries	Cherries, sweet
Cranberries	Chokeberries	Figs
Currants	Elderberries	Grapes
Gooseberries	Grapefruit juice	Guavas
Lemons	Grape juice	Nectarines
Loganberries	Loquats	Peaches
Plums	Oranges	Pears
Quinces		Plums
Raspberries		Pomegranates
Citrus skins		Strawberries

Homemade Apple Pectin

I think we can all agree that nothing compares to homemade. Making your own pectin for preserves is a rewarding all-natural way of using natural ingredients in your jams and jellies. *Makes 4 cups*

> 4 pounds tart, firm, ripe apples, peeled and cored
>
> 5 cups water
>
> 3 tablespoons lemon juice

1. Remove any bruised places on the fruit. Cut into thin slices and place in a large stockpot with the water and lemon juice. Bring to a boil, uncovered, for about 30 minutes or until the liquid reduces by half, stirring occasionally.

2. Line a strainer with a single layer of cheesecloth; set over a large pot. Pour in the apples and cooking liquid.

3. Gather the cheesecloth containing the apple pulp and squeeze it to extract any additional juice. Pour the strained juice into a measuring bowl.

4. Pour the juice back into the stockpot and boil for an additional 20 minutes. It should reduce to about 4 cups.

5. Remove from the heat and let stand for 10 minutes. Strain again, using another single layer of cheesecloth to line your strainer.

6. Use the cooked juice stock as your homemade pectin. Four cups of this stock equals about a half-bottle (3 ounces) of commercial pectin.

7. Store leftover pectin in the refrigerator, or freeze for up to a year. You can also seal the pectin in sterilized pint jars while it is still hot and process it for 15 minutes in a boiling water bath.

No-Pectin Apple Jelly

Don't throw those apples away! Use the apples from this recipe to make applesauce. *Makes 8 (½-pint) jars*

3 pounds apples, cored and quartered (peels left on)

3 cups water

3 cups sugar

1 tablespoon lemon juice (optional)

1. In a large uncovered pot, combine quartered apples and water over high heat and allow mixture to boil for 20 minutes until soft.

2. Strain the cooking liquid through a cheesecloth-lined strainer. Squeeze the cheesecloth to extract as much liquid as possible from the apples. (If you want clear jelly, don't squeeze the cheesecloth.)

3. Measure the strained liquid. For every 1 cup of juice, add 1 cup sugar. Boil together for 20 to 30 minutes. Stir frequently, ensuring that mixture is not sticking to the bottom. Allow mixture to come to the jelly point.

4. Pour mixture into hot, sterile jars, leaving ¼ inch headspace. Remove any air bubbles by inserting a knife and moving it around the jar in an up-and-down motion. Wipe rims of jars with a damp, clean paper towel. Adjust lids and rings and process in a water bath for 10 to 15 minutes.

Testing for Jelly Point

To test if jam or jelly is done, use a jelly or candy thermometer to make sure the mixture has come to 220°F. (If you live at a higher altitude, follow the recommended temperature for your area.) If you don't have a jelly or candy thermometer, try one of these tests:

- Dip a cool metal spoon into the jelly. Turn the spoon on its side on a dish. If the mixture comes off the spoon in a large drop, it's done.

- Place a small saucer in the freezer while you're preparing the jelly. When you think the jelly is done, place 1 tablespoon hot jelly on the chilled saucer and return it to the freezer for 2 minutes. If you can divide the mixture in half with your finger, the jelly point has been reached.

No-Pectin Peach Jelly

Makes 8 (½-pint) jars

> 5 pounds peaches, peeled, pitted, and coarsely chopped (11 to 12 cups)
>
> 4 cups sugar
>
> 4 to 6 tablespoons lemon juice

1. Combine the peaches and sugar in a large saucepan over medium-high heat. Slowly bring the mixture to a boil, stirring, until the sugar is completely dissolved.

2. Boil rapidly for 30 minutes, stirring frequently. Test to make sure the jelly point has been reached. Strain fruit pieces from liquid.

3. Ladle liquid into sterilized jars, leaving ½ inch headspace. Remove any air bubbles by inserting a knife and moving it around the jar in an up-and-down motion. Wipe the jar rims clean with a moistened paper towel, add the lids, and screw on the bands.

4. Process in a boiling water bath for 20 minutes.

Berry Jam

Makes 2 to 3 cups

> 5 cups berries (your choice)
>
> 1 (1.75-ounce) package no-sugar pectin

> 5 cups sugar
>
> 2 tablespoons lemon juice

1. In large a saucepan over high heat, mix together the berries and pectin and bring to a full boil. The berries will produce their own liquid when they cook down. Stir thoroughly to ensure the berries do not get scorched.

2. Stir in the sugar and lemon juice. Let come to a boil and test for jelly point. If jelly point has been reached, remove from the heat.

3. Fill sterilized jars with the jelly, leaving 1 inch of headspace. Remove any air bubbles by inserting a knife and moving it around the jar in an up-and-down motion. Wipe the jar rims clean with a moistened paper towel, add the lids, and screw on the bands.

4. Process in a boiling water bath for 10 minutes.

Ketchup

To easily peel the tomatoes for this recipe, submerge them in boiling water for 1 minute and then transfer to an ice-water bath. The skins will slide right off. *Serves 16*

6 to 7 large tomatoes, quartered, seeds removed

1 small onion, chopped or ⅓ cup dehydrated chopped onions

3 garlic cloves, minced

1 bay leaf

6 tablespoons sugar

1 tablespoon dark molasses

¾ tablespoon garlic powder

¼ teaspoon ground allspice

1½ teaspoons paprika

¼ teaspoon ground cloves

2 teaspoons salt

¼ cup distilled white vinegar

1. Peel the skin from the tomatoes, cut them in half, and remove the seeds.

2. In a blender, puree tomatoes, onions, and garlic.

3. Add to a large (12 to 16-quart) pot and bring mixture to an active simmer over medium-high heat.

4. Add the remaining ingredients and continue cooking, stirring frequently, until the sauce thickens.

5. Allow mixture to come to an active simmer and reduce heat to low for 20 minutes. Remove from the heat.

6. Fill sterilized jars with the ketchup, leaving 1 inch of headspace. Remove any air bubbles by inserting a knife and moving it around the jar in an up-and-down motion. Wipe the rims clean with a moistened paper towel, add the lids, and screw on the bands.

7. Process in a boiling water bath for 20 minutes.

BBQ Sauce

Serves 6

4 cups ketchup, purchased or made from recipe on page 188

1 jalapeño chile, left whole

2 cups water

1 cup apple cider vinegar

¼ cup packed light brown sugar

½ cup dark molasses

1 tablespoon freshly ground black pepper

1 tablespoon onion powder

1 tablespoon dry mustard

2 tablespoons lemon juice

2 tablespoons Worcestershire sauce

1. In a medium saucepan, combine all the ingredients. Bring to a boil over medium-high heat, reduce to simmer, and cook for 1 hour, uncovered, stirring frequently.

2. Remove jalapeño from mixture.

3. Fill sterilized jars with the sauce, leaving 1 inch of headspace. Remove any air bubbles by inserting a knife and moving it around the jar in an up-and-down motion. Wipe the rims clean with a moistened paper towel, add the lids, and screw on the bands.

4. Process in a boiling water bath for 20 minutes.

Enchilada Sauce

Serves 10 to 12

3 tablespoons vegetable oil

3 tablespoons all-purpose flour

3 tablespoons chili powder

1 teaspoon ground cumin

½ teaspoon cayenne pepper, or to taste

3 cups water

2 (8-ounce) cans tomato paste

2 teaspoons garlic powder

1 teaspoon onion powder

1 cup prepared salsa (page 199)

salt and pepper

1. In a large pot over medium heat, whisk the oil, flour, and chili powder together and cook for 1 or 2 minutes.

2. Add the remaining ingredients and bring to a slow simmer. Stir well to combine the seasonings and dissolve the tomato paste in the water. Leave mixture uncovered and allow it to come to a slow simmer, for at least 20 minutes, stirring occasionally. Taste and adjust the seasoning as desired. The sauce will thicken as it cools.

3. Fill sterilized jars with the hot liquid, leaving 1 inch of headspace. Remove any air bubbles by inserting a knife and moving it around the jar in an up-and-down motion.

4. Wipe the rims clean with a moistened paper towel, add the lids, and screw on the bands.

5. Process in a boiling water bath for 20 minutes.

Teriyaki Sauce

Serves 15

1 cup soy sauce

5 cups water

1½ tablespoons orange or pineapple juice

1½ tablespoons ground ginger

1½ teaspoons garlic powder

1½ cups packed light brown sugar

¼ cup honey

pepper, to taste

1 tablespoon sesame seeds

1. In a large bowl, stir together all the ingredients except for the sesame seeds.

2. In a large saucepan over low heat, toast the sesame seeds until toasted for 1 to 2 minutes. Pour in the mixture from the bowl and bring to an active simmer. Cook uncovered on low for 25 minutes, stirring often.

3. Fill sterilized jars with the hot liquid, leaving 2 inches of headspace. Remove any air bubbles by inserting a knife and moving it around the jar in an up-and-down motion. Wipe the rims clean with a moistened paper towel, add the lids, and screw on the bands.

4. Process in a boiling water bath for 20 minutes.

Meat variation: Sauté bite-sized boneless chicken or beef pieces and add to the sauce before filling the sterilized jars; leave 2 inches headspace. Pressure-can for 90 minutes at 10 pounds pressure.

Sloppy Joe Sauce

Serves 4 to 6

1 tablespoon olive oil

½ medium green or red bell pepper, diced

½ cup chopped celery

1 medium onion, chopped or ¼ cup dehydrated chopped onion

4 garlic cloves, minced

½ cup shredded carrot

1 pound ground beef or 4 cups dehydrated ground beef crumbles

½ cup ketchup, purchased or from recipe on page 188

1 (6-ounce) can tomato paste

1 tablespoon Worcestershire sauce

1 tablespoon apple cider vinegar

2 tablespoons dark brown sugar

⅛ teaspoon ground cloves

½ teaspoon dried thyme

salt and pepper

1. Heat the olive oil in a large skillet over medium-high heat. Add the bell pepper, celery, and onion and sauté for 5 minutes. Add the garlic and carrots; cook, stirring, for 5 more minutes. Remove from the heat and transfer the vegetables to a medium bowl; set aside.

2. In the same skillet over medium heat, cook the ground beef, breaking it apart with a spoon. Strain off all but 1 tablespoon of the fat from the meat.

3. Add the cooked vegetables to the skillet with the cooked ground beef. Stir in the wet ingredients and the brown sugar, mixing well. Add ground cloves, thyme, salt, and pepper. Lower the heat to medium-low and simmer for 10 minutes. Adjust the seasonings to taste, as needed.

4. Ladle into hot, sterilized quart jars, leaving 1 inch of headspace. Remove any air bubbles by inserting a knife and moving around the jar in an up-and-down motion. Wipe the rims clean with a moistened paper towel, add the lids, and screw on the bands.

5. Pressure-can the filled jars for 90 minutes at 10 pounds of pressure, following the manufacturer's directions for your pressure canner. Then turn off the heat and allow the pressure to return to zero naturally.

Plum Sauce

Makes 1 (10-serving) jar

1 cup plum jam

2 teaspoons grated orange zest

squeeze of lemon juice

1 tablespoon distilled white vinegar

1 teaspoon onion powder

¼ teaspoon ground ginger

¼ teaspoon ground allspice

dash of garlic salt

dash of red pepper flakes, optional

1. In a large saucepan, stir all the ingredients together to combine thoroughly. Bring to a boil over medium-low heat. Remove from heat.

2. Ladle hot sauce into a sterilized jar, leaving ¼ inch headspace. Remove any air bubbles and add the lid. Wipe rim and screw on band. Process in a boiling water bath for 20 minutes. Store for up to 1 year.

Pressure Canning

Low-acid foods need to be preserved at a higher temperature than required for high-acid foods. A low-acid environment promotes the growth of bacteria (including botulism—see page 178), but the high temperatures achieved by pressure canning gets foods into the safety zone. The food must reach 240°F, which can only be achieved under pressure.

Vegetables (except for tomatoes, which are actually a fruit) are low in acid and must be processed in a pressure canner. Likewise, pressure canning must be used for meats, seafood, poultry, and soups.

VEGETABLE CANNING: HOT PACK METHOD

If processing in an altitude over 1,000 feet above sea level, process at 15 pounds of pressure.

Vegetable	Preparation	Hot pack method	Pressure canner processing: pints	Pressure canner processing: quarts
Asparagus	Remove tough ends; cut to fit jars. Tie in bundles and cook in open saucepan for 2 minutes.	Place in sterilized jars and cover with hot water.	30 minutes at 10 pounds of pressure	40 minutes at 10 pounds of pressure
Beans, snap	Cut in small pieces. Add boiling water to barely cover. Boil for 5 minutes, uncovered.	Pack in hot, sterilized jars. Add 1 teaspoon salt to each quart jar. Cover with hot cooking liquid.	20 minutes at 10 pounds of pressure	25 minutes at 10 pounds of pressure

VEGETABLE CANNING: HOT PACK METHOD

If processing in an altitude over 1,000 feet above sea level, process at 15 pounds of pressure.

Vegetable	Preparation	Hot pack method	Pressure canner processing: pints	Pressure canner processing: quarts
Beets	Use young beets. Remove tops and skins, leaving bottom roots. Boil for 20 to 25 minutes in water.	Pack hot in sterilized jars. Add 1 teaspoon salt to each quart. Cover with boiling water.	30 minutes at 10 pounds of pressure	35 minutes at 10 pounds of pressure
Carrots	Using only young carrots, cut off tops and peel.	Pack whole or sliced in hot, sterilized jars. Add 1 teaspoon salt to each quart jar. Cover with boiling water.	25 minutes at 10 pounds of pressure	30 minutes at 10 pounds of pressure
Corn	Use tender, young corn. Remove husk and silk; cut kernels from cob.	Fill jars with corn kernels to 1 inch from the top. Fill jars to 1 inch from top with boiling water.	55 minutes at 10 pounds of pressure	85 minutes at 10 pounds of pressure
Lima beans	Use young, tender beans. Shell.	In a pot, add enough water to cover and bring to a boil. Pack in sterilized jars and cover with hot liquid.	40 minutes at 10 pounds of pressure	50 minutes at 10 pounds of pressure
Okra	Remove stems, cover with water, and bring to a boil.	Pack in hot sterilized jars. Cover with hot cooking water.	25 minutes at 10 pounds of pressure	40 minutes at 10 pounds of pressure
Peas	Use only young, tender peas. Shell.	Place in a saucepan with boiling water and heat. Pack in sterilized jars and add 1 teaspoon salt to each quart jar. Process immediately.	40 minutes at 10 pounds of pressure	40 minutes at 10 pounds of pressure

THE PREPPER'S ULTIMATE FOOD STORAGE GUIDE

VEGETABLE CANNING: HOT PACK METHOD

If processing in an altitude over 1,000 feet above sea level, process at 15 pounds of pressure.

Vegetable	Preparation	Hot pack method	Pressure canner processing: pints	Pressure canner processing: quarts
Peppers	Remove skins and seeds and cut into desired size.	Pack in hot jars, layering the peppers, with 1 teaspoon salt per pint. Water doesn't need to be added.	30 minutes at 10 pounds of pressure	40 minutes at 10 pounds of pressure
Potatoes (white)	Peel potatoes and cut into 1" to 2" chunks.	Pack hot and cover with boiling water.	35 minutes at 10 pounds of pressure	40 minutes at 10 pounds of pressure
Potatoes (sweet)	Boil 20 to 30 minutes until tender in center. Drain water and slip skins off and leave whole or cut into quarters or cubes.	Pack dry to top of can or to within 1" of jar top. Add ½ teaspoon salt to pints, and 1 teaspoon to quarts. Cover with fresh boiling water or hot sugar syrup (medium), leaving ¼" headspace.	65 minutes at 10 pounds of pressure	90 minutes at 10 pounds of pressure
Pumpkin, winter squash	Remove skin and seeds and cut into cubes.	Steam until tender. Pack hot to 1" from jar top in jar. Add 1 teaspoon salt per quart, or spices and brown sugar.	55 minutes at 10 pounds of pressure	90 minutes at 10 pounds of pressure

Chart inspired by *The Settlement Cook Book*, published in 1903

Step-by-Step Process

For pressure canning, you'll need this basic equipment:

- Jars
- Flats (also called snap lids)
- Rings
- Pressure canner with valves, seals, and gauges
- Rack (or use a folded towel in the bottom of the pot)
- Jar lifter
- Jar funnel

Just as for water bath canning, you can get lots of gadgets if you want to, but these are the essentials.

A number of the pressure canning steps are identical to those for water bath canning. The differences are related to the equipment. Once you've learned to use your pressure canner correctly, you'll find it every bit as easy as water bath canning.

1. Sanitize your jars, lids, and rings. You can wash them in a dishwasher, which will get hot enough to sterilize everything. Otherwise, you need to submerge them in boiling water for at least 10 minutes, lifting them carefully in and out with the jar lifter. Leave the sterilized items in the dishwasher or hot water until you're ready to use them.

2. Prepare your canner. Place your rack or folded towel in the bottom of the canner and add about 3 inches of water. In pressure canning it's not necessary for the water to cover the lids. (Always check the instructions that came with your canner and follow those.) At this point, you can turn the burner on low to begin warming the water, but don't bring it to a boil yet.

3. Fill your jars. Line up your jars on the counter near the stove. If the surface isn't heatproof, set them on a towel, because they'll be very hot when filled. Using the funnel, ladle in the prepared food, leaving the headspace recommended in your recipe.

4. Put on the lids. With a clean, dry dish towel, carefully wipe the rims of the filled jars, making sure to remove any food residue. Place a flat on each jar, then twist on a ring—you don't have to really torque it.

5. Place the jars in the canner. Place the closed jars on the rack or towel inside the canner. Be careful not to let them touch each other—not only could they break if they bump together in the boiling water, but in pressure canning the steam must be able to circulate all around the jars.

6. Build steam in the canner. Lightly apply cooking oil or Vaseline around the rim of the pressure canner lid so that it won't stick when you open it. Also check the vent pipe before each use to be sure it's clear. Place the lid firmly on the canner, latch it, and turn up the heat to bring the water to a boil. At this point, steam should be coming out of the vent pipe. Reduce the heat until a moderate amount of steam comes steadily out for 10 minutes. This is to release the air and build up the steam inside the canner.

7. Pressurize the canner. After exhausting the steam for 10 minutes, either close the petcock or place the weighted regulator on the vent pipe, depending on your canner. Turn up the heat and wait until the gauge has reached the desired pressure. (The required pressure will differ, depending on the altitude and the recipe.) This usually takes 3 to 5 minutes. (Note: if you lose pressure during processing, you must restart the processing time.) Adjust the heat to maintain the pressure—this takes practice. Monitor your canner throughout the entire processing time to be sure the pressure is maintained.

8. Release the pressure. When your processing time is over, it's time to release the pressure. It couldn't be easier. Turn off the burner. Take the canner off the burner and set it on a heatproof surface. Walk away. Allow the canner to return to room temperature and release pressure naturally.

   The pressure is completely reduced when the air vent/cover lock and overpressure plug have dropped and no steam escapes when the pressure regulator is tilted. This can take 45 minutes to an hour and cannot be rushed!

9. Open the vent. When the pressure is completely gone, open the petcock or remove the weighted regulator. Leave the lid on for another 2 to 5 minutes.

10. Remove the jars from the canner. Very carefully remove the canner lid, facing it away from you so that you aren't burned by the steam rushing out. Using your jar lifter, carefully remove the jars from the canner, one by one. Tip each jar to the side to allow the hot water to drip off the top, then place on your heatproof or towel-lined surface.

11. Allow 12 to 24 hours for the jars to cool and seal. Let the jars stand in a draft-free place where they won't be moved or bumped, usually for overnight. You'll hear a musical "pop" as a jar seals in the cool air—that's the lid being sucked down and forming a seal. When you are ready to store the jars, you can remove the rings and test the seals by pushing down with your finger. If a lid pops back and forth, it's not sealed; refrigerate to use right away. Store your sealed jars in a cool, dark place.

Canning Juices

If you have a surplus of fruit in your home, canning juice is a great way to store it. Having canned juices in your emergency food pantry provides a low-cost alternative to store-bought juices, and they can be used for food preparation or canning as well.

An average of 15 pounds of whole fruit is needed per canner load of 7 quart-size jars. There are two ways to turn your fruit into juice:

- **Juicer method:** If you have a juicer, you can be more efficient with your time. Simply follow the instructions for your juicer. Make sure that you read the section on pasteurizing juice in order to prolong the shelf life of your canned juice.

- **Stovetop method:** This may take more time, but with this method you'll be able to use the fruit for other recipes after the juice is extracted, thus making better use of your fruit. For example, for apple juice you can cook the apples on the stove, can the juice, and then use the apples to make applesauce. It's two canning projects in one!

Pasteurizing Juice

If you're canning juice, you may want to consider pasteurizing it. The Federal Drug Administration recommends that all juice be pasteurized. The pasteurization process heats juice in a high temperature environment for a short time to destroy bacteria, molds, and unwanted microorganisms that could be lurking in it. The drawback is that it kills off the good stuff, too. Most of the nutrients and minerals present in fresh juice are destroyed in the process. So why would you want to can nutrient-depleted juices? Well, having it on hand can provide you with more beverage options as well as ingredients for cooking.

HOW TO PASTEURIZE JUICE:

1. Fill a sink with cold water.

2. Sterilize all utensils that will touch the juice. Jars, lids, funnel, and ladles should be placed in boiling water for 10 minutes.

3. Use a sterilized colander lined with a coffee filter to strain the juice; remove any fruit pieces.

4. Heat the juice in the top of a double boiler, maintaining a constant temperature of 175°F for 20 minutes.

5. Ladle the juice into the jars, leaving ½ inch headspace; secure the lids.

6. Place the jars in a sink of cold water and use a cooking thermometer to check that the water bath is at 40°F. Let the jars sit in the cold water bath for 15 minutes, continuing to monitor the temperature.

7. Remove the jars and store for up to 2 weeks in the refrigerator.

8. To can juice for longer-term storage, add the hot liquid to sterilized jars; add lids and wipe the rims. Screw bands on and process in a boiling water bath for 5 to 10 minutes.

Apple Juice

If you have an electric juicer, you can use it to extract concentrated juice, then add water to your liking. Home-canned apple juice has a shelf life of 18 months to 2 years. *Serves 6*

> 8 to 10 sweet apples (such as Red Delicious, Gala, Fuji, or Rome, or use a combination)
>
> 10 cups water
>
> ½ to 1 cup granulated sugar (optional)

1. Core and slice the apples, but leave on the peels. Place in a large pot and pour in the water.

2. Cover the pot and bring the water to a boil over medium-high heat. Reduce to an active simmer and cook for 30 minutes, or until the apples are soft.

3. Discard any apple solids by straining the apple solids and separating them from the juice. If there are still solids present, use a coffee filter and strain again.

4. Sweeten the juice to taste.

5. Use the pasteurization process (page 195) to destroy any microorganisms.

6. Ladle the hot pasteurized juice into sterilized jars, leaving ¼ inch of headspace. Wipe the rims clean with a moistened paper towel, add the lids, and screw on the rings. In a hot water bath, process pint and quart jars for 5 minutes and half-gallon jars for 10 minutes.

Raspberry or Blackberry Juice

For drinking, dilute with 3 or 4 parts water to 1 part juice. *Serves 6*

> 3 to 4 pounds raspberries or blackberries
>
> water
>
> granulated sugar to taste

1. Place the berries in a large pot and add water to cover them. Bring to a boil over high heat, then remove from the burner and mash the berries to release the juices. Return the pot to the stove and bring the mixture back to a boil. Cook for 5 to 10 more minutes.

2. Remove from the heat and let cool for 5 to 10 minutes. Strain the cooled berry mixture through a colander lined with cheesecloth to remove any pulp or seeds. Mash any solid particles to extract any remaining juice. Sweeten to taste with sugar.

3. Use the pasteurization process (page 195) to destroy any microorganisms.

4. Ladle the hot pasteurized juice into sterilized jars, leaving ¼ inch of headspace. Wipe the rims clean with a moistened paper towel, add the lids, and screw on the rings.

5. Process in a boiling water bath for 5 to 10 minutes.

Grape Juice

Makes 10 ounces

> 10 pounds sweet grapes
>
> 3 cups water
>
> 1 cup sugar (optional)

1. Place the grapes in a large pot and add enough water to cover them (about 3 cups). Bring to a boil over high heat, stirring often. When mixture comes to a boil, remove from heat.

2. Pour the grape mixture into a cheesecloth-lined colander or fine mesh sieve and set over a large bowl. Mash the grapes to extract the juices. Discard any skins, seeds, or pulp. Refrigerate for 24 to 48 hours.

3. Strain the chilled juice through a coffee filter to remove any remaining solid particles. Add sugar, if desired.

4. To can juice, heat the mixture in a large pot to boiling and ladle it into sterilized jars, leaving ¼ inch headspace. Wipe the rims clean with a moistened paper towel, add the lids, and screw on the bands.

5. Process in a boiling water bath for 15 minutes for pint- or quart-size jars. For half-gallon jars, process 20 minutes.

Vegetable Stock

Serves 5

> 2 tablespoons olive oil
>
> 2 carrots, peeled and chopped
>
> 2 parsnips, peeled and chopped
>
> 2 onions, whole
>
> 2 celery stalks, chopped
>
> 1 (28-ounce) can diced tomatoes
>
> 3 garlic cloves, smashed
>
> 1 teaspoon black peppercorns
>
> 5 cups water

1. Heat the olive oil in a large (12 to 16-quart) stockpot over medium heat. Add the carrots, parsnips, onions, and celery. Cover the pot and cook, stirring occasionally, until the vegetables are soft.

2. Add the remaining ingredients and bring to a gentle simmer over medium-low heat. Cook gently for about 1 hour, or until the flavors are well incorporated.

3. Strain the stock through a cheesecloth-lined colander or fine-mesh strainer and discard the vegetable solids and peppercorns.

4. Ladle into hot, sterilized jars, leaving 1 inch of headspace. Wipe the rims clean with a moistened paper towel, add the lids, and screw on the bands.

5. Process in a pressure canner. Over medium-high heat, bring the pressure canner to a boil. Vent the steam for 10 minutes, then close the vent. When the canner reaches 10 pounds of pressure, process pint jars for 30 minutes and quart jars for 35 minutes. Allow pressure to return to zero naturally before removing jars.

Salsa

Serves 5

2 (28-ounce) cans diced tomatoes	juice of 2 lemons
7 green onions, chopped, green tops included	9 garlic cloves, minced
3 tomatoes, peeled and diced	3 tablespoons ground cumin
6 tomatillos, peeled and diced	2 tablespoons chili powder
1 bunch cilantro, finely chopped	½ cup distilled white vinegar
2 jalapeño chiles, finely diced	¼ to ½ teaspoon cayenne pepper

1. Mix all the ingredients together in a large bowl.

2. Ladle the salsa into sterilized jars. Wipe the rims clean with a moistened paper towel, add the lids, and screw on the bands.

3. Process in a boiling water bath for 45 minutes.

Packing Meat

Preserving meat is a great way to have a shelf-stable protein source available during an extended emergency. Meat can be canned in its own juices, in soups, or as canned meals. The U.S. Department of Agriculture strongly suggests that you use a pressure canner for canning meat. Beef, lamb, pork, veal, venison, poultry, and bear can all be canned.

Choose quality chilled meat and remove any large bones and as much fat as possible. Soak strong-flavored game meats for 1 hour in brine water (1 tablespoon salt per 1 quart water), then rinse.

There are two methods for packing meat in jars (always check gauge pressure for your altitude):

HOT PACK—Precook meat to the rare stage by roasting, stewing, or browning it in a small amount of fat. Add 1 teaspoon of salt per quart to the jar, if you wish. Fill hot jars with meat pieces and add boiling broth, meat drippings, water, or tomato juice (especially for wild game), leaving 1 inch of headspace. Remove air bubbles and adjust the headspace if needed. Wipe the jar rims with a dampened paper towel, add the lids and rings, and process.

RAW PACK—Add 1 teaspoon of salt to each quart jar, if desired. Fill hot jars with raw meat pieces, leaving 1 inch of headspace. Do not add liquid. Wipe the jar rims with a dampened paper towel, add the lids and rings, and process. Always check gauge pressure for your altitude.

Canned Meat

Chopped or ground meat can be substituted for boneless meat pieces. Simply prepare it as you would for any other canned meat recipe. *Serves 5*

> 1 pound boneless meat (beef, poultry, lamb, venison, ham, etc.)
>
> canning salt

1. Sterilize your jars, lids, and rings.

2. Remove any fat from the meat. Cut the meat into ½ to 1-inch pieces.

3. Fill the jars with the meat, leaving 1 inch of headspace.

4. Add ½ teaspoon canning salt to each pint or 1 teaspoon to each quart. Wipe the rims clean with a moistened paper towel, add the lids, and screw on the bands.

5. Following the manufacturer's instructions, pressure-can the filled jars for 90 minutes at 10 pounds of pressure. Then turn off the heat and allow the pressure to drop to zero naturally.

For canned beef tips: mix 1 or 2 tablespoons of cornstarch with some of the broth to make gravy. Serve beef tips and gravy on a bed of rice.

Soup: To make a delicious soup, add water, vegetables (whatever you have on hand), a can of tomatoes, and some seasonings to the canned meat.

Meat Stock

Serves 5

> 3 to 5 pounds bone-in meat, any kind
>
> 12 cups water
>
> 1 onion, whole
>
> 5 garlic cloves (optional)
>
> 2 celery stalks, whole
>
> salt, as needed

> 5 black peppercorns, whole
>
> 2 bay leaves
>
> 2 carrots, peeled, whole
>
> 2 parsnips, peeled, whole (optional, to add an earthy flavor)

1. In a large (12 to 16-quart) stockpot over medium-high heat, brown the meat on all sides. Add the water and remaining ingredients. Bring to a boil and then reduce the heat to low and allow to slowly simmer for 2 to 3 hours.

2. Remove from the heat, allow to cool, and refrigerate overnight.

3. Remove the fat that has solidified at the top. Remove the vegetables and strain the stock through a cheesecloth-lined colander.

4. Remove the meat from the stock. Heat the stock over medium-high heat until it just begins to boil.

5. Fill sterilized jars with the stock, leaving 1 inch of headspace. Remove any air bubbles by inserting a knife and moving it around the jar in an up-and-down motion. Wipe the rims clean with a moistened paper towel, add the lids, and screw on the bands.

6. Following the manufacturer's directions, pressure-can the filled jars for 90 minutes at 10 pounds of pressure. After 90 minutes, turn off heat and allow the pressure to drop to zero naturally.

Serving ideas: Use this stock for beef tips and broth, vegetable beef soup, vegetable beef stew, roast beef sandwiches, or barbecue beef.

Pea Soup with Bacon

Serves 5 to 6

1 (14-ounce) package dry split peas	2 carrots, peeled and diced
1 onion, diced	7 cups chicken broth
2 bacon slices, cooked and crumbled	salt and pepper
1 potato, peeled and diced	

1. In a large stockpot over medium heat, combine the peas, onion, bacon, potato, carrots, and broth. Add salt and pepper to taste. Cover, bring to boil, and simmer for 1½ hours, stirring occasionally.

2. Fill sterilized jars with the soup, leaving 1 inch of headspace. Remove any air bubbles by inserting a knife and moving it around the jar in an up-and-down motion. Wipe the rims clean with a moistened paper towel, add the lids, and screw on the bands.

3. Following the manufacturer's instructions, pressure-can the jars at 10 pounds of pressure. Process pint-size jars for 70 minutes and quart jars for 90 minutes. Then turn off the heat and allow the pressure to return to zero.

Spaghetti Meat Sauce

A vegetarian version of this sauce can be made by omitting the ground beef. Pressure-can the filled jars at 11 pounds of pressure for 20 minutes for pint-size jars and 25 minutes for quarts. Then turn off the heat and allow the pressure to drop to zero naturally. *Serves 4 to 5*

2 onions, chopped	2 carrots, peeled and finely shredded
4 tablespoons olive oil	3 celery stalks, chopped
8 to 10 garlic cloves, chopped	2 bay leaves
1 to 2 pounds ground beef	1 tablespoon Italian seasoning
1 cup red wine	1 tablespoon dried basil
4 (28-ounce) cans diced tomatoes	salt and pepper

1. In a large pot over medium heat, sauté the onions in the olive oil for 2 to 3 minutes. Add the garlic and sauté another 3 minutes.

2. Add the ground beef and cook thoroughly, breaking up the meat with a spoon. Pour in the wine. Add the rest of the ingredients and allow to simmer for 30 minutes, uncovered.

3. Fill sterilized jars with the hot sauce, leaving 1 inch of headspace. Remove any air bubbles by inserting a knife and moving it around the jar in an up-and-down motion. Wipe the rims clean with a moistened paper towel, add the lids, and screw on the bands.

4. Following the manufacturer's instructions, pressure-can the filled pint-size jars for 60 minutes at 10 pounds of pressure and 70 minutes for quart-size jars. After the processing time has passed, turn off the heat and allow the pressure to drop to zero naturally.

Canned Hot Dogs

Makes 2 (quart-size) jars

  12 uncooked hot dogs left whole

Place the hot dogs in sterilized jars without adding water; they will produce their own liquid. Wipe the rims clean with a moistened paper towel, add the lids, and screw on the bands. Pressure-can at 10 pounds of pressure for 90 minutes. Turn off the heat and allow the pressure to drop to zero naturally.

Canned Meat Loaf

For this recipe, use sterilized wide-mouth jars. This recipe can also be used for canning meatballs. *Makes 5 (quart-size) jars*

  5 pounds ground beef

  1 to 2 cups dry breadcrumbs or crumbled crackers

  2 teaspoons garlic salt

  1 teaspoon paprika

  ½ teaspoon pepper

  ¼ cup dehydrated onion

  ¼ cup dehydrated bell pepper

  1½ teaspoons hamburger seasoning

  ¾ cup ketchup (purchased or made from recipe on page 188)

1. In a large bowl, thoroughly mix all the ingredients together. Pack the mixture into wide-mouth jars, leaving 1½ inches of headspace.

2. With your fist, push the meat down in the middle to make an indentation. This will reduce the risk of grease spilling out of the lids.

3. Process at 10 pounds of pressure for 90 minutes. Turn off the heat and allow the pressure to drop to zero naturally.

Beef Chili

Serves 6 to 8

1 to 2 cups dried pinto beans, soaked in water overnight

2 pounds ground meat or 4 cups dehydrated beef crumbles

1 (14.5-ounce) can diced or stewed tomatoes

1 cup dried bell peppers, diced

½ cup dehydrated yellow onion or 1 cup finely minced fresh onion or 1 tablespoon onion powder

1 to 2 teaspoons dried garlic or 3 garlic cloves, minced

3 tablespoons chili powder

1 tablespoon garlic powder

1 tablespoon dried jalapeño or 1 fresh jalapeño, chopped

¼ teaspoon cayenne pepper

salt and pepper

1. Rinse the soaked beans, then cover with water and simmer for 1 hour over medium-high heat, stirring often to prevent scorching.

2. Add the meat to the beans. (If you're using fresh ground beef, cook it first and then add to beans.) Stir in the other ingredients, mixing well. Cover and cook over medium heat for about 2 more hours. Remove the lid and cook on low for another 30 minutes to allow the chili to thicken slightly.

3. Fill sterilized jars with the hot chili, leaving 1 inch of headspace. Remove any air bubbles by inserting a knife and moving it around the jar in an up-and-down motion. Wipe the rims clean with a moistened paper towel, add the lids, and screw on the bands.

4. Following the manufacturer directions, pressure-can the filled jars for 90 minutes at 10 pounds of pressure. After 90 minutes, turn off the heat and allow the pressure to drop to zero.

Sugar-Baked Ham

These directions are "per jar." This is a great way to put away those endless leftovers after Christmas or Easter dinner! *Makes 1 (8-ounce) jar*

1 teaspoon prepared grainy mustard

3 tablespoons brown sugar

1 teaspoon apple cider vinegar

4 (½-inch-thick) slices of ham

4 whole cloves

1. Make a paste of the mustard, brown sugar, and vinegar. Spread the mixture on one side of each ham slice.

2. Tightly roll up each slice with the mustard mixture inside and insert into the sterilized jar. Top each ham roll with a clove. Do not add any liquid.

3. Wipe the rim clean with a moistened paper towel, add the lid, and screw on the band.

4. Process the ham in a pressure cooker for 40 minutes at 10 pounds of pressure. After 40 minutes, turn off and allow the pressure to drop to zero.

Dehydrating Food

For centuries, dehydrating food has been used as a means of survival. Many consider this to be the safest and most affordable preservation method, and the best way to preserve the flavors of foods.

The dehydration process removes moisture from food so that bacteria, yeast, and mold can't grow. Dehydration only minimally affects nutritional content and prolongs the shelf life of your foods! In fact, due to the low heat setting during the drying cycle and the gentle air flow, 3 to 5 percent of the nutritional content of food is lost. However, you can retain much of the thiamin, riboflavin, niacin, and minerals found in dried vegetables if you use the soaking water you use to reconstitute them to then cook them.

Dehydrating vegetables and fruits for long-term storage is a great way to get needed nutrition into diets with minimal investment. You can also use a dehydrator to dry herbs, make jerky, make fruit or vegetable leather, make spices, dry noodles, and even make dough ornaments!

There are several different types of home dehydrators:

Stackable food dehydrators consist of removable trays that stack, one on top of the other. Some units house the mechanics in the bottom, others are on top of the stack.

Box-type food dehydration units are rigid and have removable shelves. The mechanical parts are either in the bottom or back of the box.

Fan dehydrators use a built-in fan to blow warm air across the food. This speeds up the drying process.

Convection food dehydrators have a heater at the bottom of the unit, so the heat rises through the food and dries it.

And let's not forget the ultimate dehydrator that harnesses the sun's power. Solar drying can be as simple as spreading a layer of fruit or vegetables in the sun, but it can also be done in a special container that catches and captures the sun's heat. The USDA recommends using high-acid fruits and vegetables, such as apricots, tomatoes, and grapes (to make raisins) for this method of dehydration. (Perishable, low-acid foods such as meat and poultry may not be dried by this method.)

Use fresh produce at the peak of ripeness for dehydrating. When overly ripe fruits and vegetables are dehydrated, the texture typically isn't as crisp.

Some vegetables need to be blanched before you dehydrate them. Use the following chart as a guideline:

Vegetable	Blanching method	Blanching time	Dehydrating time
Asparagus, cut	Steam or water	4 to 5 minutes	8 to 10 hours
Beans, green (cut)	Steam or water	2 minutes	12 hours
Broccoli, small florets	Steam or water	3 to 3½ minutes	10 hours
Brussels sprouts, halved	Steam or water	4 to 6 minutes	12+ hours
Cabbage	Steam or water	2 minutes	8 to 10 hours
Carrots and parsnips, sliced	Steam or water	4 minutes	12+ hours
Cauliflower, small florets	Steam or water	4 minutes	12+ hours
Celery, sliced	Steam or water	2 minutes	12+ hours
Corn, on cob (cut kernels after blanching)	Steam or water	2 minutes	12+ hours
Eggplant, sliced	Steam or water	3 minutes	12+ hours
Peas, shelled	Steam or water	3 minutes	12+ hours
Potatoes	Steam or water	7 minutes	12+ hours
Spinach and collard greens, trimmed	Steam or water	2 minutes	12+ hours
Summer squash, sliced	Steam or water	2 minutes	12+ hours
Winter squash, cut in chunks	Steam or water	2 minutes	12+ hours

Storing Dry Foods

Dehydrated food doesn't take up a lot of space, so it's easy to store it in an organized fashion. No need to be concerned with refrigerating it or freezing it; as long as the dried food is kept in a cool, dark area with low moisture, it will last for up to 12 months.

In most cases, dehydrated food should be consumed within a year. Any time after this and the nutrients will begin to break down. Follow these guidelines:

- Dehydrated fruits and vegetables will last for up to a year if properly stored.
- Dried meats should be consumed within two months. If they haven't been eaten after one month, store them in the refrigerator to prolong their freshness.
- Dried herbs can last for years.
- Dried noodles are best if eaten within a year.

Rehydrating Food

Rehydrating dried foods is relatively straightforward: introduce them to liquid and wait. Most foods can be rehydrated simply by soaking them in water at room temperature. However, there are some foods that require warm water or another liquid to be used. And for that matter, you can get creative about the type of liquid you use. For example, rehydrating dried food in a vegetable stock will add a richer flavor. Or, using fruit juices to rehydrate dried fruit will create a sweeter flavor. Covering the soaking foods with a lid or cover will help expedite the rehydration process.

To rehydrate dried food requiring hot liquid: pour boiling water or liquid over the dried food and cover it with a lid. Let it sit for 20 to 30 minutes to absorb the moisture. If you're adding salt, do so after the rehydration process is completed.

Once the food is rehydrated, it will not look the same or have the exact texture it had before being dried. Use the following charts to estimate the amounts of dried food and amount of time needed to rehydrate the goods.

REHYDRATING DRIED FRUIT
Use room temperature water

Product	Water (added to 1 cup dried food)	Soaking time (minimum)
Apples, sliced	1½ cups	60 minutes
Pears, sliced	1¾ cups	75 minutes
Peaches, sliced	2 cups	75 minutes

Source: University of Georgia

REHYDRATING DRIED VEGETABLES
Use boiling water

Product	Water (added to 1 cup dried food)	Soaking time (minimum)
Asparagus	2¼ cups	90 minutes
Beans, lima	2½ cups	90 minutes
Beans, green and snap	2½ cups	60 minutes
Beets	2¾ cups	90 minutes
Cabbage	3 cups	60 minutes
Carrots	2¼ cups	60 minutes
Corn	2¼ cups	30 minutes
Okra	3 cups	30 minutes
Onions	2 cups	30 minutes
Peas	2½ cups	30 minutes
Pumpkin	3 cups	60 minutes
Squash	1¾ cups	60 minutes
Spinach	1 cup	30 minutes
Sweet potatoes	1½ cups	30 minutes
Turnip greens and other greens	1 cup	45 minutes

Source: University of Georgia

THE PREPPER'S ULTIMATE FOOD STORAGE GUIDE

REHYDRATING DRIED GRAINS AND MEATS
Use boiling water

Product	Water (added to 1 cup dried food)	Soaking time (minimum)
Beans	1 cup	60 to 120 minutes
Beef crumbles (ground)	1 cup	30 minutes
Pasta	1 cup	60 minutes
Poultry	1 cup	30 minutes
Rice—white, brown, or wild	1 cup	60 minutes
Textured vegetable protein (TVP)	1 cup	30 minutes

Source: University of Georgia

Fruit Leather

If you have a lot of fruit on hand that isn't being eaten, you can quickly turn it into fruit roll-ups. Some of my family's favorite fruits are apples, pears, strawberries, raspberries, blueberries, apricots, peaches, and plums. *Makes 1 baking sheet full of fruit leather*

2 to 3 pounds fresh fruit

½ cup water

sugar or other sweetener, as needed

1 teaspoon lemon juice (optional)

dash of cinnamon, nutmeg, or other spices (optional)

vegetable or olive oil, for brushing pan

OVEN METHOD

1. For stone fruits, remove the pits and chop the fruit. For apples or pears, peel, core, and chop. For grapes, remove the stems and seeds. Taste to see how sweet the fruit is. If it's very sweet, you won't need to add any sugar.

2. Place the fruit in a large saucepan. Add ½ cup water for every 4 cups chopped fruit. Bring to a simmer, cover, and cook over low heat for 10 to 15 minutes, or until the fruit is soft.

3. Use a blender or food mill to puree the fruit to a very smooth consistency.

4. Return the fruit to the saucepan. Add sugar in small amounts until the fruit is as sweet as you want it. Continue to simmer and stir until the sugar is completely dissolved and the puree has thickened, 5 to 10 minutes (or more).

5. To brighten the flavor and prevent food discoloration during the drying process, stir in the lemon juice, if using. If you wish, add cinnamon, nutmeg, or other spices.

6. Line a rimmed baking sheet with sturdy plastic wrap (the microwave-safe kind). Brush on a small amount of vegetable or olive oil to keep the fruit from sticking. Pour in the puree to a thickness of ⅛ to ¼ inch.

7. Place the baking sheet in the oven; don't let the plastic wrap touch the oven sides or racks, and make sure it hasn't folded back onto the puree. (If that happens, the puree won't dry out.) Heat the oven to the lowest setting (usually around 170°F). Use the convection setting if you have one—it will speed up the process. Let dry for as long as it takes to form fruit leather that's smooth and no longer sticky. We usually keep ours in the oven overnight, 8 to 12 hours.

8. Roll up in the plastic wrap and cut into strips, or use cookie cutters to cut the fruit leather into fun shapes. Store in an airtight container in a cool, dark place.

FOOD DEHYDRATOR METHOD

1. Follow steps 1 through 5 for the oven method (above).

2. Line food dehydrator trays with microwave-safe plastic wrap. Pour in the fruit puree to a thickness of ⅛ to ¼ inch.

3. Set the dehydrator to 135°F and let the fruit dehydrate for 8 to 12 hours. The fruit leather is ready when it is smooth and no longer sticky, and easy to peel.

4. Roll up the fruit leather and cut into strips in its plastic wrap, or use a cookie cutter to cut it into shapes. Store in a cool, dry place.

Dehydrated Meat

Dehydrating meat is a minimalistic way of extending the shelf life of your meats. Realistically, you don't need any additional seasonings or special cures to dehydrate meat. Simply place it on a tray and turn on the dehydrator. Taking the extra step of cooking ground meats before dehydrating them helps give them a "crumbled" look.

Although the USDA recommends that poultry be cooked until it has heated to an internal temperature of 165°F before it is dehydrated, many people dehydrate raw poultry just like they would dehydrate raw beef. If you feel more comfortable cooking the poultry before dehydrating it, follow this procedure:

Cut poultry into thin slices ¼ inch thick and place on dehydrator trays or, if you are using the oven method to dehydrate, place sliced poultry on a cookie sheet. Maintain a constant dehydrator temperature of 130°F to 140°F during drying or in the oven at the lowest setting. Meat is best if used within a month of dehydrating.

Preparing the Meat

Partially freeze meat to make slicing easier. The thickness of the meat strips will make a difference in the safety of the methods recommended in this book. Slice meat into ¼-inch strips. For tougher jerky, slice the meat with the grain; for tender jerky, slice across the grain. Trim off any excess fat to prevent the meat from going rancid. Marinating the jerky gives the meat added flavor.

Ground Meat

I recommend using only lean or extra-lean ground meat, either beef or poultry. Meat with high fat content produces beads of oil as it dehydrates, and these have to be blotted off throughout the drying process. Look for meat that has less than 15 percent fat content, preferably in the 7 to 10 percent range. *Makes 4 cups dried meat crumbles*

> 1 pound lean ground meat (beef, turkey, or chicken)
>
> ¾ cup dry breadcrumbs
>
> salt and pepper

1. In a bowl, combine the ground meat and breadcrumbs.

2. In a skillet over medium heat, cook the meat mixture thoroughly, breaking it up with a spoon; season with salt and pepper to taste. Drain off the excess grease and allow the meat to cool for a few minutes.

3. Transfer to dehydrating trays and set the dehydrator to 145°F. Dehydrate for 2 or more hours, until the meat is completely dried. Dried meat crumbles can be safely stored in an airtight container in a cool, dark, low-moisture environment for up to 1 month, or in an airtight container at room temperature for up to 1 month or in the refrigerator for up to 6 months to a year.

Ham

Use a lean cut, well cured ham that is trimmed of fat. Cut a fully-cooked smoked ham into ¼-inch cubes or very thin slices. Spread a single layer of the cubes or slices on each dehydrator tray. Dry at 145°F for about 4 hours, stirring occasionally. Reduce the temperature to 130°F and continue drying and occasionally stirring until the meat is hard and thoroughly dried, about 2 more hours. Store dried ham pieces in an airtight container in the refrigerator for up to 1 month. To rehydrate, combine 1 cup of dried ham and 1 cup of boiling water in a saucepan. Cover and cook on low heat for about 1 hour.

Basic Meat Jerky

Cut across the grain of the meat for crispy jerky, and with the grain for chewy jerky. *Makes 50 to 60 strips*

3 to 4 pounds uncooked meat (beef, pork, or poultry), trimmed of fat

5 ounces liquid smoke

5 ounces soy sauce

5 tablespoons Worcestershire sauce

1 tablespoon salt

1 tablespoon pepper

1 tablespoon garlic powder

½ tablespoon onion powder

1. Trim the fat and slice the meat into very thin strips.

2. Mix the remaining ingredients in a small bowl. Place a layer of strips in a large bowl or crock and sprinkle on part of the seasoning mixture. Continue to layer and season until all the meat has been used.

3. Weigh down the meat with a plate or other heavy object. Cover and let marinate, refrigerated, for at least 12 hours.

4. Drain the strips and carefully pat dry with paper towels. Arrange on a rack in a shallow baking dish and bake in a 250°F oven until dehydrated, about 4 hours. Once removed from oven, allow jerky to air-dry for 24 hours, or use a dehydrator on the highest setting until the meat is completely dried, up to 6 hours.

Teriyaki Jerky

Makes about 50 strips

2 pounds uncooked meat (beef, pork, or poultry) trimmed of fat and sliced in thin strips

½ cup Worcestershire sauce

⅔ cup soy sauce

1 tablespoon liquid smoke

2 tablespoons honey

1 tablespoon granulated sugar

2 teaspoons pepper

2 teaspoons onion powder

1 tablespoon ground ginger

1 teaspoon paprika

1. Place the meat in a large bowl or crock.

2. In another bowl, stir together the remaining ingredients. Pour the marinade over the meat, cover, and refrigerate for 24 hours.

3. Drain off and discard the marinade and carefully pat the meat dry with a paper towel. Place the meat strips on dehydrator trays. Dehydrate at 250°F until the meat is completely dried, up to 6 hours. Store in an airtight jar.

Black Pepper Jerky

Makes about 50 strips

2 pounds uncooked meat (beef, pork, or poultry), trimmed of fat and sliced into strips

1 cup Worcestershire sauce

¼ cup soy sauce

2 tablespoons salt

3 tablespoons finely ground black pepper

1 tablespoon garlic powder

1 tablespoon onion powder

1 teaspoon paprika

1. Place the meat in a large bowl or crock.

2. In another large bowl, stir together the remaining ingredients. Pour the marinade over the meat, cover, and refrigerate for 24 hours.

3. Drain off and discard the marinade and place the meat on dehydrator trays. Dehydrate at 250°F until the meat is completely dried, up to 6 hours. Store in an airtight jar.

Dehydrated Seafood

Dehydrating seafood doesn't create the most pleasant odor. To avoid smelling up the house, plug in your dehydrator outdoors. Do this during the day so that you won't attract unwanted nighttime animal visitors. *Makes 3 ounces*

1 pound medium or large shrimp

1 pound fish, deboned and filleted

1. To dehydrate fish or shellfish, remove any shells, devein shrimp, and remove any bones from fish.

2. Cut or break into small pieces.

3. In a large pot of boiling salted water, cook fish or shrimp 2 to 3 minutes until firm. Drain waste and pat meat dry with a paper towel.

4. Spread flat on a dehydrating tray. Dehydrate at 155°F for 4 to 6 hours, until crispy. Dried shrimp is best stored in an airtight container for up to 1 month at room temperature. Refrigerate to store longer.

Dried Soup Mixes

Premade dry soup mixes are a great emergency food to have stored away. All you need to do is add water, and you have an instant meal. Store the following soup mixes in airtight containers and plan to enjoy them within a year.

For the following recipes, 1 cup of dry mix yields 8 cups of soup. To serve, bring 8 cups of water to a boil in a 4-quart saucepan and add 1 cup of dry soup mix. Turn off the heat and cover the pan. Let it sit for 20 minutes, or until the soup mixture is tender.

The best way to dry vegetables for soup mixes is to whirl them in a blender until they're the size of small, minced flakes. Then spread on a dehydrating tray and dehydrate for 4 to 5 hours at 145°F, or until completely dry. Once dried, store in labeled wide-mouth pint-size jars.

VEGETABLE SOUP MIX

1 cup dried vegetable flakes (any combination: onions, peas, carrots, zucchini, squash, celery)

½ cup dried tomato puree

3 tablespoons onion flakes

½ cup pearl barley or lentils

1 teaspoon dried parsley

½ teaspoon garlic powder

½ teaspoon onion powder

3 tablespoons chicken or beef bouillon

salt and pepper

CREAMY COUNTRY SOUP MIX

2 cups nonfat dry milk

¼ cup chicken bouillon granules

3 tablespoons dried vegetable flakes (such as potatoes, corn, beans, carrots, zucchini, or squash)

2½ teaspoons onion powder

1 teaspoon dried chives

½ teaspoon dried thyme

¼ teaspoon garlic salt

2 teaspoons pepper

CREAMY POTATO SOUP MIX

2 cups instant potato flakes

2 tablespoons powdered butter

2 cups nonfat dry milk

2 tablespoons chicken bouillon granules

2 teaspoons dehydrated minced green onion

1 teaspoon dried parsley

½ teaspoon dried thyme

1¼ teaspoons seasoning salt

pepper, to taste

bacon bits or dried ham bits (optional)

CHICKEN AND RICE SOUP MIX

½ cup dried chicken pieces, stored separately from soup mix

1 cup dehydrated cooked white or brown rice (see page 214)

3 tablespoons chicken bouillon granules

2 tablespoons dried celery

2 tablespoons dried onion flakes

¼ cup dried carrots

2 teaspoons dried garlic flakes

½ teaspoon dried thyme

1 teaspoon white pepper

salt and black pepper, to taste

Rehydrate the chicken in water for 30 minutes before preparing soup. Then bring 8 cups of water (including the water from rehydrating the chicken) to a boil in a 4-quart saucepan over medium-high heat, and add 1 cup soup mix. Turn off the heat, cover, and let sit 20 minutes. Then turn the heat to low and simmer, covered, for 30 to 35 minutes, or until the rice is tender.

TURKEY NOODLE SOUP MIX

½ cup dried turkey bits

1 cup uncooked egg noodles

3 tablespoons chicken bouillon granules

1 tablespoon dried onion

1 tablespoon dried celery

½ tablespoon dried carrots

½ teaspoon dried thyme

⅛ teaspoon celery salt

½ teaspoon garlic powder

½ teaspoon pepper

1 bay leaf

For 8 servings, rehydrate the turkey in water for 30 minutes. Then bring a total of 8 cups of water (include the water for rehydrating the turkey) to a boil in a 4-quart saucepan over medium-high heat and add 1 cup of the soup mix. Turn the heat to low and simmer, covered, for 30 to 35 minutes, or until noodles and turkey are tender.

HEARTY BEAN SOUP MIX

2 cups dehydrated split peas

2 cups dehydrated small lima beans

2 cups dehydrated pinto beans

2 cups dehydrated Great Northern beans

1 cup dehydrated ham bits

1 cup dehydrated minced onions

1 cup dehydrated carrots

1 cup dehydrated celery

¼ cup dehydrated tomato puree

1 ½ teaspoons ground cumin

1 teaspoon dried marjoram

1 ½ teaspoons garlic powder

2 tablespoons chicken bouillon granules

1 teaspoon onion salt

¼ teaspoon pepper

To rehydrate beans, soak in cool water for 45 to 60 minutes, or cook in simmering water for 10 to 15 minutes. Rehydrate the ham in water for 30 minutes. Bring 8 cups water (include the water for rehydrating the ham) to a boil in a 4-quart saucepan over medium-high heat, add rehydrated beans and 1 cup soup mix, and cook on medium-high heat for 30 minutes. Turn off the heat, cover, and let sit 20 minutes.

CREAMY CHEESE SOUP

¼ cup dehydrated sharp cheddar cheese or 1 packet of powdered cheese mix from a box of macaroni and cheese

1 tablespoon chicken bouillon granules

½ teaspoon pepper

¼ cup dehydrated carrots

1 tablespoon onion powder

3 tablespoons celery salt

3 tablespoons dried parsley

3 cups dry nonfat milk or powdered coffee creamer

2 to 3 tablespoons instant mashed potatoes

Instant White Rice

Serves 4

> 1 cup uncooked white rice
>
> salt and pepper

Cook the rice according to the package directions, or follow the directions on page 259. Allow to cool and then spread evenly on a dehydrator tray. Dehydrate at 135°F for 12 hours. Halfway through the drying process, break up any rice that is stuck together. Store in an airtight container in a cool, dark place for up to 6 to 12 months.

Instant Brown Rice

Serves 4

> 2 cups uncooked brown rice
>
> salt and pepper

Cook the rice according to the package directions, or follow the directions on page 259. Allow to cool. To dehydrate, cover your dehydrator trays with parchment paper or the mesh liners that came with your unit. Do not use waxed paper in your dehydrator as it will melt. Spread the rice in a single layer and dehydrate at 125°F for 5 hours or until completely dry. Halfway through the drying process, break up any rice that is stuck together. Allow to cool to room temperature before storing in an airtight container.

Dehydrated Beans

Dehydrating beans will expedite cooking times during extended emergencies and cut down on fuel usage.

> 1 pound small beans (such as pinto beans, navy beans, or lentils), uncooked

1. Rinse the beans in a colander under cool water to remove any grit.

2. Bring a large pot of water to a boil, add the beans, and cook until soft, 2 to 3 hours. Drain the beans in a colander to remove any excess water.

3. Lay the beans on the dehydrator tray in a single layer. Pat with towels to remove excess moisture. Arrange the beans so that air can circulate around them.

4. Set the temperature on the dehydrator to 140°F.

5. Place the tray in the dehydrator. Dry for 5 to 8 hours, turning the beans and rotating the trays every 2 to 3 hours to ensure even drying. Check the dryness periodically. When you touch the beans they should be dry and brittle and have no pockets of moisture present. Remove the tray from the dehydrator. Allow the beans to cool completely.

6. Place the beans in an airtight container such as a jar or plastic freezer bag. Store the beans in a cool, dark place.

7. To rehydrate, add 1 cup of boiling water to ¾ cup dehydrated beans and allow to sit for 15 to 20 minutes.

Dried Breadcrumbs

Makes 1 cup

    5 thin slices bread

Lay thinly sliced bread slices on a dehydrator tray and heat at 145°F for 2 to 3 hours, or until the bread easily crumbles. Crush into crumbs and store in an airtight plastic bag or jar away from moisture.

Dehydrated Noodles

Serves 8

    1 (16-ounce) bag dry egg noodles, cooked

Cook noodles according to directions, but undercook them by 2 to 3 minutes. Drain and allow to cool. Spread evenly on a dehydrator tray, ensuring that pasta is not touching and dehydrate and dry at 130°F for 2 to 4 hours or until the noodles are firm and completely dry. Once the pasta is completely dry (it should be brittle and crisp), it can be stored in an airtight container in a cool, dark space for up to 6 months. To rehydrate, add 1 cup boiling water to 1 cup dried pasta and allow to sit for 5 to 10 minutes, or until soft.

CHAPTER 4

Breakfast

There's something to be said for breakfast being the most important meal of the day. You have to admit that after a good breakfast you have more energy, enhanced concentration, and a better overall mood. Experts suggest that a balanced breakfast kick-starts your metabolism and supplies a continuing source of energy throughout the day—and when an emergency occurs, you'll want to have that energy to keep up with whatever activity the situation calls for.

Breakfast can be an easy way to get needed protein, carbohydrates, and vitamins into your body. In a time of emergency, keep simplicity in mind—after all, your fuel may be limited or your food reserves may run low. A simple breakfast could be oatmeal, grits, toast with peanut butter, or dry cereal. That said, you may prefer a more substantial breakfast or just a change from the ordinary. The following recipes—using ingredients commonly stored in emergency food pantries—could easily be incorporated into your daily breakfast planning.

Griddle Cakes

Offer powdered sugar, fruit compote, or syrup to top these pancakes.

Makes 12

1½ cups fine unseasoned dry breadcrumbs

1½ cups hot milk

2 tablespoons butter, melted

2 eggs, well beaten

½ cup all-purpose flour

3½ teaspoons baking powder

½ teaspoon salt

1 tablespoon granulated sugar

1. Stir all the ingredients together in a large bowl to make the griddle cake batter.

2. Heat a greased skillet over medium heat.

3. Spoon batter into the skillet, using about ¼ cup for each griddle cake. Cook for 1 to 2 minutes on each side, or until golden brown. Serve warm.

Protein Pancakes

Serves 2

1 (1-ounce) scoop vanilla protein powder

water, as needed

1 tablespoon vegetable oil, vegetable shortening, or butter

pancake toppings (such as fruit, applesauce, or syrup)

1. Mix the protein powder with enough water to make a lumpy batter the same consistency as regular pancake batter.

2. Add oil, shortening, or butter to a hot skillet over medium heat until a drop of water dropped onto its surface sizzles.

3. Pour in batter by large spoonfuls and cook for 1 to 2 minutes on each side. Add your toppings of choice to serve.

Easy French Toast

Serves 4

1 egg

1 cup milk

1 tablespoon ground cinnamon

1 teaspoon vanilla extract

¼ teaspoon finely grated orange zest

dash of salt

4 slices bread

butter or oil, as needed

syrup or jam, for serving

1. In a large bowl, whisk together the egg, milk, cinnamon, vanilla, orange zest, and salt.

2. Over medium heat, melt butter or oil in a skillet until a drop of water dropped onto the surface sizzles.

3. Dip the bread slices in the egg mixture to coat thoroughly.

4. Cook, turning once, until both sides of the bread are lightly browned and crisp. Serve hot, topped with syrup or jam.

Cinnamon Rolls

Makes 12 rolls

¾ cup milk

1 packet (2¼ teaspoons) active dry yeast

2 cups all-purpose flour

1 egg yolk

FILLING

3 tablespoons brown sugar

1 tablespoon ground cinnamon

3 tablespoons powdered sugar

2½ tablespoons butter, melted

dash of salt

¼ cup (½ stick) butter, softened

½ cup raisins (optional)

1. Heat the milk to lukewarm. In a small bowl, dissolve the yeast in the warm milk; whisk for 1 minute and set aside.

2. In a large bowl, combine the flour, egg yolk, powdered sugar, melted butter, and salt. Mix for 8 minutes or until the dough becomes smooth and no longer sticks to a wooden spoon.

3. Cover the dough with greased plastic wrap and place in the refrigerator for 3 to 24 hours. Bring to room temperature before shaping.

4. In a small bowl, combine all the ingredients for the filling and mix well. Set aside.

5. On a floured surface, roll the dough into a 12 x 9-inch rectangle. Spread the dough with the filling mixture. Sprinkle with raisins, if desired.

6. Roll the dough from the long side, jelly-roll style; pinch the seam to seal. Cut into 12 equal-size pieces and place in lightly greased muffin cups. Cover and let rise in a warm place until doubled in size, about 30 minutes. Preheat the oven to 375°F.

7. Bake for 20 minutes, or until lightly browned. Remove from the muffin tin and let cool on a wire rack. Serve warm.

Homemade Cake Donuts

Makes 16

1 cup granulated sugar

4 teaspoons baking powder

1½ teaspoons salt

½ teaspoon ground allspice

2 eggs, lightly beaten

1 cup milk

¼ cup (½ stick) butter, melted

3 cups all-purpose flour

vegetable oil for frying

COATING

2 to 3 tablespoons granulated or powdered sugar

⅛ teaspoon ground cinnamon

1. In a large bowl, stir together the sugar, baking powder, salt, and allspice.

2. Stir in the eggs, milk, and melted butter. Add the flour 1 cup at a time, beating until blended. The dough should be soft and sticky but firm enough to handle. Cover with plastic wrap and chill for 1 hour.

3. Remove the chilled dough from the refrigerator. Begin heating about 1 inch of oil to 360°F in a large skillet.

4. Working on a floured surface with half the dough at a time, roll to about ½ inch thickness. Cut circles using the floured top of a glass. Use your thumb to make a hole in the center of each circle.

5. Gently drop the doughnuts in batches into the hot oil. Flip them over as they puff; turn a couple more times as they cook, about 2 to 3 minutes total or until golden. Remove from the oil and place on paper towels to drain.

6. Mix the sugar and cinnamon in a paper bag. Carefully shake the warm donuts in the bag, one at a time, to cover with the sugar mixture.

Applesauce Oat Muffins

Makes 12

2 (1-ounce) packets instant plain oatmeal

1¼ cups all-purpose flour

½ cup sugar

½ teaspoon baking soda

1 teaspoon baking powder

¼ teaspoon salt

1 teaspoon apple pie seasoning (page 163)

1 cup buttermilk

1 egg

⅔ cup applesauce

½ teaspoon vanilla extract

1. Preheat the oven to 400°F. Grease the cups of a standard 12-cup muffin tin.

2. Mix all the dry ingredients together in a medium bowl (oatmeal through apple pie seasoning).

3. In a large bowl, whisk together the buttermilk, egg, applesauce, and vanilla. Combine with the dry ingredients, mixing just until well incorporated.

4. Spoon into the prepared muffin tin. Bake for 12 minutes, or until golden brown on top.

Egg in the Middle

Serves 4

4 slices bread

3 eggs

4 tablespoons butter

salt and pepper

1. On a cutting board, use a cookie cutter or small round cup to cut a 3-inch hole in the middle of each slice of bread. Keep the holes and toast them while the eggs are being prepared.

2. In a small bowl, whisk the eggs until well mixed.

3. In a skillet over medium heat, melt 1 tablespoon of the butter. Add a slice of bread, flipping it so that both sides are coated in butter.

4. When the bread begins to toast on one side, ladle about ¼ of the beaten eggs into the hole in the bread. When the egg mixture begins to cook and adhere to the bread, turn the bread over to cook the other side.

5. Sprinkle with salt and pepper and serve immediately. Repeat for each slice of bread.

Creamy Grits

Serves 6

4 cups water, or more as needed

¼ teaspoon salt

1 cup grits (not instant)

¼ teaspoon ground cinnamon

cream or milk, for serving

toasted almonds, dried fruit, honey, maple or fruit syrup (optional)

1. In a medium saucepan over medium-high heat, bring the water to a boil. Stir in the salt and grits and reduce the heat to medium-low.

2. Cover saucepan with lid and allow the grits to simmer for at least 30 to 35 minutes, until soft.

3. If the grits become too thick or dry, add more water, ¼ cup at a time until the mixture is the right creamy consistency.

4. Spoon the warm grits in bowls with a splash of cream or milk and your choice of toppings.

Luke's Sliced Grits

Serves 4

3 cups water

1 teaspoon salt

1 cup plain grits or yellow cornmeal

1 teaspoon granulated sugar

2 to 3 tablespoons unsalted butter

maple syrup, powdered sugar, or pecans, for serving

1. In a medium saucepan, heat the water to boiling on high. Reduce the heat to medium; stir in the salt and cornmeal.

2. Reduce the heat to low and add the sugar. Cook, stirring regularly, until the mixture is thick, about 10 minutes.

3. Spoon into a lightly greased 9 x 5-inch loaf pan. Cover and refrigerate overnight.

4. In the morning, melt the butter in a skillet over medium heat. Cut the cornmeal mush into 1-inch-thick slices. When the butter is melted, add slices of grits. Cook on one side for 5 minutes, turn, and cook 5 minutes more (add more butter or oil before cooking the second side, if desired).

5. To serve, drizzle with maple syrup, sprinkle with powdered sugar, or top with pecans.

Southern Biscuits and Gravy

Southern cooks are real pros at taking a small amount of something and making it feed a lot of people. Biscuits and gravy is one of those creations—how else can you make half a pound of bacon, ham, or sausage feed four hungry people and leave them thoroughly satisfied? *Serves 4*

BISCUITS

2 cups all-purpose flour

1 tablespoon baking powder

½ teaspoon salt

½ cup vegetable shortening

¾ cup milk

1. Preheat the oven to 450°F.

2. In a large mixing bowl, sift together the flour, baking powder, and salt. Cut in the shortening with a fork or pastry blender until the mixture resembles coarse crumbs. Pour in the milk while stirring with a fork. Mix until the dough is soft and moist and pulls away from the sides of the bowl.

3. Turn out the dough onto a lightly floured surface and toss with flour until no longer sticky. Roll to ½ inch thickness.

4. Cut out your biscuits using a floured biscuit cutter, cookie cutter, or glass top. Press together the dough scraps and cut more biscuits.

5. Place the biscuits on an ungreased baking sheet. Bake until golden brown, about 10 minutes.

BREAKFAST GRAVY

Breakfast gravy, by its very nature, is not healthy, low in cholesterol, or heart-friendly. It is, however, a tasty source of calories and protein that can power you through a morning of hard physical labor.

½ pound bacon, sausage, or ½ cup ham, or ¼ cup dehydrated meat crumbles

3 tablespoons vegetable shortening or butter

¼ cup all-purpose flour

3 cups milk (can be reconstituted nonfat dry milk)

salt and pepper to taste

1. In a large cast-iron skillet, brown the meat, breaking it into bite-size pieces. If using ham, cut into cubes before browning.

2. Add the shortening and flour to the pan, stirring constantly to create a roux.

3. When the roux begins to brown lightly, stir in the milk; season with salt and pepper. Stir constantly until your gravy is the consistency you want.

4. Serve over fresh-baked biscuits.

Power Oatmeal

Serves 2

1 cup rolled oats

½ to 1 cup milk

1 (1-ounce) scoop vanilla protein powder

1 cup dried fruit (such as apples or raisins)

2 tablespoons chopped nuts (walnuts or pecans are delicious)

1. Cook the oats according to the package directions.

2. Add the milk and protein powder. Thoroughly stir the mixture until all ingredients are combined. Thoroughly mix in the protein powder.

3. Top the individual servings with fruit and nuts.

Instant Oatmeal Mix

Makes 14 (½-cup) servings

6 cups quick-cooking oats

⅓ cup dry powdered milk

¼ cup powdered sugar

¼ cup packed brown sugar

3 teaspoons ground cinnamon

1 teaspoon salt

1 cup dried fruit or nuts

1. In a large bowl, combine all of the ingredients. Then store in airtight container in a cool, dry place for up to 1 month.

2. To prepare oatmeal, place ½ cup of mix and add ½ cup boiling water or milk to the mix and stir until oats are softened, 2 to 3 minutes.

Breakfast Quinoa

Serves 6

1 cup milk

1 cup water

1 cup quinoa

½ teaspoon ground cinnamon

¼ teaspoon ground cumin

fresh or dehydrated fruit (optional)

⅓ cup chopped toasted pecans

6 teaspoons honey

1. Combine the milk, water, and quinoa in a medium saucepan and bring to a boil over medium heat.

2. Reduce the heat to low; cover and simmer 15 minutes, or until most of the liquid has been absorbed. Turn off the heat; let stand on the burner, covered, for 5 minutes.

3. Stir in the cinnamon, cumin, and fruit, if using. Top each serving with pecans and drizzle with 1 teaspoon honey.

Wheat Berry Cereal

Serves 1

½ cup cooked wheat berries

⅛ cup chopped almonds or walnuts

½ cup fresh or dehydrated fruit

1 cup milk

Combine wheat berries, nuts, and fruit in a bowl and add milk.

Kolaches

The Czech people are famous for their pastries, and the kolache is one of their most acclaimed. The name is related to a word meaning "pocket," describing the way the fillings are tucked into the middle of a sweet roll. This versatile dough can also be fried to make donuts. Just sprinkle with powdered sugar and voilà! *Makes 20 kolaches*

¾ cup lukewarm milk

1 packet (2¼ teaspoons) active dry yeast

3 tablespoons powdered sugar

2½ tablespoons butter, melted

dash of salt

2 cups all-purpose flour (for rolling)

½ cup jelly or favorite kolache filling

1 egg yolk

1. In a bowl, add the yeast to the lukewarm milk and whisk for 1 minute. Set aside for 15 minutes.

2. In a large bowl, combine the yeast mixture along with the powdered sugar, butter, and salt. Mix for 8 minutes or until the dough becomes smooth and no longer sticks to a wooden spoon. Cover dough and leave in a warm place to rise until doubled.

3. Preheat the oven to 400°F. Roll out the dough on floured surface to a 12 x 9-inch rectangle about ¼ inch thick. Pull off small pieces of dough, roll into 2-inch balls, and flatten into 3 to 4-inch circles. On a greased cookie sheet, place dough 2 inches apart. With the backside of a spoon, push into dough to create an indentation. Dollop a spoonful of jelly or other filling into each indentation.

4. Beat the egg yolk in a small dish and brush on the exposed dough. Bake for 15 to 20 minutes, until golden.

Homemade Bran Flakes

Serves 4

1 cup wheat bran

1 cup whole wheat flour

⅔ cup almond flour or other finely ground nuts

¼ cup packed light brown sugar

½ teaspoon baking powder

½ teaspoon salt

½ cup milk

1. Preheat the oven to 350°F. Cut parchment or wax paper to fit 2 large baking sheets that will fit side by side in your oven.

2. Pour all of the dry ingredients into a large mixing bowl and combine well with a fork. Stir in the milk and mix well. You will now have a wet dough.

3. Place one of the cut pieces of parchment or wax paper on your work surface and use your hands to flatten ¼ of the dough on the paper. Cover with plastic wrap and use a rolling pin to completely flatten the dough. It may be so thin in some places that you can see through it. Remove the plastic wrap and transfer the bran flake–covered paper onto the baking sheet.

4. Repeat the process with the second piece of parchment or wax paper and another ¼ of the dough. Bake the 2 sheets of dough for 5 minutes and then check—you want your giant bran flakes to have the consistency of a large cracker. Continue baking until the flakes have the right crispness, checking every couple of minutes so you don't burn them.

5. Let the completed flakes cool completely on the baking sheets.

6. Repeat the process with the rest of the dough.

7. Reduce the oven temperature to 275°F. Tear or break your giant flakes into normal cereal-size pieces and spread them out over the paper-covered baking sheets. Bake for 20 minutes, stirring the flakes every 5 minutes.

8. Store in an airtight container for up to 2 weeks.

Homemade Corn Flakes

Serves 3

> 1 cup fine or medium-fine cornmeal
>
> ¼ cup granulated or powdered sugar (optional)
>
> water

1. Set an ungreased metal skillet over medium heat. Sift a thin layer of cornmeal into the skillet.

2. Fill a spray bottle with water and spray the cornmeal until it is moistened but not soaked.

3. Without touching the cornmeal mixture, let it cook slowly until the water is halfway evaporated; immediately sift sugar over the top, if using.

4. Cook until the water has completely evaporated and the flakes begin releasing from the bottom of the skillet. The flakes will be large.

5. Store in an airtight container for up to 2 weeks.

Hot Rice Cereal

Serves 2 to 3

1¼ cups water	½ teaspoon salt
1¼ cups milk	2 to 3 teaspoons sugar or maple syrup
1 cup uncooked white or brown rice	1 tablespoon butter or margarine (optional)

1. Mix the water and milk in a 4-quart saucepan and bring to a boil over medium heat.

2. Stir in the remaining ingredients, reduce the heat to low, and cover tightly.

3. Simmer for 20 minutes, or until the rice is tender and the liquid has been absorbed.

Rice Tortitas

This is a great recipe for leftover rice. *Serves 4 to 5*

2 cups cooked white or brown rice, cooled	1 teaspoon vanilla extract
3 eggs, beaten	2½ teaspoons baking powder
½ cup granulated sugar	½ to 1 cup all-purpose flour
¼ teaspoon salt	vegetable oil, for deep frying
1 teaspoon ground cinnamon	powdered sugar for topping
½ teaspoon ground nutmeg	

1. In a large bowl, combine the cooked rice, eggs, sugar, salt, cinnamon, nutmeg, vanilla, and baking powder. Add just enough flour to hold the batter together.

2. Pour 2 to 3 inches oil into a skillet and heat over medium-high until oil begins to sizzle. Drop batter by heaping spoonfuls into the hot oil.

3. Fry until golden brown and crisp, 6 to 8 minutes.

4. Drain on paper towels and generously sprinkle with powdered sugar.

CHAPTER 5

Lunchtime Favorites

A midday meal can do wonders for renewing your energy level and keeping your metabolism active. Lunch can be anything from last night's leftovers to a simple sandwich, or it can be more substantial. Served with rolls, cornbread, or crackers, a steaming bowl of soup makes a satisfying complete meal. Typically, lunches should be between 300 and 500 calories, and they should include an array of the vitamins your body needs for proper functioning.

Beef Minestrone Soup

Serves 6 to 8

1 jar spaghetti meat sauce or use the recipe for Spaghetti Meat Sauce (page 201)

4 cups vegetable broth

1 (15-ounce) can red kidney beans, undrained

1 (15-ounce) can small white or Great Northern beans, undrained

¼ cup green beans, fresh or dehydrated

¼ cup chopped zucchini, fresh or dehydrated

½ cup sliced carrots, fresh or dehydrated

2 tablespoons dried parsley

1 teaspoon dried oregano

1 teaspoon salt

½ teaspoon pepper

¼ teaspoon dried thyme

1½ cups water

⅓ cup uncooked small shell pasta

3 cups fresh baby spinach

grated Parmesan cheese, for topping (optional)

1. Pour the spaghetti sauce and vegetable broth into a large stockpot. Add the canned beans, vegetables, seasonings, and water.

2. Bring the soup to a boil over medium-high heat, then reduce the heat to low and allow to simmer uncovered for 20 minutes.

3. When almost ready to serve, add the pasta and cook for an additional 20 minutes, or until the soup has the desired consistency.

4. Ladle the soup into bowls and stir in fresh spinach. Top the individual servings with Parmesan cheese, if desired.

Vegetarian Chili

Adding 2 cups of wheat berries can add carbohydrates and boost this meal's nutrition.

Serves 3

1 (15.4-ounce) can black beans

1 (15.4-ounce) can red kidney beans

1 (15.4-ounce) can whole kernel corn

1 (14.5-ounce) can diced tomatoes

1 (14.5-ounce) can crushed tomatoes

¼ cup dehydrated green bell peppers

2 tablespoons dried onion flakes

2 tablespoons chili powder

1 tablespoon garlic powder

hot sauce, to taste

1. Rinse and drain the beans and corn. Place in a large saucepan.

2. Stir in all the remaining ingredients except the hot sauce.

3. Bring to a boil over medium heat, then reduce the heat to low and simmer for at least 30 minutes, until the flavors are well blended.

4. Add hot sauce to taste.

Sweet Potato Chili

Serves 4 to 6

1 sweet potato or yam, peeled and cubed or 1 (15-ounce) can sweet potatoes, drained

1 onion, diced

1 bell pepper, diced

1 apple, peeled, cored, and cubed

4 garlic cloves, minced

1 (28-ounce) can diced tomatoes, undrained

1 (15.5-ounce) can black beans, undrained

1 (15.5-ounce) can navy beans, undrained

1 cup water

1 tablespoon ground cumin

1 tablespoon chili powder

1 teaspoon unsweetened cocoa powder

¼ teaspoon ground cinnamon

salt and pepper

1 (12.5-ounce) can of chunk chicken breast (optional)

hot sauce

In a large pot, combine all the ingredients except the hot sauce along with the liquid in cans. Bring to a boil over medium heat, then reduce the heat and simmer, uncovered, for at least 30 minutes, until the flavors are well blended. Stir in hot sauce to taste.

Baked-Bean Chili

Serves 4 to 5

1 pound ground beef (or other ground meat) or 1 cup freeze-dried beef or 4 cups dehydrated beef

2 (15.5-ounce) cans baked beans

1 (14.5-ounce) can diced or stewed tomatoes

¼ cup barbecue sauce

¼ cup packed brown sugar

3 tablespoons chili powder

1 tablespoon onion powder

1 tablespoon garlic powder

salt, to taste

1. Rehydrate any dehydrated meat for 1 hour. Combine all the ingredients in a large pot and bring to a boil over medium heat. If using ground beef, brown meat in a skillet, breaking up ground meat with a spoon.

2. Reduce the heat to low, cover, and simmer for 1½ hours, stirring frequently to ensure the beans do not get scorched (or until the ground meat is thoroughly cooked, if using fresh meat).

3. Remove the lid and simmer for another 30 minutes.

3-Can Black Bean Soup

Serves 4

1 (15-ounce) can whole kernel corn, undrained

1 (15-ounce) can black beans, undrained

1 (28-ounce) can diced tomatoes, undrained

1 tablespoon chili powder

3 teaspoons garlic powder

¼ teaspoon cayenne pepper

1 tablespoon dried onion flakes

2 tablespoons chicken bouillon granules

1 tablespoon dried parsley

salt and black pepper, to taste

cilantro, coarsely chopped (optional)

tortilla chips or baked flour tortilla crisps

1. Pour the corn, beans, and tomatoes into a 16-quart stockpot along with the can liquids.

2. Stir in the following 7 ingredients (chili powder through salt and pepper).

3. Bring the mixture to a boil over medium heat, then reduce the heat to low and simmer, uncovered, for 20 to 30 minutes.

4. Stir in cilantro to taste, if desired. Ladle the hot soup into bowls and top with crumbled tortilla chips or crisps to serve.

Creamy Corn Chowder

Serves 2 to 3

1 (15-ounce) can whole kernel corn, drained and rinsed

1 (15-ounce) can creamed corn, undrained

2 cups milk or ⅔ cup instant nonfat milk mixed with 2 cups water

⅔ cup instant mashed potato flakes, or as needed

salt and pepper

1. In a 4-quart saucepan, combine both kinds of corn and the milk. Bring to a boil over medium heat, then reduce the heat to low and simmer, uncovered, for 5 minutes.

2. Stir in the instant mashed potato flakes, a little bit at a time, until the chowder is as thick as you want it.

3. Season to taste with salt and pepper.

Split Pea Soup

Serves 4 to 6

1 pound split peas

5 cups water or vegetable broth, or more as needed

1½ cups diced carrots or 1 (15-ounce) can carrots or 1 cup diced dehydrated carrots

2 tablespoons olive or vegetable oil

3 tablespoons dried onion flakes

2 cups diced ham (smoked, canned, or dehydrated)

1 tablespoon seasoning salt

2 bay leaves

1 tablespoon dried thyme

pepper, to taste

1. Rinse and sort the peas to remove any dirt or stones.

2. Combine all the ingredients in a 4-quart saucepan. Bring to a boil over medium heat.

3. Reduce the heat and simmer the soup, uncovered, for 2 hours, or until the peas have disintegrated, stirring frequently and add water if needed.

4. Remove the pot from the heat and let the soup stand for 15 minutes to thicken. Remove and discard the bay leaves before serving the soup.

Leftover Chowder

Serves 8

1 leftover cooked chicken carcass

8 cups water

5 bacon strips, cooked and chopped

2 garlic cloves, minced

2 onions, diced

2 medium red potatoes, peeled and diced

4 carrots, peeled and sliced or 2 cups sliced dehydrated carrots

kernels from 2 ears of corn or 2 cups dehydrated corn kernels

1 ½ teaspoons prepared Cajun seasoning, or use the recipe on page 163

1 mild or spicy chile, diced (optional)

2 tablespoons all-purpose flour

milk or heavy cream, for serving (optional)

1. In a covered large stockpot over low heat, simmer the chicken carcass in the water for 7 hours. Add more water if needed.

2. Lift out the chicken and allow it to cool. Strain the broth through a sieve into 16-quart stockpot; discard the bones, skin, and other remnants.

3. When the chicken is cool enough to handle, pick any remaining meat off the bones.

4. Add the chicken meat to the broth along with all the remaining ingredients except the flour and milk. Allow the chowder to simmer actively over medium heat for 15 to 25 minutes, or until the vegetables are soft.

5. To thicken the soup, whisk 1 cup of the broth together with 2 tablespoons of flour in a medium bowl. Stir into the chowder.

6. To make the soup creamy, pour a splash of milk or cream into the individual bowls before ladling in the chowder.

Cream of Asparagus Soup

Serves 3

2 (10.5-ounce) cans asparagus

4 cups milk or 1 ½ cups instant nonfat dry milk mixed with 4 cups chicken broth or water

2 chicken bouillon cubes (if not using broth)

1 tablespoon garlic powder

1 ½ teaspoons dried thyme

1. Using a blender, puree the asparagus with the liquid from the cans. Alternatively, use a potato masher to produce the consistency you want.

2. Transfer the pureed asparagus to a 4-quart saucepan and stir in the milk or dry milk mixture. Add the bouillon (if using), garlic powder, and thyme; blend well.

3. Over medium heat, bring the soup to a low simmer. Simmer until heated through.

Potato Cheese Soup

Serves 3

1 (15.4-ounce) can condensed cheese soup

⅔ cup nonfat dry milk

1 cup water

1¼ cups instant mashed potato flakes

1 tablespoon onion powder

salt and pepper

freeze-dried or dried chives, to taste

2 tablespoons bacon bits (optional)

1. Combine the canned soup, dry milk, and water in a 9-quart saucepan over medium heat. Bring to a simmer, but do not boil. Let simmer for 5 minutes.

2. Stir in the potato flakes, onion powder, salt, and pepper, mixing well. Continue to simmer until heated through.

3. Top individual bowls of hot soup with chives and bacon bits, as desired.

Dr. Mom Chicken Noodle Soup

Leave the skin on the onion to create a golden brown broth. *Serves 6*

2 (14.5-ounce) cans chicken broth or 4 cups hot water mixed with 2 chicken bouillon cubes

2 (12.5-ounce) cans chunk chicken

2 tablespoons dried garlic flakes or 6 garlic cloves, minced

2 tablespoons dried minced onion or 1 whole onion, chopped

2 tablespoons dried parsley

1 tablespoon dried oregano

1 (15.4-ounce) can peas and carrots, drained

½ (12-ounce) package egg noodles

1. Combine the first 6 ingredients in a large saucepan over medium heat.

2. Simmer, uncovered for 1 to 2 hours to allow flavors to meld.

3. Add the drained peas and carrots and the egg noodles. Bring to a low boil and cook as long as the package directs for al dente noodles.

Vegetable Beef and Barley Soup

Serves 6

1 pound ground or cubed beef, 1 cup dehydrated beef or 12 ounces dried beef

1 (12–ounce) can V8 or tomato juice

1 (15-ounce) can peas and carrots, undrained

1 (15-ounce) can whole kernel corn, undrained

1 (15-ounce) can green beans, undrained

1 (15-ounce) can white or red kidney beans, undrained

½ cup uncooked pearl barley

2 bay leaves

1 tablespoon dried minced garlic

1 tablespoon dried onion flakes

½ teaspoon dried marjoram

½ teaspoon chili powder

½ teaspoon dried thyme

salt and pepper

1. If you are using dehydrated ground beef, rehydrate in water for 30 minutes before adding to a large pot. If you are using ground or cubed beef, brown it in a skillet, breaking up the ground beef with a spoon. When browned, drain the grease.

2. In a large stockpot, combine the beef with all the remaining ingredients.

3. Bring to a boil over medium heat, then reduce to a low simmer and cook for 2 hours, covered, until the beef is completely cooked and the barley is tender. Stir often during the cooking process.

Lucky Bean Soup

Serves 8

1 pound Hearty Bean Soup Mix (page 213)

1 (28-ounce) can diced tomatoes

1 medium onion, chopped

½ cup chopped green bell pepper

½ cup chopped celery

1 or 2 garlic cloves, chopped

1 tablespoon chili powder

½ teaspoon ground cumin

10 to 12 cups water, or as needed

1 pound smoked sausage or ham

salt and pepper

1. Rinse the beans and cover with water to soak overnight, or at least 12 hours. Drain.

2. In a 9-quart stockpot, combine everything except the sausage or ham, salt, and pepper. The water should cover the other ingredients. Bring to a boil over medium-high heat.

3. Reduce the heat and simmer for 1 to 2 hours, uncovered, until the beans are tender. Add the sausage or ham and season to taste with salt and pepper. Cook until the flavor of the meat is well blended into the beans.

Potato Soup

Serves 4

2 tablespoons chopped dehydrated green onions

2 tablespoons chopped dehydrated celery

2 tablespoons butter or margarine

4 cups milk, or as needed

4 servings instant potato flakes

½ teaspoon chicken bouillon granules

salt

¼ teaspoon pepper

dash of garlic powder

paprika, parsley, bacon bits, or grated cheese, for garnish (optional)

1. In a 4-quart saucepan over high heat, rehydrate the onion and celery in ¾ cups boiling water for 5 minutes.

2. Over low heat, sauté the rehydrated onion and celery in the butter or margarine.

3. Add the milk, potato flakes, bouillon, salt, pepper, and garlic powder. Heat to almost boiling, stirring constantly. If the soup seems too thick, thin with more milk or with water.

4. Remove from the heat. Garnish individual servings with paprika, parsley, bacon bits, or grated cheese, if you wish.

Taco Soup

This soup is good served over rice or tortilla chips. *Serves 4*

2 cups dehydrated or fresh ground beef, cooked

1 onion, chopped

1 (15.5-ounce) can kidney or black beans

1 (15.5-ounce) can pinto beans

2 (28-ounce) cans stewed tomatoes

1 (10-ounce) can Rotel diced tomatoes and green chiles

1 (1.5-ounce) packet taco seasoning

1 (1.5-ounce) packet ranch dressing mix

1 to 2 cups water

Without draining the cans, pour all the ingredients into a large saucepan or stockpot. Stir to combine. Simmer over medium heat, covered, for 30 minutes.

Goulash

Serves 5

¼ cup vegetable oil

1 pound bone-in pork or beef

½ cup dried onion flakes or 1 whole onion, sliced

1 teaspoon dried garlic flakes or 2 garlic cloves, minced

2 tablespoons paprika

3 to 5 cups prepared sauerkraut

3 cups water

salt and pepper

sour cream, for serving (optional)

1. Heat the oil in a large pot over medium-high heat. When the oil is sizzling, add the meat and sear 4 to 5 minutes on each side.

2. Reduce the heat to medium and add the onions, garlic, and paprika and continue cooking until the meat is cooked, 20 to 30 minutes. Remove the meat to a cutting board.

3. Scrape up the browned bits from the bottom of the pot. Add the sauerkraut and water and bring to a simmer over medium heat.

4. When the meat has cooled enough to handle, cut it into cubes and return it to the pot. For the richest flavor, add the meat bones, too. Season to taste with salt and pepper. Simmer on low heat, uncovered, for 1 to 2 hours.

5. Top with sour cream to serve, if you wish.

Pantry Chicken and Dumplings

Serves 6 to 8

2¼ cups biscuit mix (such as Bisquick)

⅔ cup milk or ⅔ cup water mixed with ½ cup nonfat dry milk

2 (12.5-ounce) cans chunk chicken

2 (14-ounce) cans chicken broth or 4 cups water mixed with 2 chicken bouillon cubes

1 tablespoon dried parsley

1 tablespoon garlic powder

1 tablespoon onion powder

salt and pepper

1. In a medium bowl, combine the biscuit mix and the milk to make the dumpling dough.

2. Place the chicken, broth, and seasonings in a 9-quart stockpot and bring to a boil over medium-high heat.

3. While the broth is coming to a boil, flatten out the dough to ¼ inch thick on a cutting board. Once the soup is boiling, tear off medium-sized pieces of dough and drop into the liquid.

4. After 1 minute, stir very gently to make sure all the dumplings are completely moistened. Reduce the heat, cover, and simmer for 10 minutes.

Asian Ramen Salad

For a heartier meal, add 1 cup cooked chicken to this salad. *Serves 6*

DRESSING

⅓ cup peanut butter

⅓ cup water

½ teaspoon garlic powder

1 tablespoon soy sauce

2 tablespoons sesame seed oil

2 tablespoons apple cider vinegar

salt and pepper

NOODLES

2 (3-ounce) packages ramen noodles, broken up, spice packet discarded

½ head cabbage, shredded

1 cup diced celery

¼ cup chopped onion

¼ cup diced carrots

¼ cup roasted, salted peanuts

4 tablespoons fresh cilantro or 2 tablespoons dried cilantro

salt and pepper

1. In a small bowl, whisk together all the dressing ingredients. Set aside.

2. Cook the ramen noodles according to the package directions. (Do not add the spice packet.) Drain.

3. In a large mixing bowl, combine the cooked noodles with the remaining salad ingredients. Gently toss with the dressing. Serve immediately.

Southern Chicken Salad

Serves 4

1 (12.5-ounce) can chunk chicken or 1 cup chopped cooked chicken

¼ cup cashews, pecans, or walnuts

2 tablespoons finely diced yellow onion or 1 tablespoon rehydrated diced onion

½ cup finely diced red apple

¼ cup dried cranberries, blueberries, or other berries

¼ cup diced purple grapes

¼ cup mayonnaise

½ teaspoon curry powder

salt

Mix all the ingredients well. Use on crackers, in salads, or as a sandwich filling.

Use Your Noodle!

Ramen noodles are a prepper favorite. Those little cubes of ultra-cheap carbohydrates are a mainstay in many preppers' pantries! They are inexpensive and quick to prepare, and they add some easy-to-digest carbs to a meal for extra energy. But the just-add-water packets will get dull very quickly. Try these additions to cooked, unflavored ramen noodles, in whatever proportions you like.

- Chives, canned baby corn (drained), soy sauce, ramen seasoning packet

- Marinara sauce, grated Parmesan cheese, beef seasoning packet

- Condensed cream of chicken soup, canned mixed vegetables (drained), chicken seasoning packet

- Diced pineapple (drained), diced canned ham, dried bell pepper, ramen seasoning packet

- 1 (15.5-ounce) can of green beans (drained), 1 (15.5-ounce) can of kidney beans (drained), (15.5-ounce) can of lima beans (drained), Italian salad dressing (serve cold or at room temperature)

Garden Tuna Salad

Serves 3 to 4

1 (5-ounce) can tuna, drained

2 hard-cooked eggs, shredded

1 large dill pickle, finely diced

¼ cup minced yellow onion

¼ cup mayonnaise

½ teaspoon lemon pepper seasoning

salt and pepper

Mix all the ingredients well. Use on crackers, in salads, or as a sandwich filling.

Spicy Tuna Salad

Serves 3 to 4

1 (5-ounce) can tuna, drained

¼ cup mayonnaise

1 teaspoon chili powder

1 teaspoon lemon pepper seasoning

⅛ teaspoon garlic powder

dash of cayenne pepper

1 teaspoon peach jelly

salt and pepper

Mix all the ingredients well. Use on crackers, in salads, or as a sandwich filling.

Deviled Ham Salad

Serves 3 to 4

1 (4.25-ounce) can deviled ham

1 large dill pickle, finely diced

1½ tablespoons finely diced jalapeño chiles

3 tablespoons mayonnaise

½ teaspoon dry mustard

¼ teaspoon onion powder

salt and pepper

Mix all the ingredients well. Use on crackers, in salads, or as a sandwich filling.

Egg Salad

Serves 3 to 4

6 hard-cooked eggs

½ cup mayonnaise

1 teaspoon dry mustard

1 tablespoon sweet pickle relish

dash of cayenne pepper

salt and pepper

Using a cheese grater, shred the eggs. Combine with the remaining ingredients, mixing well. Use on crackers, in salads, or as a sandwich filling.

Chicken Macaroni Salad

Serves 4

2 cups cooked macaroni

1 (12.5-ounce) can chunk chicken, drained

½ cup mayonnaise, or as needed

¼ cup onion, chopped

¼ cup celery, chopped

¼ cup sweet pickle relish

2 teaspoons granulated sugar

2 teaspoons white vinegar

½ teaspoon prepared yellow mustard

salt and pepper

Combine all the ingredients in a large bowl and stir well. Add a little more mayonnaise, if necessary. Taste and adjust the seasonings as needed. Cover and chill for several hours before serving.

Pasta Italiano

Serves 4

2 cups cooked pasta

1 (3.25-ounce) can pitted black olives, drained and sliced

½ fresh or dehydrated red bell pepper, diced

¼ cup coarsely chopped dehydrated tomatoes

2 tablespoons fresh finely chopped red onion

½ cup mayonnaise

2 tablespoons prepared Italian salad dressing

2 tablespoons lemon juice

2 tablespoons dried basil

1 tablespoon dried parsley

¼ teaspoon pepper

½ teaspoon salt, or to taste

Combine all the ingredients in a medium bowl and stir well. Add a little more mayonnaise, if necessary. Taste and adjust the seasonings as needed. Cover and chill for several hours before serving.

Ham and Pea Salad

Serves 6

4 cups cooked macaroni pasta

1 cup thinly sliced celery

1 cup diced onion

1 cup diced ham

1½ cups frozen green peas, thawed

¼ cup mayonnaise

½ cup prepared ranch dressing

1 teaspoon dried basil

dash of garlic powder

salt and pepper

Combine all the ingredients in a large bowl and stir well. Add a little more mayonnaise, if necessary. Taste and adjust the seasonings as needed. Cover and chill for several hours before serving.

Momma's Fish Patties

Serves 4 to 5

1 (16-ounce) can salmon or other fish	¼ teaspoon salt
½ cup saltine cracker crumbs or cornmeal	¼ teaspoon pepper
¼ cup cornmeal	dash of Tabasco sauce
2 eggs, lightly beaten	vegetable oil for frying

1. Drain the juices from the canned fish; reserve.

2. Flake the fish, making sure that all the skin and bones have been removed.

3. Combine the cracker crumbs with the reserved fish liquid. Allow to stand for 5 minutes, or until the liquid has been absorbed. Stir in the flaked fish, cornmeal, eggs, salt, pepper, and Tabasco. Shape the fish mixture into patties.

4. Pour oil into a heavy skillet to a depth of ¼ inch. Heat the oil over medium heat. Fry the patties 2 to 3 minutes on each side in the hot oil until browned. Drain on paper towels and serve warm.

Bean Patties

Serve these patties hot with warm flatbread or as a sandwich filling. *Serves 6 medium or 12 small patties*

1 (15.5-ounce) can beans (such as chickpeas, lentils, black, or pinto beans), drained	3 tablespoons chopped dehydrated tomatoes, rehydrated
1 large onion, finely chopped	2 teaspoons chili powder
2 garlic cloves, finely chopped	2 tablespoons cornmeal
1 teaspoon ground cumin	salt and pepper
3 tablespoons chopped dried fresh parsley	1 tablespoon all-purpose flour
	vegetable oil for frying

1. In a medium bowl, combine the beans, onion, garlic, cumin, parsley, tomatoes, chili powder, cornmeal, salt, and pepper. Mix well. Stir in the flour.

2. Mash the beans, mixing the ingredients well. You can also combine the ingredients in a food processor. You want the result to be a thick paste.

3. Form the mixture into balls about the size of ping-pong balls. Flatten slightly.

4. In a deep skillet, heat 2 inches of oil until it sizzles when a drop of water hits oil. Fry the patties in the hot oil until sides are golden brown, turning every 5 to 7 minutes. Drain on a paper towel and serve warm.

Tuscan Bean Salad

Serves 6

2 (15.4-ounce) cans navy beans or cannellini beans, drained

1 (6-ounce) can pitted black olives, chopped

1 small onion, chopped, or ½ cup chopped dehydrated onion, rehydrated

¼ cup dehydrated chopped tomatoes

¼ cup olive oil

2 tablespoons balsamic vinegar

2 cups coarsely chopped fresh spinach

1 tablespoon Italian seasoning

dash of cayenne pepper

salt and pepper

Combine all the ingredients in a medium bowl and stir well. Add a little more mayonnaise, if necessary. Taste and adjust the seasonings as needed. Cover and chill for several hours before serving.

Chicken Bean Wraps

To make a crispier version, brush a small amount of oil on both sides of the tortillas and crisp in a 345°F oven for 5 minutes, or until the tortillas are as crisp as desired. *Serves 4 to 5*

1 (16-ounce) can refried beans

dash of chili powder

4 or 5 flour tortillas

1 (12.5-ounce) can chunk chicken, drained

shredded lettuce or sprouts

1 cup prepared salsa (page 199)

shredded sharp cheddar cheese (optional)

Recipe variation: Use 1 cup ground beef crumbles instead of chicken.

1. On low heat, in a small pot, heat refried beans with the chili powder until they reach desired temperature. In a skillet, heat and warm tortillas 30 seconds on each side. Slather the warm tortillas with refried beans.

2. Top each tortilla with chicken chunks, lettuce or sprouts, salsa, and cheese, if using.

CHAPTER 6

Supper

In many families, dinner is the only meal of the day at which everyone is present. For that reason, lots of us choose to make it the most delicious and comforting meal possible. The recipes in this chapter bring to mind a cozy warm country kitchen! Keep in mind that on average, dinner should consist of 30 percent of your daily calories, or between 500 and 800 calories. When you don't have a particular fresh ingredient, use the following chart for a substitute, which can be used for the recipes in this book and for your own familiar favorites.

DRIED FOOD SUBSTITUTES FOR FRESH INGREDIENTS

Fresh ingredient	Substitution
Apples	Dehydrated apple slices, applesauce
Beef	Freeze-dried ground beef, freeze-dried sliced beef, dehydrated beef crumbles, canned beef, chipped beef, beef pouches, TVP, jerky
Bell peppers	Dehydrated peppers, freeze-dried peppers
Butter	Canned butter, freeze-dried butter powder, shortening
Carrots	Dehydrated carrots, freeze-dried carrots
Celery	Dehydrated celery, freeze-dried celery
Cheese	Freeze-dried shredded cheese, Cheez Whiz, Velveeta processed cheese, canned cheese soup
Chicken	Canned or chunk chicken, freeze-dried chicken, dehydrated chicken pieces
Eggs	Freeze-dried powdered eggs, 1 tablespoon soy flour plus 1 tablespoon water, 1 tablespoon applesauce
Ham	Canned flaked ham, Spam, canned ham, freeze-dried ham, dehydrated ham bits
Milk	Nonfat dry powdered milk, nonfat dry milk, freeze-dried milk powder, canned evaporated milk
Mushrooms	Canned mushrooms, freeze-dried mushrooms, dehydrated mushrooms
Onions	Onion powder, freeze-dried onion, dehydrated onion, onion soup mix
Sausage	Freeze-dried sausage crumbles, pepperettes, or little smokies
Turkey	Canned flaked turkey, freeze-dried turkey, dehydrated turkey pieces

A Note about Freeze-Dried Foods

Freeze-dried foods can be a great addition to any prepper's pantry. The beauty of freeze-dried food isn't just the nutrition and variety it can add to your family's diet, but that it can last 25 years or more. Foods that would normally be off limits during a disaster can be neatly lined up on your shelves, awaiting the addition of hot water to provide a burst of vitamins, minerals, and flavor.

Learn in good times to reconstitute freeze-dried foods and use them in your normal recipes—it will totally change your outlook toward surviving with the contents of your pantry!

Meats—Investing in freeze-dried meats will allow you to make all your normal recipes with only slight adaptations. Try these in freeze-dried form:

- Beef strips
- Chicken breast
- Ground beef
- Ham
- Sausage crumbles
- Turkey breast

Vegetables—Some veggies that you can't get in cans are available in freeze-dried form. Bell pepper, for example, might be hard to find in the middle of a winter blackout. But if you have a well-stocked section of freeze-dried foods, a scoop of peppers will be at your fingertips. Some useful freeze-dried vegetables:

- Broccoli
- Cauliflower
- Celery
- Diced carrots
- Green bell peppers
- Mushrooms
- Onions
- Spinach
- Zucchini

Eggs and dairy products—These may be lacking in your pantry, since they need to be refrigerated or frozen. However, freeze-dried foods will let you add cheesy goodness to casseroles or enjoy a hot breakfast omelet. How great would it be to be able to make your kids a Friday-night pizza in the midst of a grid-down situation? Think about stocking up on #10 cans of the following:

- Shredded cheddar and mozzarella cheeses
- Powdered cheese
- Powdered milk, buttermilk
- Powdered whole eggs, egg whites, and egg yolks
- Powdered butter
- Powdered shortening

Tater Skins

This has become an American favorite. *Serves 8*

6 medium russet or Idaho potatoes, scrubbed (about 7 pounds)

olive oil, as needed

1 cup chopped bacon or ham

salt and pepper

½ cup shredded fresh or freeze-dried cheddar cheese

sour cream or yogurt, for dipping (optional)

3 green onions, finely chopped

1. Preheat the oven to 400°F. Rub the potatoes with olive oil and bake 30 minutes. (To conserve fuel, do this while you're cooking something else.)

2. Cook the bacon or ham in a skillet until crispy, then drain on a paper towel.

3. Slice the baked potatoes in half and scoop out the centers until there is only ½ inch of potato flesh left on the skin. Reserve the scooped-out flesh for another use.

4. Increase the oven temperature to 450°F.

5. Rub the potato skins inside and out with olive oil and sprinkle with salt and pepper.

6. Spread the potato skins on a baking sheet and cook for 10 minutes on one side, then turn them over and cook for another 10 minutes, until crisp and lightly browned.

7. Remove the potatoes and set the oven on broil. Arrange the potatoes skin-side down and sprinkle with the cheese and cooked bacon or ham. Return them to the oven and broil for 2 minutes.

8. To serve, top with sour cream or yogurt (if using) and the chopped green onions.

Reuben Casserole

Serves 2 to 3

1 (15-ounce) can corned beef, chopped

1 (10-ounce) can condensed cream of mushroom soup

1 (12-ounce) jar sauerkraut

1 (12-ounce) package egg noodles, cooked and drained

1 cup shredded mozzarella or Swiss cheese (optional)

1. Preheat the oven to 325°F. Lightly grease a medium 1.8-liter casserole dish.

2. Mix all the ingredients together in the prepared dish.

3. Bake for 45 minutes, or until the top is lightly browned.

Potato Dumplings

Serve these dumplings with hot soup or a hearty stew. *Serves 8*

2 whole russet potatoes (about 2 pounds), cooked and mashed

1 teaspoon salt, plus salt for cooking water

1 cup all-purpose flour, plus more for rolling

2 eggs, lightly beaten

lukewarm water, as needed

3 tablespoons butter, optional

1. In a medium bowl, mash the cooked potatoes until smooth.

2. Bring a large pot of salted water to a boil over high heat while you prepare the dumplings.

3. In a large bowl, combine salt, flour, and eggs. If the dough seems too dry, add 1 or 2 tablespoons lukewarm water. Add potatoes and mix everything together to make a smooth, medium-thick dough.

4. Place the dough on a lightly floured surface and knead the mixture until smooth. Add 1 tablespoon flour if dough is sticky. Divide the dough in half. With floured hands, shape the dough into 1½-inch balls.

5. Carefully transfer the dough pieces into the boiling water. Reduce the heat to medium, cover the pot, and cook for 10 to 15 minutes or until dumplings rise to the surface. If the dumplings stick to the bottom of the pot, use a wooden spoon or a spatula to unstick them. Drain in a colander. Drizzle with melted butter, if preferred.

6. Use a slotted spoon to lift the dumplings out of the water and allow to dry for a few minutes on a paper towel–lined plate and then turn over to dry the other side.

Shepherd's Pie

Serves 3 to 4

1 pound ground beef, cooked and crumbled, or 4 cups dehydrated beef crumbles

1 (10-ounce) can condensed cream of mushroom soup

1 (10-ounce) can creamed corn

1 (10-ounce) can peas and carrots, drained

½ teaspoon dried thyme

1 tablespoon dried minced onion

1 tablespoon dried garlic flakes

salt and pepper

⅔ cup instant potato flakes, reconstituted according to the package directions

2 tablespoons butter, melted (optional)

1. Preheat the oven to 375°F. Lightly grease a 1.8-liter casserole or baking dish.

2. Combine everything except for potato mixture and butter in the prepared dish, mixing well.

3. Top with the potato mixture and brush with butter, if using.

4. Bake, uncovered, for 40 minutes, until lightly golden and heated through.

Dottie's Easy Chicken Pot Pie

Serves 4 to 5

1 Basic Pie Crust recipe (page 302)

1 (12.5-ounce) can chunk white chicken, drained

1 (15-ounce) can mixed vegetables, drained

1 (10-ounce) can condensed cream of mushroom soup

salt and pepper

1. Prepare the pastry dough, wrap in plastic, and refrigerate at least 30 minutes.

2. Preheat the oven to 350°F.

3. Divide the pie dough in half. On a floured surface, use a floured rolling pin to roll half of the dough to a 12-inch round. Transfer it into a 9-inch pie pan, letting the edges hang over.

4. In a large bowl, mix together the chicken, vegetables, and mushroom soup. Season with salt and pepper to taste. Pour the mixture into the pie shell.

5. Roll the rest of the dough to an 11-inch round. Carefully transfer the dough round onto the pie. Trim the edges to ½ inch, fold under, press together, and crimp. Slit the top to make steam vents.

6. Bake until the crust is golden brown, 40 to 45 minutes.

Creamed Tuna

Serves 3 to 4

¼ cup diced onions

2 tablespoons butter

1 tablespoon all-purpose flour

½ teaspoon salt

⅛ teaspoon freshly ground pepper

1 cup milk

1 (5-ounce) can tuna, drained

1 (10-ounce) can peas, drained

toast or cooked rice, for serving

1. In a medium saucepan over medium-high heat, sauté the onions in the butter until tender but not browned. Stir in the flour, salt, and pepper.

2. Add the milk all at once; cook, stirring constantly, until the mixture thickens and bubbles.

3. Break up the tuna with a fork, and add the tuna and peas to the creamed mixture and simmer for 5 minutes.

4. To serve, spoon over toast or rice.

Scalloped Potatoes and Ham

Serves 4 to 6

6 medium potatoes, peeled and thinly sliced (about 4 to 6 pounds)

1½ cups chopped ham (fully cooked or dehydrated)

1 cup sliced carrots (fresh or dehydrated)

½ cup peas (fresh or dehydrated)

1 teaspoon dehydrated minced garlic or 1 garlic clove, minced

3 tablespoons chopped dehydrated onion or 1 medium onion, chopped

2 (10-ounce) cans condensed cream of mushroom soup

½ cup unsweetened condensed milk

salt and pepper

1. Preheat the oven to 350°F. Lightly grease a 1½ to 2-quart casserole dish.

2. Place a layer of potatoes in the bottom of the dish. Add a layer of ham and then sprinkle on a layer of carrots, peas, garlic, and onion. Continue to alternate layers until all the potatoes, ham, and vegetables have been used.

3. In a large bowl, stir together the mushroom soup, condensed milk, salt, and pepper. Pour over the layered ingredients in the casserole dish.

4. Cover and bake for 1 hour, until the potatoes are tender.

Tuna Noodle Casserole

Serves 3 to 4

1 (10-ounce) can tuna, drained well

1 (10-ounce) can condensed cream of mushroom soup or other condensed cream of vegetable soup

1 (15-ounce) can peas, drained

½ (12-ounce) package egg noodles, cooked and drained

½ to 1 cup French-fried onions or ½ cup fine breadcrumbs

1. Preheat the oven to 400°F. Lightly grease a medium 1.8-liter casserole dish.

2. Mix the tuna, soup, and peas in the prepared dish until well combined. Gently stir in the cooked noodles.

3. Top with the French-fried onions or breadcrumbs.

4. Bake, uncovered, for 30 minutes, or until lightly browned.

Chicken with Lemon Basil Sauce

Serves 4 to 6

3 tablespoons olive oil, divided

1 tablespoon distilled white vinegar

¼ (.4-ounce) packet ranch dressing mix (optional)

pasta, cooked al dente

2 (12.5-ounce) cans chunk chicken, drained

2 garlic cloves, chopped

2 tablespoons fresh lemon juice

1 teaspoon grated lemon zest

1 cup low-salt chicken broth

1 cup spinach (canned, fresh, or dehydrated)

½ cup chopped fresh basil or 1 tablespoon dried basil

salt

pepper

1. In a small bowl, make a sauce for the pasta by whisking together 1 tablespoon of the oil, the vinegar, and the ranch dressing mix (if using). Add to the cooked pasta and stir to combine. Set aside.

2. Heat the remaining 2 tablespoons olive oil in a wide, heavy skillet over medium-high heat. Add the chicken and sauté until browned. Add the chicken to the bowl of pasta. Leave the juices in the pan.

3. In same skillet, reduce heat to medium, add the garlic to the pan and sauté for 2 minutes. Add the lemon juice and lemon zest. Stir until well blended. Add the chicken broth and spinach; simmer until reduced to sauce consistency, about 8 minutes. Stir in the basil and season to taste with salt and pepper.

4. Spoon the warm sauce over the chicken and pasta and serve.

Creamy Chicken Pasta

Serves 4

1 (4-ounce) package Knorr Pasta Sides of choice (such as Creamy Garlic Rafaello)

1 (12.5-ounce) can chunk chicken

1 (14-ounce) can creamed spinach or 1 (10.75-ounce) can creamed asparagus soup, drained well

grated Parmesan cheese, to taste

1. Prepare the pasta side dish according to the package directions.

2. Stir the chicken and spinach (or asparagus) into the hot pasta. Cover the pan tightly and let stand for 5 minutes. At this point it should be heated through; if not, turn on the burner to low and stir the mixture continuously until hot.

3. Top with Parmesan cheese and serve.

Beef Stroganoff

Serves 4 to 5

1 (1.6-ounce) packet mushroom gravy

3 cups egg noodles, cooked or 3 cups prepared rice

1 cup dried beef crumbles, rehydrated or 1 (12-ounce) can roast beef and gravy

1 cup dried peas, rehydrated

3 tablespoons dehydrated minced onions

1 teaspoon garlic powder

dash of nutmeg

salt and pepper

In a large skillet over medium-high heat, prepare the gravy according to the packet instructions. In the same skillet, combine all remaining ingredients and reduce heat to medium-low. Heat until the gravy begins to bubble. Serve hot.

Taco Pie

Serves 4 to 6

4 large flour or corn tortillas

1 (16-ounce) can refried beans

1 cup prepared mild salsa (page 199)

8 ounces Velveeta, cubed

1. Preheat the oven to 400°F.

2. In a greased pie pan, layer the ingredients 3 times in this order: tortilla, refried beans, ⅓ cup salsa, cheese. Top with the final tortilla and any remaining salsa and cheese.

3. Bake for 20 minutes, or until hot and bubbly.

4. Let stand for 10 minutes to thicken and then slice into wedges to serve.

Baja Fish Tacos

Serves 6

BAJA SAUCE

¾ cup sour cream

juice of 1 lime

1 teaspoon chili powder

½ teaspoon ground cumin

1 teaspoon garlic powder

½ teaspoon onion powder

2 jalapeño chiles, finely chopped

TACOS

6 corn tortillas

1 to 2 pounds cod fish fillets, pan-fried

3 cups fresh shredded purple cabbage

1 bunch fresh cilantro, chopped

½ onion, thinly sliced

1. In a small bowl, stir together all the sauce ingredients until thoroughly blended.

2. In a skillet, warm the tortillas over medium heat for 30 seconds on each side. To assemble the tacos, fill each tortilla with a piece of fish, shredded cabbage, cilantro sprigs, and sliced onion.

3. With a spoon, add the Baja Sauce to the tacos.

Crispy Chicken Tostadas

Serves 4

4 (5-inch) flour tortillas

vegetable oil, for coating tortillas

1 (15.5-ounce) can refried beans

1 (12.5-ounce) can chicken breast

shredded cheddar cheese

1 (2.25-ounce) can black olives, drained, sliced

lettuce or sprouts

salsa, for serving

1. Preheat the oven to 375°F.

2. Brush the tortillas with oil on both sides. Place on a baking sheet and bake for 5 to 8 minutes, until golden brown. Remove from the oven and let cool.

3. Top each tortilla with refried beans, chicken, cheese, and olives. Return to the oven for 5 minutes.

4. Top with lettuce or sprouts and serve with salsa.

Mexi-Tacos

For a crispier version, brush a light amount of oil on small corn tortillas, and bake them at 375°F for 8 minutes, flipping them over halfway through. Serves 5

1 tablespoon vegetable oil

½ onion, chopped

1 (15.4-ounce) can black beans, rinsed and drained

1 (15.4-ounce) can corn, rinsed and drained

¼ cup dehydrated red or green bell peppers, rehydrated

1 to 2 tablespoons coarsely chopped pickled jalapeños

1 tablespoon chili powder

¼ cup prepared salsa

salt and pepper

5 taco shells

1. Heat the oil in a skillet over medium heat. Sauté the onion in the oil until soft.

2. Stir in all the remaining ingredients except the taco shells and cook until heated through.

3. Spoon the hot filling into the taco shells and serve warm.

Chicken and Rice

Serves 4 to 6

1 cup uncooked rice

2 tablespoons vegetable oil

½ onion, chopped or 3 tablespoons dehydrated chopped onion

1 garlic clove, minced

2 (12.5-ounce) cans chunk chicken, chopped

1 (6-ounce) can sliced mushrooms

3 cups water

1 tablespoon paprika

salt and pepper

1 to 2 tablespoons all-purpose flour

1. Cook the rice according to the package directions.

2. While the rice is cooking, heat the oil in a skillet over medium heat. Sauté the onion and garlic in the oil until soft. Add the chicken and mushrooms and cook until everything begins to sizzle.

3. Pour the water into the skillet. Stir in the paprika and season to taste with salt and pepper. Cover and cook for 10 minutes, or until bubbly.

4. Spoon out 1 cup of the liquid into a bowl. Whisk in 1 tablespoon of flour, stirring until thickened. Add another tablespoon if not thick enough. Add back into the skillet and stir until the sauce has thickened.

5. Serve over the warm rice.

Spaghetti Casserole

Serves 4 to 5

1 pound spaghetti, cooked al dente and drained

1 (15-ounce) can spaghetti sauce

1 (14-ounce) can creamed spinach

1 (8-ounce) can sliced mushrooms, drained

½ cup fine breadcrumbs

¼ cup grated Parmesan cheese

2 tablespoons dried parsley

1. Preheat the oven to 400°F. Lightly grease a medium 1.8-liter casserole dish.

2. Mix the cooked spaghetti, spaghetti sauce, spinach, and mushrooms in the prepared casserole dish.

3. In a small bowl, stir together the breadcrumbs, Parmesan, and parsley. Sprinkle over the top of the casserole and bake for 30 minutes, or until heated through. If the top begins to get too brown, cover with foil.

Chicken Jambalaya

Serves 4 to 5

1 (12.5-ounce) can chunk chicken

1 cup uncooked white rice

½ cup stewed tomatoes

1 medium onion, chopped, or ⅓ cup dehydrated onion flakes

4 green onions, chopped, or 4 tablespoons dehydrated green onions

¼ cup chopped green bell peppers

⅓ cup chopped celery or 3 tablespoons dehydrated chopped celery

2 teaspoons Cajun seasoning, or more for extra heat

salt and pepper

¼ cup dry breadcrumbs

2 tablespoons butter, melted

1. Preheat the oven to 350°F. Lightly grease a 1.8-liter casserole dish.

2. In 4-quart a saucepan over medium heat, mix together the chicken, rice, and tomatoes. Allow to simmer, covered, for 10 minutes.

3. Add the onion, green onion, green pepper, and celery. Stir in the Cajun seasoning, salt, and pepper and stir well.

4. In a small bowl, combine the breadcrumbs and butter and stir until mixed thoroughly. Turn the jambalaya mixture into the baking dish and cover with the buttered crumbs. Bake for 1 hour.

King Chicken Casserole

Serves 8

1 (10-ounce) can Rotel tomatoes and chiles

1 (10-ounce) can condensed cream of mushroom soup

1 (10-ounce) can condensed cream of chicken soup

1 cup chopped yellow onion, fresh or ⅓ cup dehydrated yellow onion

2 (12.5-ounce) cans chunk chicken, drained

12 small corn tortillas, broken into pieces, or 4 cups crumbled tortilla chips

1 cup chicken broth

16 ounces Velveeta cheese, shredded and divided or 3 cups dehydrated shredded sharp cheddar cheese

1. Preheat the oven to 350°F. Lightly grease a 1.8-liter casserole dish.

2. In a large bowl, combine the tomatoes, soups, onion, and chicken.

3. In a medium bowl, soften the tortilla pieces or tortilla chips in the broth.

4. Layer the tortilla pieces, chicken mixture, and cheese in the baking dish. Repeat with remaining ingredients. Pour any remaining broth on top. Bake for 30 to 40 minutes.

Mandarin Orange Chicken

Serves 4 to 5

1 tablespoon vegetable oil

2 (12.5-ounce) cans chunk chicken, drained

¾ cup mandarin oranges, undrained

¼ cup soy sauce

1 tablespoon cornstarch

¾ teaspoon prepared yellow mustard

1 tablespoon distilled white vinegar

¼ teaspoon garlic powder

1 tablespoon minced onions (fresh or dehydrated)

½ cup fresh green bell pepper, diced or ⅓ cup dehydrated diced bell peppers

cooked rice, for serving

1. Heat the oil in a skillet over medium heat. Sauté the chicken in the hot oil.

2. Meanwhile, whisk together the juice from the mandarin orange can with the soy sauce, cornstarch, yellow mustard, and vinegar in a small bowl; set aside.

3. In the skillet, add onions and bell peppers and stir. Add the marinade and pour over the chicken in the skillet.

4. Reduce heat to low and allow it to simmer. Add the oranges, cover with a lid, and cook 5 more minutes. Serve with rice.

Bandito's Casserole

Serves 4 to 6

1 pound ground beef (fresh or 1 cup dehydrated ground beef crumbles)

1 medium onion, chopped, or ⅓ cup dehydrated onion, rehydrated

1 (4.3-ounce) box Spanish rice

1 (15.4-ounce) can pinto beans, drained

2 cups water

1 tablespoon taco seasoning

1 teaspoon ground cumin

salt and pepper

1. In a skillet over medium-high heat, brown the beef or cook the rehydrated beef for 5 minutes. Add the onion and allow to cook for 2 to 3 minutes.

2. Add the remaining ingredients to the pan and allow the mixture to come to an active simmer. Cover and reduce the heat to low.

3. Cook for 15 minutes until the rice is tender and serve warm.

Slow-Cooker Tropical Ham

Serves 10

1 pound canned ham

1 (15-ounce) can crushed pineapple

1 cup orange juice

3 tablespoons light brown sugar

1 teaspoon ground allspice

1. Remove the ham from the can, draining the juices. Place the ham in a slow cooker.

2. In a medium bowl, mix the pineapple with the orange juice. Pour over the ham. Sprinkle the brown sugar and allspice on top.

3. Cover and cook on low for 8 hours.

Chipped Beef on Toast

This recipe—a Great Depression staple—can be adapted to whatever you have on hand. Instead of the beef, you can add bacon, ham, or Spam.

Serves 4 to 5

2 tablespoons butter

2 tablespoons all-purpose flour

1½ cups milk

2 cups dried beef crumbles or 1 (12-ounce) jar chipped beef

½ teaspoon garlic powder

½ teaspoon Worcestershire sauce

dash of cayenne pepper

salt and pepper

toast or cooked rice

1. In a 4-quart saucepan over medium heat, melt the butter. Whisk in the flour, stirring until a thick roux forms.

2. Reduce heat to low, and add the milk a little at a time, stirring continuously until the mixture thickens and comes to a steady simmer.

3. Stir in the beef and seasonings. Serve over toast or over rice.

Chili Mac

For a speedy version of this dish, simply stir a can of chili with beans into a prepared box of macaroni and cheese. *Serves 4 to 5*

1 pound ground beef

2 tablespoons chili powder

1 tablespoon onion powder

1 tablespoon garlic powder

1 (15-ounce) can pinto beans, rinsed and drained

1 (3-ounce) can tomato paste

2 cups uncooked elbow macaroni

1. In a skillet over medium-high heat, brown the ground beef, breaking it up as it browns. Once the beef is cooked through, drain it and add seasonings. Then, stir in the beans and tomato paste.

2. Meanwhile, cook the macaroni al dente according to the package directions.

3. Drain the cooked pasta and stir it into the ground beef mixture in the skillet. Heat through, stirring gently.

Beef and Potato Nachos

Serves 4 to 5

1 pound ground beef

1 (15-ounce) can kidney beans, rinsed and drained

1 tablespoon onion powder

1 (1-ounce) packet taco seasoning

1 (4.5-ounce) can tomato paste

½ cup water

3 cups cooked diced potatoes

1 (4.5-ounce) can diced green chiles

1 (10-ounce) can condensed cheddar cheese soup

1 cup milk

½ teaspoon sugar

tortilla chips, for serving

1. Preheat the oven to 350°F.

2. In a skillet, cook the ground beef thoroughly, breaking it up with a spoon, drain any residual grease.

3. Stir in the beans, onion powder, taco seasoning, tomato paste, and water. Spread this mixture in the bottom of a greased 1.8-liter casserole dish.

4. In a medium bowl, stir together the potatoes and chiles. Pour over the beef mixture in the pan.

5. Using the same bowl as for the potatoes, mix together the soup, milk, and sugar. Pour evenly over the casserole in the pan.

6. Bake, covered, for 1 hour. Uncover and bake another 15 minutes. Let stand for 10 minutes before serving. Serve over tortilla chips.

Macaroni and Tomatoes

Serves 4 to 6

1 (8-ounce) package elbow macaroni

2 tablespoons butter, divided

1 small onion, chopped or ⅓ cup dehydrated chopped onions, rehydrated

1 (14.5-ounce) can tomato paste or 1 cup ketchup (purchased or made from recipe on page 188)

½ teaspoon granulated sugar

1 (14-ounce) can diced tomatoes

salt and pepper

1. Cook the macaroni according to the package directions until al dente. Drain and add to a bowl with 1 tablespoon of butter. Stir pasta to melt the butter, set aside.

2. In a skillet over medium heat, melt the remaining butter and sauté the onion until tender. Stir in the tomato paste (or ketchup) and sugar and let simmer for 5 minutes.

3. Add the tomatoes and then the cooked macaroni. Season with salt and pepper to taste.

4. Stir and simmer, uncovered, over low heat for 15 minutes.

Pasta e Fagioli

Serves 4 to 5

1 tablespoon olive oil

2 tablespoons dried minced onion

2 tablespoons dried minced garlic

¼ cup dehydrated or freeze-dried carrots

1 tablespoon dried basil

2 teaspoons dried oregano

dash of red pepper flakes

1 (14.5-ounce) can diced tomatoes, with juices

3 cups low-sodium chicken broth or vegetable broth, or 3 bouillon cubes mixed with 3 cups water, plus more as needed

1 (15.8-ounce) can Great Northern beans, rinsed and drained

1 cup uncooked tiny pasta shells (ditalini)

2 tablespoons parsley

grated Parmesan cheese and freshly ground black pepper, for topping

1. In a large, heavy pot over medium heat, combine the olive oil, onion, garlic, and carrots. Cook for 3 minutes, stirring, until carrots soften, about 5 minutes.

2. Add the dried basil, oregano, and red pepper flakes and toss to coat with the oil. Stir in the tomatoes and broth; bring to a boil.

3. Reduce the heat low and simmer, uncovered, for 30 minutes.

4. If the sauce seems too thick, add 1 cup of stock or water to thin, then stir in the beans and pasta. Simmer for 6 to 8 minutes, or until the pasta is tender. Stir in the parsley.

5. Serve hot, topped with grated Parmesan and freshly ground black pepper.

Spaghetti Salad

Serves 6

8 ounces uncooked spaghetti

2 teaspoons seasoning salt

3 tablespoons lemon juice

¼ cup Italian dressing

1 tomato, diced or ⅓ cup dehydrated diced tomato

1 cup diced fresh green bell pepper or ¼ cup dehydrated diced celery, rehydrated

½ cup chopped fresh celery or ¼ cup dehydrated chopped celery, rehydrated

½ cup diced onion, fresh or 4 tablespoons dehydrated chopped onion, rehydrated

1 (3.25-ounce) can sliced black olives, drained

¼ teaspoon ground black pepper

2 teaspoons grated Parmesan cheese

1. Cook the spaghetti according to the package directions. Drain.

2. In a large bowl, mix the cooked spaghetti and remaining ingredients and stir to combine. Serve chilled or at room temperature.

Mac and Cheese

Serves 5

1 (8-ounce) package elbow macaroni

4 tablespoons butter, divided

3 tablespoons all-purpose flour

1 garlic clove

2 cups milk

2 cups shredded cheddar cheese or 2 cups dehydrated shredded sharp cheddar cheese

1 teaspoon dry mustard

1 cup dry breadcrumbs

salt and pepper

1. Cook the macaroni according to the package directions. Meanwhile, preheat the oven to 425°F.

2. Drain the pasta and add to a lightly greased, 2.8-liter casserole dish along with 2 tablespoons of the butter. Stir until butter has melted.

3. Melt the remaining 2 tablespoons butter in a saucepan over low heat and slowly whisk in the flour. Cook, stirring, for 3 minutes until the mixture looks paste-like.

4. Add the garlic clove and slowly stir in the milk, whisking continuously until the sauce comes to a boil. Stir and cook an additional 5 minutes to let the sauce thicken.

5. Stir in the cheese, dry mustard, and season to taste with salt and pepper. Remove the garlic clove.

6. Pour the sauce over the cooked macaroni in the casserole dish. Top with the breadcrumbs.

7. Bake for 15 minutes, until the breadcrumbs are lightly toasted and the casserole is heated through.

Potato Gnocchi

6 fist-sized russet white potatoes

2 cups all-purpose flour

½ cup olive oil

1 egg

¼ teaspoon salt

marinara sauce or pesto, to serve

1. Boil the potatoes in their skins until soft. Once cooled, remove the skins.

2. Mash with a fork, or puree in the blender or food mill until the texture is similar to creamy mashed potatoes.

3. Bring a medium pot of water to a boil. On the counter next to the stove, prepare an ice bath with 6 cups ice and 6 cups water (or just use cold water).

4. In a large mixing bowl, combine the potatoes, flour, oil, egg, and salt, mixing well to create a dough. Knead the dough for 4 to 5 minutes, or until it feels dry to the touch.

5. Roll out the dough to ¾ inch thick, then cut it into strips with a pizza cutter or a knife.

6. Pick up the strips with a fork and drop them into the boiling water for 1 minute; when they are done they will float to the top of the water.

7. Immediately remove the cooked gnocchi and place it in the ice bath until cooled.

8. Drain the gnocchi well and serve with marinara sauce or pesto sauce.

CHAPTER 7

Beans & Rice

Beans and rice are the best pantry budget stretchers, bar none. Forming a complete protein when served together, they can serve 20 people for less than $5! Their tremendous amount of fiber is filling, and adding some tasty seasonings can make these humble ingredients into a delicious, satisfying meal.

Beans, Beans, the Magical Fruit

Most bean eaters today open a can and dump it out. But beans purchased in cans are far less tasty and a lot pricier than beans cooked from scratch. Canned beans are a great pantry addition for those times when cooking facilities are limited or when time is a factor, but you can't beat home-cooked beans for taste and economy.

STEP 1: Rinse and sort. Dried beans are often dirty, and you might even find the occasional insect. Not to worry—the first step gets rid of all that. Take a handful at a time, scanning for dried or withered legumes. Put them in a pot and cover with water. Swish them around and then drain them in a colander. Rinse briefly under running water.

STEP 2: Soak. Most beans cook far more quickly if they've been soaked first for 8 hours or more. (Split peas, lentils, black-eyed peas, lima beans, and fava beans don't require soaking.) To soak, cover the beans with water by about 2 inches and let them soak for 8 hours or longer. The beans will expand a great deal, so make sure to use a big enough container.

Soaking beans has another significant benefit—it loosens the outer skin and removes the oligosaccharides, the indigestible complex sugars that can cause intestinal gas.

Quick-soak method—If you forget to start soaking your beans far enough ahead of time, you can use this method to speed things up. Place the rinsed and sorted beans in a pot, cover them with water by about 2 inches, and bring to a boil. Cover the pot, remove from the heat, and let the beans soak. This can reduce your soaking time to 2 to 3 hours.

STEP 3: Cook. After soaking your beans, dump out the soaking water (plants love this water!) and rinse the beans. Place in a large stockpot and cover with 3 to 4 times as much water as beans. Bring to a boil, then reduce to a simmer. Note: Kidney, cannellini, and butter beans must be boiled on high for 10 minutes to neutralize a toxin that can cause extreme intestinal distress.

Expect to cook beans for 1 to 1½ hours, until they are tender and slightly soft. Split peas only take 30 to 45 minutes. All legumes and beans should be cooked thoroughly for ease of digestion.

Rice 101

Rice is the primary food staple of more than three billion people worldwide. It is inexpensive, versatile, and nutritious. Rice contains eight essential amino acids and 15 vitamins and minerals, and it's a great source of complex carbohydrates.

A single grain of rice is made up of several layers. The outer layer is an inedible hull. Only this hull is removed in the processing of brown rice, leaving the other nutritious layers intact. Sometimes brown rice is milled further, removing the bran and the germ, leaving it less nutritious. This is when brown rice starts getting stripped of its nutritional content. For white rice, the processing is taken a step further and the grain is polished, removing most of the nutritional value.

The downside to brown rice is that because it contains the oil-rich wheat germ, it's less stable. Brown rice can become rancid in as little as six months. That's why white rice, though far less nutritious, still has a place of value in a food storage pantry.

Cooking Techniques

The easiest way to cook rice is to bake it. It's absolutely foolproof. In a grid-down situation, if your oven is gas, you may still be able to use this method.

2 cups rice

4 cups water or stock

seasonings of choice

FOR BROWN RICE:

1. Preheat the oven to 375°F.

2. Put the rice and water or stock in a 4-quart saucepan and bring to a boil on the stovetop over medium-high heat.

3. Cover tightly with a lid and immediately place the pan in the oven.

4. Cook for exactly 1 hour—no peeking. Perfect fluffy rice!

FOR WHITE RICE:

1. Preheat the oven to 350°F.

2. Put the rice and water in a saucepan and bring to a boil on the stovetop over medium-high heat.

3. Cover tightly with an ovenproof lid and immediately place the pan in the oven.

4. Cook for exactly 30 minutes—no peeking. Perfect fluffy rice!

20 Ways to Eat Beans and Rice

A simple pot of cooked beans and rice can offer amazing variety with nothing more than a change of herbs, spices, and other additions. Prepare your beans and rice as directed, season them abundantly—and don't be afraid to adjust the seasonings to suit your family's preferences.

Most of the following recipes don't include step-by-step instructions. They are really just ways to jazz up your already-cooked beans and rice. Simply combine all the ingredients in a 6-quart saucepan and simmer over medium heat for about 10 minutes.

Arroz con Frijole

Serves 5 to 6

4 cups prepared white or brown rice

1 (15-ounce) can pinto beans, undrained and rinsed

1 tablespoon chili powder

2 teaspoons ground cumin

1 teaspoon garlic powder

1 teaspoon onion powder

1 tablespoon beef bouillon granules

1 (3-ounce) can tomato paste

Rice Fagioli

Serves 5

4 cups prepared white or brown rice

1 (15-ounce) can cannellini beans (white kidney beans), undrained

1 tablespoon garlic powder

1 tablespoon chicken bouillon granules

2 cups fresh spinach leaves

2 teaspoons Italian seasoning

grated Parmesan cheese, for serving

salt and pepper

Baltimore Beans and Rice

Serves 5 to 6

4 cups prepared white or brown rice

3 to 4 cups cooked black-eyed peas

1 cup fresh kale or spinach, chopped

1 tablespoon apple cider vinegar

1 tablespoon Worcestershire sauce

1 (15-ounce) can whole kernel corn, rinsed and drained

2 tablespoons Old Bay or Chesapeake seafood seasoning

Asian Beans and Rice

Serves 5 to 6

4 cups prepared white or brown rice

3 to 4 cups cooked black beans or adzuki beans

1 cup cooked diced carrots

¼ cup diced green onions or freeze-dried chives

1 teaspoon ground ginger

2 tablespoons soy sauce

1 (11-ounce) can mandarin oranges with juice

1 teaspoon Chinese five-spice powder

Mediterranean Beans and Rice

Serves 5 to 6

4 cups prepared white or brown rice

3 to 4 cups cooked cannellini beans (white kidney beans)

1 (6-ounce) jar marinated artichoke hearts, drained and chopped

1 teaspoon celery seed powder

1 tablespoon garlic powder

½ cup whole pitted green olives

1 tablespoon lemon juice

1 tablespoon dried parsley

1 teaspoon dried dill weed

salt and pepper

Indian Beans and Rice

Serves 5 to 6

4 cups prepared white or brown rice

3 to 4 cups cooked chickpeas

1 tablespoon curry powder

½ teaspoon ground cinnamon

1 cup canned diced tomatoes with green chiles

1 teaspoon ground ginger

salt and pepper

1 tablespoon chopped fresh cilantro (if available)

Lentil Stew with Rice

Serves 5 to 6

4 cups prepared white or brown rice

3 to 4 cups cooked brown lentils

1 teaspoon onion powder

1 teaspoon garlic powder

1 (15-ounce) can diced or stewed tomatoes

1 tablespoon dried thyme

East Indian Lentils and Rice

Serves 5 to 6

- 4 cups prepared white or brown rice
- 3 to 4 cups cooked brown lentils
- 1 cup cooked diced carrots
- 1 tablespoon minced garlic
- 1 teaspoon ground coriander
- 1 teaspoon ground cumin
- salt and pepper

Dal with Rice

Serves 5 to 6

- 4 cups prepared white or brown rice
- 3 to 4 cups cooked red lentils
- 1 teaspoon ground coriander
- 1 teaspoon ground cumin
- 1 tablespoon garlic powder
- 1 teaspoon curry powder
- 2 tablespoons lemon juice
- salt and pepper

New Orleans Red Beans and Rice

Serves 5 to 6

- 4 cups prepared white or brown rice
- 3 to 4 cups cooked red kidney beans
- 1 tablespoon dehydrated onion flakes
- 1 tablespoon dried minced garlic
- 1 tablespoon dehydrated bell pepper
- 1 cup diced ham
- 1 teaspoon cayenne pepper
- 1 teaspoon dried thyme
- 1 teaspoon dried sage
- 1 teaspoon dried parsley
- 1 tablespoon Cajun seasoning

New Year's Day Hoppin' John

Serves 5 to 6

- 4 cups prepared white or brown rice
- 3 to 4 cups cooked black-eyed peas
- 1 cup diced ham or meat from 1 leftover ham bone
- salt and pepper
- 1 teaspoon garlic powder
- 1 tablespoon onion powder
- crushed red pepper flakes, to taste

Creole Hoppin' John

Serves 5 to 6

- 4 cups prepared white or brown rice
- 3 to 4 cups cooked black-eyed peas
- 1 tablespoon onion powder
- 1 teaspoon garlic powder
- 1 teaspoon paprika
- 1 tablespoon chili powder
- ½ teaspoon cayenne pepper
- 1 teaspoon dried thyme
- 1 cup diced fresh tomatoes

Cuban Beans and Rice

Serves 5 to 6

- 4 cups prepared white or brown rice
- 3 to 4 cups cooked black beans
- 1 tablespoon dried bell peppers (or 1 tablespoon fresh, if available)
- 1 tablespoon chili powder
- 1 teaspoon garlic powder
- 1 teaspoon onion powder
- 1 tablespoon lemon or lime juice
- 1 tablespoon chopped fresh cilantro (if available)

Cuban Beans and Rice II

Serves 5 to 6

- 4 cups prepared white or brown rice
- 3 to 4 cups cooked black beans
- 1 (15-ounce) can Rotel tomatoes with chiles
- 1 (15-ounce) can whole kernel corn, rinsed and drained
- 1 tablespoon chili powder
- 1 tablespoon garlic powder
- 1 teaspoon onion powder
- 1 tablespoon lemon or lime juice
- 1 tablespoon chopped fresh cilantro (if available)

Louisiana Country Beans and Rice

Serves 5 to 6

- 4 cups prepared white or brown rice
- 3 to 4 cups cooked red kidney beans
- 1 (15-ounce) can Rotel tomatoes with green chiles
- 1 tablespoon dehydrated onion flakes
- 1 tablespoon dried minced garlic
- 1 tablespoon dried oregano
- dash of hot sauce, or to taste

Lemon Black Beans and Rice

Serves 5 to 6

4 cups prepared white or brown rice

3 to 4 cups cooked black beans

1 tablespoon lemon juice

1 teaspoon garlic powder

1 tablespoon chopped fresh cilantro (if available)

Pirate Beans and Rice

Serves 5 to 6

4 cups prepared white or brown rice

3 to 4 cups cooked black beans

1 tablespoon dark rum

2 tablespoons dark brown sugar

½ cup diced carrots, cooked

1 tablespoon garlic powder

1 tablespoon onion powder

1 tablespoon dried parsley

salt and pepper

Beefy Enchilada Beans and Rice

Serves 5 to 6

4 cups prepared white or brown rice

3 to 4 cups cooked pinto beans

1 pound ground beef, cooked, or 1 cup dehydrated meat crumbles

½ cup canned diced green chiles

1 (10-ounce) can tomato paste

1 tablespoon chili powder

1 teaspoon ground cumin

1 tablespoon garlic powder

1 teaspoon onion powder

Bean Fried Rice

Serves 5 to 6

4 cups prepared white or brown rice

3 to 4 cups cooked black beans

1 teaspoon ground ginger

1 teaspoon Chinese five-spice powder

¼ cup chopped green onions or chives

1 cup canned peas and carrots, drained

1 tablespoon soy sauce

1 tablespoon plum sauce

CHAPTER 8

Kid-Approved Snacks

Caring for kids in the midst of a crisis can be difficult; when children are in a chaotic and unpredictable environment, they pick up on the stress and may act out, regress, or withdraw. Including your children in preparations can help them learn to adapt to the situation at hand. One woman shared that when her family was in the middle of an emergency, they sat together and said, "We're not scared, because we're prepared." Repeating this simple sentence helped her family find a sense of peace, knowing that Mom and Dad had the situation handled.

Let your kids feel like part of the solution by allowing them to ask questions and give their input. Enlist their assistance—most kids love helping out Mom or Dad! Adding some of their favorite foods to the emergency menu will help give them a sense of normality.

Graham Crackers

Makes 4 dozen

½ cup vegetable shortening

¾ cup packed light brown sugar

1½ teaspoons vanilla extract

1½ cups whole wheat flour

½ cup all-purpose flour

1 teaspoon baking powder

½ teaspoon baking soda

¼ teaspoon salt

1 teaspoon ground cinnamon

½ cup milk

½ cup ground flax seed or wheat germ, or 2 tablespoons honey (optional)

1. In a medium bowl, cream together the shortening and brown sugar with a spoon. Stir in the vanilla.

2. In a large bowl, combine the whole wheat and all-purpose flours, baking powder, baking soda, salt, and cinnamon. Beat into the creamed mixture alternately with the milk. Stir in the flax seed, wheat germ, or honey, if using. Cover and chill until firm.

3. Preheat the oven to 350°F. Grease two baking sheets.

4. On a lightly floured surface, roll the dough to a ⅛-inch thickness. Cut into 2-inch rectangles for mini graham crackers or cut into 4-inch rectangles for traditional-size crackers. Place ½ inch apart on the prepared cookie sheets.

5. Bake for 10 to 12 minutes in the preheated oven, until crisp. The edges will be golden brown. Remove from baking sheet to cool on wire racks. Store in an airtight container for up to 2 weeks.

Applesauce

Serves 4

6 sweet apples (such as Gala, Jonathan, or McIntosh), peeled, cored, and quartered

1 teaspoon ground cinnamon (optional)

¾ cup water

3 tablespoons brown sugar (optional)

1. Place the apples in a medium saucepan over medium-low heat. Sprinkle with cinnamon, if you wish. Add the water and cook, covered, until the apple bits become soft, about 10 minutes.

2. Using a blender or a potato masher, mash the apples until the sauce has the texture you want.

3. Stir in brown sugar, if desired, and mix well.

Oatmeal Snack Mix

Serves 3 to 4

2 cups rolled oats

½ cup honey

1 teaspoon ground cinnamon

1 teaspoon salt

1 cup dried apple cubes or other dried fruit (or a combination)

½ cup nuts (whatever you have on hand, such as pecans, walnuts, or almonds)

2 cups square cereal pieces (oat, corn, or rice)

1. Preheat the oven to 325°F.

2. Lightly spray a rimmed baking sheet with cooking spray. Spread the oatmeal on the sheet and drizzle with the honey. Sprinkle with the cinnamon and salt.

3. Bake for 20 minutes, removing from the oven every 5 minutes to stir.

4. Stir in the fruit, nuts, and cereal squares. Let cool and then store in an airtight container.

Homemade Saltine Crackers

Makes 30 crackers

2 cups all-purpose flour

¾ teaspoon salt, plus more for sprinkling

⅔ cup milk

3 tablespoons butter, melted, plus more for brushing

½ teaspoon baking soda

10 ounces shredded cheddar cheese or 1 (1-ounce) packet ranch dressing mix (optional)

1. Preheat the oven to 400°F. Grease a baking sheet.

2. In a large bowl, stir together the flour, ¾ teaspoon salt, milk, butter, and baking soda. If you want to make flavored crackers, stir in cheese or ranch dressing mix. Knead the dough well for 1 or 2 minutes.

3. On a floured surface, roll the dough very thin, about ⅛ inch thick. Transfer in one piece to the baking sheet.

4. Score the dough with a pizza cutter or knife. Brush the top very lightly with butter and sprinkle with a little salt. (You can leave out this step if you want unsalted crackers.)

5. Bake for about 12 minutes. Let crackers cool on a wire rack. They will harden once they start to cool. Break into pieces and store in an airtight container.

Chunky Peanut Butter Balls

To add a special touch, roll the balls in crushed graham crackers or cookies before chilling them. *Makes 20 balls*

1 cup chunky peanut butter

1 cup quick-cooking rolled oats, toasted in the oven

⅓ cup crushed dehydrated apples

¾ teaspoon vanilla extract

½ teaspoon ground cinnamon

dash of salt

1 bar dark chocolate, melted, for drizzling (optional)

1. Combine all ingredients except the melted chocolate, if using, in a medium bowl and stir well to combine.

2. Spoon out a heaping tablespoon of the mixture and roll between your hands to form a ball. Place on a plate. Repeat to make the rest of the peanut butter balls.

3. Cover and refrigerate for a couple of hours. If using the melted chocolate, drizzle the chocolate on the chilled peanut butter balls before serving. Chill for an additional 20 minutes for chocolate to set.

Chocolate Crackers

Makes 20 crackers

about 20 saltine crackers, either store-bought or Homemade Saltine Crackers (page 267)

¾ cup unsalted butter

¾ cup packed brown sugar

¼ teaspoon vanilla extract

4 cups semisweet chocolate chips

½ cup toffee bits, peanut butter chips, cookie sprinkles, or other topping (optional)

1. Preheat the oven to 375°F.

2. Line a rimmed baking sheet with foil and arrange the crackers on the foil so they aren't touching.

3. In a 1-quart saucepan over low heat, stir together the butter, brown sugar, and vanilla until the butter is melted and the sugar is well incorporated. Pour the mixture over the crackers and place in the oven for 5 minutes.

4. Remove from the oven and sprinkle the chocolate chips onto the crackers. As the chocolate begins to melt, spread it over the cracker tops until they are evenly coated. If you wish, sprinkle on toffee bits, peanut butter chips, or your favorite topping.

5. Place the partly cooled baking sheet in the refrigerator to chill completely. Store in an airtight container.

Yummus Hummus

Accompany this dip alongside raw veggies, pita chips, or crackers. It can also be used as a sandwich spread. *Serves 2 to 3*

1 (15-ounce) can chickpeas, rinsed and drained

2 tablespoons lemon juice

¼ cup extra-virgin olive oil, plus more for drizzling

2 garlic cloves, crushed and minced

½ teaspoon sea salt

1½ teaspoons ground cumin

⅛ teaspoon cayenne pepper

chopped parsley, for garnish

Place the chickpeas, lemon juice, ¼ cup olive oil, garlic, salt, cumin, and cayenne in the bowl of a food processor. Process until smooth. To serve, drizzle with more olive oil and garnish with parsley.

Carrot-Orange Salad

Serves 4 to 5

5 to 7 carrots, peeled

2 apples, peeled and cored

juice of 1 orange or other citrus fruit

chopped pineapple (optional)

1. Shred the carrots and apples in a food processor or with a cheese grater. (If you have a food processor, it will save you time and energy!)

2. Transfer the shredded carrots, apples, and chopped pineapple, if using, to a large bowl and squeeze orange juice over them.

3. Cover and refrigerate for 1 hour to allow the flavors to meld. Serve chilled.

Good Ol' Bean Dip

Offer homemade tortilla chips or crisp vegetables for dipping. To make a spicier dip, add a dash of cayenne pepper. *Serves 2 to 3*

1 (15-ounce) can refried beans

1 tablespoon brine from bottled jalapeño slices

½ teaspoon ground cumin

½ teaspoon salt

½ teaspoon white pepper

½ teaspoon granulated sugar

1 teaspoon chili powder

Mix all the ingredients together in a bowl until thoroughly blended. Cover and chill for at least 1 hour before serving.

Cowboy Crackers

Makes about 25 crackers

1 sleeve of packaged saltine crackers or 38 Homemade Saltine Crackers (page 267)

1 (.4-ounce) packet ranch dressing mix

1⅓ cups vegetable oil

⅛ to ¼ teaspoon crushed red pepper flakes

1. Preheat oven to 250°F. Place the crackers in a 1-gallon zip-top plastic bag.

2. Whisk together the remaining ingredients in a small bowl. Pour the mixture over the crackers and shake to coat.

3. Lay the bag flat and flip it over every 10 minutes for 1 hour to make sure all the crackers are generously coated.

4. Place spiced crackers on a baking sheet and bake for 20 minutes.

Cinnamon Apple Protein Snack

Serves 3 to 4

> 1 tablespoon ground cinnamon
>
> 1 (1-ounce) scoop vanilla protein powder
>
> 3 large apples, peeled, cored, and sliced

Pour the cinnamon and protein powder into a resealable plastic bag. Add the apples, seal the bag, and shake until the slices are coated with the cinnamon mixture. Serve immediately.

Granola

Serves 8

> 3 cups rolled oats
>
> ½ cup sweetened flaked coconut
>
> ½ cup coarsely chopped nuts (such almonds, pecans, or peanuts)
>
> ½ cup unsalted shelled sunflower seeds
>
> ½ cup honey or maple syrup
>
> ⅓ cup vegetable oil
>
> ¼ teaspoon ground cinnamon
>
> dash of almond extract
>
> dash of coconut extract
>
> ½ to 1 cup dried fruit (cherries, apples, bananas, cranberries, raisins, or blueberries are great choices)
>
> ¼ cup semisweet chocolate chips (optional)

1. Preheat the oven to 300°F.

2. Combine all the ingredients in a large bowl and stir thoroughly. Spread on a rimmed baking sheet.

3. Bake for 20 to 25 minutes, or until lightly toasted. The granola will crisp up more as it cools. Allow to cool completely, then store in an airtight container.

PB and Jelly Oat Bars

Serves 8 to 10

1 cup firmly packed dark brown sugar

¾ cup unsalted butter or vegetable shortening

½ cup peanut butter

2 cups all-purpose flour

1 teaspoon salt

½ teaspoon baking soda

1½ cups instant rolled oats

½ cup unsalted shelled sunflower seeds

dash of vanilla extract

⅓ cup water

1 cup jelly (your choice of flavor)

1. Preheat the oven to 400°F. Grease a 13 x 9-inch baking pan.

2. In the bowl of an electric mixer, combine the brown sugar, butter or shortening, and peanut butter. Beat on medium speed until well blended.

3. In a medium bowl, stir together the flour, salt, and baking soda. At low speed, gradually add the dry ingredients to the creamed mixture. Stir in the oats, sunflower seeds, and vanilla until well blended. With the mixer running, add the water 1 tablespoon at a time.

4. Divide the dough in half and press half of it into the bottom of the greased pan. Spread evenly with the jelly.

5. Flatten small amounts of the remaining dough between your hands and arrange evenly on top of the jelly so that the dough sections are touching. Fill in any spaces with dough so that the jelly is completely covered.

6. Bake for 25 to 30 minutes, or until the top is golden brown and the edges are slightly brown. Do not overbake.

7. While warm, cut into bars about 2½ by 2 inches. Allow to cool completely and store in an airtight container.

Cheese Crackers

Add extra seasonings for different cracker flavors. Red pepper flakes, taco seasoning, or ranch dressing mix will add flair to this recipe.

Makes about 75 crackers

¼ cup (½ stick) butter, at room temperature

1¾ cups shredded cheddar cheese

½ teaspoon sea salt, plus a bit more to sprinkle on top

¾ cup all-purpose flour, plus more for dusting

2 tablespoons milk

1. In a large bowl, cream the butter, cheese, and salt together until completely blended. Add the flour and mix until the dough is soft and crumbly. Add 1 tablespoon of milk at a time until the dough comes together.

2. Refrigerate the dough, covered, for 1 hour.

3. Preheat the oven to 350°F.

4. On a floured surface, roll the chilled dough to a thickness of about ⅛ inch. Divide in half. On a piece of parchment paper, roll half of the dough into a very thin 12 x 9-inch rectangle. Cut into 1-inch squares, using a pizza cutter; arrange on parchment paper and lift the sheet of parchment onto a baking sheet. Repeat with the other half of the dough.

5. Using a fork or toothpick, poke holes in the center of each cracker and sprinkle with salt.

6. Bake for 10 to 15 minutes, or until the crackers are puffed up and beginning to brown on the edges. Transfer the crackers to a wire rack or plate to cool. When completely cool, store in an airtight container.

CHAPTER 9

Side Dishes

Incorporating vegetables into a meal to go along with the main dish is a great opportunity to add vitamins and other nutrients and provide a more complete meal for your family. Many of the following dishes can be refined to suit your individual preference or situation. Keep in mind that many can be adapted using freeze-dried or dehydrated ingredients to provide nutrition not only in the summertime, but all year—see the chart on page 241.

Sautéed Spinach

Serves 4 to 5

1 tablespoon olive oil

2 garlic cloves, sliced

5 cups spinach, washed and chopped

salt and pepper

Heat the oil in a skillet over medium heat. Sauté the sliced garlic in the oil for 1 minute. Add the spinach and cook for 1 minute. Serve warm.

Spiced Vegetable Medley

This makes a great vegetarian taco filling. Add a cup of beans, and you're set! For a spicier version, chop and sauté a jalapeño chile in with vegetables. *Serves 4 to 5*

1 tablespoon olive oil

½ onion, chopped

3 garlic cloves, minced

kernels from 2 ears of corn

1 zucchini, diced

1 yellow squash, diced

1 bell pepper, chopped

2 tablespoons chili powder

salt and pepper

1 cup spinach, chopped

1. Heat the olive oil in a large skillet over medium heat. Sauté the onion in the oil for 2 minutes. Add the garlic and sauté for an additional minute.

2. Add the corn, zucchini, summer squash, and bell pepper. Cook for 4 minutes, stirring frequently, or until the vegetables begin to soften.

3. Season with the chili powder, salt, and pepper, stirring well.

4. Turn off heat and stir in the spinach. Serve warm.

Sautéed Cabbage and Bacon

Serves 6

3 bacon slices, cooked and chopped, or ¼ cup bacon bits

½ onion, chopped

1 head cabbage, chopped

salt and pepper

1. In a large pan, heat the bacon pieces over medium heat to release the bacon grease. Add the onion and sauté with the bacon for 2 minutes.

2. Add the cabbage and sauté, stirring, for 4 minutes.

3. Season with salt and pepper to taste.

Peas with Lemon Pepper

Serves 4

1 (10-ounce) package frozen peas, thawed, or 1 (15-ounce) can peas

1 tablespoon water

2 tablespoons butter

2 teaspoons lemon pepper seasoning

⅛ teaspoon dried dill

salt and pepper

Combine all the ingredients in a 4-quart saucepan over medium heat. Heat, stirring, until the mixture reaches an active simmer.

Corn Fritters

Serves 6

2 cups cornmeal

2 eggs, lightly beaten

¾ cup all-purpose flour, sifted

½ teaspoon salt

1 tablespoon sugar

¼ teaspoon white pepper

1 teaspoon baking powder

vegetable oil, for frying

1. Mix together the cornmeal and eggs. Stir in the flour, salt, sugar, pepper, and baking powder.

2. Heat oil in a skillet over medium-high heat. Drop tablespoons of batter into the hot oil. Cook the fritters 2 to 4 minutes, or until golden on both sides, turning once.

Stewed Lentils

Serves 4 to 6

1 cup lentils	1 (28-ounce) can diced tomatoes
2½ cups water	2 vegetable or beef bouillon cubes
2 teaspoons olive oil	2 teaspoons mild curry powder
1 cup dehydrated carrots	2 teaspoons dried thyme
1 tablespoon minced dried garlic	1 tablespoon red wine vinegar
1 tablespoon minced dried onion	salt and pepper

1. Rinse and pick over the lentils to remove any stones or debris.

2. Place the lentils in a 4-quart saucepan and pour in the water. Add the olive oil, carrots, garlic, onion, tomatoes, bouillon, curry, and thyme.

3. Bring to a boil over medium-high heat, then lower the heat to medium-low and simmer, covered, for about 40 minutes, or until the lentils are tender. Check occasionally to be sure the liquid is still simmering; add more water if needed.

4. Remove from the heat and allow the lentils to sit, covered, for another 10 minutes. Stir in the vinegar, season to taste with salt and pepper, and serve hot.

Creamed Peas

Serves 4

1 (10-ounce) package frozen peas, thawed, or 1 (15-ounce) can peas	salt and pepper
1 tablespoon butter	1 tablespoon breadcrumbs or cracker crumbs (optional)
⅓ cup heavy cream or Heavy Cream Substitute (page 321)	

1. In a medium saucepan, combine the peas, butter, and cream or substitute. Season to taste with salt and pepper. Over medium heat, bring the mixture to an active simmer, stirring frequently.

2. Remove from the heat. If you wish, add 1 tablespoon breadcrumbs or cracker crumbs to thicken the sauce.

Potato Croquettes

Serves 4

1½ cups water

4 cups instant potato flakes

2 tablespoons milk

¼ cup dehydrated onions

1 teaspoon garlic powder

½ teaspoon salt

¼ teaspoon pepper

3 dashes of Tabasco sauce (optional)

1 egg

1½ cups dry breadcrumbs

vegetable oil for frying

1. In a saucepan over high heat, bring the water to a rapid boil. Stir in the instant mashed potatoes. Add the milk and dehydrated onions, garlic powder, salt, pepper, and Tabasco sauce, stirring well until combined.

2. Using an ice cream scoop, form balls of mashed potatoes.

3. Beat the egg in a small bowl. Place the dry breadcrumbs in another small bowl or rimmed pan. Dip the potato balls in egg and then dredge in breadcrumbs.

4. Pour oil to a depth of 2 inches in a deep skillet. Heat the oil in the skillet over medium-high heat. Fry the potato balls in the oil until the breadcrumbs become golden brown, flipping to brown completely, about 3 to 4 minutes.

Hominy Casserole

Serves 4

3 tablespoons unsalted butter

1 cup chopped onion

2 (15-ounce) cans hominy, undrained

1 (4-ounce) can chopped green chiles, rinsed and drained

½ pound Velveeta, cubed or ¾ cup dehydrated sharp cheddar cheese

1 cup sour cream

½ teaspoon ground cumin

2 garlic cloves, minced

½ cup rehydrated meat crumbles, such as ham or ground beef (optional)

salt and pepper

1. Preheat the oven to 350°F.

2. In a large skillet over medium heat, melt the butter and sauté the onions until soft. Add hominy in a saucepan over medium heat until the liquid from the can has evaporated. Add salt and pepper.

3. Mix in the chiles, cheese, sour cream, cumin, garlic, and meat crumbles (if using). Pour into an ungreased 1.8-liter casserole dish and bake for 30 minutes.

Un-fried Refried Beans

Un-fried refried beans are great served with rice as a main dish or side dish for a Tex-Mex meal. Use them as a tortilla filling or dip. Spice things up with hot sauce as desired. *Serves 4*

2 tablespoons dried onion flakes

2 tablespoons dried garlic flakes

2 tablespoons dried chopped bell pepper

¼ cup boiling water

1 (15.4-ounce) can pinto beans, rinsed and drained, or 1 cup dried pinto beans, cooked

3 tablespoons tomato paste

1 tablespoon chili powder

1 tablespoon ground cumin

salt, to taste

1. In a small bowl, combine the onion, garlic, and pepper. Pour the boiling water over the mixture.

2. While the vegetables are rehydrating, combine the other ingredients in a small saucepan over low heat, stirring frequently.

3. Stir in the rehydrated vegetables and continue to heat until warmed through.

Stuffed Spaghetti Squash

Serves 3 to 4

1 spaghetti squash, halved and seeded (about 2 pounds)

1 (15.5-ounce) can white beans, drained and rinsed

1 (15.5-ounce) can black-eyed peas, drained and rinsed

1 garlic clove, minced

¾ teaspoon salt

3 tablespoons balsamic vinegar

1 tablespoon Dijon mustard

1 teaspoon honey

3 tablespoons olive oil

1½ tablespoons Italian seasoning

1. Preheat the oven to 375°F. In a large baking dish, arrange the squash halves and pour in 1-inch of water. Bake for 45 minutes, or until tender.

2. In a 4-quart saucepan over medium-high heat, combine the beans, black-eyed peas, and garlic and heat through.

3. In a small bowl, whisk together the vinegar, mustard, honey, olive oil, and Italian seasoning.

4. Using a fork, loosen the squash pulp from the shell. Top with the bean mixture and drizzle the balsamic vinaigrette over the top.

Mashed Potatoes

Serves 4 to 5

3 to 5 red or russet potatoes (about 6 pounds), peeled

1 to 2 tablespoons butter

½ cup milk

½ teaspoon salt

1. Cook the potatoes in a large pot of boiling water over medium-high heat, ensuring that all the potatoes are covered. Cook the potatoes until soft, and drain in a colander.

2. Add the butter to the potatoes and mash with a potato masher.

3. Pour milk into potatoes and add the salt, continuing to mash potatoes.

4. Mash until potatoes are smooth. Serve warm.

Green Bean Salad

Serves 4

¼ cup olive oil

3 tablespoons red wine vinegar

1½ teaspoons Dijon mustard

1 teaspoon salt

¼ teaspoon pepper

3 cups cooked green beans

½ cup chopped fresh basil leaves

1 tablespoon Italian seasoning

4 ounces feta cheese, crumbled

In a small bowl, whisk together the olive oil, vinegar, mustard, salt, and pepper. Place the green beans and remaining ingredients in a medium bowl and pour the dressing over them; toss well.

Personal Eggplant Marinara

Serves 4 to 6

2 or 3 small eggplants (2 to 3 pounds)

olive oil, as needed

1 to 2 tablespoons Italian seasoning

1 (24-ounce) jar marinara sauce or 5 cups homemade Spaghetti Meat Sauce (page 201)

1 cup grated Parmesan cheese

1. Preheat the oven to 375°F.

2. Cut the eggplants into ½-inch-thick slices. Brush the eggplant with olive oil and sprinkle with Italian seasoning.

3. Spoon marinara sauce into the bottom of a large baking dish, and arrange the eggplant slices in the dish. Top each slice with 1 or 2 spoonfuls of marinara sauce and sprinkle on the cheese.

4. Bake for 20 minutes, covered, or until the cheese is golden brown and the eggplant is soft.

Broccoli-Cauliflower Medley with Cheese Sauce

Serves 4

1 tablespoon butter

1 tablespoon all-purpose flour

1 cup half and half or Heavy Cream Substitute (page 321)

1½ cups cubed Velveeta cheese or ½ cup dehydrated shredded sharp cheddar cheese (1-inch cubes)

salt and pepper

½ teaspoon garlic powder

⅛ teaspoon paprika

4 cups cooked broccoli and cauliflower florets

1. In a skillet over medium heat, melt the butter and whisk in the flour.

2. Gradually whisk in the half and half or cream substitute and bring to an active simmer. Whisk until smooth.

3. Add the Velveeta and seasonings and continue to stir until the cheese is melted and completely incorporated.

4. Pour the sauce over the vegetables just before serving.

Baked Potato Chips

Serves 4 to 6

5 to 6 unpeeled russet potatoes, very thinly sliced (about 4 pounds)

¼ cup olive oil

1 tablespoon chili powder or other seasoning (such as ranch dressing mix or Italian seasoning)

salt and pepper

cooking spray

1. Preheat the oven to 400°F. Spray two rimmed baking sheets with cooking spray.

2. Boil the potato slices in water, uncovered, for 8 minutes; drain.

3. In a large bowl, combine the olive oil and chili powder or other seasoning, and mix until incorporated. Add the potatoes to the bowl and gently toss to coat.

4. Spread the potato slices in a single layer on each prepared baking sheet. Cook for 10 to 15 minutes and then flip the slices over. Bake for an additional 10 to 15 minutes.

5. Let the potato chips cool for 10 minutes before serving.

Baked Kale Chips

You can make a dehydrated version of kale chips the same way as this recipe—just dehydrate the kale until crispy rather than baking it. Store in a zip-top bag. *Serves 2*

1 bunch kale

1 tablespoon olive oil

1 teaspoon seasoning salt

1 teaspoon red wine vinegar (optional)

1. Preheat the oven to 350°F. Line a baking sheet with parchment paper.

2. Using a knife or kitchen shears, cut the kale leaves from the thick stems. Tear into bite-size pieces. Wash and thoroughly dry the leaves, using a salad spinner.

3. Spread the kale on the prepared baking sheet and drizzle with the olive oil. Sprinkle with seasoning salt, and use a spray bottle to spritz the kale with the red wine vinegar, if using.

4. Bake until the edges of the kale have browned but aren't burnt, 10 to 15 minutes. Store the baked chips in an airtight container.

Tomatoes Balsamico

This side dish is great cooked or uncooked! To make it more filling, spread a few spoonfuls of fresh ricotta or farmer's cheese over the tomatoes before topping them with the other ingredients. Add a spoonful of marinara sauce to each serving. *Makes 6 (2-slice) servings*

3 or 4 medium to large tomatoes, thickly sliced

3 tablespoons balsamic vinaigrette dressing (page 283)

1 garlic clove, minced

¼ cup grated Parmesan cheese

1 tablespoon dried or 2 tablespoons fresh basil

salt and pepper

1. Preheat the oven to 400°F.

2. Spread the tomatoes on a baking sheet lined with foil. Brush with the vinaigrette, and sprinkle on the garlic and Parmesan cheese. Add the salt and pepper to taste.

3. Top with basil and roast for 20 minutes.

Poppaw's Turnip Greens

Serves 6

1 pound turnip greens

5 or 6 turnip roots, peeled and quartered (about 3 pounds)

juice of 1 lemon

1 onion, chopped

4 bacon slices, cooked and chopped, drippings reserved

salt and pepper

1. Rinse the turnip greens several times to remove any grit and tear the leaves into bite-size pieces.

2. Place the turnip roots and greens in a large pot and fill halfway with water. (The greens will greatly reduce in volume while cooking, so don't use too much water.) Add the lemon juice.

3. Place the chopped onion, chopped bacon, and bacon drippings in the pot with the turnips and greens.

4. Cook over medium heat, covered, until the turnips are tender, about 30 minutes. Season with salt and pepper to taste.

Jessica's Sweet Kale Salad

Serves 4 to 6

1 bunch kale, chopped

½ cup raisins or dried cranberries

½ cup raw, unsalted shelled pumpkin seeds

1 unpeeled green apple, cored and diced

1 avocado, chopped

olive oil

Celtic sea salt, pepper, ground coriander, and ground cumin, to taste

Mix together the kale, raisins or cranberries, pumpkin seeds, apple, and avocado. Drizzle with olive oil. Season as you like with salt and pepper, coriander, and cumin. Toss gently to combine.

Sweet Potato Bake

Serves 4 to 6

3 sweet potatoes, mashed

¼ cup milk

2 teaspoons vanilla extract

PECAN CRUMBLE TOPPING

½ cup finely chopped pecans

½ cup packed brown sugar

½ cup packed brown sugar

¼ teaspoon salt

3 tablespoons all-purpose flour

¼ cup (½ stick) butter, softened

1. Preheat the oven to 375°F.

2. Combine the sweet potatoes, milk, vanilla, brown sugar, and salt; mix well. Transfer to a lightly greased baking dish.

3. Work the topping ingredients together to form a crumbly mixture. Sprinkle over the sweet potato mixture.

4. Bake, uncovered, for 25 minutes.

Mixed Vegetables with Dijon Mustard Sauce

Serves 4 to 5

4 cups mixed fresh vegetables (such as broccoli, cauliflower, carrots, and asparagus)

salt and pepper

1 cup sour cream

2 tablespoons red wine vinegar

¼ cup Dijon mustard

2 teaspoons sugar

⅛ teaspoon cayenne pepper

1. Steam the vegetables for 4 to 5 minutes, to the desired degree of doneness.

2. Meanwhile, whisk together the remaining ingredients in a small saucepan. Warm the sauce over low heat until it just begins to simmer.

3. Serve the sauce with the cooked vegetables.

Creamed Corn and Carrots

Serves 5

1 tablespoon olive oil

2 medium red potatoes, diced

1 carrot, peeled and chopped

½ medium onion, diced

2 cups water

2 (8.5-ounce) cans cream-style corn, undrained

1½ teaspoons salt

pepper

½ cup milk

½ cup cooked diced bacon or bacon bits

1. In a large sauté pan over medium heat, add the olive oil and sauté the potatoes, carrot, and onion until the onion pieces are soft.

2. Add the water, corn, salt, and pepper and simmer for 20 minutes.

3. Stir in the milk and bacon pieces and bring to an active simmer.

Zucchini Boats

Serves 6

3 zucchini squash halved lengthwise

3 tablespoons olive oil

½ cup shredded mozzarella cheese

¾ teaspoon dried basil

½ teaspoon Italian seasoning

2 garlic cloves, minced

2 tablespoons dried onion flakes

2 or 3 small tomatoes, thinly sliced

¼ cup dry breadcrumbs

¼ cup grated Parmesan cheese

salt and pepper

1. Preheat the oven to 350°F.

2. With a spoon, scrape out the seeds from the zucchini halves.

3. Place the zucchini halves on a baking sheet and coat with olive oil. Sprinkle on the mozzarella cheese, basil, Italian seasoning, garlic, onion flakes, salt, and pepper.

4. Arrange tomato slices on the zucchini. Top with the breadcrumbs and Parmesan cheese.

5. Bake for 25 minutes, or until the tops are golden.

Onion Gratin

Serves 4

2 large yellow onions, cut into ¼-inch slices	1 tablespoon all-purpose flour
1 tablespoon olive oil	1 cup Heavy Cream Substitute (page 321)
1 cup dry breadcrumbs	¼ teaspoon garlic powder
salt and pepper	¼ cup white wine
3 tablespoons dried thyme	½ cup grated Parmesan cheese
1 tablespoon butter	

1. Preheat the oven to 375°F.

2. Spread the onions on a rimmed baking sheet and drizzle with the olive oil. Coat with the breadcrumbs, season with salt and pepper to taste, and sprinkle with thyme. Bake for 15 minutes.

3. Meanwhile, make a roux by melting the butter in a medium sauté pan over medium heat and whisking in the flour. Add the heavy cream substitute and garlic powder and whisk until the mixture thickens. Add the wine and stir until the mixture bubbles.

4. Transfer the onions to a 4-quart baking dish and spoon the cream sauce onto them. Top with Parmesan cheese. Cover with foil and bake for 35 minutes, or until the top is golden brown.

5. When ready to serve, drizzle the sauce in the dish over the onions.

Balsamic Vinaigrette Dressing

Serves 6

¼ cup extra virgin olive oil	1 teaspoon prepared mustard
¼ cup red balsamic vinegar	1 teaspoon Italian seasoning
1 clove garlic, minced	salt and pepper

In a medium bowl, add oil and vinegar and aggressively stir until combined. Add remaining ingredients and stir until mixed.

CHAPTER 10

Grains

A savory side dish of grains can really help fill out a meal, elevating the simplest main dish meat to the status of "dinner" and adding an energizing serving of inexpensive carbohydrates. This is a great way to extend your food supply!

Easy Cheesy Rice

You can use more cheese or a different type of cheese—adapt this to whatever you have on hand. *Serves 5*

4 cups water

2 teaspoons chicken bouillon granules

2 tablespoons butter or margarine

1½ cups uncooked medium-grain rice

3 slices American cheese

1. In a 4-quart saucepan over medium-high heat, bring the water, boullion granules, and butter to a boil.

2. Stir in the rice, cover, and reduce the heat to low. Cook for 15 to 20 minutes or until the rice is tender, adding more water if needed.

3. Remove from the heat, tear the cheese into small pieces, and stir it into the rice until completely melted.

Baked Brown Rice

Serves 5

2½ cups broth, or 2½ cups water with 1 chicken or beef bouillon cube

1½ cups brown rice and wild rice mixture

2 garlic cloves, finely minced

salt and pepper

1. Preheat the oven to 375°F.

2. In a 3-quart oven-safe saucepan, bring the broth (or water and bouillon cube) to a boil over medium heat.

3. Add the rice, garlic, and salt and pepper to taste; immediately put the lid on to seal the pot tightly.

4. Place in the oven and bake for exactly 1 hour and you'll have a pot of perfect fluffy rice.

Creamy Risotto-Style Rice

For a complete meal, add dehydrated meat strips and vegetables while rice is steaming.
Serves 5 to 6

1 tablespoon olive oil

1 cup minced onion

2 garlic cloves, minced

1¼ cups uncooked white rice

3 tablespoons white wine

2½ cups water

2 cups milk

1 medium tomato, peeled, seeded, and chopped

1⅓ cups fresh or dehydrated corn kernels

1 teaspoon Italian seasoning

½ teaspoon salt

freshly ground pepper, to taste

½ cup grated Parmesan cheese

1. Heat the oil in a large sauté pan, over medium heat. Sauté the onion and garlic in the oil until soft.

2. Add the rice and toast over medium heat for 2 minutes. Stir to prevent from burning.

3. Stir in the white wine.

4. Add the water, milk, tomato, corn, Italian seasoning, salt, and pepper. Heat until the mixture comes to an active simmer.

5. Cover, reduce the heat to low, and cook for 15 minutes. Then turn off the heat but leave the rice on the burner, covered, for 10 more minutes.

6. Stir in the Parmesan cheese and serve warm.

Rice and Broccoli Casserole

To turn this comforting casserole into a complete meal, simply add a 12.5-ounce can of chunk chicken. *Serves 4 to 6*

2 cups fresh or frozen broccoli florets, thawed

1 cup shredded sharp cheddar cheese or Cheez Whiz, or 1 (10.75-ounce) can condensed cheddar cheese soup, plus more (optional) for sprinkling

1 cup condensed cream of mushroom soup

¾ cup milk

1 cup uncooked instant rice or 2 cups cooked rice

salt and pepper

1. Preheat the oven to 350°F.

2. Mix all the ingredients together in a large bowl. Pour the mixture into a greased casserole dish. If you have it, sprinkle additional cheese on top.

3. Cover with a casserole lid or foil. Bake for 45 minutes if you are using uncooked instant rice. If you're using cooked rice, bake until the dish is hot all the way through and the cheese is bubbly, about 30 minutes.

Quick Rice Pilaf

Serves 4

1 cup water

1 tablespoon chicken or beef bouillon granules

1 (15-ounce) can peas and carrots or mixed vegetables

1 cup uncooked instant rice

1. In a 4-quart saucepan over medium-high heat, bring the water, bouillon, and veggies to a boil.

2. Stir in the rice.

3. Cover, remove from the heat, and let sit for 5 minutes. Fluff with a fork and serve.

Pepper-Oat Pilaf

Serves 4

1 to 2 tablespoons vegetable oil

½ cup chopped roasted red peppers (canned or fresh)

1 (4.5-ounce) can sliced mushrooms, drained or ½ cup sliced fresh mushrooms

1¾ cups rolled oats

1 egg, beaten well

1 tablespoon dried minced onion

1 tablespoon dried minced garlic

¾ cup broth

2 tablespoons dried thyme

salt and pepper

grated Parmesan cheese, for serving (optional)

1. Heat the oil in a large saucepan over medium heat. Sauté the peppers and mushrooms in the oil until they are starting to brown slightly.

2. In a medium bowl, stir together the oats, egg, onion, and garlic until the oats are coated.

3. Stir the oats into the mixture in the saucepan and cook, stirring frequently, until the oats are dry and separated, 5 to 10 minutes.

4. Stir in the broth, thyme, and salt and pepper to taste; cook for a few more minutes, stirring until the liquid has been absorbed.

5. Sprinkle with Parmesan cheese, if you wish, and serve hot.

Basic Wheat Berries

Serves 4

> 1 cup dry wheat berries
>
> 1 teaspoon salt
>
> 3½ cups water

1. Sort through the wheat berries, discarding any stones. Rinse well.

2. In a large saucepan over medium heat, bring the wheat berries, water, and salt to a boil.

3. Reduce the heat to low, cover, and simmer for 1 hour, or until the wheat berries are tender. (Undercooked wheat berries have an unpleasant texture—make sure you've cooked them thoroughly!)

Wheat Berry Rice Pilaf

Serves 6

> 2 teaspoons olive oil
>
> 1 (4-ounce) can sliced mushrooms, drained or ½ cup sliced fresh mushrooms
>
> 1 tablespoon soy sauce
>
> 1 tablespoon dried minced onion
>
> 1 tablespoon dried minced garlic
>
> 1½ cups cooked Basic Wheat Berries
>
> 1½ cups cooked brown or white rice
>
> ½ cup beef or chicken broth
>
> 1 tablespoon dried thyme
>
> salt and pepper

1. Heat the oil in a large saucepan over medium heat. Sauté the mushrooms in the oil until soft, about 3 minutes.

2. Sprinkle the mushrooms with the soy sauce, then stir in the onion and garlic. Cook for 2 more minutes, stirring constantly.

3. Stir in the rest of the ingredients and cook for 5 to 10 minutes, stirring, until the broth has been absorbed and the pilaf is heated through.

Wheat Berry Cranberry Salad

Prepare this recipe a day ahead for the best flavor. *Serves 8*

2 cups cooked Basic Wheat Berries (page 287)

½ cup walnuts, chopped

½ cup fresh parsley, coarsely chopped

DRESSING

3 tablespoons olive oil

2 tablespoons lemon juice

½ cup dried cranberries

4 tablespoons dehydrated green onions or ¼ cup sliced fresh green onions, sliced (optional)

dash of salt

1 teaspoon honey

salt and pepper

1. In a large bowl, mix together all the salad ingredients.

2. In a small bowl, whisk together the dressing ingredients. Pour the dressing over the salad and gently toss. Refrigerate the dressed salad to allow the flavors to meld before serving.

Basic Quinoa

The trick to delicious, lightly sweet quinoa is washing it well to remove its bitter coating. Rinse the quinoa in a mesh strainer under running water until the water is clear, not frothy. If running water isn't available, "swish" the quinoa in a large bowl of water and drain well. Use fresh water for cooking it. Quinoa can be used wherever you'd normally use rice or pasta—under sauces or stir-fries, as a side dish, even as a hot breakfast cereal. It's all a matter of how you season it. *Serves 4*

2 cups water

1 cup quinoa

1. Rinse the quinoa and drain well.

2. In a medium saucepan over medium-high heat, bring the water to a boil. Add the quinoa, reduce the heat to low, cover, and simmer for 15 minutes.

3. Remove from the heat, place the lid on the pan, and let sit for 5 minutes. Fluff with a fork before serving.

Quinoa Pilaf

Serves 4

1 cup quinoa

2 cups water

2 cubes chicken or vegetable bouillon

¼ cup dehydrated carrots

¼ cup dehydrated green or red bell peppers

2 tablespoons dried minced onion

½ teaspoon dried oregano

salt and pepper

¼ cup dried cranberries

1. Rinse the quinoa and drain well.

2. In a medium saucepan over medium heat, combine the quinoa, water, and all remaining ingredients except for the cranberries. Bring to a boil, then reduce the heat to low, and simmer for 15 minutes, uncovered.

3. Remove from the heat and stir in the cranberries. Place the lid on the pan and let sit for 5 minutes. Fluff with a fork before serving.

Quinoa Tabouli

This Middle Eastern salad is easily made from pantry ingredients.

Serves 5 to 6

2 cups cooked Basic Quinoa (page 288)

½ cup dried parsley

½ cup sliced green onions or 1 teaspoon onion powder

1 teaspoon garlic powder

1 tablespoon dried mint

½ teaspoon basil

½ cup lemon juice

¼ cup olive oil

salt and pepper

Greek seasoning

1. Place the quinoa in a large bowl. Lightly stir in the remaining ingredients until mixed.

2. Cover and refrigerate for at least 12 hours to allow the flavors to meld. Serve chilled.

Uncle Terry's Cheese Grits

Serves 4 to 5

1 cup uncooked plain grits

8 ounces Cheez Whiz or Velveeta, diced

¼ cup (½ stick) unsalted butter

¾ teaspoon salt

¼ teaspoon garlic salt

2 eggs, lightly beaten

1. Prepare the grits according to the package directions.

2. While the grits are cooking, preheat the oven to 350°F. Grease an 8 x 8-inch baking dish.

3. Stir the remaining ingredients into the hot grits until the cheese and butter are melted. Pour into the prepared dish and bake for 35 to 40 minutes.

Cornbread Salad

Serves 9

1 (9 x 13-inch) pan cooked cornbread, crumbled

1 cup chopped celery

½ cup chopped onion

3 hard-cooked eggs, chopped

1 green bell pepper, chopped

½ cup bacon bits or 4 cooked bacon slices, drained and crumbled

1 or 2 tomatoes, chopped

1½ cups mayonnaise

salt and pepper

1 (1-ounce) packet ranch dressing mix (optional)

Gently toss all the ingredients together in a large bowl. If using the ranch dressing mix, no additional salt and pepper is needed. Cover and refrigerate to serve chilled.

Mexican Rice

Serves 5

½ cup uncooked white rice

1 small onion, chopped, or ⅓ cup dehydrated onion

1 garlic clove, minced

1 tablespoon butter or vegetable oil

1 cup beef broth, or 1 cup water and 1 beef bouillon cube

1 cup canned diced tomatoes

1 (4-ounce) can diced green chiles, chopped

2 teaspoons ground cumin

salt and pepper

1 teaspoon chili powder

1. In a large skillet over medium heat, sauté the rice, onion, and garlic in the butter or oil until golden brown.

2. Add the beef broth or water and bouillon. Stir in the tomatoes, chiles, cumin, salt, pepper, and chili powder.

3. Cover and cook over low heat for 25 to 30 minutes, or until the rice is tender.

CHAPTER 11

Breads & Biscuits

Bread and biscuits can go a long way toward making any simple fare more filling. And they have the added bonus of helping you get that last little bit of delicious soup or sauce at the bottom of your bowl!

Quick Buttermilk Biscuits

Makes 8

½ cup (1 stick) butter

2 cups self-rising flour

¾ cup buttermilk

2 tablespoons melted butter, for brushing

1. Preheat the oven to 425°F. Lightly grease a 9 x 9-inch baking pan.

2. In a medium bowl, work the butter into the flour until the mixture resembles coarse meal. Add the buttermilk, stirring just until the flour mixture is moistened.

3. Turn the dough out onto a lightly floured surface and knead 3 or 4 times. Roll to a ¾ inch thickness; cut with a 2-inch biscuit cutter. Place the biscuits on the prepared pan.

4. Bake for 13 to 15 minutes, until tops are golden. Brush the tops of the hot biscuits with melted butter and serve warm.

Pop's Beer Bread

Makes 1 loaf

3 cups self-rising flour

1 tablespoon granulated sugar

2 tablespoons honey

1 (12-ounce) bottle of beer

1. Set the oven to its lowest setting. Grease a 9 x 5-inch bread pan.

2. Place all the ingredients in a large bowl and mix together with a spoon. Pour into the prepared bread pan and place, uncovered, in the warm oven for 15 minutes.

3. Increase temperature to 375°F and bake for 40 minutes. Allow to cool for 15 minutes on a wire rack.

Yeast Biscuits

Makes 8

2 tablespoons sugar

1 cup warm water (110°F)

1 packet (2¼ teaspoons) active dry yeast

2 cups all-purpose flour

½ cup nonfat dry milk

¼ teaspoon salt

½ cup vegetable shortening

1. In a small bowl, stir together the sugar, warm water, and yeast. Let stand for 10 to 15 minutes.

2. In a large bowl, mix together the flour, powdered milk, and salt. Cut in the shortening using a fork. Stir in the yeast mixture. Cover bowl with a towel and allow it to rest for 1 hour. Dough should be very sticky.

3. After the dough has risen, scrape it out onto a well-floured surface and knead for 4 minutes then roll out and shape into 8 biscuits.

4. Place the biscuits on a greased baking sheet and cover with a clean dish cloth to allow to rise until nearly doubled in size, 30 to 45 minutes. Meanwhile, preheat the oven to 400°F.

5. Bake the biscuits for 10 to 12 minutes, until lightly browned.

Butter Biscuits

To make garlic cheese biscuits, add ½ teaspoon garlic powder and 1¼ cups grated cheddar cheese to the batter. *Makes 8*

2½ cups Bisquick baking mix

dash of salt

¼ cup (½ stick) cold unsalted butter, cubed

¾ cup cold milk

1. Preheat the oven to 400°F.

2. Using a large fork, combine the Bisquick and salt with the cold butter in a medium bowl. Small chunks of butter should remain, about the size of peas. Stir in the milk until combined, but don't overmix.

3. Drop ¼-cup portions of dough onto an ungreased baking sheet, using an ice cream scoop.

4. Bake for 15 to 17 minutes, or until the tops of the biscuits begin to turn light brown.

Cornbread

Serves 8

1 egg, beaten

2 tablespoons butter, melted

1 cup milk

¾ cup cornmeal

1 cup all-purpose flour

¼ cup granulated sugar

1 tablespoon baking powder

½ teaspoon salt

1. Preheat the oven to 425°F. Grease an 8 x 8-inch baking pan.

2. Mix the egg, butter, and milk in a small bowl. Set aside.

3. In a separate bowl, stir together the cornmeal, flour, sugar, baking powder, and salt. Beat in the milk mixture. Spread evenly in the prepared pan.

4. Bake for 20 minutes. Allow to cool for 10 minutes on a wire rack before serving.

Quick and Easy Corn Muffins

Serves 8

⅓ cup baking mix (such as Bisquick)

1 cup yellow cornmeal

6 tablespoons granulated sugar

⅔ cup milk

2 eggs

1. Preheat the oven to 400°F. Grease an 9 x 13-inch pan or 8 cups of a standard muffin tin.

2. Whisk together the baking mix, cornmeal, and sugar in a bowl. Add the milk and eggs, stirring until the lumps are gone.

3. Pour the mixture into the prepared baking pan or fill the muffin cups half full. Bake 15 to 20 minutes, or until the muffin tops are slightly browned. If using a 9 x 13-inch pan to cook the cornbread, bake for 20 to 25 minutes or until a toothpick inserted into the cornbread comes out clean. Remove from the oven and let it cool slightly on a wire rack and serve warm.

Tip: For a sweet addition to your corn muffins, sauté ½ cup minced dried or fresh fruit (peaches, pineapple, mango, apples, or cranberries) in 3 tablespoons butter for 5 minutes to use as a tasty spread.

Quick-Knead Bread

Makes 1 loaf

3 cups all-purpose flour

¼ teaspoon active dry yeast

½ teaspoon salt

1 tablespoon sugar

1½ cups warm water (110°F)

1. In a large bowl, mix all the ingredients together until well incorporated (the dough will be very soft and sticky). Cover with plastic wrap or put in an airtight container and let sit for 18 hours. (My microwave serves as the resting spot for this step.)

2. After the 18 hours, place the dough on a floured surface. Dampen your hands with a little water (this keeps the dough from sticking to you) and knead for 4 minutes. Shape the dough into a ball.

3. Transfer the dough to a lightly greased 9-inch baking dish or Dutch oven with a lid. Allow the dough to rest for another 1½ to 2 hours or until it begins to rise again.

4. Preheat the oven to 500°F. Bake, covered, for 30 minutes. Remove the lid and reduce the oven temperature to 450°F. Bake an additional 15 minutes, until golden brown and the center is hollow when tapped.

5. Allow to cool completely on a wire rack.

White Bread

Makes 1 loaf

2 packets (4½ teaspoons) active dry yeast

2 tablespoons granulated sugar

1 cup warm water (110°F)

2 teaspoons salt

5 cups all-purpose flour, divided

1½ cups warm milk (110°F),

½ teaspoon baking soda dissolved in 1 tablespoon water

cornmeal, for bread pan

1. In a large bowl, dissolve the yeast and sugar in the water. Set aside for 15 minutes to let the yeast activate.

2. After 15 minutes, beat in the salt, 3 cups of the flour, and 1 cup of the milk. Stir in the dissolved baking soda until well blended.

3. Beat in the remaining ½ cup milk and 1½ to 2 cups more flour, to make a stiff dough. Mix until the dough becomes too sticky to mix with a spoon (about 3 minutes).

4. Allow bread to rise covered in a warm place for 2 hours or until it has doubled in size. On a lightly floured surface, knead the dough for 5 minutes.

5. Grease a 9 x 5-inch loaf pan and coat with cornmeal. Shape the dough into a loaf and place in the pan. Cover and let rise in a warm place for 45 to 60 minutes, until doubled in size.

6. Preheat the oven to 375°F. Once the bread has risen, bake for 25 to 30 minutes, or until the top of the loaf is golden brown.

Simple Wheat Bread

Makes 2 loaves

4 teaspoons active dry yeast

2 cups warm water (110°F)

⅓ cup granulated sugar

⅓ cup honey

3 tablespoons olive oil

5 cups whole wheat flour (or 3 cups whole wheat flour and 2 cups all-purpose flour)

1. Stir the yeast into the warm water in a small bowl. Set aside to let the yeast activate, about 10 minutes.

2. In a large bowl, stir together the sugar, honey, and olive oil. Add the flour and yeast mixture and mix thoroughly.

3. Transfer the dough to a lightly greased bowl, cover with a dish towel, and allow the dough to rest and rise in a warm place until doubled in size, about 2 hours (I set mine inside my microwave). After the dough has risen, punch it down and then knead it for about 2 minutes. Shape it into 2 loaves. Place in lightly greased 9 x 5-inch loaf pans.

4. Allow the loaves to rest in the unheated oven for another hour. Place a bowl of hot water in the oven to help the dough rise faster.

5. Remove the bread and bowl of hot water, and preheat the oven to 400°F. Bake the loaves for 30 minutes.

Poor Man's Village Bread

This is extremely adaptable bread that can be baked, pan-fried, or grilled. Additional ingredients can also be added according to your taste. This specialty bread can be served with soup, as an addition to any meal, or on its own for a snack. *Serves 8 to 10*

2 cups sauerkraut, drained

1 cup all-purpose flour

¾ teaspoon salt

optional additions: sprouts, diced peppers, finely chopped herbs, caraway seeds, chopped garlic, julienned spinach

olive oil, for greasing pan

1. Preheat the oven to 350°F. Grease a baking sheet with olive oil.

2. Mix the sauerkraut and flour together to make a sticky dough. If the dough seems too dry, add 1 to 2 tablespoons water or sauerkraut liquid until you have the desired consistency.

3. Add the salt and any optional additions and mix until dough stays at a sticky consistency.

4. Flour your hands and shape the dough into small flattened balls about the size of the palms of your hands. Repeat until all dough has been used.

5. Place the flattened dough balls on the prepared baking sheet and use a fork to poke holes in the tops so steam can escape.

6. Bake for 6 to 8 minutes and then turn to cook on the second side. If you wish, when you flip the bread over you can sprinkle on a desired amount of flavorings or spices such as garlic, spinach, or herbs, or drizzle on olive oil.

7. Bake for an additional 6 to 8 minutes. Serve warm.

Oat Rolls

These delicious rolls can be served with whipped honey butter.

Makes 18

2½ cups water, divided	1¾ teaspoons salt
1 cup rolled oats	2 tablespoons active dry yeast
⅔ cup packed dark brown sugar	5 to 6 cups all-purpose flour
3 tablespoons butter	

1. In a 4-quart saucepan over medium heat, bring 2 of the cups of the water to a boil. Stir in the oats and reduce the heat to a simmer until oats are soft. Remove from the heat and allow to cool until it reaches 110°F.

2. Stir in the remaining ½ cup water and the brown sugar, butter, and salt. Stir in the yeast. Let rest for 15 minutes and then stir in the flour, 1 cup at a time. Mix until all the flour has been absorbed and the dough is smooth and elastic.

3. Place the dough in a greased bowl and cover with a towel. Let the dough rise in a warm place until doubled, about 1 hour, then punch it down.

4. Shape the dough into rolls on a greased baking sheet and cover; allowing to rise for another 30 minutes in a warm place until it begins to rise again.

5. Preheat the oven to 350°F. When the rolls have risen, bake them for 15 to 20 minutes.

Ezekiel Bread

Makes 2 loaves

4 cups warm water (110°F)	½ cup millet
1 cup honey	¼ cup dry green lentils
½ cup olive oil	2 tablespoons dried Great Northern beans
2 (2¼-teaspoon) packets active dry yeast	2 tablespoons dried kidney beans
2½ cups wheat berries	2 tablespoons dried pinto beans
1½ cups spelt flour	2 tablespoons salt
½ cup barley	

1. Grease two 9 x 5-inch loaf pans. Set aside.

2. In a large bowl, stir together the water, honey, olive oil, and yeast. Let sit for 10 minutes.

3. In a second large bowl, stir all of the grains and beans together until well mixed. Grind them in a hand-crank or electric flour mill. Add the fresh-milled flour and the salt to the yeast mixture; stir until well mixed, about 10 minutes. The dough will be like batter bread dough.

4. Pour the dough into the prepared pans. Cover and let rise in a warm place for about 1 hour, or until the loaves have risen to the tops of the pans.

5. Preheat the oven to 350°F. When the dough has finished rising, bake the loaves for 45 to 50 minutes, or until they are golden brown.

Corn Tortillas

Makes about 15

2 cups masa harina	1½ cups hot water (110°F)
½ teaspoon kosher salt	vegetable oil, for the griddle

1. In a medium bowl, mix together the masa harina, salt, and hot water until thoroughly combined. Turn the dough onto a lightly floured surface and knead until it is pliable and smooth.

Tip: If the dough is too sticky, add more masa harina; if it begins to dry out, sprinkle with water.

2 Cover the dough tightly with plastic wrap and let stand for 30 minutes at room temperature.

3. Coat a griddle or skillet with oil and heat over medium-high heat.

4. Measure out heaping table spoons of dough and roll them into balls. Cover with a plastic bag or plastic wrap and roll them as flat as possible. The size can vary according to what you are using them for (tacos, burritos, etc.).

5. Working in batches, place the flattened tortillas on the hot, oiled griddle (or in the skillet) and cook for 2 to 3 minutes, until dark spots appear and the edges begin to curl upward. Then turn over and cook for another 20 seconds.

6. Transfer the cooked tortillas to a plate and cover with a towel to keep them warm while you finish cooking the remaining tortillas. You can place a paper towel or napkin in between tortillas to remove excess oil. Serve warm.

7. To store tortillas, wrap them in foil and place them in an airtight container. To reheat, place foil-wrapped tortillas into a 350°F oven for 10 minutes.

Jessica's Bread

Makes 1 loaf

2 cups self-rising flour

1 teaspoon nonfat dry milk

water, as needed

toppings of choice (see instructions)

1. Combine the flour and milk powder in a bowl. Mix in water until you have a smooth, elastic dough. Form into a ball.

2. Heat a lightly greased cast-iron skillet over medium heat.

3. Flatten the dough ball to about ½ inch thick and place in the hot skillet. Cook for 5 to 10 minutes, flipping it over several times.

4. Serve warm topped with butter, herbs, and garlic for a savory flavor, or with butter and reconstituted dried fruit for a sweet flavor.

Breadsticks

Makes 16

1½ cups warm water (110°F)

1 tablespoon active dry yeast

2 tablespoons granulated sugar

1 teaspoon salt

4 cups all-purpose flour

melted butter, for baking sheet and breadsticks

garlic powder, to taste

½ cup shredded cheddar or mozzarella cheese and/or ¼ cup grated Parmesan cheese, or cinnamon and sugar

1. In a large bowl, mix together the warm water, yeast, and sugar. Let sit for 5 minutes.

2. Stir in the salt. Stir in the flour, 1 cup at a time, mixing well with your hands until the dough pulls away from the side of the bowl.

3. Grease the inside of a large bowl or spray with cooking spray. Place the dough in the bowl, turning it to grease all sides, and cover with a damp towel.

4. Allow the dough to rise in a warm place for 20 minutes or until doubled in size. Butter a baking sheet.

5. Place the dough on a floured work surface and knead it for 2 to 5 minutes. Roll the dough to ¼ inch thickness.

6. Cut the dough into 1 to 2-inch-wide slices and transfer them to the prepared baking sheet. Brush with melted butter and dust with garlic powder. If you wish, sprinkle cheddar, mozzarella, Parmesan cheese, or cinnamon and sugar on top of the breadsticks.

7. Allow the breadsticks to rise, covered, for another 20 minutes in a warm place. Meanwhile, preheat the oven to 375°F.

8. Bake for 15 minutes. Transfer the breadsticks to a wire rack to cool.

Potato Bread

Makes 1 loaf

1 cup unseasoned mashed potatoes (you can make them with instant flakes)

2 teaspoons active dry yeast

2½ tablespoons sugar

1 cup warm water

3 cups all-purpose flour

1 teaspoon salt

1. Preheat the oven to 375°F. Grease a bread pan or baking sheet, depending on whether you are making a single loaf or buns.

2. In a large bowl, beat together the mashed potatoes, yeast, sugar, and water until no lumps remain.

3. Sift together the flour and salt. Mix into the potato mixture.

4. On a floured surface, knead the dough until it is smooth. Form into a loaf or individual buns and transfer to the prepared pan or baking sheet.

5. Bake until the bread starts to brown, about 35 minutes for a loaf or 25 minutes for buns. Let cool on a wire rack.

Homemade Flour Tortillas

Because of the shortening in the dough, it's usually not necessary to use oil for "frying" these tortillas. If you notice any sticking, use a small amount of cooking spray or oil. *Makes 12 tortillas*

3 cups all-purpose flour, plus more for rolling

2 teaspoons baking powder

1 teaspoon salt

4 to 6 tablespoons vegetable shortening

1¼ cups warm water (110°F)

1. Mix the dry ingredients in a large bowl. Cut in the shortening, using a fork or pastry blender (or your clean hands).

2. Add warm water, a little at a time, until your dough is soft but not sticky.

3. Working on a floured surface, knead the dough for a couple of minutes. Divide into 12 balls and cover, allowing dough to rest for 10 to 15 minutes.

4. Heat a skillet over medium-high heat.

5. Dust each ball of dough with a little flour, then roll it into a fairly thin (about ⅛ inch thick), 3 to 4-inch round tortilla. If you don't have a rolling pin, you can use a glass or even your hands to shape the dough.

6. Lay the tortilla in the hot skillet. Watch carefully—it only takes a few seconds to cook. Flip the tortilla to the other side. You know it's done when you see many brown spots. Place the cooked tortillas on top of one another on a plate and cover with a clean dish towel until ready to serve.

Homemade Baked Tortilla Chips

Makes 16 chips

4 flour tortillas corn tortillas or wheat tortillas, quartered

2 tablespoons vegetable oil, or cooking spray

salt, to taste

1. Preheat the oven to 350°F. Lightly brush oil onto a baking sheet.

2. Brush a light coating of oil on one side of each tortilla. Sprinkle with salt.

3. Stack the tortillas, greased side up, in an even pile. Cut in half, then in quarters, then in eighths. Separate and arrange the pieces, greased side up, on the prepared baking sheet.

4. Toast the chips in the oven for about 10 minutes, or until they are crisp and just beginning to brown lightly. Serve immediately or store in an airtight container.

THE PREPPER'S ULTIMATE FOOD STORAGE GUIDE

Pizza Dough

Makes 1 pie or 8 servings

3 cups all-purpose flour

1 (2¼-tablespoons) packet active dry yeast

1 teaspoon salt

1 tablespoon sugar

1 cup warm water (110°F)

2 tablespoons vegetable oil

pizza toppings of choice

1. In a large bowl, combine the flour, yeast, salt, sugar, and warm water.

2. Add the oil to the bowl. Stir until the dough is well mixed. Transfer to a lightly oiled large bowl; cover and allow to rest in a warm place until doubled, about 90 minutes.

3. Preheat the oven to 375°F. Grease a large pizza pan.

4. Working on a floured surface, knead the dough and shape it. Roll the dough into a ball and allow to rest, covered, for 30 additional minutes. Transfer the dough to your work surface, lightly sprinkled with cornmeal. Shape the dough with lightly floured hands into a 9-inch disk, about ¼ inch thick. Brush the outer edge lightly with olive oil. Top as desired. Bake until the crust is golden brown, and the cheese is bubbling, 8 to 12 minutes.

Pita Bread

For pita chips, brush the cooked pita bread with oil, cut into quarters and bake at 375°F until crispy. *Makes 8 pitas*

1 (2¼-teaspoons) packet active dry yeast

1¼ cups warm water (110°F)

2 teaspoons salt

3 cups all-purpose flour, plus more for rolling

1. In a medium bowl, dissolve the yeast in the warm water. Allow mixture to sit for 10 minutes.

2. Stir in the salt and beat in the flour to form a soft dough.

3. Turn the dough onto a floured surface and knead until smooth and elastic, about 6 to 8 minutes. Do not let the dough rise at this point. Divide into 6 pieces; knead each piece for 1 minute and roll into a 5-inch circle about ¼ inch thick. Arrange the kneaded dough pieces on a greased baking sheet. Cover and let rise in a warm place until doubled, about 45 minutes.

4. Preheat the oven to 500°F. Bake for 4 minutes until the bread puffs up. Turn over and bake for 2 minutes more.

5. Remove each pita with a spatula from the baking sheet and add additional pitas for baking. Use the spatula to gently push down puff. Immediately place in storage bags.

Desserts & Baked Goods

Many of my childhood memories of family get-togethers include a long table brimming with desserts. My wonderful family still loves sweets, and I've raided their recipe boxes to bring you some favorites that can be made from ingredients in your storage pantry.

Basic Pie Crust

For sweet pies, add 2 tablespoons granulated sugar to the dough. *Makes 1 pie crust*

1 stick butter, softened	4 to 5 tablespoons cold water
1½ cups all-purpose flour	⅛ teaspoon salt

1. Stir the ingredients together until well combined.

2. Shape the dough into a flattened disk; wrap in plastic wrap and refrigerate at least 30 minutes, or overnight.

3. Allow the dough to come to room temperature. On a floured surface, use a rolling pin to roll the dough to a 12-inch round. Ease the dough circle into a 9-inch glass pie pan, gently pressing it against the side. Trim the dough edge, leaving a 1-inch overhang. Fold the edge under and pinch to give decorative look.

4. Fill pie crust with filling and bake as directed. For a prebaked crust, preheat the oven to 425°F. Line the dough with foil and fill pan with pie weights (or dried beans, pennies, rice, or marbles). Bake the pie shell for 10 to 12 minutes, or until it is beginning to set. Remove the foil with the weights and bake 15 to 18 minutes longer, or until golden. If the shell puffs while baking, press it down with the back of a spoon. Set on a wire rack to cool.

Graham Cracker Pie Crust

Makes 1 pie crust

1½ cups crushed graham crackers (about 16 crackers; see page 265)

¼ cup white sugar

7 tablespoons butter, melted

1. Preheat the oven to 350°F. Mix the graham cracker crumbs and sugar together until combined. Add melted butter and mix with a fork until completely moistened.

2. Press into a 9-inch pie pan.

3. Bake for 8 to 10 minutes, until golden and the edges are crispy.

Chocolate PB Balls

Makes 9 (4-ball) servings

1 cup chocolate protein powder

1 cup peanut butter

½ cup honey

½ cup rolled oats

extra protein powder, or powdered sugar or unsweetened cocoa powder, for rolling

1. In a medium bowl, stir the first four ingredients together to combine thoroughly.

2. Form the dough into walnut-size balls. Place on waxed paper.

3. Roll the balls in protein powder, powdered sugar, or cocoa (this will make them less sticky to handle). Refrigerate for 1 hour before serving.

Protein Granola Bars

Serves 9

1 cup quick-cooking rolled oats

½ cup vanilla or chocolate protein powder

½ cup wheat and barley nugget cereal (such as Grape-Nuts)

½ teaspoon ground cinnamon

⅓ cup unsweetened applesauce

½ cup honey

2 tablespoons peanut butter

2 eggs, well beaten

¼ cup unsalted shelled sunflower seeds

¼ cup dried fruit, chopped

¼ cup chopped pecans or other nuts

1. Preheat the oven to 325°F. Line a 9-inch square baking pan with foil and grease the foil for easy removal of the bars.

2. In a large bowl, stir together the oats, protein powder, cereal, and cinnamon.

3. In a medium bowl, combine the applesauce, honey, peanut butter, and eggs. Stir into the oat and cereal mixture.

4. Add the sunflower seeds, dried fruit, and nuts.

5. Spread evenly in the prepared pan. Bake for 30 minutes, until firm and lightly browned around the edges.

6. Let cool on a wire rack, then use the foil to lift out of the pan. Cut into bars or squares.

Country Berry Crumble Pie

Serves 6

1 Basic Pie Crust recipe (page 302)

4 cups fresh blackberries, blueberries, strawberries, or your choice

¾ cup granulated sugar

¼ cup all-purpose flour

CRUMB TOPPING

½ cup all-purpose flour

½ cup granulated sugar

½ teaspoon ground cinnamon

2 teaspoons lemon juice

grated zest of 1 lemon

1 teaspoon vanilla extract

½ cup (1 stick) butter, cut into slices

1 cup rolled oats

1. Prepare the pastry dough, wrap it in plastic wrap, and refrigerate for at least 30 minutes.

2. Preheat the oven to 375°F. Meanwhile, on a floured surface, roll half the dough into a 12-inch round. Fit the dough round into a lightly greased 9-inch deep dish pie pan. Trim the edge, leaving a 1-inch overhang; fold under and crimp.

3. Lay a sheet of foil over the crust and fill it with pie weights or dry beans. Bake for 15 minutes, then remove from the oven and lift off the foil liner and beans.

4. While the pie shell is baking, mix together the filling ingredients in a large bowl (berries through vanilla). In a separate bowl, work the topping ingredients into a crumbly mixture.

5. Pour the filling into the pie shell. Sprinkle the crumb mixture evenly over the top.

6. Return the pie to the oven and bake for about 1 hour, until the topping is golden brown. Don't let the crumb topping get too dark. If the pie begins to get too brown, cover loosely with foil. Remove from the oven and let cool a bit on a wire rack before serving.

Dessert Mousse

Serves 4 to 6

1½ cups milk

1 (6-serving) package instant pudding mix, any flavor

1 (8-ounce) container whipped topping, or 1 to 2 cups made from recipe (page 320)

1. In a large mixing bowl, beat together the milk and pudding mix.

2. Fold in the whipped topping until it is completely blended.

3. Spoon into individual dessert dishes and refrigerate to serve chilled.

Chocolate Éclair Cake

Serves 9

1 (14.4-ounce) package graham crackers

4 cups milk

2 (4-serving) packages instant vanilla pudding mix

1 (12-ounce) container frozen whipped topping, thawed, or 2 cups homemade Whipped Topping (page 320)

1 (16-ounce) container prepared chocolate frosting

1 teaspoon vanilla

1. Line the bottom of a 9 x 13-inch baking pan with one-third of the graham crackers.

2. In a large bowl, combine the milk and vanilla pudding mix, following the package directions.

3. Fold the whipped topping into the prepared pudding. Spread a layer with half of the pudding mixture over the graham crackers.

4. Add another layer of graham crackers, another pudding layer, and a final layer of graham crackers. Cover with a lid and refrigerate for 1 hour.

5. In a small saucepan over low heat, warm the frosting just enough that you can stir it easily with a spoon. Pour over the cake. Refrigerate for at least 12 hours, or overnight. Cut in squares to serve.

Auntie's Caramel Sauce

This delectable sauce can be used as an ice cream topping, to make caramel popcorn or caramel apples, or as a flavorful addition to pies and cakes. *Makes 4 cups*

1 cup (2 sticks) butter

2 cups packed dark brown sugar

1 (14-ounce) can sweetened condensed milk

2 teaspoons vanilla extract

⅛ teaspoon salt

1. In a 4-quart saucepan, combine the butter, brown sugar, and condensed milk; bring to a boil over medium-high heat until the mixture begins to thicken, about 2 minutes.

2. Continue to cook, stirring constantly, for an additional 2 minutes.

3. Remove from the heat and stir in the vanilla and salt.

4. Serve warm. Refrigerate to thicken sauce.

Chocolate Sauce

Serves 4 to 6

¼ cup water, plus 1 or 2 more tablespoons as needed

½ cup sugar

2 tablespoons cocoa powder

2 tablespoons butter

dash of salt

½ teaspoon vanilla extract

1. In a 4-quart saucepan over medium heat, bring the water and sugar to a boil. Continue to cook until the mixture becomes a syrup, about 5 minutes.

2. Reduce the heat to low, and add the cocoa, butter, and salt, and cook, stirring, until combined.

3. Remove from the heat, and stir in the vanilla. Allow to cool 5 to 10 minutes before serving.

Gingerbread

Serves 9

1 cup hot water

½ cup (1 stick) butter or margarine, softened

½ cup granulated sugar

1 egg

1 cup dark molasses

2½ cups sifted all-purpose flour

½ teaspoon salt

½ teaspoon ground cloves

1 teaspoon ground ginger

1½ teaspoons ground cinnamon

1½ teaspoons baking soda

1. Preheat the oven to 350°F. Grease and flour a 9 x 9-inch pan.

2. Bring the water to a boil in a small saucepan over high heat. Turn off the heat.

3. In a large bowl, cream the butter with the sugar. Beat in the egg and molasses.

4. Sift together the flour, salt, spices, and baking soda. Add to the wet mixture and mix well. Then add the hot water and beat until smooth.

5. Pour into the prepared pan and bake for 35 to 40 minutes, until a knife inserted into the gingerbread comes out clean.

Fried Fruit Pies

Makes 10 to 12 pies

2 Basic Pie Crust recipes (page 302)

2½ cups canned fruit slices or berries, or rehydrated dried fruit

¾ cup packed light brown sugar

1 teaspoon ground cinnamon

ICING

1 cup powdered sugar

1 tablespoon milk or water

½ teaspoon vanilla extract

½ teaspoon ground nutmeg

¼ teaspoon ground allspice

1 tablespoon all-purpose flour

vegetable oil, for frying

1. Double the basic recipe for a basic pie crust, wrap it in plastic wrap, and refrigerate for at least 30 minutes.

2. Drain the fruit and chop it into small pieces. In a medium bowl, stir together the fruit, brown sugar, cinnamon, nutmeg, allspice, and flour.

3. Allow the dough to come to room temperature. On a floured board, use a floured rolling pin to roll the dough pieces to a thickness of ⅛ inch. Cut into 5-inch circles.

4. Spoon ¼ cup of pie filling onto half of each dough circle. Moisten the pastry edges with water, fold the dough over the filling, and press the edges with the tines of a fork to seal.

5. In a skillet, heat 2 inches of oil to 350°F. Fry the pies, a few at a time for 3½ to 4 minutes, or until golden brown. Drain on paper towels.

6. Stir together the icing ingredients in a small bowl. Lightly drizzle icing over the warm pies.

Sand Tarts

Makes 4 dozen

1 cup (2 sticks) unsalted butter

½ cup powdered sugar, plus more for rolling

1¼ teaspoons vanilla extract

2 cups sifted all-purpose flour

1½ cups chopped walnuts or pecans

dash of salt

1. Preheat the oven to 350°F.

2. Cream the butter. Beat in the ½ cup powdered sugar and the vanilla.

3. Add the flour, salt, and nuts, mixing well.

4. Form into small balls, as desired. Transfer to an ungreased baking sheet and place 1 inch apart. Bake for 30 minutes, or until golden.

5. Remove from the oven and roll on a plate of powdered sugar while still warm. Cool on wire racks and store in an airtight container.

Caramel Popcorn

Serves 16

4 quarts popped corn

½ cup (1 stick) butter

1 cup packed light brown sugar

1 cup granulated sugar

¼ cup light corn syrup

½ teaspoon baking soda

½ teaspoon salt

1 teaspoon vanilla extract

1 cup peanuts (optional)

1. Preheat oven to 250°F. Place the cooked popcorn aside.

2. In a saucepan over medium heat, melt the butter. Stir in the brown sugar, granulated sugar, and corn syrup. Bring mixture to a boil, stirring constantly. Without stirring, boil mixture for 4 additional minutes.

3. Remove from heat, add baking soda, salt, vanilla, and nuts, if using.

4. On a shallow baking sheet, pour over popcorn and toss. Bake popcorn for 1 hour and 15 minutes. Allow to cool completely and store in an airtight container.

Easy Pumpkin Muffins

Makes 1 dozen muffins

1 package yellow cake mix

1 (15-ounce) can pumpkin puree

1½ teaspoons ground cinnamon

½ teaspoon ground nutmeg

¼ teaspoon ground cloves

1. Preheat the oven to 350°F. Grease a standard 12-cup muffin tin or line with paper liners.

2. In a large bowl, stir all the ingredients together until combined.

3. Spoon the batter into the prepared muffin compartments. Bake for 20 to 25 minutes or until a toothpick inserted in middle comes out clean. Cool on a wire rack.

Apple Enchiladas

Makes 10 enchiladas

½ cup (1 stick) butter

1½ cups water

1 cup granulated sugar, plus more for sprinkling

1 (21-ounce) can apple pie filling

10 (7 to 8-inch) flour tortillas

cinnamon for sprinkling

1. Preheat the oven to 350°F. Coat the inside of a 9 x 13-inch baking dish with cooking spray or vegetable oil.

2. Combine the butter, water, and 1 cup sugar in a medium saucepan over medium heat; bring to a boil, then remove from the heat.

3. Working on a flat surface, spread 2 generous tablespoons of apple pie filling along the center of each tortilla. Roll up, enchilada-style.

4. Lay in rows in the prepared dish, seam side down. Sprinkle with cinnamon and sugar and then pour the sugar syrup over the top.

5. Cover with foil and bake for 35 minutes. Serve warm.

No-Bake Chocolate Cookies

Makes 3 dozen

3 tablespoons unsweetened cocoa powder

2 cups granulated sugar

½ cup milk

½ cup (1 stick) butter

3 cups quick-cooking rolled oats

½ cup crunchy peanut butter

1 tablespoon vanilla extract

1. Combine the cocoa, sugar, milk, and butter in a 4-quart saucepan over medium heat. Bring to a boil very slowly, then boil for no longer than 1½ to 2 minutes.

2. Using a big wooden spoon, stir together the oats, peanut butter, and vanilla in a bowl.

3. Pour the hot mixture over the oatmeal mixture and stir to combine. Form into small balls and drop onto waxed paper. Let cool until set.

Crazy Cake (No-Egg Cake)

Serves 6 to 8

1 cup granulated sugar

¼ cup unsweetened cocoa powder

1 teaspoon baking soda

1½ cups all-purpose flour

1 tablespoon white vinegar

1½ teaspoons vanilla extract

7 tablespoons vegetable oil

1 cup water or coffee

pecans, chocolate chips, or toffee pieces, for topping (optional)

1. Preheat the oven to 350°F.

2. In a large bowl, sift together the sugar, cocoa, baking soda, and flour.

3. Make a well in the center and add the vinegar, vanilla, and oil. Pour in the water or coffee and stir until well combined.

4. Pour the batter into a lightly greased 8 x 8-inch pan. Add any additional toppings to the top of the batter, if desired. Bake for 40 minutes. Cool completely on a wire rack.

Peach Cobbler

Serves 6 to 8

½ cup (1 stick) butter or margarine, plus 1 tablespoon for the dish

1 teaspoon ground cinnamon

½ teaspoon ground nutmeg

2 cups granulated sugar, divided

1 (29-ounce) can sliced peaches, drained

1 cup baking mix (such as Bisquick, or made from recipe on page 319)

1 cup milk

1. Preheat the oven to 350°F. Butter an 8 x 8-inch baking dish.

2. In a small pan, melt the butter or margarine on stovetop. Pour into a small bowl and set aside.

3. In a 4-quart saucepan over medium heat, mix the spices and 1 cup sugar, with the peaches; bring to boil. Pour into prepared baking dish.

4. In a large bowl, mix together the baking mix, milk, and remaining 1 cup sugar. Add the melted butter and mix until combined. Pour the batter into the pan over the spiced peaches.

5. Bake for 35 to 40 minutes or until golden. Let cool on a wire rack.

Mandarin Orange Cake

Serves 9

1 package yellow cake mix

1 teaspoon ground cinnamon

3 eggs

1 cup vegetable oil

1 (11-ounce) can mandarin orange segments

1 (8-ounce) container frozen whipped topping, thawed

1 (20-ounce) can crushed pineapple with juice

1 (4-serving) package instant vanilla pudding mix

1. Preheat the oven to 350°F. Grease a 9 x 13-inch pan.

2. In a large bowl, combine the cake mix, cinnamon, eggs, oil, and mandarin oranges with their juices. Stir until smooth. Pour the batter into the prepared pan.

3. Bake 35 to 40 minutes, or until a toothpick inserted into the center of the cake comes out clean. Allow to cool.

4. To make the topping: In a large bowl, softly beat together whipped topping, pineapple with juice, and dry pudding mix until blended. Spread on cake.

Orange Jell-O Dessert Salad

Serves 6

1 (20-ounce) can crushed pineapple

1 (3-ounce) package orange Jell-O

8 ounces whipped topping, purchased or made from recipe on page 320

½ cup chopped walnuts or pecans

1. Drain the pineapple, retaining the juice for making the Jell-O.

2. Prepare the Jell-O according to the package directions, replacing part of the water with the drained pineapple juice.

3. Stir the Jell-O until it begins to dissolve, then mix in the drained pineapple and the whipped topping. Top with the chopped nuts. Chill overnight until the Jell-O is firm. Cut into squares to serve.

Homemade Vanilla Wafers

Makes 2 dozen

½ cup (1 stick) unsalted butter, softened

1 cup granulated sugar

¼ cup packed brown sugar

1 egg

2 tablespoons milk

2 teaspoons vanilla extract

1½ cups all-purpose flour

1 teaspoon baking powder

¼ teaspoon salt

1. Preheat the oven to 350°F.

2. In a medium bowl, cream the butter with the sugar. Beat in the egg, milk, and vanilla.

3. In a large bowl, combine the flour, baking powder, and salt. Add to the wet mixture, mixing well.

4. Drop by spoonfuls onto greased baking sheets, spacing 2 inches apart. Bake for 12 to 15 minutes, or until the edges are golden brown. Move to a wire rack to cool.

Icebox Pie

Serves 6

1 (6-ounce) container frozen lemonade, thawed

1 (14-ounce) can sweetened condensed milk

6 ounces whipped topping, purchased or made from recipe on page 320

1 prepared Graham Cracker Pie Crust (page 302)

Mix together the lemonade, condensed milk, and whipped topping. Pour into the pie shell, smoothing the top. Chill in the refrigerator at least 1 hour before serving.

Rice Pudding

Serves 4

1 tablespoon butter, softened

2 cups cooked white rice

3 cups milk

1 egg, well beaten

¼ cup packed dark brown sugar

¼ teaspoon ground cinnamon

½ teaspoon ground nutmeg

1 teaspoon vanilla extract

dash of salt

⅓ cup raisins or dried fruit pieces (optional)

1. Preheat the oven to 350°F. Butter a 1.8-liter casserole dish.

2. In a large saucepan over medium-high, heat the rice and milk and bring to a slight simmer.

3. In a medium bowl, combine the egg, brown sugar, cinnamon, nutmeg, vanilla, and salt. Mix and add to the milk and rice mixture. Stir well until all ingredients have combined, about 3 minutes. If desired, add raisins or dried fruit pieces into the mixture and stir. Pour the mixture into the prepared dish.

4. Bake for 15 minutes. Serve warm.

No-Bake Fruit Crisp

Serve this crisp in bowls with ice cream, as a breakfast topping for warm cereals, or as a sweet treat all by itself. *Serves 6 to 8*

1 pound peaches, berries, or other fruit

¼ cup (½ stick) butter

1 cup packed dark brown sugar

1 teaspoon ground cinnamon

¼ teaspoon ground nutmeg

¾ cup rolled oats

¼ cup sliced almonds

1. Peel and slice the peaches or other fruit as necessary.

2. Melt the butter in a large skillet over low heat. Whisk in the brown sugar, cinnamon, and nutmeg. Bring to a simmer over medium heat.

3. Stir in the fruit. Cook for 5 to 8 minutes, stirring frequently, until the fruit is tender.

4. Remove from the heat and stir in the oats and sliced almonds.

Sugar Cream Pie

Serves 6

3 tablespoons all-purpose flour

⅛ teaspoon salt

1 cup granulated sugar

1 cup heavy cream

½ cup evaporated milk

1 teaspoon vanilla extract

⅛ teaspoon ground nutmeg

1 baked Basic Pie Crust shell (page 302)

1. Preheat the oven to 425°F.

2. In a medium bowl, stir together the flour, salt, and sugar. Beat in the cream, evaporated milk, vanilla, and nutmeg to make a smooth paste. Pour into the baked pie shell.

3. Bake for 15 minutes, then reduce the oven temperature to 375°F and bake for another 30 minutes. Serve warm.

Chocolate Fudge

Makes 50 squares

2 cups granulated sugar

2 teaspoons light corn syrup

1 cup milk

5 tablespoons unsweetened cocoa powder

2 tablespoons butter

⅛ teaspoon salt

2 teaspoons vanilla extract

marshmallows, chopped nuts, or toffee pieces (optional)

1. Butter an 8 x 8-inch baking dish; set aside.

2. In a 4-quart saucepan over medium heat, combine the sugar, corn syrup, milk, and cocoa powder. Stir slowly until the mixture reaches the soft-ball stage, 8 to 10 minutes. To test for the soft-ball stage, take a spoonful of mixture and drop it in a dish of cold water. Grab the spoonful out of the water and squeeze between your fingers. If it is flexible and stays in a ball shape, it is ready. Add the butter, and salt.

3. Remove from the heat and allow the mixture to cool. When the surface dents when touched, slowly stir in the vanilla, marshmallows, nuts, or toffee, if desired.

4. Pour into the prepared pan. Refrigerate and allow the fudge to harden fully. Cut into squares. Store in an airtight container for up to 1 week.

Chocolate Ramen Noodles

Makes about 40 squares

1 package ramen noodles (flavor packet discarded)

2 cups semisweet chocolate chips

2 tablespoons butter

1 teaspoon vanilla

1 (14-ounce) can sweetened condensed milk

powdered sugar, for dusting

1. In a medium bowl, break up the noodles into very small pieces.

2. In a small saucepan, melt the chocolate chips. Add the butter, vanilla, and condensed milk and stir well.

3. Add the crushed noodles to the chocolate mixture and stir until thoroughly mixed.

4. Line an 8 x 8-inch baking dish with foil and spray the foil with cooking spray. Pour the chocolate mixture into the dish and refrigerate for 2 hours, until hardened.

5. To serve, remove from the refrigerator and cut into bite-size pieces.

Basic Pudding Mix

Serves 4

3 cups nonfat dry milk

1¾ cups granulated sugar

1 cup cornstarch

¼ teaspoon salt

Stir all the ingredients together until well blended. Store in a covered container or in individual 1-cup packages.

To make pudding, place 1 cup pudding mix in a small saucepan. Slowly sir in 2 cups boiling water. Cook over medium heat for 3 to 5 minutes, stirring constantly, until the mixture is thickened. Let the mixture cool slightly and then pour into individual containers to make homemade pudding cups or into a single container. Cover and keep refrigerated.

Vanilla pudding—Stir in 1 teaspoon vanilla extract and 1 tablespoon butter once the pudding has thickened.

Chocolate pudding—Add 2 tablespoons of cocoa powder to 1 cup of dry mixture before cooking. Stir in ½ teaspoon vanilla and 1 tablespoon butter once the pudding has thickened.

Italian Ice

For flavoring, add 1 cup of your favorite juice or 1 teaspoon of vanilla along with the water in the recipe. *Makes 2 cups*

2 cups water, divided

½ cup granulated sugar

1. In small a saucepan over medium heat, combine 1 cup of the water and the sugar, stirring often, until the sugar has dissolved.

2. Remove from the heat, add the remaining 1 cup water, and let cool for 20 minutes.

3. Pour into a freezer-safe container (I use a large cake pan) and place in the freezer. Add any flavoring and stir every hour for 5 hours, or until the ice becomes difficult to stir.

4. To serve, scoop into individual dessert bowls.

CHAPTER 13

Beverages

As previously mentioned, water should be the main liquid that you drink. That said, there often comes a time when you want something else. I do not advise storing a large assortment of sodas as they tend to dehydrate us more than hydrate. But having some stored for a special treat will be a nice morale booster. Drink mixes are also great for storage pantries. These days, there are many flavored mixes to choose from, including teas, fruit punches, and individual fruit drinks.

A great way to have fruit on hand for flavoring drinks is to dehydrate fruit slices such as lemons and oranges. Fruits can really lift a drink out of glum and up to "yum!"

Spiced Tea

⅔ cup instant black tea

1 cup powered orange-flavored drink mix

⅓ cup powdered lemonade

¼ cup sugar

¾ teaspoon ground cinnamon

½ teaspoon ground cloves

1. Mix all the ingredients together and stir thoroughly.

2. To serve, stir 1½ teaspoons drink mix into 1 cup hot water.

Mock Hot Toddy

1 tablespoon honey

1 teaspoon lemon juice

¼ teaspoon ground cinnamon

⅛ teaspoon ground cloves

7 ounces hot black tea

lemon wedge, for garnish

Combine the honey, lemon and spices in a mug. Add hot water and stir. Top with hot, brewed tea and stir again. Garnish with a lemon wedge.

Hot Cocoa Mix

2 cups dry milk powder

½ cup non-dairy creamer

¾ cup sugar

½ cup unsweetened cocoa

dash of spice such as cinnamon, nutmeg or cayenne or pepper

1. Mix all the ingredients together and store in a cool, dry space.

2. To serve, add 1 cup of warm milk or water to 1 to 2 tablespoons of cocoa mix.

Basic Almond Milk

1 cup raw almonds

4 cups filtered water

1. Soak the almonds in water for at least 4 hours. Discard the soaking water.

2. In a high-speed blender, blend nuts and the 4 cups water for about 2 minutes until the nuts are completely blended.

3. Line a colander with several layers of cheesecloth and strain the milk through twice. Leftover strained nuts can be use in baking recipes or to make almond butter. Almond milk will last 3 to 4 days. Adding a dash of salt can act as a preservative. Adding a dash of vanilla can make the mixture richer.

Oat Milk

8 tablespoons rolled oats

pinch of salt

1½ quarts filtered water

optional: sweetened coconut, agave nectar, or sugar, for sweetening

½ teaspoon vanilla

1. Place the oats, salt, water, and desired sweetener (optional), in a pitcher. Stir until mixed.

2. Allow mixture to soak in the refrigerator overnight.

3. After mixture has soaked overnight, pour the contents of the pitcher into the blender. Blend until well blended.

4. Pour the contents of the blender into a fine mesh sieve that is placed over a large bowl, and strain it thoroughly. Strain again if needed. The leftover strained oats can be cooked and used for oatmeal or used in baking recipes.

5. Add vanilla and stir.

6. Chill and shake before use. Oat milk lasts up to 5 days.

Rice Milk

1 cup uncooked white or brown rice

6 to 8 cups water

½ teaspoon sea salt

3 tablespoons maple syrup, agave nectar, or honey, to taste

½ teaspoon vanilla extract, plus more to taste

¾ teaspoon ground cinnamon, plus more to taste

1. Place the rice, 6 cups of water, and salt in a pan.

2. Cover and bring to a boil over high heat. Reduce the heat to low and simmer for 3 hours, or until the rice is very soft. (This can also be done in a slow cooker overnight on low heat.)

3. In a blender, puree rice mixture with the remaining ingredients. You will have to do it in 2 batches. Puree each batch at least 2 to 3 minutes to completely liquefy the rice. Add more water if you prefer a thinner consistency.

4. Strain mixture through a cheesecloth or a fine mesh sieve. Flavor with vanilla and sugar to taste. Chill, and serve over ice.

Old-Fashioned Root Beer

1 teaspoon active dry yeast

½ cup warm water

2¼ cups granulated sugar

1 gallon filtered water

3 to 4 teaspoons root beer extract

1. Dissolve the yeast in the warm water.

2. In a gallon size-jar, dissolve the sugar in the water.

3. Add the yeast mixture to the jar along with the root beer extract. Fill the jar with more warm water and stir until all ingredients are well combined.

4. Cover jar and allow it to sit in the warm sun for 4 hours. The root beer will be ready to drink the next day. Chill before serving.

Vanilla Cream Soda

2 cups sugar

1 cup water

1½ tablespoons vanilla extract

1 bottle seltzer or club soda

ice cubes

1. Make a simple syrup by combining the sugar and water in a small saucepan over medium-low heat. Continuously stir and bring to a boil.

2. Once the mixture turns from cloudy to clear, take it off the heat and allow to cool for about 5 minutes.

3. Once mixture is cooled, add the vanilla extract and seltzer or club soda, and serve over ice.

Spiced Cider Mix

2 tablespoons sweetened lemonade drink mix

½ teaspoon ground nutmeg

1½ teaspoons ground cinnamon

¼ teaspoon ground cloves

¼ teaspoon ground allspice

hot apple juice

1. Mix all dry ingredients together and store in a cool, dry space.

2. To serve, add 1 tablespoon of the mix into a cup of hot apple juice.

3. To make a large batch, add the entire mix to 1 gallon of hot apple juice in a large pan and bring to an active simmer for 5 to 10 minutes.

Amish Tea

3 cups boiling water

4 bags black tea

3 cups apple juice

⅓ cup honey

1. Pour the boiling water over the tea bags in a large heatproof container. Allow to steep for 5 minutes.

2. Remove and strain the tea bags and add the honey and apple juice. Mix well.

Citrus Tea

2 cups prepared orange-flavored drink

2 cups sugar

1 teaspoon ground cinnamon

1 (.15-ounce) package unsweetened lemon drink mix

In a pitcher, mix all the ingredients together and stir thoroughly. Chill for 1 hour before serving.

CHAPTER 14

Alternative Ingredients

One of the main reasons I am writing this book is to equip you with knowledge that can make you self-reliant during times when many won't be. Having the skills to prepare favorite recipes even when the grid is down will keep spirits up and tummies full. In this section you'll find do-it-yourself alternatives for common ingredients that you may not have on hand.

Bisquick Substitute

Makes 1 cup

- 1 cup all-purpose flour
- 1 ½ teaspoons baking powder
- ¼ teaspoon salt
- 1 tablespoon vegetable shortening, added at time of use

Stir together the flour, baking powder, and salt; store in an airtight container. To use the mixture, work in 1 tablespoon shortening.

Self-Rising Flour

- 1 cup all-purpose flour
- ½ teaspoon baking powder
- ½ teaspoon salt

Mix all the ingredients together and store in airtight container.

Powdered Sugar

- 1 cup granulated sugar
- 1 tablespoon cornstarch

In a blender, whirl the sugar with the cornstarch until it is powdered.

Brown Sugar

For dark brown sugar, add another tablespoon of molasses

  1 cup sugar

  1 tablespoon molasses

In a medium bowl, mix together the sugar and molasses until completely blended. Store in an airtight container until ready for use.

Whipped Topping

Makes 3 cups

  1 cup nonfat dry milk

  1 cup cold water

  4 teaspoons sugar

  1 teaspoon vanilla extract

1. In a chilled medium bowl, combine the dry milk and water. Beat with a chilled wire whisk for 5 to 10 minutes or until stiff.

2. Add the sugar and vanilla to the milk. Beat the mixture until blended, about 5 minutes.

Buttermilk Substitute

Makes 1 cup

  1 cup milk

  1 tablespoon distilled white vinegar or lemon juice

Mix together and allow to sit for 5 minutes. Use immediately in recipes calling for buttermilk.

Sweetened Condensed Milk

  1 tablespoon butter

  ½ cup hot water

  1 cup nonfat dry milk

  ¾ cup sugar

1. In a small saucepan over medium heat, melt the butter in the hot water and stir until combined.

2. Pour into a medium bowl and stir in the dry milk powder and sugar. Mix well until the sugar and milk powder are dissolved.

Homemade Butter

If you are off the grid, you can also pour the mixture into a canning jar and shake vigorously until the butter separates from the buttermilk. *Makes 1 cup*

2 cups heavy cream

¼ teaspoon salt (optional)

1. Pour the cream and salt into the bowl of a food processor or blender. Process for 10 minutes, or until the butter separates from the buttermilk.

2. Press the butter into a small bowl with the back of a spoon to remove any remaining liquid. Save the buttermilk to use in cooking.

Butter Substitute

This has a different consistency than regular butter, but it can be substituted in cooking and baking. For a more spreadable butter, add another tablespoon of olive or sunflower oil to the mixture when processing. *Makes ¾ cup*

¾ cup nonfat dry milk

⅓ cup water

¼ cup olive oil or sunflower oil

⅛ teaspoon salt

¼ teaspoon butter flavoring extract (optional)

1. In the bowl of a food processor, blend the milk with the water.

2. With the processor running, slowly add the oil through the feed tube until the mixture has thickened.

3. Add the salt and butter flavoring, if using, and process until all the ingredients are well incorporated. Refrigerate after use.

Heavy Cream Substitute

Makes 1¼ cups

1 cup milk

¼ cup nonfat dry milk

Whirl the milk and dry milk powder in a blender until thoroughly mixed. Use in baking or cooking dishes that call for heavy whipping cream.

Easy Sour Cream

¾ cup raw unpasteurized milk, sour

⅓ cup butter

Beat together all the ingredients until mixture begins to thicken.

Mason Jar Yogurt

Be sure to reserve 1 tablespoon of the yogurt as a starter for your next batch. To make a thick yogurt that has the consistency of sour cream, drain it in the refrigerator using a coffee filter. *Makes 4 cups*

4 cups milk (can be reconstituted from nonfat dry milk)

1 tablespoon plain yogurt (for your starter)

2 tablespoons nonfat dry milk (optional)

1. In a medium saucepan over medium heat, heat the milk until it reaches 190°F to 200°F. (Use a candy thermometer to monitor the temperature.) Take care not to let the milk come to a boil.

2. Quickly cool the milk to 120°F by placing the pan in a sink filled with cold water.

3. Whisk in the yogurt. To make a richer flavored yogurt, add a tablespoon of nonfat dry milk and stir well. Pour the milk and yogurt mixture into a 1-quart Mason jar.

4. To maintain the temperature and allow the cultures to activate, wrap the jar in a dish towel and place it in a small cooler. Pour in hot tap water so the jar is submerged, but not floating. Close the cooler.

5. Your yogurt will be ready in 6 to 8 hours. If you prefer a tangier yogurt, allow it to sit in the cooler for an additional 2 hours. Store, covered, in the refrigerator.

PART 3

Canning

Introduction

From time immemorial, preserving the harvest has been a vital step in preparing for the barren winter months ahead. Indeed, the agrarian lifestyle was based on producing food and then preserving enough of it to last until your next harvest. Now we can combine agrarian tradition with science and modern food safety. The tools and knowledge available today allow us to preserve our harvests in ways our ancestors never dreamed of.

Different methods of preservation have been used throughout the ages and many of them are still used today, but hands down, my favorite method of preservation is canning. Canning is the perfect solution for those seeking natural food sources, for gardeners, for those seeking a more self-reliant life, and for those interested in preparedness.

A prepper's pantry is usually loaded to the rafters with things like beans, rice, and wheat, but many food stockpiles are lacking when it comes to storing proteins, fruits, and vegetables. Home canning fills in the gaps in a pantry stocked with store-bought goods, and does so at a very reasonable price. For home canners, a hot meal during a power outage situation can be as simple as opening a jar, pouring the contents into a pot, and placing it on the wood stove for about half an hour.

Once you have a pressure canner (and you conquer the fear of blowing yourself up with it!), you can preserve nearly anything. By creating meals right in jars, you can provide your family with instant, tasty nutrition. These items are very simple to prepare. If you use garden produce when possible and use ingredients purchased on sale, you can have many "instant" meals prepared at a very affordable price—and the best part is, you know exactly what's in each of them.

In this book, we'll go through canning step by step. First we'll discuss why canning is a great way for preppers to preserve their food, we'll discuss safety, and we'll talk about the basics of canning. Even if you've never canned before, you'll have all of the information you need to get started.

Next you'll find the recipes. If you've never canned before, water bath canning jams and condiments is a great way to get started. Once you've gotten your feet wet with these recipes, you can move on to pressure canning individual ingredients. Then, for the crowning jewel of canning projects, we'll can some entire meals that are ready to heat and eat. You'll turn to those meals again and again over the course of the year. If you're a veteran canner, you'll find new charts to refer to and new recipes to try. I hope that this book becomes a reference you will turn to again and again.

Because food scientists are constantly learning and updating their findings, all recipes in this book have been updated to reflect the newest information as of 2017.

So dust off your canner, and let's use some modern technology to get prepared the old-fashioned way.

CHAPTER 1

A Guide to Canning

Most preppers have cupboards, attics, and spare rooms full of beans, rice, and other grains. Some stash grocery-store bargain finds made of cheap, non-nutritious ingredients. However, there are several problems with pantries that hold only these types of supplies.

- Beans, rice, and whole grains take a long time to cook, not to mention eating the same thing again and again is boring.

- A limited pantry means limited variety in nutrients.

- Shelf-stable meat can be very expensive to purchase, and the price for a high-quality product can be completely out of reach for many families.

- Relying on the power grid to keep your meat, fruits, and vegetables preserved is risky. Even with a generator, eventually you'll run out of fuel, and then all of that food will go to waste.

While these items may have a place in your pantry, there's another way to build your food supply: home canning. Canning is an old-fashioned art that when combined with modern food safety science can create a safe, healthy, and delicious food supply for your family.

When you preserve your own food, you know exactly what is in the jars on your shelves. You can avoid allergens, genetically modified ingredients, and excess salt or sugar. What's more, you won't be reliant on a grid that could fail at any time, either for storing your food or for consuming it—when you can your own meals in jars, your food is always fully cooked. Although it will be more appetizing heated up, you can safely consume canned food straight from the jar.

If a grid-down situation goes on for an extended time, it will be important to have a long-term, grid-independent method for preserving your harvest and your meat. In my family, we practice the concept of an agrarian pantry. An agrarian pantry is similar to what our ancestors had. Most purchases are made during the growing season and only small shopping trips are needed to supplement these throughout the year. To build an agrarian pantry, stock up on a year's supply of basics like grains, baking items, tea, coffee, and dried beans. Then focus your efforts on acquiring items when they are in season and preserving them when they are at their peak. Try your hand at canning, dehydrating, and root cellaring. Items can be grown on your own property or purchased by the bushel from local farms and orchards.

Look into purchasing a side of beef and a side of pork to add to your pantry. One purchase per year is sufficient for most families and the price per pound drops dramatically when you buy meat in these large quantities. Remember not to put all of your faith in the deep freezer, however, because losing power unexpectedly could leave you with a smelly mess and a large lost investment. Try canning, smoking, salting and dehydrating for the bulk of your meat purchases.

An agrarian pantry must be replenished every year. The items in your pantry are purchased and stored under the assumption that they will be consumed within the next 12 months. Extra supplies should ideally be stored to make up for shortfalls caused by a poor harvest.

Canning Is a Cost-Effective Way to Build Your Pantry

For the frugal among us, (and let's face it, prepping and frugality go together like peanut butter and jelly), canning can save you a lot of money. Home canning can be a great way to cost-effectively build your pantry for several reasons:

- you can buy in bulk
- you can take advantage of good sales
- you can buy in-season produce at better prices than off-season produce
- it costs less to put together canned meals than it does to buy processed foods
- you don't risk losing your stockpile to power outages like you would with your freezer

Thrifty Canning Tips

If the purpose of canning your own food is to save money, these tips can help!

DON'T GO SHOPPING JUST FOR A CANNING RECIPE; BE FLEXIBLE. It's okay to have a general idea of what you want to can, but if you have recipes that require specific ingredients beyond your pantry basics, you may end up spending a lot of money. For example, one day I went to a garden exchange and swapped some money and home-canned goodies for other people's surplus produce. When I got the items home, I looked at my bounty and decided what to make based on that. Had I gone to the store or market specifically looking for certain things, I would have spent far more. Be flexible when canning and learn to adapt the ingredients you have on hand.

FILL YOUR CANNER. If you only have enough ingredients for five jars of whatever you're making but your canner holds seven jars, fill the other two jars with beans (see Chapter 11). You'll be using the same amount of electricity or gas whether the canner is full or not.

BUY CHEAP AND GET CREATIVE. Recently, I went to a local orchard that had a huge sale on just-picked pears. Half bushels were on sale for $9. And it got even better—they were buy one, get one free! When you get a bounty like this, try to can the food in a way that provides you with some variety, instead of simply canning them all the same way.

Are you sold on canning as a way to stock your pantry yet? Read on, and I'll show you exactly how it's done.

The Healthy Canner's Manifesto

A lot of people look at my canning projects and they shake their heads. "Why would you work that hard when you can just go to the grocery store?" The list of reasons is long and distinguished.

I DON'T WANT TO SERVE FOOD-LIKE SUBSTANCES. I don't want food that has been concocted in a factory after being created by chemists who throw around words like "mouthfeel" and "sodium ethyl parahydroxybenzoate." I don't want to eat something that was chemically modified to taste like a different item, all to give a higher profit margin to Kraft or Kellogg's.

I DON'T WANT TO SERVE GENETICALLY MUTATED ORGANISMS. I don't want anything that was created in a petri dish at the labs of Monsanto, which infects more than 80 percent of food in the grocery store aisles. Many of the foods at the grocery store, even those in the produce aisle, are the result of a genetically sterilized seed. Corn and soy products are especially prone to modifications. These foods were altered to contain pesticides and mutations that allow them to grow bigger, faster, and more brightly colored. GMO foods were not thoroughly tested before being rushed to the market by Monsanto in their desire to create a world food monopoly. In independent studies,[1] laboratory animals that are fed a GMO diet develop multiple organ failure, sterility, greater allergic responses, high rates of offspring mortality, and premature death.

I CAN'T AFFORD TO HIT THE HEALTH FOOD STORE FOR EVERY BITE OF FOOD. These stores come to mind for most people when they think about organic or natural foods. But for most of us, specialty stores are financially out of reach. I can save money by getting locally grown foods when they are in season, cleaning them carefully, and preserving them for the winter ahead. This allows room in my budget for weekly grocery items like organic hormone-free milk.

EATING SEASONALLY PROVIDES NUTRITIONAL BENEFITS. I grow as much organic produce as I can on my small lot. I supplement what I grow with produce from a couple of local farms, where I have been lucky enough to forge a relationship with the farmers. Our food does not come from thousands of miles away, where it is picked while green and left to ripen in a box. It is picked and home-processed at the peak of its freshness as often as possible, which lets us conserve as many nutrients as we can for the winter ahead.

I EAT HUMANELY RAISED MEAT. I refuse to consume the growth hormones, antibiotics, and other medications that are given to factory-farmed animals. I spend a little bit more money and buy our meats in bulk from a local Mennonite butcher shop or a farmer that I know personally. They do not use any chemicals on their animals and the livestock is fed what livestock naturally eats— grass, hay, bugs, and seeds. Furthermore, the animals are farmed humanely, reducing hormones like cortisol that are released when any animal is under stress.

HOME-CANNED FOOD IS THE FASTEST "FAST FOOD" AROUND. By preserving entire meals in jars, I can get a healthy and delicious meal on the table in a fraction of the time it would take to drive to a McDonald's and get the food home. Quite literally, a pot of homemade soup is steaming in a bowl in less than 5 minutes.

During the growing season, the work that I put in to cooking the food that will last us for the rest of the year probably requires less hands-on time than it would if I were producing the same meals throughout the year, one meal at a time. The reason for this is that I produce 8 to 16

---

1   http://www.organiclifestylemagazine.com/doctors-against-gmos-hear-from-those-who-have-done-the-research

meals at a time. Altogether, this consumes about two hours of preparation time and two hours of inactive processing time, when I can do other things. That is an average 20 minutes per meal, and half of that time is *not* spent in the kitchen.

I DON'T HAVE TO RELY ON THE POWER GRID TO KEEP MY FOOD FRESH. Tons of food—literally tons—is thrown out every year due to power outages. Most people stash meat and vegetables in their freezers, which is great as long as the power is up and running.

Canning might not be for everyone. It might not be for every meal. But as someone who firmly believes that our nutritional choices are the basis for our overall long-term physical and mental health, as the parent of a child with allergies and chemical sensitivities, and as an activist who refuses to support the food monopoly and toxic practices of companies like Monsanto and Dow Chemical, I have chosen along with my family to take the old-fashioned, healthy route to a pantry full of food.

CHAPTER 2
Food & Food Safety

If you've never canned before, you need to know the basics first. When you purchase your canning gear, be sure to thoroughly read the instructions. If you are new to this, you'll refer to this section of the book again and again while you get the hang of your new skill, so go ahead and fold down the corners of the pages that you find important. If your instruction manual disagrees with anything I say here, the instruction manual wins, as the instructions I provide are based on my own equipment.

With these types of recipes, it's very difficult to predict what the yield will be. The recipes aim for a canner load of six or seven jars, but there are a lot of variables, like these:

- the density of your fruits and vegetables
- the cooking duration
- the temperature and humidity conditions in your kitchen
- the weather on the day that you're canning
- the altitude where you're canning
- the different varieties of fruits and vegetables

You get the idea. It's difficult to really set your heart on a specific yield, so many of these recipes don't even try to predict the amount you'll end up with. I'll provide an estimate where possible and suggest a jar size where it makes sense, but when you are canning in a prepper-type situation, you're using up the food that you have on hand. Often, these quantities will not come in nice, neat, carefully weighed bushels. In any preparedness situation, adaptability is key.

Safety Tip: Beware of Botulism

Every recipe in the book will tell you whether you should use a water bath canner or pressure canner. Water bath canning is *only* for high-acid foods like fruits and pickles. For everything else, you should use a pressure canner.

This is because of the risk of botulism. The absolute scariest part of canning is the thought that you might preserve your food incorrectly and subject your family to the risk of botulism.

Botulism isn't very common. Over the past 10 years, fewer than 300 cases were reportedly due to home-canned food. The percentages are on your side, particularly if you process your food carefully and according to USDA guidelines.

Botulism is caused by a germ called *Clostridium botulinum*. It lives in soil and thrives in an environment that is moist and free of oxygen, so canned food is the perfect medium in which it can thrive.

This toxin can cause a serious, life-threatening emergency with even a few bites of food.[2] Some of the symptoms of botulism are:

- double vision
- blurred vision
- drooping eyelids
- slurred speech
- difficulty swallowing
- dry mouth
- muscle weakness

When in Doubt, Throw It Out!

There are other ways home-canned food can be contaminated. If there is any doubt in your mind about whether your food is safe, discard it safely where it won't be eaten by humans or animals. (Pets can also die from botulism.)

Here are some warning signs that your canned food might be spoiled:

- a container that is swollen, bulging, misshapen, or leaking
- a container that looks cracked or damaged
- an eruption of liquid or foam when the jar is opened
- a bad smell
- discoloration
- visible mold

For the love of all things cute and fluffy, don't taste questionable food to see if it's okay. When in doubt, throw it out. It's not worth your life, and if you are consuming this food during a preparedness emergency, you may not have access to medical care.

I know all of the warnings about botulism are scary. It's scary stuff! That's why I get so aggravated when people say that a pressure canner is unnecessary. I get emails all the time from people who tell me things like this: "My Great Grandma Ida always processed her meat and green beans in a water bath canner for just three hours, and she lived to be 117 years old."

Anecdotes are not viable justifications for taking risky shortcuts. My granny did things like that too. She did all sorts of stuff that we don't do any longer. As recently as 30 years ago, folks didn't put their children in car seats. Most kids survived, but there were a few that bulleted through the front windshield.

---

2 http://www.cdc.gov/features/homecanning

We now possess the capability to make things safer than did our ancestors. If you have the ability and the equipment to avoid any risk of botulism, isn't your family worth the effort? Maybe they didn't have the equipment to do these things a century ago, but we have it now. Think how awful you would feel if your spouse or child died or suffered permanent physical damage because of something you fed them against standard advice.

To use a water bath canner for low-acid foods like meat and vegetables is to risk the lives of your family. It's that simple, and it's not worth the risk. We get to have the best of both worlds: old-fashioned skills combined with modern food science. Take advantage of them both.

Now that the botulism lecture is out of the way, let's move on and discuss canning practices that are safe and healthy.

Best Practices for Cleaning Fruits and Vegetables

While I would love for every bite we consume to be organic and fresh from the garden, budgetary restrictions don't always allow for that. Furthermore, even USDA-certified organic produce (particularly orchard fruits) might have an application of antibiotics. Organic veggies might even have some toxins because of spraying from nearby farms.

Of course, just because something isn't labeled organic doesn't necessarily mean it's slathered in chemicals. Many people don't realize the high price of becoming certified organic—it literally costs tens of thousands of dollars. Because of the price, a lot of local produce is traditionally grown and pesticide free but is not certified organic. It helps to purchase produce from local farms and to have a good relationship with a few favorite farmers. This way, you can quiz them about what, if anything, is sprayed on the goodies before you bring them home.

So what can you do about those fruits and veggies that do get sprayed? Apples, for example, can have more than 48 different pesticides on them, according to a report by the Environmental Working Group.[3] You can clean off more than 95 percent of pesticides if you are diligent in your process. I use the process below for cleaning all of our food before consuming or preserving it. Not only does it remove pesticides and traces of fertilizer, it also removes plain old ordinary dirt.

1. Put 1 cup of baking soda and some all-natural dish soap into a sink full of hot water. Use cool water for more delicate produce like berries or lettuce.
2. Allow your produce to soak in the solution for about 20 minutes. An alarming white film of gunk may rise to the top of the sink.
3. Drain the sink and rinse the produce. Rinse hearty produce under running water. For delicate produce, scrub your sink clean, fill it with fresh water, and swish the produce around in the clean water to rinse it.
4. Use a cloth and scrub the outside of thick-skinned, firm produce. Allow delicate produce to drain in a colander.

---

3 http://www.cbsnews.com/news/apples-top-list-for-pesticide-contamination

5. If you are still able to see a film or if the rinse water is cloudy, clean out your sink with white vinegar and repeat until your rinse water is clear.

The process is a bit time-consuming, but if you are putting in the effort to home-can so that your family has wholesome, delicious food, it's worthwhile to make certain your produce is as pristine as you can make it.

What Not to Can

There are some things that you should never can because, according to the food scientists at the USDA,[4] it simply cannot be done safely:

- barley
- butter
- milk
- cheese
- cornstarch
- cruciferous vegetables, unless pickled
- eggs
- flour of any type
- grains
- oats
- pasta
- purees
- rice
- summer squash and zucchini, unless pickled

---

4   http://nchfp.uga.edu/questions/FAQ_canning.html

CHAPTER 3

Canning 101

If you are canning for preparedness' sake, you'll want to stock up on some particular supplies. The amount of supplies you'll need will be based on the size of your family, how much food you go through, and what you intend to can.

Jars

Our family of three uses about 400 jars per year for our canning projects and keeps about 100 extra just in case. These jars are ready to be reused as soon as they are washed.

I purchase name-brand jars, like Ball, because I've found that the cheaper jars are more likely to shatter during pressure canning, and that creates a heckuva mess, let me tell you. I have had excellent luck finding name-brand jars at thrift stores and yard sales. Be sure to run your finger over the rim of each jar when buying second hand. You want to feel for little nicks or chips that will keep your jars from sealing properly. Also, flip them over and inspect the bottoms for hairline cracks.

Rings

Most of the time when you buy jars, they come with rings. I remove the rings before putting full jars into storage so I don't require as many rings as I do jars. Of course, if you're filling your jars with water when they aren't filled with food, you'll want to keep more rings on hand.

Lids

I purchase lids (also known as flats) by the case and always keep at least 400 on hand to sustain us throughout the year, though generally I have something closer to a two-year supply. Be sure to have lids for both regular and wide-mouth jars, if you use both kinds. Try to keep your lids at a moderate temperature year round. If they get too hot, the adhesive will be gummy ahead of time and may fail to seal. If they get too cold, the adhesive will be brittle and may fail to seal.

I avoid the cheap generic lids, especially for pressure canning. I have a higher rate of failure with those. I recommend Ball lids, which are BPA free.

Reusable Lids

"But what about reusable lids?" In principle, reusable lids should be a prepper's best friend. We love stuff that we can use over and over and never replace, right? I have a confession. I have tried reusable lids, and I really, really didn't like them. I found that they were a bit more difficult to use because you have to make sure the stars are aligned, pray, sprinkle in the tears of a Tibetan maiden, and can only at midnight. Well, not really, but you get the general idea. There are many steps to using reusable lids, and everything must be perfect.

It's also unclear how safe these lids are, especially those of the Tattler brand. For example, *The Natural Canning Resource Book* by Lisa Rayner noted that the National Center for Home Food Preservation "documented higher levels of seal failure rates on Tattler lids" compared to other brands. Further studies have shown that many compounds, including alcohol, acids, chlorine, and sunlight can break down the plastic in the lids, which means that the plastic can leach into your food.

These lids also allow oxygen to survive in the headspace. Because the lid is largely inflexible and is only sealed after processing because of the way the band is tightened, it's tough to guarantee that all oxygen has been flushed out of the headspace; compare this with metal lids, where the vacuum itself is what creates the seal. This could create conditions where it is possible for nasty microorganisms to grow. As a precaution, I'll only use my current Tattler lids for processing high-acid foods like fruit.

Please use your own judgment when deciding which kind of lids will be best for your family.

Canning Salt

I stock up on vast amounts of canning salt, also known as pickling salt. It's a preservative and an integral part of canning. It doesn't contain anti-caking additives, which can make canning liquid turn murky, or iodine, which can discolor fruits and veggies. You can also use kosher salt or sea salt, but keep in mind that sea salt is measured differently than canning salt. Take care not to overdo it.

Sugar

Sugar, like salt, is a preservative, and it has a place in even the healthiest diet. You can purchase sugar in bulk and repackage it to last for a very long time. The key is to keep out moisture and bugs.

My favorite is turbinado sugar. Sucanat crystals are pure and unprocessed, but turbinado takes it a step further. The crystals are washed in a centrifuge to remove the surface molasses. This reduces the mineral content but makes turbinado sugar appropriate for recipes that call for white sugar.

When I have a recipe that calls for brown sugar, I turn to muscovado sugar. Muscovado is a very dark, unrefined sugar that has the highest molasses content of the natural sugars. It has an incredibly rich flavor and a texture like moist beach sand.

I primarily store organic, less processed sugar for my stockpile, although I do have a stash of inexpensive cane sugar stocked away just in case I run out of the good stuff. If you go with a less expensive sugar, cane sugar is the best option. If it doesn't say "cane sugar" on the package, it is most likely beet sugar. There's nothing inherently wrong with sugar made from beets, but sugar beets are usually genetically modified.[5]

Although it isn't genetically modified, that doesn't mean that non-organic cane sugar is actually a *good* option. It is often doused in Roundup (a brand of glyphosate) at harvest time to make certain the cane dies down evenly, increasing the yield. My suggestion? Go organic if you can.

Lemon Juice

Unless you live in a place where lemons and limes grow, you could have difficulty getting a hold of lemon juice in a long-term disaster. Stock up on the plastic squeeze bottles of lemon juice, which will last for about a year, according to the labels. Lemon juice is an essential ingredient for many things you will be canning. Keep in mind that they are often preserved with sulfites, which some people can't tolerate. To make sure your lemon juice is good after a longer period of time, do *not* add it directly to your recipe. Put some in a little dish. Make sure it isn't murky and that it still smells OK. Dip your finger in and take a little taste. If it doesn't pass any of those three tests, discard it and use citric acid instead.

Ascorbic/Citric Acid

This is not usually my first choice when canning, but I do stash away vitamin C tablets for the purpose of being able to add them to canning recipes if lemon juice is unavailable. Use six 500-milligram tablets per gallon of product or liquid.[6] You can also purchase citric acid or ascorbic acid on its own. The cheap citric acid is made from genetically modified mold (yuck!), so go with an organic source. You can often find a better quality citric acid where cheese-making supplies are sold.

Vinegar

I keep both white vinegar and apple cider vinegar on hand in large quantities. Vinegar is a preservative, so it's safe to say that it will stay fresh on your pantry shelves almost indefinitely.[7]

The other bonus to vinegar is that you can make it yourself, often from food scraps that would otherwise be thrown away. However—and this is important—if you make your own vinegar, you must test the pH if you want to use it for canning. The safety of most canning recipes is based on the acidity levels of commercial vinegar. All you need to do this is grab a

---

5 http://www.non-gmoreport.com/articles/jun08/sugar_beet_industry_converts_to_gmo.php
6 http://nchfp.uga.edu/how/can_01/ascorbic_acid.html
7 http://www.eatbydate.com/other/condiments/how-long-does-vinegar-last

pack of inexpensive pH strips.[8] You'll want a pH of 2.4 or lower, because the lower the pH, the higher the acidity level is.

Jar Prep

Your preserved food is only as sanitary as the vessels you store it in. For some items, you will need to sanitize your jars, rings, and flats. Some folks get really stressed out about this. Please keep in mind that you are not performing open-heart surgery. Nearly all canning recipes have to be processed for more than 10 minutes, which, in conjunction with the pre-sterilization you have performed, should keep your food safe and healthy. In fact, the National Center for Home Preservation[9] recently said that it's *unnecessary* to sanitize the jars of foods that are going to be processed for 10 minutes or longer.

Because I store my jars outside in a shed, I do generally sanitize them by running them through the dishwasher. If you want to sanitize your jars or if your canning process will last less than 10 minutes, there are several methods for doing so.

THE DISHWASHER METHOD. This is the easiest method. Just run the sanitizing cycle right before you begin canning. The dishwasher will keep the jars hot until you are ready to fill them. The heat from the dishwasher will also make the rubber on the jar lid more pliable and ready to seal.

THE WATER BATH CANNER METHOD. Assuming that your jars are clean and all you need to do is sanitize them, you can use your water bath canner for this.

1. Place them on the rack in the canner.
2. Pour in enough water to go over the opening of the jars and fill them.
3. Bring the canner to a boil and allow it to boil for 10 minutes.
4. Use your jar lifter and remove the jars, placing them upside down on a towel or drying rack to drain.

Time-Saving Hint: Reuse the hot water for canning once the jars are filled and lidded.

THE OVEN METHOD. You can also use your oven to sanitize your jars.

1. Preheat your oven to 225°F.
2. Place your jars in a roasting pan and slide them into the oven for at least 20 minutes.
3. Turn off the heat, but leave the jars in there until they are ready to be packed.

Warning: This is kind of a "duh," but the jars will be hotter than heck when you take them out of the oven, so don't burn yourself when filling them and placing them in the canner!

Sanitizing the Lids

Dont's forget you'll need to sanitize the lids!

---

8   http://www.culturesforhealth.com/learn/kombucha/testing-acidity-strength-vinegar
9   http://nchfp.uga.edu/how/can_01/sterile_jars.html

1. In a small saucepan, bring enough water to a simmer to cover your lids and rings. Do not bring the lids to a rolling boil, as this could damage the sealing compound.
2. Keep the lids in the hot water and remove them with sanitized tongs or a lid lifter (a cool little magnetic wand) when you are ready to put them on the jars.

Water Bath Canning

Water bath canning is a safe method for preserving high-acid foods. Some examples of foods that can be canned in a water bath are:

- jams and jellies
- fruit
- applesauce
- pickles
- tomato products

For water bath canning, you must have the following tools:

- big canning pot
- rack or folded towel
- jar lifter
- jar funnel
- jars
- lids
- rings

These items are the minimum tools you need for canning properly and safely. There are all sorts of other gadgets out there, like items that help you measure headspace and lid lifters with a little magnet on the end, but if you have the above items, you are ready to can!

Step-by-Step Water Bath Canning

While your product is on the stove, bubbling merrily away, follow these steps.

1) WASH YOUR JARS, LIDS, AND RINGS. If you have a dishwasher, you can wash them in the dishwasher. The heat from it is enough to sanitize everything. If you are processing for longer than 10 minutes, you'll be golden. If not, you need to use one of the sanitation methods recommended previously. You can also add 10 minutes to your processing time in the water bath, but this can affect the quality of your product. Personally, I'm notoriously lazy and use the dishwasher.

2) PREPARE YOUR CANNER. Place your canner on the stove or burner and place the rack or folded towel on the bottom of your canner. Fill your canner with water, leaving about 3 to 5 inches at the top to allow for room for your filled jars. Bring your water to a boil. Because it takes forever and a day to bring that much water to a boil, I generally get it started while I am prepping my food.

3) FILL YOUR JARS. Line up your jars on a heatproof surface near the stove. You can place a towel on the counter to protect it from the hot, filled jars. Using the funnel, ladle your prepared product into the jars, leaving the recommended amount of headspace.

4) PUT ON YOUR LIDS. With a dry, clean dish towel, carefully wipe the lip of the filled jars to remove any residue. Place the lids on each jar, then tighten the rings by hand. You don't have to use much torque on them. The rings simply hold the lids in place until they seal.

5) PLACE YOUR JARS IN THE CANNER. With your handy-dandy jar lifter, place the closed jars carefully into the canner. Put them in gently because as you know, boiling water hurts when it splashes on you. Be careful not to let the jars touch each other because they could break, and that makes a big mess you won't want to deal with. Make sure the lids are all completely submerged. They don't have to be under by inches, just covered.

6) PROCESS THE JARS. Put the lid back on your canner and bring the water to a rolling boil. Don't start clocking your processing time until the water is at a full boil. Then just leave the jars in the water bath for the time required by your recipe.

7) REMOVE THE JARS FROM THE CANNER. Using your jar lifter, carefully remove the jars from the boiling water. Tip the jars to the side to allow the hot water to drip off the top. Then place the jars on your towel or heatproof surface.

8) LEAVE 'EM ALONE! ALLOW 12 TO 24 HOURS FOR THE JARS TO COOL AND SEAL. You will hear musical "pop," "plink," and "ping" noises as the jars seal in the cool air; that is the lid getting sucked down and forming a seal to the lip of the jar.

9) REMOVE THE RINGS. When you are ready to store the jars, you can remove the rings. This keeps your rings from rusting because of moisture trapped between the metal ring and the jar.

10) TEST THE SEALS. Test the seal by pushing down with your finger. If it pops back and forth, it is not sealed. Another way to check is by picking up your jar by the lid. It should remain firmly adhered to the rim of the jar. If it is not properly sealed, put it in the refrigerator and use the unsealed product in the next few weeks. You can also reprocess your food, as long as it's done within 24 hours.[10] Use a new lid if you do this.

11) PUT IT AWAY. Store your sealed little gems in a cool, dark place. It's okay to peek in and admire them from time to time.

Pressure Canning

Low-acid foods have to be preserved at higher temperatures than do high-acid foods. The low-acid environment welcomes the growth of bacteria like botulism, a form of food poisoning that can cause permanent nerve damage or even death. (Remember botulism from page 329?) The temperature must reach 240°F, which can only be achieved through steam under pressure. Pressure canning exceeds the temperature of water bath canning, getting your product into the

---

10   http://nchfp.uga.edu/questions/FAQ_canning.html#1

safety zone that prevents the possibility of botulism. All vegetables (except for tomatoes, which are botanically a fruit), meats, seafood, and poultry must be preserved in a pressure canner.

I'll be honest—I was utterly terrified the first time I used my pressure canner. I was certain I was going to blow up my kitchen. This fear was backed up when I put the regulator (that little black round thing you see on the top) on askew, which led to my screaming and dropping the regulator, and the canner's making a gosh-awful whistling noise.

But after successfully pressure-canning a couple of times, I'm actually equally as comfortable using this method as I am using the water bath method. Some recipes can be made using either canner, but when it's an option I nearly always choose the pressure canner because it is far faster for those recipes.

Pep talk is over—let's pressure-can!

For pressure canning, you need:

- pressure canner with valves, seals, and gauges
- rack or folded towel
- jar lifter
- jar funnel
- jars
- lids
- rings

Like water bath canning, you can get all the fancy gadgets if you want to, but the ones listed above are the essentials.

The instructions in this book are for a dial gauge canner. If you happen to have a weighted gauge canner, you can only apply pressure during canning at either 5, 10, or 15 pounds. If the pressure required for canning a certain food does not exactly match any of these values, go up to the next highest pressure. For example, if the recipe calls for 11 pounds of pressure (PSI), then use the 15-pound weight setting.

Step-by-Step Pressure Canning

One thing you will notice about pressure canning is that it is actually very similar to water bath canning. Differences are really only related to the equipment. Once you have learned to use your pressure canner correctly, you will find it every bit as easy as water bath canning. Remember to always check the instructions on your individual canner. If there is a discrepancy between what you read here and in the instructions, go with the instructions that came with your product.

1) **WASH YOUR JARS, LIDS, AND RINGS**. You'll be processing them for long enough and at hot enough temperatures that sanitizing them is unnecessary.

2) **PREPARE YOUR CANNER**. Place your canner on the stove or burner. Place your rack or folded towel in the bottom of your canner and add about 3 inches of water to the canner. Most pressure canners have a line to which they should be filled with water. In pressure canning, it is not necessary for the water to cover the lids. At this point, you can turn the burner on low to begin warming the water, but don't bring it to a boil yet.

3) FILL YOUR JARS. Line up your jars on the counter near the stove. If the surface is not heatproof, place a towel on the counter first because the filled jars will be very hot. Ladle the prepared product into the jars using the funnel, leaving the headspace recommended in your recipe.

4) PUT ON YOUR LIDS. With a dry, clean dish towel, carefully wipe the lip of the filled jars, making sure to get off any food residue. Place the lids on each jar, then tighten the rings—you don't have to really twist too hard, as the lids will seal in the canner. If you are canning a fatty food, you can use a cloth dampened with vinegar to remove any fat on the rim that might prevent a good seal.

5) PLACE YOUR JARS IN THE CANNER. Be careful not to let the jars touch because not only could they could break when they bump together in the boiling water, but in pressure canning, the steam must be able to completely surround the jars.

6) BUILD STEAM IN THE CANNER. Before putting the lid on the canner, check the vent pipe to be sure it is clear. Place the lid firmly on the canner, latching it as per the specifics of your canner, and increase the heat to bring the water to a boil. At this point, steam should be coming out of the vent pipe. Reduce the heat until a moderate amount of steam is coming steadily out of the pipe for 10 minutes. The purpose of this is to release the air and build up the steam inside the canner. If you don't give it the whole 10 minutes, your canner will not build pressure. As patience is not my strong point, I learned this from experience.

7) CLOSE THE VENT. After exhausting the steam for 10 minutes, either close the petcock valve or place the weighted regulator on the vent pipe, depending on your canner. When I place the regulator on, I always put a dish towel around my hand, because steam is hot. It sometimes makes a loud, high-pitched noise when you are putting the regulator on. Don't be alarmed by the various rattling, whistling, and bubbling noises. Pressure canning is loud business.

8) PRESSURIZE THE CANNER. Turn up the heat on the burner and wait until the gauge has reached the desired pressure. (Pressure will differ based on altitudes and recipes—see page 341 for altitude adjustments). This usually takes 3 to 5 minutes. Note that if you lose pressure while processing, you must start the processing time from the beginning.

9) ADJUST THE HEAT TO MAINTAIN THE PRESSURE. This part takes practice. Monitor your canner while it is processing to be sure the pressure is maintained. I have found that turning the dial on my electric stove to somewhere around four keeps my pressure between 10 to 12 pounds quite steadily.

10) RELEASE THE PRESSURE. When your processing time is over, it is time to release the pressure. It couldn't be easier. Turn off the burner. Take the canner off the burner and put it on a heatproof surface. Walk away. Allow the canner to return to room temperature and release pressure naturally. Don't try to cool it down faster—that is how people get hurt while pressure canning. The pressure is completely reduced when the air vent/cover lock and overpressure plug have dropped, and when no steam escapes when the pressure regulator is tilted. The gauge, if your canner has one, should be completely at zero. This entire process can take more than 45 minutes and must not be rushed!

11) OPEN THE VENT. When the pressure is gone, open the petcock or remove the weighted regulator. If the regulator doesn't want to come off, there is likely still some pressure in the canner. Don't force it—walk away for another 15 minutes. Once the vent is open, leave the canner for another 2 to 5 minutes.

12) REMOVE THE JARS FROM THE CANNER. Use pot holders to protect your hands while you unlatch the lid of your pressure canner. Very carefully, remove the lid from canner, turning it away from you so that you are not burned by the steam that will rush out. Using your jar lifter, carefully remove the jars from the canner one by one. Then place the jars on your towel or heatproof surface.

13) ALLOW 12 TO 24 HOURS FOR THE JARS TO COOL AND SEAL. Let the jars stand overnight in a draft-free place where they will not be moved or bumped. Jars that are sealed properly will bubble away on the counter for quite some time after they have been removed from the pressure canner. You will hear a musical "pop" as the jars seal in the cool air—that is the sound of the lid getting sucked down and forming a seal on the jar. When you are ready to store the jars, remove the rings. This will keep your rings from rusting because of moisture trapped between the metal ring and the jar.

14) TEST THE SEAL BY PUSHING DOWN WITH YOUR FINGER. If it pops back and forth, it is not sealed. Another way to check is by picking the jar up by the lid. The lid should remain firmly adhered to the rim of the jar. If it is not properly sealed, put it in the refrigerator and use the unsealed product within the next few weeks. You can also reprocess your food as long as it's done within 24 hours. Use a new lid if you do this.

15) STORE YOUR JARS IN A COOL, DARK PLACE.

Altitude Adjustment

It's time to talk science, which so much of canning is. At sea level and up to 1,000 feet above sea level, water boils at 212°F. However, once you get above the 1,000-foot mark, the changes in atmospheric pressure mean that the boiling point is actually *lower* than 212°F.

Altitude (feet)	Water Boiling Point
0 (Sea Level)	212°F
2,000	208°F
4,000	204°F
6,000	201°F
8,000	197°F
10,000	194°F

Because of these differences in boiling point, we must add extra processing time in order to make our food safe. It simply isn't worth the risk to miss a few minutes of canning time, so learn your altitude and adjust your times accordingly. I had to re-calculate all of the times and pressures that I had been using when I moved from sea level to my new home 3,000 feet the mountains.

Water Bath Canning Adjustments

Food safety requirements state that the goodies inside your jars should reach 212°F when water bath canning, and if they don't, you have to add to your processing time in order to make your preserved food safe.

For water bath canning, add 2½ minutes of processing time for every 1,000 feet above sea level. Use the following chart as a reference on how to increase processing time based on your elevation.

WATER BATH CANNING ADJUSTMENTS

Elevation	Additional time
1,000–2,999	+5 minutes
3,000–5,999	+10 minutes
6,000–7,999	+15 minutes
8,000–10,000	+20 minutes

Pressure Canning Adjustments

Pressure canning requires that your food reach 240°F. When pressure canning at higher altitudes, you need additional pressure as opposed to additional time.

The standard rule is to add 1 pound of pressure for every 1,000 feet above sea level. However, you will rarely ever adjust more than 5 pounds, regardless of your elevation.

For safety reasons, pressure canners should never be used above 17 pounds of pressure.

PRESSURE CANNING ADJUSTMENTS

Elevation	Additional pressure
1,000–1,999	+ 1
2,000–3,999	+ 3
4,000–5,999	+5
6,000–7,999	+5
8,000–10,000	+5

For the recipes included in this book, times and pressures are given based on sea level altitudes, so use these charts to adjust according to your location.

CHAPTER 4

Traditional Canning Tips & Recipes

This section of the book deals with preserving the basics. In the type of long-term sustainability scenario many of us are concerned about, being able to *preserve* the food you raise is every bit as important as being able to raise the food. The only way you'll make it through the time between growing seasons is by storing food, and canning is a method that will work for many different foods. Let's get started on the nitty gritty basics that will make up the backbone of your home-preserved food store!

Condimental Fare

Chapters 5 through 7 will teach you how to can your own condiments. You can make the simplest fare tastier, more elegant, and even more nutritious with the right condiment. I'm not talking about squirting ketchup on a burger—I'm talking about a mouth-watering relish made of garden vegetables, a surprisingly luscious fruit salsa, a decadent homemade jam, or a sweet and savory chutney that you can use to turn relatively bland prepper pantry items into instant gourmet.

Nearly all of the condiments in this book have an acidity level that allows for water bath canning, unless otherwise noted. For that reason, I've put it first in the book. Jams and condiments are a wonderful, immediately gratifying way to get your feet wet with canning.

Having shelves full of chutneys and relishes will add a boost of nutrition and flavor to your meals. Furthermore, many chutneys are of the "kitchen sink" variety, which means that you can use up those odds and ends of produce that are not quite enough to make a full batch based on any single item. When your garden is producing more than you can eat, consider preserving some leftovers as condiments to add to the variety on your groaning pantry shelves. With your pantry full of jams and condiments, you can get your fancy on at any time!

The Nitty Gritty Basics

Chapters 8 through 11 focus on the basic ingredients that make up most of the meals you'll be cooking. When you have fruit, vegetables, and meat in your pantry, you can combine these basics in untold ways to make delicious meals. Because these prepared foods have little in the way of seasoning, they will be adaptable to many different types of cuisine when they're needed.

Canned foods of this nature don't have an extremely long shelf life when compared with grains and dried beans. They are not meant to be in long-term storage. Rather, this process is a nod to our agrarian ancestors, who stored food each year to get them through to the next harvest plus a little extra, in case the harvest was poor. Home-canned food lasts for "at least a year"[11] according to the USDA, although some people maintain that the food is safe and tasty long after that time.

Generally, I can my produce all summer and fall. In the winter and spring, I can my meat. Doing it this way, I have a nice, rotating supply and I'm not doing everything at once.

Tomato, Tomahto: An Important Note

Since you'll be using tomatoes in a lot of the recipes in this book, I wanted to give you some tips on how to handle them up front. Come back and reference this page every time a recipe calls for prepped tomatoes.

Get More Tomatoes

Here's my recommendation for your end-of-summer food preservation: you'll need 100 pounds of tomatoes. I can hear your shock from here: "100 pounds? Are you insane?"

Get 100 pounds of tomatoes or more if you can. No other item of produce increases in nutrients when cooked and stored like tomatoes. Canning tomatoes is like loading your shelves with vitamins and tasty meals throughout the winter, when fresh, locally grown fruits and veggies are expensive and scarce.

I plant more tomatoes in my garden than anything else because we love them so much. You can often find tomatoes by the bushel for $1 to $2 per pound at your local farmer's market or, if your friends have an overabundance, you can barter for finished products.

Trust me. Get as many tomatoes as you can get your hands on, and you won't regret it.

Prepping Your Tomatoes

Everyone loves tomato season, or, as I like to call it, "Make Your Kitchen Look Like a Crime Scene" season!

I'm not gonna lie—there is nothing messier than a bushel of tomatoes getting jarred. It's a fair bit of work to process your own tomato products, but the intensely flavored results make it all worthwhile.

These are some short cuts to speed along your tomato processing procedures.

---

11 http://nchfp.uga.edu/questions/FAQ_canning.html#5

Mess-Free Tomato Peeling

Lots of people already know this little trick but it bears repeating, especially when you are looking at an entire bushel of those bad boys!

1. Begin boiling a pot of water on the stove. At the same time, prep a large bowl with very icy water.
2. Slide tomatoes into the pot of boiling water for 1 to 2 minutes. You will know they are ready to come out because the skin will start to wrinkle up.
3. Use a slotted spoon to remove the tomatoes and drop them instantly into the ice bath, where you can leave them for as long as you need to.
4. Once the tomato is cool enough to touch, you can easily slide the skin off with your fingers.

This process also works like a charm on thin-skinned fruits like peaches, nectarines, and apricots.

Coring the Tomatoes

There's more than one way to skin a cat—er, core a tomato! You can simply use a paring knife and cut it out. Or, you can use an old-fashioned hand crank food mill that spits the bad stuff out one end and the good stuff out the other.

Turning Tomatoes into a Sauce-Like Consistency

You can turn your tomatoes into a sauce-like consistency in three different ways.

- Dump the whole mess of cored and peeled tomatoes into a big stockpot, as is or roughly chopped, and cook them down.
- Puree them by batches in a food processor or blender and then cook them down.
- Put them through the food mill, then cook them down in the stockpot.

For me, the choice relies on what I am making. For spaghetti sauces, I prefer the consistency of the tomatoes that come out of the food mill. If I'm making sauces, like ketchup or barbecue sauce, I prefer to use the food processor.

Consider your tomatoes officially prepped. From this point on, you'll be ready to proceed with your recipes!

CHAPTER 5

Jazz Things Up with Jams

One of the easiest things to can is jam or jelly. It is a quick water bath canning project that can be done in just a few hours and is quite satisfying. Learn how to make jam and you'll be able to supply your family with jam for the entire winter ahead.

The typical way to make jam is with boxed or bottled pectin. It's also possible to make jam without pectin (see page 348). Both methods are universal recipes, meaning you can follow the same set of instructions to make any type of jam. On page 349, you'll find a chart that provides specific instructions and processing times for different types of fruit.

How to Make Jam with Boxed Pectin

If you will be using boxed pectin to make your jam, here are the basic instructions. The amounts of fruit, sugar, lemon juice, and pectin that you will be using will vary based on the recipe you are making; this is a general set of instructions for making jam with pectin. Note that pectin comes in different sized packages, so when in doubt, follow the instructions that come with your pectin.

1. Prep your fruit by washing it and cutting it up if necessary.
2. Smush your fruit. You can do this with a potato masher, food processor, blender, or food mill. For some fruits, I like to puree them for a smoother jam and for others, I like chunkier jam—it's up to personal preference.
3. In a small bowl, use a fork to mix ¼ cup of the sugar with one packet of pectin, unless the directions on your packet specify a different amount.
4. In a saucepan, add the fruit, lemon juice, and pectin together. Mix well.
5. Bring the mixture to a boil over medium heat, stirring frequently.
6. Once mixture is boiling, stir in the sugar and return to a boil for 1 minute.
7. Test your jam (see below).
8. Ladle the jam carefully into your jars, wipe the rims, and cap your jars with lids and rings.
9. Process in a hot water bath canner, according to the ingredients chart.

Jam Making Rule of Law: Always Test Your Jam!

Keep a spoon in the freezer. To test your jam, drip a bit of the hot jam into the spoon, which will allow it to quick cool. The consistency the jam will reach is the same consistency your finished product will have. After testing, I nearly always end up adding another quarter to half package of pectin. I use the cheaper pectin to "top it up." Then, I return my jam mixture to a simmer for a couple of minutes and test again. Omitting this step may result in a very tasty ice cream topping or waffle syrup, but not jam!

The Scoop on Pectin

For years when I made jam, I reached for a box of pectin from the store. But when I spent some time reading up on store-bought pectin, I was very unhappy to discover that the jams I'd been making for my family had been tainted with GMOs. I had unknowingly been contaminating my carefully sourced fruit and pricey turbinado sugar with the very things I strive to avoid, and I hadn't even given it a second thought.

Most brands breathlessly exclaim "all natural pectin" or "made from real fruit." And this is true—pectin does originate from fruit. But don't be deceived. This misleading label makes it sound as though boxed pectin is nothing more than some powdered fruit. Here are the ingredients from the box of pectin lurking in my canning cupboard: citric acid, dextrose, and fruit pectin.

Dextrose is generally made from cornstarch, the main ingredient in good old high-fructose corn syrup. And don't let anyone tell you that citric acid is "just vitamin C." It is derived from GMO mold (see page 335 for more on this). Plus, not only does store-bought pectin contain unsavory ingredients, but it is also very highly processed. So, if you want to avoid GMOs and processed foods, what's a homemade-jam making mama to do?

Jam has been around for thousands of years. The first known book of jam recipes was written in Rome in the first century.[12] Since I'm pretty sure our ancestors didn't have those handy little boxes of Sure-Jel or Certo sitting in their pantries, I set out to learn how they made thick, delicious preserves to spread on their biscuits.

My first attempt at breaking up with the box was to make my own pectin with green apples. I made a tasty product, but it wasn't really jam-like. It's possible, considering the time of year, that the apples were too ripe to allow this to work for me, but I assume that unripe apples were not always available in the past when people wanted to make jam from the currently ripe harvest.

I continued to read recipes and methods from days gone by. It soon became clear that adding pectin wasn't really necessary at all. In days past, the sugar and the fruit worked hand-in-hand to create the desired consistency.

I combined bits from a few different methods and finally came up with a jam that I was happy with. In comparison with the boxed pectin jam, it doesn't gel quite as much, but after trying this jam, the texture of the others now seems slightly artificial to me. This produces a softer preserve with an incredibly intense fruit flavor. Also, when using this method, you don't get that layer of foam that you have to skim off the top like you do with the boxed pectin method.

The instructions for basic non-pectin jams are pretty much the same regardless of what jam you'll be making. You'll only need to make minor modifications for different fruits. When making non-pectin jams, you'll wind up with a fantastic by-product; when you drain the fruit, the juice collected can be turned into a delicious syrup and processed at the same time as your jam.

---

12   https://www.encyclopedia.com/food/encyclopedias-almanacs-transcripts-and-maps/jams-jellies-and-preserves

Your yield for this recipe will vary based on the fruit used. See Basic Jam-Making Guidelines on page 349.

Pectin-Free Jam and Fruit Syrup

Makes approximately 6 (1-pint) jars

7 pounds (14 to 20 cups) fresh or frozen fruit

¼ cup lemon or lime juice

5 cups and 2 tablespoons sugar, divided

clean cotton fabric for draining (I used a flour sack towel. This will be permanently stained, so don't use something you want to keep pretty.)

1. Prepare your fruit. For berries, this means washing them, sorting them, and removing little leaves and twigs, as well as shriveled berries. Leave the odd green berry in, because less ripe fruit has more naturally occurring pectin than ripe fruit. For fruits like apples or peaches, this might mean blanching and peeling them, then removing the cores.

2. Mash, finely chop, or puree your fruit. I used a blender to puree half of the fruit, and a food processor to finely chop the other half. We prefer a slightly rough texture.

3. Pour your mixture into a large crock or non-reactive bowl, layering your fruit with 3 cups of sugar. I use the ceramic insert from my slow cooker for this.

4. Leave the fruit and sugar mixture in your refrigerator overnight. The juice from the fruit will combine with the sugar and form a slightly jelled texture. Some liquid will separate from the sugar and fruit.

5. The next day, line a colander with a piece of fabric. Place the colander into a pot to catch the liquid from the fruit and sugar mixture.

6. Pour your fruit and sugar mixture into the fabric-lined colander. Put this back in the refrigerator for at least an hour to drain. You can let it drain for longer with no ill effect; in fact, this will result in an even thicker jam.

7. When you're ready to make jam, scoop the fruit out of the fabric-lined colander and place it in a pot, leaving lots of extra space for liquid to evaporate. This helps it cook down faster.

8. The approximately 2 pints of liquid that you caught in the other pot will form the basis for your fruit syrup. Place that pot on the stove and bring it to a rolling boil. Add ¼ cup of sugar and a tablespoon of lemon juice per pint and reduce heat to a simmer. I like to add one big spoonful of jam to this to add a little texture to the syrup.

9. On another burner, bring your fruit and sugar mixture to a simmer, stirring frequently. Taste test and add up to 2 cups of additional sugar. After about an hour, the texture will have thickened. If you still have a great deal of liquid, you can use a fabric-lined sieve to strain some more out. You can add this liquid to the syrup.

10. Fill sanitized jars with your finished products. Process the water bath canner according to the type of fruit you are canning (see Basic Jam-Making Guidelines below, and make adjustments for your altitude).

Making Basic Jams

While recipes are helpful if you are making a fancy jam with multiple ingredients, you don't actually need a recipe for basic jams. You can use this chart to figure out the water bath canner processing times and special instructions for whatever fruit you happen to have on hand. Remember to always adjust for altitude!

BASIC JAM-MAKING GUIDELINES

Fruit	Special Instructions	Processing Time
Apricot	Peel, slice in half to pit	5 minutes
Blackberry	Optional step: mill to remove seeds	10 minutes
Blueberry	Optional step: puree	7 minutes
Cherry	Pit with a cherry pitter, chop before cooking	10 minutes
Grape	Mill to remove seeds	10 minutes
Huckleberry	Check for stems	10 minutes
Peach	Peel, slice in half to remove pits	10 minutes
Plum	Slice in half to remove pits	5 minutes
Raspberry	Crush with a potato masher	10 minutes
Strawberry	Remove cores, mash with a potato masher	10 minutes

Blueberry Lemon Jam

This stuff is like the Muse of Jams. Everyone that has tried it has been struck with sudden inspiration: "Oh my gosh, can you imagine this on pancakes?" "Wow! What if you used it in shortbread thumbprint cookies?" "This is just begging for some good English scones!"

You get the idea. You've gotta try it!

Makes approximately 7 (1-pint) jars

> 7 to 8 pints fresh or frozen blueberries
>
> 4–5 cups sugar, to taste, separated
>
> ¾ cup lemon or lime juice, separated

1. Wash and sort your berries. Look out for the little woody stems that like to hide in the berries and create a sneaky, unpleasant texture in your finished product.

2. Smush your berries. I like to use my blender or food processor to puree the daylights out of them, but some people want more texture, in which case you could use a potato masher.

3. Pour your berries into a crock and layer them with 3 cups of the sugar. Top with ½ cup of lemon juice. Leave this in your fridge overnight.

4. The next day, place a fabric-lined colander in a bigger pot. Drain your berries and sugar mixture for at least an hour.

5. When you're ready to make jam, scoop the fruit out of the fabric-lined colander and place it in a pot, leaving lots of extra space to help it cook down faster.

6. Bring your fruit and sugar mixture to a simmer, stirring frequently. After about an hour, the texture will have thickened. If you still have a great deal of liquid, you can use a fabric-lined sieve to strain some more out.

7. Stir in ¼ cup of lemon or lime juice and 1 cup of sugar. Increase heat to bring mixture back to a simmer.

8. Optional: Use the 1 to 2 pints of liquid that you caught in the other pot as the basis for a fruit syrup. Place that on the stove and bring it to a rolling boil. Add ¼ cup of sugar and 1 tablespoon of lemon juice per pint, and reduce heat to a simmer. You can add one big spoonful of jam to add texture.

9. When it has reached the desired texture, ladle the jam carefully into your awaiting jars, wipe the rims, and cap your jars with lids and rings. If you made any, ladle the syrup into jars, too.

10. Lid your jars and process them in a water bath canner for 7 minutes, adjusting for altitude. After allowing your little gems of blueberry-lemon jam to cool, greedily hide them away so you don't have to share.

Dandelion Blossom Jam

If you live in or visit an area that you are *absolutely certain* does not spray pesticides, you can join the bees and enjoy some dandelion nectar—except yours will be in the form of jam. So far, this jam has only been made successfully with added pectin. You'll be left with a topaz-toned honey-like substance that will give you a new understanding of the minds of bees. You only need the yellow flowers from the top of the dandelions; you can break them off right at the top of the stem. Pick 10 to 12 cups worth of blossoms.

Makes approximately 6 (1-pint) jars

10 to 12 cups dandelion blossoms	1 packet of pectin (size varies with brand)
2 tablespoons lemon juice	4½ cups sugar

1. Prepare the blossoms by pinching them between your fingers and snipping off the green part with scissors.

2. Place the petals in a large glass bowl and cover them with 4 cups of boiling water. That's it for today! You're going to sleep while the petals brew up a golden yellow, room temperature dandelion tea.

3. The next morning, drain the tea through a coffee filter into another container. You should have 3 to 4 cups of dandelion tea.

4. Pour the strained tea into a saucepan and stir in the lemon juice.

5. Following the instructions on your pectin package, add the pectin and sugar to the contents of the saucepan. (See page 346 for instructions on using pectin for jam making.)

6. Test your jam. When the consistency is right, remove it from the heat and immediately ladle it into sanitized jars.

7. Lid your jars and process them in a water bath canner for 10 minutes, adjusting for altitude.

Spiced Cherry Amaretto Jam

More than 90 percent of cherries tested positive for at least one pesticide, according to the Environmental Working Group's annual "Dirty Dozen" report.[13] I strongly recommend that you use organic cherries to make this jam. Bing cherries are especially delicious. If you do use non-organic cherries, wash your fruit well in a baking soda bath, then rinse well to get as much residue off as possible (see page 331 for more thorough instructions). Also note that unlike with most pectin-free recipes, cherries don't need to sit overnight or be drained of excess liquid.

Makes approximately 6 (1-pint) jars

4 pounds sweet cherries	1 teaspoon ground cinnamon
4½ cups sugar	½ teaspoon ground cloves
¼ cup amaretto	¼ teaspoon ground allspice
½ cup lemon juice	¼ teaspoon ground nutmeg
¼ teaspoon salt	

1. Using a cherry pitter, remove the pits from the cherries.

2. In batches, roughly chop the cherries using your food processor.

3. Place the cherries into a saucepan and stir in sugar, amaretto, lemon juice, salt, and spices.

4. Bring the mixture to a boil, then reduce heat and simmer until you've reached the desired consistency.

5. Ladle the hot jam into sanitized pint jars, allowing ¼ inch of headspace.

6. Lid the jars and process in a water bath canner for 10 minutes, adjusting for altitude.

---

13 https://www.ewg.org/foodnews/summary.php

Slow Cooker Plum Butter

This incredibly simple, hands-off recipe requires practically no attention from the time you put it in the slow cooker until the time you put it in jars for canning!

Makes approximately 8 (1-pint) jars

14 pounds plums

4 cups sugar

1 teaspoon ground nutmeg

2 tablespoons vanilla extract

1. Remove pesticides from the skins of the plums. Once they are clean, slice your plums in half, remove the stones, and toss the plums in the slow cooker.

2. Stir in the sugar and nutmeg.

3. Set the slow cooker on low, put the lid askew, and cook for about 10 hours or until the plum butter has reached the desired thickness. Keep in mind, the butter will thicken a tiny bit more as it cools.

4. Add the vanilla, stirring well to infuse the entire batch with its deliciousness. Adding the vanilla earlier in the process will cause the vanilla to dissipate as the plums cook down. It's much better when you add it at the end.

5. Ladle the plum butter into pint jars.

6. Process in a hot water bath canner for 10 minutes, adjusting for altitude.

Ginger Peach Jam

It's like a taste of summer with a bite of spice! You will *not* want to share, so plan to make a second batch for gifts. Peaches can be peeled just like tomatoes (see page 345). Blanch for a minute in boiling water then drop them into ice water, and the skin will slide right off!

Makes approximately 6 (1-pint) jars

6 pounds peeled, chopped peaches

5 cups sugar, divided

2-inch piece fresh ginger, grated

1 teaspoon ground cinnamon

¼ cup lemon juice

1 teaspoon ground nutmeg

vanilla extract (optional)

1. Prep your peaches by blanching them in hot water, then dipping them in an ice bath to remove the peel. Remove the pit.

2. Mash or roughly puree the peaches. Layer them with 3 cups of sugar in a crock and place them in the fridge overnight.

3. Using a fabric-lined colander over a bowl, drain the puree for 3 hours.

4. In a large saucepan, bring drained peaches, ginger, cinnamon, lemon juice, nutmeg, and vanilla, if using, to a boil. Reduce heat and simmer.

5. Meanwhile, in another pot, simmer your peach juice with ¼ cup of sugar per pint. You can add a little vanilla extract to the syrup for a different flavor.

6. Add the remaining sugar to the jam, stir well, and simmer until it reaches the consistency you prefer.

7. When it reaches the consistency you like, ladle into your sanitized jars.

8. Process the jars in a water bath canner for 10 minutes, adjusting for altitude.

Brown Sugar Peach Preserves

This is a holiday favorite at our house. I use half-pint jars, which contain the perfect amount to pour over cream cheese, yogurt cheese, or baked Brie. This sophisticated appetizer is best served with simple, hearty crackers. Trust me; you'll look fancy when you serve it!

Makes approximately 7 (1-pint) jars

7 pounds fresh peaches

2 cups white or turbinado sugar

¼ cup lemon juice

2 cups brown or muscovado sugar

¼ cup finely chopped jalapeño peppers (optional)

1. Prep your fruit by washing it carefully. If the peaches are not organic, make a baking soda rinse (see page 331) to help remove the pesticides.

2. Smush your fruit. For this particular jam, I like to puree most of the fruit (including the skins) and then finely chop a few for added texture.

3. Layer the peaches and the white or turbinado sugar in a large crock and leave it in the refrigerator overnight.

4. The next day, drain the peaches using a fabric-lined colander over a large bowl for at least 2 hours.

5. In a stockpot, stir the peach puree, peach chunks, and lemon juice together well.

6. Bring the mixture to a boil over medium heat, stirring frequently.

7. Once mixture is boiling, stir in the brown or muscovado sugar and the jalapeños, if using, then reduce to a simmer. Be sure to stir frequently until it reaches the desired consistency.

8. Ladle the jam carefully into your awaiting sanitized jars, wipe the rims, and cap your jars with lids and rings.

9. Process in a water bath canner for 10 minutes and make adjustments for your altitude.

Variation: For some sweet and spicy goodness, add jalapeños. To make both recipes at once, ladle out your Brown Sugar Peach Preserves into one set of jars and then add jalapeños to the remaining jam for two flavors in one batch: Brown Sugar Peach Preserves and Sweet and Spicy Pepper Peach Jam. Keep the seeds in your jalapeños for a spicier flavor.

Raspberry Jalapeño Jam

Every year at Christmas, I dump this recipe out over a block of cream cheese and serve it with crackers. I could honestly just eat that and nothing else, although people seem to frown on guests that don't eat some of the turkey. This jam makes a lovely and elegant appetizer, a tasty glaze for chicken or fish, and a delightful condiment on a turkey and Swiss cheese sandwich.

Makes approximately 7 (1-pint) jars

8 cups raspberries

4 cups sugar, divided

2 to 4 jalapeño peppers

¼ cup lemon juice

1. Prep the raspberries by washing them gently. Roughly puree in the food processor.

2. In a large bowl, layer the raspberry puree with 2 cups of sugar. Leave this in the refrigerator overnight. The next morning, there won't be very much juice. You most likely will not have enough to make syrup.

3. Carefully prep your jalapeños by wearing gloves, mask, and hazmat suit. (Okay, not really, but be careful 'cause those suckers can really make you burn if you touch your face after playing with them.) I use the food processor to get teeny tiny bits of jalapeño without massive pain and pepper juice exposure.

4. Stir raspberries, peppers, and lemon juice together in a large pot, bringing the mixture to a simmer.

5. Gradually stir in the remaining sugar and allow it to simmer until it reaches the desired texture.

6. Ladle the jam into your ready-and-waiting sanitized jars. Process in a water bath canner for 10 minutes, adjusting for altitude.

Variation: You can pair jalapeños with many different fruits. I've successfully married hot peppers with blackberries and peaches, and the results have been delicious.

Spiced Fig Merlot Jam

This is another jam that looks super-fancy. Fresh figs are such a fantastic texture that they are basically in jam consistency as soon as you smush them. You can substitute any other red wine for the Merlot.

Makes approximately 8 (1-pint) jars

8 pounds fresh figs

2 cups lemon juice

3 cups sugar

1 tablespoon ground cinnamon

½ teaspoon ground cloves

1 cup of Merlot

1. Wash figs and remove stems.

2. Roughly puree figs in the blender or food processor.

3. In a stockpot, stir in all ingredients except the wine, and bring to a boil.

4. Once mixture is boiling, add the wine and reduce to a simmer until the jam is the consistency you desire.

5. Ladle the hot jam into sanitized jars.

6. Process the jars for 13 minutes, adjusting for altitude.

Rockin' Rhubarb and Strawberry Jam

This is a wonderful seasonal combo. Strawberries and rhubarb ripen at about the same time, and they go together like peas and carrots.

Makes approximately 7 (1-pint) jars

2 pounds strawberries	3 to 4 cups of sugar, to taste
1½ pounds rhubarb	¼ cup lemon juice

1. Prep your fruit by washing it carefully. Remove the stems of the strawberries and roughly chop the rhubarb.

2. Smush your fruit. We like this jam better if it's a little bit chunky, so don't go crazy unless you truly hate chunky jam.

3. Layer the fruit and 3 cups of sugar in a large crock and leave it overnight in the refrigerator.

4. The next day, drain the concoction using a fabric-lined colander over a large bowl for at least 2 hours.

5. In a stockpot, stir your fruit mixture and lemon juice together well.

6. Bring the mixture to a boil over medium heat, stirring frequently.

7. Once the jam is boiling, taste test it, taking care not to burn a layer of skin off your tongue. Stir in the extra sugar if necessary. Reduce to a simmer. Stir frequently until the jam reaches the desired consistency.

8. Ladle the jam carefully into your awaiting sanitized jars, wipe the rims, and cap your jars with lids and rings.

9. Process in a water bath canner for 10 minutes and make adjustments for your altitude.

12 Ways to Use Homemade Jam That Don't Involve Toast

If you're anything like me, sometimes you can go a teeny little bit…well…overboard…with the jam making. And by overboard, I mean that at the end of summer you have to resort to stashing jars under your bed and in the cabinet beneath the television to make room for them all.

Since there's only so much toast that one family can consume, here are some other delicious ways to use your jam.

1. Top your yogurt with it. You know those icky, artificially flavored fruit-bottom yogurts you can get at the store? Well, you make your own version of these by adding a hefty spoonful of peach jam to some vanilla-flavored yogurt. I always make my own yogurt, so this is a nice scratch meal from start to finish. You can even enthusiastically stir it into the yogurt to come up with a deliciously sweet, fruity yogurt.

2. Serve it with cheese and crackers. If you want to look fancy, set up a cheese plate with a tart-flavored jam in the middle. Top a cracker with a slice of cheese and a teeny dollop of jam. I like peach, blackberry, and Raspberry Jalapeño (page 354) for this. If you serve wine along with this dish, people will think they've stumbled into cocktail hour at the Waldorf Astoria.

3. Turn it into a pancake topping. Thin your blueberry jam with a little bit of fruit juice. I like grape juice because it is mild and absorbs the flavor of the jam. Warm the mixture in a saucepan, ladle over pancakes or waffles, and top with whipped cream. Serve immediately.

4. Add it to smoothies. Just a couple of tablespoons of jam will add a new twist to your favorite smoothies. Strawberry jam in a chocolate protein smoothie is a favorite in our house.

5. Make a marinade with it. Using a food processor, mix peach preserves (or pepper peach preserves, if you like it spicy), soy sauce, garlic, and a dash of orange juice. Place in a large zip-top bag to marinate pork or chicken before grilling. Make some extra marinade for basting.

6. Make jam-filled muffins. Line a muffin tin with muffin cups. Fill each cup halfway with batter. Add a tablespoon of blackberry jam, then fill the cup to the top with batter. Bake as usual. The jam will be ridiculously, blazingly hot when fresh out of the oven, so don't eat these until they have thoroughly cooled.

7. Make thumbprint cookies. Make your favorite shortbread batter and place cookie-sized amounts on a baking sheet. Press your thumb into the raw cookie, then fill the indentation with your fanciest jam. We use Spiced Fig Merlot Jam (page 354) or Blueberry Lemon Jam (page 349) for this. Bake as usual.

8. Crepe filling: Using a food processor, mix ¼ cup of Rockin' Rhubarb and Strawberry Jam (page 355) with 8 ounces of cream cheese and process it until it's fluffy. Add this filling to crepes. To serve, drizzle a little of the pancake topping on them, add some slivered almonds, and top with a dollop of whipped cream.

9. Have an ice cream social. Using a fork, stir some red grape juice into strawberry or raspberry jam until it reaches the desired consistency. Top your ice cream with this for sundaes.

10. Make a fancy baked Brie. This is another yummy holiday recipe. Roll out some pastry; you can make your own or use refrigerated crescent roll dough. Add a peeled wheel of Brie to the center. Top the Brie with your favorite jam—Spiced Fig Merlot (page 354) or blackberry works beautifully for this. Pull the pastry up over the top and pinch it together. Bake according to the directions on the pastry dough, or according to your recipe. Check the dough to be sure it's done—you may need to bake it a bit longer, and if it is becoming overly brown, cover the top lightly with a sheet of tinfoil. Allow this to sit at room temperature for half an hour before serving. Slice into triangles and enjoy the gooey goodness.

11. Add it as a layer in a cake. When making a layer cake, add a layer of jam in the center instead of frosting. Try blueberry jam in a lemon layer cake for a delicious taste sensation.

12. Dehydrate into fruit leather. I do this at the end of summer when I need to free up some jars for the year's harvest. If you have a dehydrator, line your dehydrator sheets with parchment. Spread your jam onto the sheets in an even layer. Place in the dehydrator on low or at 135°F. Check it after 6 hours. Depending on the humidity in your area, it will take anywhere from 6 to 12 hours to dehydrate. Slice it while it's still warm, then allow it to cool before putting it away. (I have tried making fruit leather in the oven but have never had satisfactory results, although lots of folks on the Internet claim to have the magic touch, if you want to try it out!)

There you go! Jam: it's not just for biscuits and toast anymore!

CHAPTER 6

Getting Condimental

Sassy Salsa Fresca

This recipe can be made more mild by reducing the amount of jalapeños, or more spicy by keeping all of the seeds from the peppers. If you *hate* cilantro, you can use parsley instead. You can use a food processor to make this recipe quicker or you can hand chop every single bit of it—it's all up to your personal combination of time and laziness.

Makes approximately 6 (1-quart) jars

8 pounds prepped tomatoes (see tomato prep, page 344)

4 cups seeded, chopped bell peppers

½ cup chopped jalapeño peppers, white pith removed

5 cups chopped onion

4 cloves garlic

4 to 6 tablespoons fresh cilantro or parsley leaves

1½ cups lemon or lime juice

1 teaspoon chili powder

1 (6-ounce) can tomato paste (optional)

1. Using your food processor, add the tomatoes, peppers, onion, garlic, and cilantro or parsley. Process on the "chop" function until you've reached the desired chunkiness.

2. Place a cotton towel in a colander over a large bowl or pot, then pour the chopped veggies in. Allow mixture to drain overnight in the refrigerator.

3. Once your veggies have adequately drained, add them into a large bowl or stockpot, then stir in your lemon or lime juice, chili powder, and tomato paste, if you're using it.

4. Ladle the salsa into the prepared jars.

5. Wipe the lip of the jars, place the lids and rings on them, and place them in the water bath canner.

6. Process for 15 minutes, adjusting for altitude.

"It's Easy Being Green" Tomato Salsa

This can be mixed with a basic white sauce to create the best enchilada sauce on the planet! Note that this salsa has a little more liquid than other types.

Makes approximately 8 (1-pint) jars

7 cups prepped green tomatoes (see tomato prep, page 344)

3 jalapeño peppers

1 green bell pepper

2 large onions

3 cloves garlic

½ cup cilantro

2 teaspoons ground cumin

1 teaspoon salt

½ cup lime juice

1. Using a food processor, chop tomatoes, peppers, onions, and garlic until they reach the desired chunkiness.

2. Pour the processed veggies into a large stockpot. Stir in cilantro, cumin, salt, and lime juice.

3. Bring to a boil, then reduce heat and simmer for 5 minutes.

4. Ladle green salsa into your ready-and-waiting pint jars, leaving a ½ inch of headspace at the top.

5. Process the jars in a water bath canner for 20 minutes, adjusting for altitude.

Peachy-Keen Salsa

This sweet-and-spicy salsa is mouth-watering over rice, chicken, pork, or fish. Pop a bow on this pretty little jar of peachy goodness for a lovely and elegant homemade gift.

Makes approximately 8 (1-pint) jars

INGREDIENTS

8 cups chopped, peeled peaches

1 large red onion, finely chopped

4 to 6 jalapeño peppers, seeded and finely chopped

1 red bell pepper, diced

6 cloves garlic, finely minced

½ cup cilantro

1 tablespoon ground cumin

½ cup apple cider vinegar

1 cup sugar

1. In a large stockpot, combine all ingredients except sugar. Mix well and bring to a boil.

2. Reduce heat. Stir in the sugar and return to a boil for 1 minute.

3. Ladle the salsa into your prepared jars.

4. Process in a water bath canner for 15 minutes, adjusting for altitude.

The Real Tomato Ketchup

Once you try this taste-of-summer condiment, those little packets and squirt bottles will never satisfy your ketchup craving again. This is a big project but it will keep you, and possibly your neighbors and friends, in the red stuff for a year. Using your blender will definitely speed things along. Use Roma, San Marzano, plum, or other paste tomatoes for this recipe.

Makes approximately 9 (1-pint) jars

12 pounds prepped paste tomatoes (see tomato prep, page 344)

1 pound quartered onions

½ pound green bell peppers, sliced into strips

½ pound red bell peppers, sliced into strips

4½ cups apple cider vinegar

1 cup brown sugar

2 tablespoons canning salt

1 tablespoon dry mustard

½ tablespoon crushed chili peppers

¼ teaspoon ground allspice

½ tablespoon ground cloves

¼ teaspoon ground cinnamon

1. In batches, puree your tomatoes, peppers, and onions. Pour each pureed batch into a large stockpot.

2. Bring the mixture to a boil, then reduce heat and simmer for 1 hour, uncovered.

3. Stir in the vinegar, sugar, and spices and then pour the entire mixture into your slow cooker. You are going to cook this on low heat for about 12 hours, uncovered. My slow cooker is oval, so I always put the lid on sideways to retain a bit of the heat while allowing the steam to escape.

4. Once the ketchup is at your preferred consistency, give it a taste and adjust the seasonings if necessary. When it's perfect, ladle it into pint jars.

5. Lid the jars and process them in a water bath for 15 minutes, adjusting for altitude.

Renegade Taco Sauce

I invented this sauce when a raccoon raided my tomato patch. The Renegade Raccoon took a single bite out of each of my newly ripe tomatoes and knocked some green ones to the ground. This sauce was my effort to salvage what was left, and it was so good that it has become a regular item in my pantry. You can include up to 1 pound of green tomatoes without changing the product.

Makes approximately 6 (1-pint) jars

5 pounds prepped tomatoes (see tomato prep, page 344)

1 large bell pepper

2 to 6 jalapeño peppers

3 cloves garlic

¼ cup cilantro leaves

1 large onion

½ cup white vinegar

1 can tomato paste

3 tablespoons chili powder

| 1 tablespoon ground cumin | 1 teaspoon salt |

1. Use your food processor and puree the tomatoes, peppers, garlic, cilantro leaves, and onions.

2. Pour the puree into a stockpot and stir in the remaining ingredients.

3. Bring the sauce to a boil and then reduce the heat. Simmer for 10 minutes, stirring frequently.

4. Taste time! Check to see if the spices need adjustment.

5. Ladle the hot sauce into pint jars.

6. Process the jars in a hot water bath for 20 minutes, adjusting for altitude.

Honey Vidalia BBQ Sauce

Your barbecues will never be the same after you make this sauce. People will clamor for a jar to take home, so you might want to consider making a double batch and doling the extras out for Christmas! This is a pressure canning recipe. Other sweet onions can be swapped out for the Vidalias.

Makes approximately 9 (1-pint) jars

12 pounds prepped Roma tomatoes (see tomato prep, page 344)

2 cups chopped Vidalia onion

2 cups chopped red bell pepper

6 cloves garlic, crushed

1½ cups honey

1½ cups apple cider vinegar

1 tablespoon dry mustard

1 tablespoon smoked Hungarian paprika

1 tablespoon canning salt

1 teaspoon black pepper

1 teaspoon cayenne pepper

1. Using a blender or food processor, puree tomatoes, onions, peppers, and garlic.

2. Pour the puree into a large stockpot and stir in all other ingredients.

3. Bring to a boil until honey is well absorbed, then pour the mixture into your slow cooker.

4. Taste test to see if your seasonings need any adjustment.

5. With the lid on sideways or askew so steam can escape, let sauce reduce for about 4 to 6 hours, stirring every once in a while. Check your consistency and keep in mind it will thicken a little more as it cools.

6. Ladle the sauce into your prepared jars, leaving ½ inch of headspace.

7. Process in a pressure canner for 25 minutes at 10 PSI, adjusting for altitude.

Cha-Cha Chili Sauce

This complex sauce, based on one my Granny used to make, is sweet, spicy, and tangy all at once. It's a delightful topping for all things savory and especially nice when the cold sauce contrasts against a hot food. All good Southerners know that pinto beans are not pinto beans without a little bit of chili sauce on top!

Makes approximately 8 (1-pint) jars

10 cups prepped ripe tomatoes

2 cups chopped white onions

2 cups chopped green bell peppers

2 cups chopped, peeled plums

2 jalapeño peppers, finely diced

1½ cups brown sugar

2 cups apple cider vinegar

5 teaspoons salt

1 teaspoon ground cinnamon

1 teaspoon dry mustard

2 tablespoons pickling spices, in a spice bag

1. Coarsely chop the tomatoes, reserving juice.

2. Combine all ingredients in a slow cooker and cook on low for 4 to 6 hours, with the lid askew to allow steam to escape.

3. Once the sauce has reached the desired consistency, remove spice bag and ladle sauce into pint jars.

4. Lid your jars and process in a water bath canner for 15 minutes, adjusting for altitude.

Asian Plum Sauce

You can only eat so much plum jam and plum butter, but if you're lucky enough to have a plum tree, you probably still have plums to spare. A great use for these plums is this Asian Plum Sauce, which you can use as a dipping sauce or a stir-fry sauce. Add crushed chili peppers to make a spicy version of this sauce, or an extra cup of sugar to make the sauce super sweet. Keep in mind that the flavors will intensify as it sits on the shelf.

Makes approximately 6 (1-pint) jars

6 pounds plums

3 cups packed brown sugar

1 cup apple cider vinegar

1 medium onion

6 cloves garlic

1 tablespoon fresh ginger, minced

1 tablespoon salt

1 tablespoon dry mustard

1 teaspoon crushed chili peppers (optional)

1 cup brown sugar (optional)

1. Wash plums well, then remove the pit. Puree them roughly in a food processor or blender, leaving the skins on.

2. In a stockpot, combine all ingredients except the additional cup of sugar, if using.

3. Simmer the mixture for 2 to 3 hours. The consistency will be thick and slightly sticky.

4. Do a taste test. If you want a sweeter plum sauce, add the remaining sugar and simmer until it is thoroughly incorporated.

5. When you are happy with the taste and texture, go ahead and fill your jars, leaving a ½ inch of headspace.

6. Lid your jars and process in a water bath canner for 15 minutes, adjusting for altitude.

Heatwave Sweet and Spicy Hot Sauce

This recipe provides a great way to use up those random hot peppers. Serrano, Anaheim, jalapeño—they all work well in this recipe. In our garden, we tend to have several different types growing. We put all of them into this sweet and spicy conglomeration that can be drizzled on just about anything to make it hotter and just plain better. But you've been warned: it's pretty darned hot!

Makes approximately 4 (1-pint) jars

3 pounds hot peppers, chopped with seeds in	3 cups apple cider vinegar
8 cloves garlic, smashed	½ cup of sugar
2 medium onions, chopped	2½ cups water
2 pounds prepped tomatoes (see page 344)	

1. Add all of the ingredients to a large stockpot and bring it to a boil for 20 minutes, or until the vegetables are tender.

2. Use a blender or food processor to puree the mixture.

3. Add the puree to sanitized pint jars, leaving ½ inch of headspace.

4. Wipe the rims of the jars, put the lids on, and then process them in a water bath canner for 10 minutes, adjusting for altitude.

CHAPTER 7

In a Pickle

Pickles are that marvelous and delicious exception to the rule stating that vegetables must be processed in a pressure canner. Because of the acid used in the pickling process, pickles may be water bath canned.

Always use a vinegar that is a distillation of at least 5 percent. This won't be difficult; nearly all vinegars, even the cheapest brands, are distilled to that percentage. However, be sure to check, because if you use a vinegar with a lower acidity, you could be putting your family at risk for… wait for it…botulism.

Note that different jar sizes are recommended for different recipes. Relishes are often jarred in half-pint jars to prevent contamination after opening. Larger items, such as pickles, are often canned in larger jars.

A Dilly of a Relish

This recipe can be made with zucchini or cucumbers, or even a combination of the two. You can use whatever type of onion you'd like for this relish, but red onions add a lovely color.

Makes approximately 8 (½-pint) jars

6 pounds finely chopped pickling cucumbers	4 cloves garlic, finely minced
½ cup canning salt	⅓ cup white sugar
2 teaspoons ground turmeric	2 tablespoons dill seeds
3 cups water	3 cups white vinegar
2 large onions, finely chopped	

1. Place chopped cucumbers in a glass bowl, sprinkle with salt and turmeric, and cover with water for 2 hours. This will help to draw the liquid out of your cukes (or zukes) so that your relish isn't runny.

2. Drain cucumbers and rinse under cold water in a colander, squeezing out the excess water with your hands.

3. Combine cucumbers, onions, garlic, sugar, dill seeds, and vinegar in a saucepan and bring to a boil.

4. Reduce heat and simmer 10 minutes.

5. Ladle into jars leaving ½ inch of headspace.

6. Process in a water bath canner for 15 minutes, adjusting for altitude.

Holy Jalapeño Relish

Use jalapeño relish to add more heat on anything you'd like to be spicier. It's great on chili, tacos, sausages, and more! This relish gets a workout at our house because some family members like spicy food and some do not, so we can customize the heat to suit ourselves. Most of the heat is in the seeds. Use or do not use the seeds accordingly to turn up (or down) the heat in your finished product. If you want a condiment with less heat, replace up to half of the jalapeños with green bell peppers.

Makes approximately 8 (½-pint) jars

5 pounds finely chopped jalapeño peppers	4 cups white vinegar
2 cups sugar	½ cup cilantro leaves (optional)

1. In a food processor, finely chop the peppers. Don't turn them into a pureed mush; make them the consistency of a relish.

2. In a large pot, stir the sugar into the vinegar and bring to a boil. Immediately turn off the heat once boil is achieved.

3. Use your food processor to chop the cilantro leaves, if you are using them, then stir them into your chopped peppers.

4. Ladle the uncooked peppers and cilantro into your canning jars, then spoon the liquid over the mixture, allowing ½ inch of headspace.

5. Process the jars in a water bath canner for 10 minutes, adjusting for altitude.

Warning: Hot peppers are the evil, vindictive uncles of the vegetable garden family. Handle them with care because when you cut them up, they fight back. Use rubber gloves and do not rub your eyes, nose, mouth, or any other mucous membrane after handling them.

Southern Belle Kitchen Sink Chow-Chow

You can make this with any veggie combination—zucchini, green tomatoes, cabbage, summer squash, cauliflower, or whatever else you've got. You can use brown or white sugar, too. Chow-chow is generally served in the South as a condiment for pinto beans or field peas with cornbread. However, it lends a sweet and spicy crunch to any simple fare.

Makes approximately 6 (1-pint) jars

8 cups chopped assorted veggies	2 whole allspice berries
1 cup finely chopped onion	3 whole cloves
1 cup diced red bell pepper	2 cups apple cider vinegar
¼ cup finely minced jalapeño pepper	2 cups sugar
2 teaspoons celery seeds	2 teaspoon dry mustard
2 teaspoons whole white mustard seeds	1 teaspoon ground turmeric
2 teaspoons coriander seeds	1 teaspoon ground ginger

1. Place all veggies in a colander over a bowl and sprinkle them with salt. Leave this in the fridge overnight to remove extra moisture.

2. Fill a spice bag with celery seeds, mustard seeds, coriander, allspice, and cloves.

3. Mix the remaining ingredients in a large, non-reactive stockpot to create a brine. Add the spice bag to the brine.

4. Bring brine to a boil then drop it to a simmer for 10 minutes, stirring often to dissolve the sugar.

5. Stir in the veggies and heat through for about 5 minutes, or until warm.

6. Ladle this mixture into jars no larger than 1 pint, leaving ½ inch of headspace.

7. Lid the jars and process in a water bath canner for 10 minutes, adjusting for altitude.

Sweet-as-Can-Be Relish

Brighten up your burgers with this sweet and simple cucumber relish. Once you taste the freshness of your own relish, you will never eat the artificially colored and high-fructose corn syrup–laden grocery store relish again!

Makes approximately 6 (½-pint) jars

4 pounds finely chopped pickling cucumbers	3 cloves garlic, finely minced
½ cup canning salt	2 tablespoons celery seeds
½ cup white vinegar	2 cups diced red bell pepper
2⅓ cups sugar	2 cups finely chopped white onion
4 tablespoons mustard seeds	

1. Place cucumbers in a large glass bowl and stir in the salt. Allow them to sit on the counter at room temperature for 4 hours.

2. Drain cucumbers and rinse in a colander under cold water, squeezing out the excess water with your hands.

3. Combine garlic, sugar, mustard seeds, celery seeds, and white vinegar in a saucepan and bring to a boil.

4. Reduce heat and stir in cucumbers, onions, and peppers, then return to a full boil.

5. Reduce heat and simmer the mixture for 10 minutes.

6. Ladle the hot relish into pint or half-pint jars, allowing ½ inch of headspace.

7. Lid the jars and process in a hot water bath canner for 10 minutes, adjusting for altitude.

British Branston Pickle

This sweet and sour condiment makes excellent use of random bits of garden produce. It is especially complimentary to dishes made with cheddar or blue cheese.

Makes approximately 5 (½-pint) jars

4 cups (about 20 ounces) chopped, peeled rutabaga

1 head cauliflower

3 carrots

2 onions

2 small zucchinis

2 Granny Smith apples, peeled and cored

1 cup chopped dates

12 gherkin pickles, diced

5 cloves garlic, minced

1 cup packed brown sugar

2⅔ cups malt vinegar

2½ cups water

⅓ cup lemon juice

¼ cup Worcestershire sauce

2 teaspoons salt

2 teaspoons mustard seeds

1½ teaspoons ground allspice

¼ teaspoon cayenne pepper

1. Using a food processor, finely chop the first 9 ingredients in batches.

2. Pour the veggies into a large saucepan and stir in remaining ingredients.

3. Bring the mixture to a boil, then pour into a slow cooker. Keeping lid askew, cook on low for 4 to 6 hours until the sauce has reached the desired consistency.

4. Ladle into pint jars, allowing ½ inch of headspace.

5. Lid your jars and process a water bath canner for 15 minutes, adjusting for altitude.

Dill-icious Sour Garlic Pickles

Grape or blackberry leaves are used for these pickles because the tannin helps keep the pickles crisp.

Makes approximately 8 (1-quart) jars

10 pounds cucumbers, 3 to 4 inches in length

2 tablespoons black peppercorns

2 tablespoons mustard seeds

2 tablespoons coriander seeds

2 tablespoons dill seeds

1 tablespoon allspice berries

12 bay leaves, crumbled

4 cups white vinegar

4 cups water

½ cup canning salt

1 grape leaf per jar

2 heads dill per jar

2 cloves crushed garlic per jar

a few flakes of crushed chili peppers per jar (optional)

1. Scrub your cucumbers with a vegetable brush, then soak them in an ice water bath for 2 to 6 hours.

2. Combine peppercorns, mustard, coriander seeds, dill seeds, allspice, and crumbled bay leaves in a small bowl. Mix well. This will serve as your spice mix.

3. Combine white vinegar, water, and canning salt in a stockpot and bring to a rolling boil for 5 minutes.

4. Place a grape leaf in the bottom of each jar. Then add to each jar approximately 6 to 8 cucumbers, a tablespoon of your spice mix, the fresh dill, and the garlic. You can process the cucumbers whole or cut them into spears, depending on your personal preference.

5. Pour the hot brine over the contents of each jar.

6. Lid your jars and process in a water bath canner for 10 minutes, adjusting for altitude.

7. Remove the jars from the canner *immediately* for a crisper pickle.

8. This is the hard part—wait 7 to 10 days before popping open a jar for best results.

I Like Bread and Buttah Pickles

You have to sing that song by the Newbeats when making these pickles—it's the rule!

Makes approximately 6 (1-quart) jars

5 to 7 pounds (4- to 6-inch) cucumbers, cut into ¼-inch slices

2 pounds white onion, thinly sliced into rings

½ cup canning salt

3 cups white vinegar

2 cups white sugar

2 tablespoons mustard seeds

2 teaspoons ground turmeric

2 teaspoons celery seeds

1 teaspoon ground ginger

1 teaspoon peppercorns

1 grape leaf per jar

1. Place cucumber and onion slices in a large glass bowl, layering with canning salt.

2. Cover the salted veggies with ice cubes and allow them to stand in the refrigerator for 2 hours.

3. Drain veggies in a colander, then rinse and drain again.

4. Combine all other ingredients except for grape leaves in a large saucepot; bring to a boil.

5. Pack your sanitized jars with one grape leaf in the bottom of each, if using. Top with the cucumbers and onions.

6. Pour the hot brine over the contents of your jars, leaving ½ inch of headspace.

7. Lid the jars and process in a water bath canner for 10 minutes, adjusting for altitude.

8. These pickles, like all pickles, get better with time. Wait for a week before opening them.

Southern-Style Sweet Pickles

These are the kind Granny used to make, if your Granny is a sweet little Southern old lady like mine was.

Makes approximately 7 (1-quart) jars

8 pounds (3- to 4-inch long) pickling cucumbers

⅓ cup canning salt

1 tablespoon black peppercorns

1 tablespoon mustard seeds

1 tablespoon coriander seeds

½ tablespoon allspice berries

4 whole cloves

3 bay leaves, crumbled

2 teaspoons celery seeds

4½ cups white sugar

3½ cups white vinegar

1 grape leaf, per jar

1. Place scrubbed cucumbers in a large glass bowl, layering with canning salt.

2. Cover the salted veggies with ice cubes and allow them to stand in the refrigerator for 2 hours.

3. Drain veggies in a colander, then rinse and drain again.

4. Make pickling spice by thoroughly mixing peppercorns, mustard seeds, allspice berries, cloves, bay leaves, and celery seeds.

5. In a large saucepan, combine sugar and vinegar with 3 tablespoons of pickling spice and bring to a boil.

6. Cut off the hard ends of the cucumbers and pack them into jars on top of a grape leaf.

7. Pour hot syrup over the contents of the jars, leaving ½ inch of headspace.

8. Process in a hot water bath canner for 10 minutes, *immediately* removing the jars when the processing time is up.

Random Pickled Veggies

When you have too much produce left in your garden to eat right away but not enough to can any one thing at the end of the season, make yourself some Random Pickled Veggies to enjoy throughout the winter. The ingredients list is flexible; it's actually more of an ingredients *suggestion* list. Go with what you have, but just try to keep the total sum of veggies the same. You can make these spicy if you include hot peppers. If you don't have hot peppers, you can substitute crushed chili peppers.

Makes approximately 6 (1-quart) jars

1 pound zucchini, cut into ¼-inch slices

1 pound green or yellow beans, ends removed

1 pound carrots, cut into ¼-inch coins

1 pound cauliflower, cut into large florets

½-pound baby pearl onions, peeled or 1 pound white onion, sliced

2 bell peppers, cut into strips

3 cups apple cider vinegar

2 cups brown sugar

2 tablespoons dry mustard

2 tablespoons mustard seeds

1 ½ tablespoons canning salt

1 teaspoon ground cinnamon

1 teaspoon ground ginger

hot peppers, sliced lengthwise (optional)

1. Combine all veggies in a large bowl and set aside.

2. Add remaining ingredients in a large saucepan and bring the mixture to a boil.

3. Immediately reduce heat, stir in the veggies, and return to a boil. Reduce heat and simmer for 15 minutes.

4. Pack veggies and liquid into pint jars, allowing ½ inch of headspace.

5. Lid the jars and process in a water bath canner for 15 minutes, adjusting for altitude.

Crazy Carrot Pickles

I passionately detest canned carrots, so I was seeking to preserve them in a way I might actually enjoy. After some tweaking and experimenting, I came up with these "crazy" carrot pickles.

Makes approximately 6 (1-quart) jars

6 pounds carrots, peeled and trimmed to fit your jars

4 cups water

4 cups apple cider vinegar

½ cup brown sugar

4 tablespoons canning salt

1 tablespoon dill seeds

½ tablespoon black peppercorns

6 cloves garlic, crushed

1. Cut your carrots into spears. The size of your jars will determine the size of your carrot pieces.

2. Combine water, vinegar, sugar, and salt in a saucepan and bring it to a boil.

3. Add the other spices evenly across your sanitized jars, then fill jars snugly with carrots.

4. Pour the brine over the contents of the jars, leaving a ½ inch of headspace.

5. Wipe the lip of the jar, put on the lid, and process the carrot pickles in a boiling water bath for 10 minutes, adjusting for altitude.

Pleasantly Pickled Red Onions

Pickled onions create a milder and sweeter flavor than you'd get by just topping a burger or sandwich with a slice of raw onion, and they're far more elegant. They are also a lovely addition to a salad.

Makes approximately 8 (½-pint) jars

- 5 cups red onion, thinly sliced into rings
- 2 cups red wine vinegar
- 2 cloves garlic, smashed
- 1 whole clove
- ¼ cup brown sugar

1. Thinly slice red onion.

2. Cry.

3. Once you can see again, bring vinegar, garlic, clove, and brown sugar to a boil in a saucepan, then immediately reduce heat and simmer for 5 minutes.

4. Fish out the large pieces of garlic and discard.

5. Stir the onions into the pot and return to a boil, stirring constantly.

6. Reduce heat and simmer for about 5 minutes, until the onions are soft.

7. Ladle the onions into pint jars and disperse liquid evenly, allowing ½ inch of headspace.

8. Lid the jars and process them in a water bath canner for 10 minutes, adjusting for altitude.

A Peck of Pickled Peppers

These spicy pickled peppers are great for topping sandwiches, nachos, or even salads. Anything you want to jazz up with a little bit of "bite" will be made better with these pickled peppers. You can use any peppers you like.

Makes approximately 8 (1-pint) jars

- 8 pounds peppers
- 1 cup water
- 5 cups white vinegar
- 1 cup white sugar
- 4 tablespoon canning salt
- 1 onion
- 4 cloves garlic, crushed

1. Use only fresh, firm peppers for this. Wash your peppers and slice them into rings.

2. Bring water, vinegar, sugar, and salt to boil in a saucepan.

3. Thinly slice your onion and distribute it evenly across your jars. Top this with crushed garlic, then pepper rings.

4. Ladle the hot brine over the veggies in the jars, leaving ½ inch of headspace.

5. Process for 10 minutes in a hot water bath canner, adjusting for altitude.

CHAPTER 8

Fruit Frenzy

Fruit is loaded with vitamins, including vitamin C. A lack of vitamin C for an extended period will cause the deficiency disease scurvy. Scurvy starts out with symptoms of paleness, lethargy, and feelings of depression. If the deficiency is not corrected, the sufferer will begin bleeding from the gums and other mucous membranes. As it worsens, tooth loss, jaundice, neuropathy, and eventually death will occur.

Imagine being able to skip a trip to the grocery store because all of your important nutrients are already preserved and waiting on your shelves. So when the fruit trees are groaning with their bounty, take a break from biting into those fresh, juicy peaches and store up some jars of sunshine for the winter.

Be sure to use the canning liquid from your fruit. You can make a snazzy and delicious mixed drink for grown-ups, use it as the basis of a smoothie, or let the kids sip it exactly how it is. You can be fancy and pour some sparkling water over ice, then spike it with some fruity syrup from your jars. In the summer, you can also make some very tasty ice pops. Here is a reference for fruit canning. These times are all based on the raw-pack method of canning fruit in quart jars.

FRUIT CANNING QUICK REFERENCE

Fruit	Time at Sea Level
Apple slices	25 minutes
Apricots	35 minutes
Berries	25 minutes
Cherries	30 minutes
Figs	55 minutes; add 2 tablespoons lemon juice
Grapefruit	15 minutes
Grapes	25 minutes
Nectarines	35 minutes
Oranges	15 minutes
Peaches	35 minutes
Pears	30 minutes
Pineapple	25 minutes
Plums	30 minutes

If you are canning a combination of fruits, look up the times for each ingredient individually. Always go with the longest time to make certain that your food is canned safely.

Canning Fruit in a Simple Syrup

The most basic way to can fruit is in a simple syrup. If you don't have the time or ingredients to be fancy, just about any fruit can be preserved this way. Here are the basic instructions; on page 372, you can find a chart with the processing times for different fruits.

There are light, medium, and heavy syrups. The difference between each of these is the proportion of sugar to water. You might want to vary the type of syrup based on the sweetness and flavor of the fruit. You can add a dash of vanilla, cinnamon, or cloves to jazz things up.

These amounts are based on what you'd need for a 7-quart canner load. An optional ingredient is 2 tablespoons of lemon or lime juice per each jar.

Light Syrup	Medium Syrup	Heavy Syrup
9 cups of water	8 cups of water	7 cups of water
3 cups of sugar	4 cups of sugar	6 cups of sugar

1. For whichever type of syrup you decide to make, bring the ingredients to a boil in a large stockpot, stirring frequently to combine the sugar. Once the sugar is dissolved, turn off the heat.

2. Pack your jars with raw fruit that has been prepped based on its type.

3. Top each jar of fruit with 2 tablespoons of lemon juice, if you're using it.

4. Ladle the hot syrup over the fruit.

5. Wipe the rim of the jar, put the lids on, and process for the appropriate amount of time based on the chart on page 372, adjusting for altitude.

No-Sugar Canning

For those who are avoiding sugar, canning fruit in juice may be the best option. You can use apple juice, white grape juice, or purple grape juice. I like to use a juice that corresponds to the fruit I'm canning, so I use apple juice for apples, white grape juice for light colored fruits like peaches, pears, or nectarines, and purple grape juice for darker fruits, like plums or berries.

For a 7-quart canner load, you'll need approximately 12 cups of the juice of your choice. I always add 2 tablespoons of lemon or lime juice to each jar of fruit but this is optional for most fruits, except as noted on the chart on page 372.

1. Bring your juice to a boil in a large stockpot, then immediately turn off the heat.

2. Pack your jars with raw fruit that has been prepped based on its type.

3. Top each jar of fruit with 2 tablespoons of lemon juice, if you're using it.

4. Ladle the hot juice over the fruit.

5. Wipe the rim of the jar, put the lids on, and process for the appropriate amount of time based on the chart on page 372, adjusting for altitude.

"How 'Bout Those Apples" Applesauce

This recipe is perfect as baby food because it has only two ingredients: apples and water. None of that nasty high-fructose corn syrup slop in *this* applesauce! Because of my inherent laziness, I used the "blender method" of making applesauce. This is the easy method. Shoot me if I one day have to try the difficult method, because this required almost three hours of hands-on work. The blender method requires far less cooking time and does not require you to peel the apples; this helps keep the vitamin content high. If you are leaving the peel on, it is especially important to clean the fruit carefully (see page 331).

Makes approximately 14 (1-quart) jars

> 1 bushel (40 pounds) cleaned apples
>
> water, as needed

1. Chop and core the apples.

2. In batches, use a blender or food processor to puree the apples, skins and all, with just enough water to allow the blender to work.

3. Pour the puree into a large stockpot. Cook the sauce only long enough to heat it up.

4. As soon as the applesauce is merrily bubbling away, it's hot enough to ladle into your prepared jars. Be sure to allow at least ½ inch of headspace.

5. Lid your jars and process in a water bath canner for 20 minutes, adjusting for altitude.

Spiced Applesauce

If you'd like a little more flavor in your applesauce, this will fit the bill. I can't even express how great your house will smell while this simmers on the stove. No sugar is needed for this batch of fragrant deliciousness.

Makes approximately 14 (1-quart) jars

> 1 bushel (40 pounds) apples
>
> lemon juice, as needed
>
> ½ cup ground cinnamon

> ⅛ cup ground ginger
>
> 2 tablespoons ground allspice
>
> 1 tablespoon ground cloves

1. Prep your apples by cleaning them as per the instructions on page 331.

2. Core the apples and cut them into chunks.

3. Using your blender or food processor, puree your apple chunks in batches. Add enough lemon juice to each batch to allow it to puree.

4. Pour the puree into the stockpot. Stir in all of the spices and bring to a light simmer. You aren't cooking the applesauce; you are merely heating it to help the flavors meld.

5. Lean over the pot and *smellllllllll* how fantastic that spiced applesauce smells. Do not skip this vital step, or your entire applesauce making process will be disrupted and the whole batch could fail based on this alone.

6. Pour the hot applesauce into your prepared jars. Clean off the lip of the jar and top it with a lid and a ring.

7. Process your applesauce in a hot water bath canner for 20 minutes, adjusting for altitude.

Cranberry Apple Slices

These treats simply beg and plead to be topped with a crisp crumb topping, baked, and then smothered in vanilla ice cream. Of course, you can also grab a spoon and dig right into the jar! Because of the tartness of the cranberries, I do add sugar; however, it's only 2 cups divided across 6 quarts.

Note: If a pile of pears happens to fall into your lap, they are equally delicious when preserved this way!

Makes approximately 6 (1-quart) jars

6 pounds apples, washed well	3 cups cranberries
1 cup lemon juice	6 cinnamon sticks
5 cups apple juice	6 cloves
2 cups brown sugar	

1. Core and slice apples, dipping them immediately in lemon juice to prevent browning.

2. Bring apple juice and brown sugar to a boil.

3. Carefully pour apple slices and cranberries into boiling juice and simmer for 5 minutes.

4. Place 1 cinnamon stick and 1 clove into each quart jar, then ladle fruit mixture and liquids into jars.

5. Make sure there are no air pockets, lid the jars, and process in a water bath canner for 25 minutes, adjusting for altitude.

Spicy Apple Rings

This is another recipe from the Granny files. I used to eat these until my mom had to pry the jar out of my sweaty little hands. So delicious!

When it comes to choosing apples for this recipe, I find that firm, tart apples like Granny Smith, Winesap, or Arkansas Black work best. With regard to red food coloring, you can get a natural one instead of using an artificial one. Unless you like eating bugs (cochineal is a red food color made from beetles), look for a red food color made from beets or other vegetables.

Some folks take a shortcut and throw in a handful of those little cinnamon heart candies to impart the traditional red color and spicy sweet flavor. This recipe has no red-hot hearts, but if you want to add some, replace the spices and half of the sugar with red-hot hearts. Even when you make it from scratch, this certainly isn't health food, but it adds some nice old-fashioned flair to a holiday dinner table.

Makes approximately 14 (1-pint) jars

12 pounds apples	3 tablespoons whole cloves
1 cup lemon juice	3 tablespoons ground cinnamon
10 to 12 cups sugar	1 teaspoon ground allspice
6 cups water	1 cinnamon stick per jar
1½ cups cider vinegar	1 teaspoon red food coloring (optional)

1. Prep your apples by washing them well and peeling them.

2. To make rings, slice the apples into circles, cutting across the diameter. Then remove the core by using a shot glass to push out the center, or carefully cut around it with a knife.

3. Dip the apple rounds in lemon juice and set them aside.

4. Combine all of the other ingredients except for the cinnamon sticks in a large stockpot. If using the food coloring, add it to the stockpot.

5. Bring the syrup to a boil, then reduce the heat and simmer it for 5 minutes. Stir frequently to dissolve the sugar.

6. Stack your apple rings into your quart jars. Pop a cinnamon stick down the center of the rings.

7. Ladle your deliciously spicy syrup over the apples. If possible, divvy up your cloves and allspice across the jars, because it looks purty.

8. Wipe the rims of the jars, put the lids on, and process in a hot water bath for 15 minutes, adjusting for altitude.

Spiced Mulled Pears

To take a break from regular sliced pears, try this decadently spiced version. This looks elegant and difficult, but honestly, it couldn't be easier! If you don't have all of the spices listed here, just double up on the ones you do have. Remember, versatility is key when it comes to canning!

Makes approximately 6 (1-quart) jars

10 pounds very firm pears	6 star anise pods
4 cups red grape juice	6 cinnamon sticks
1 cup orange juice	12 whole cloves
2 tablespoons vanilla extract	12 black peppercorns
½ cup brown sugar	

1. Peel pears, then cut them into eighths, discarding the cores.

2. In a stockpot, bring the grape juice, orange juice, vanilla, and brown sugar to a boil.

3. In each prepared jar, place 1 anise pod, 1 cinnamon stick, 2 cloves, and 2 peppercorns.

4. Pack the jars with pear sections, leaving ½ inch of headspace.

5. Ladle the syrup over the pears and remove any air pockets.

6. Lid the jars and process in a water bath canner for 20 minutes, adjusting for altitude.

Merlot-Spiced Pears

This is the be-all and end-all canned pear recipe. Not only does it taste decadent, but the way your house smells when you make it will bring everyone to the kitchen just to inhale it. When choosing a wine, opt for a drier red than you would usually drink. White sugar can be used in place of the turbinado.

Makes approximately 6 (1-quart) jars

10 pounds very firm pears	2 tablespoons ground cinnamon
2 bottles Merlot	1 teaspoon ground cloves
1 cup water	2 cups turbinado sugar

1. Pour the wine and water into a saucepan and bring to a simmer on low heat.

2. Mix the spices and sugar in a bowl until well combined.

3. While the wine mixture is simmering, stir in the sugar mixture. Stir with a whisk until the mixture is dissolved in the wine. Simmer on low heat for 15 minutes.

4. While the wine syrup is simmering, pack sliced pears into 6 sanitized quart jars.

5. Ladle the hot wine syrup over the pears, leaving ½ inch of headspace.

6. Process in a water bath canner for 20 minutes, adjusting for altitude.

Plain and Simple Pear Sauce

Another great way to use an abundance of pears is to make pear sauce. Slightly sweeter than applesauce, it can be used in baking or substituted in any recipe in which you would normally use applesauce. I like to leave the skins on the pears since so many of the nutrients lurk there.

Note: Pear sauce sometimes separates during the canning process. Don't be alarmed—it won't affect the quality or the taste. Simply shake the jar well before serving. Pear sauce generally has a thinner consistency than applesauce, so use the smallest amount of water possible.

Makes approximately 6 (1-quart) jars

> 15 pounds pears
>
> dash of vanilla extract (optional)
>
> water, as needed

1. Wash the pears carefully using the method described on page 331. If the pears are not organic, this will help to remove the pesticides if they have been sprayed.

2. Remove the cores and any dark spots.

3. Using a blender or food processor, puree the pears on a high setting, adding a teeny splash of vanilla if you're using it and water as needed to assist the blending.

4. Pour pear mixture into sanitized jars.

5. Process in a water bath canner for 20 minutes, adjusting for altitude.

"Everything Is Peachy" Peach Slices

A bushel of peaches will give you 20 to 24 quarts of peach slices to enjoy over the long winter. They are like bites of sunshine. Select freestone peaches; this will make your life far easier, as they give up the pit without the vast effort required to remove the pit from clingstone peaches. Trust me on this one.

Peaches can be peeled just like tomatoes. Dip them in boiling water for about a minute, then dunk them in ice water, and the skin will almost get up and walk off by itself. (Okay, I confess, you'll have to help it a little.)

Makes 20 to 24 (1-quart) jars

> 1 bushel peeled peaches
>
> 1 cup lemon juice
>
> 12 cups white grape juice
>
> 8 cups water
>
> 4 cups sugar

1. Cut peeled peaches in half, then slice them. Immediately dip slices in lemon juice and then place them in a bowl.

2. In a stockpot, bring white grape juice, sugar, and water to a boil.

3. Place your peach slices into quart jars, leaving ½ inch of headspace.

4. Dump your bowl of lemon juice into the hot syrup.

5. Ladle the syrup over your peaches, then put the lids on the jars.

6. Peaches can be processed either in a water bath canner for between 30 and 40 minutes *or* in a pressure canner for 10 minutes at 5 PSI, adjusting for altitude. I prefer the pressure canner because I feel more vitamins are preserved in the shorter cooking time.

Plum Easy Cinnamon-Spiced Plums

The easiest thing about this plum recipe is that there is virtually *no work,* unless you choose to slice the plums in half and remove the stone at the time of processing. You will end up with a mushier plum this way, but a thicker sauce. You can use either grape juice or apple juice for this recipe.

Makes approximately 7 (1-quart) jars

14 pounds small plums	7 cups white grape or apple juice
7 cinnamon sticks	7 cups water
14 whole cloves	3 cups sugar (optional)

1. Wash plums well, using the method described on page 331.

2. If you are slicing the plums, cut them in half and remove the stone. If you are preserving them whole, poke the plums at each end using a fork—otherwise, your plums will explode in your jars during processing.

3. Pack your jars with plums.

4. Add one cinnamon stick and a couple of cloves to each jar.

5. On the stove, bring your mixture of juice, water, and sugar, if using, to a boil.

6. Ladle the hot liquid over the raw-packed plums in quart jars. Lid the jars.

7. To process, you can either process for 25 minutes in a water bath canner, *or* process for 1 minute at 5 PSI in a pressure canner, adjusting for altitude.

Tutti-Frutti Mixed Jars

Warning: Once you've tried this homemade fruit cocktail, you'll never be able to choke down that nasty, syrupy stuff from the store again. Your family will insist that you make this every single year! The mint adds a hint of fresh summery flavor to every jar, but is entirely optional.

This is a wonderful recipe for using whatever you have on hand. The proportions don't matter; use whatever is cheap and abundant for you. For this reason, there are no measurements with this recipe; it will be different every time. Use apple juice or white grape juice.

SUGGESTED FRUITS

Mixture of apples, apricots, cherries (pitted), grapes, nectarines, peaches, pears, and plums

1 cup lemon juice

3 tablespoons sugar per quart jar (optional)

1 cup apple or white grape juice for every cup of water

fresh mint (optional)

1. Wash all fruit carefully.

2. Cut fruit into bite-sized pieces and dip the pieces in lemon juice, then place them into jars, evenly dispersing the different types of fruit across your batch.

3. If you are adding sugar, spoon it on top of the fruit in the jars.

4. Fill a stock pot with equal parts juice and water.

5. Bring mixture to a boil and then ladle it over the fruit in your ready-and-waiting sanitized quart jars.

6. Add a sprig of mint, if using, to each jar. Lid the jars and process in a water bath canner for 20 minutes, adjusting for altitude.

Very, Very Orange Cherries

This sweet, sunny recipe turns out better if you process it in a pressure canner, but alternate instructions are present for those who don't have one. The main issue is one of texture. The pressure-canned cherries are significantly more firm.

Also, if you don't have one, get a cherry pitter. For less than $10, this investment will literally save you hours!

Makes approximately 7 (1-quart) jars

10 pounds sweet cherries

3 cups red grape juice

3 cups orange juice

1 cup sugar

1. Using a cherry pitter, remove the pits from the cherries. Place cherries in quart jars.

2. In a stockpot, heat the juices and sugar until boiling.

3. Ladle the hot liquid into the jars, then run a rubber spatula around the inside of the jar to remove any air pockets.

4. Lid the jars and process them in a pressure canner for 10 minutes at 5 PSI, adjusting for altitude.

Note: If you do not have a pressure canner, add the cherries to the boiling juice and cook for 10 minutes before placing them in the jars. Then process them in a water bath canner for 20 minutes, adjusting for altitude.

Bring on the Berries

Berries are among the easiest fruits to can because they require practically *no* prep work, and are actually best when a raw-pack canning method is used.

This method works well with every berry that I have tried: blueberries, blackberries, raspberries, huckleberries, and strawberries have all been successful. You can also mix your berries for even more yumminess! Use whichever type of grape juice you prefer for this recipe.

Makes 1 quart jar

2 tablespoons lemon juice per quart jar

assorted berries, just under 2 pints per quart jar

2 tablespoons sugar per jar, optional

grape juice and water, in an equal ratio

1. Clean berries.

2. Place 2 tablespoons of lemon juice into each quart jar, then add in the berries, leaving ½ inch of headspace. Top with sugar if you're using it.

3. Bring your juice and water mixture to a boil in a large stockpot.

4. Ladle the liquid over the berries, lid the jars, then gently turn or shake them to remove air pockets from the bottom of the jar.

5. Berries can be processed either in a hot water bath canner for 20 minutes, *or* in a pressure canner for 10 minutes at 5 PSI, adjusting for your altitude.

CHAPTER 9

Venerable Vegetables

Ahh, vegetables. They are the reason I began gardening in the first place, and then from there, canning. My yearning for year-round, affordable, organic, non-GMO produce provided the jumping off point for my two favorite hobbies.

We eat lots of vegetables. I would be hard-pressed to afford them all at the natural food store. In the summer, the perfect solution is to raise my own veggies or hit up the farmer's market. But of course, we want vegetables in the winter too.

Taking it one step further, there may come a time when you must be self-sufficient and will only be able to eat what you can grow and preserve. Learning the best ways to store your garden bounty for the cold days ahead is vital.

Most of the vegetables listed here are canned simply with very little seasoning. It's not that we dislike flavor, but if there is less seasoning in the jar, you can cook them up however you want in the winter. This allows them to be used as ingredients in whatever meal you happen to be making and makes them far more versatile.

I use the raw-pack method whenever possible because, well… because I'm lazy. Running a close second to my laziness is that veggies that have been cooked and then canned are often too mushy. Canned veggies by their very nature are fairly mushy, and as an al dente veggie lover, it's a bit of an adjustment. If you don't like the textural result of some of your canning projects, be creative and think of other ways to use them. Try pureeing them and adding them to soup or mashed potatoes, for example.

If you are using salt, place the desired amount in the bottom of your sanitized canning jars. When you pour water over the contents, the salt will disperse. Our preference is ⅛ teaspoon in pint jars and ¼ teaspoon in quart jars. I recommend a non-iodized salt, like canning salt or sea salt, if you plan to add salt to your vegetables. Iodized salt can make the veggies turn ugly colors.

Note: Take advantage of the vitamins stored in the liquid by adding it to soup stock or using it for cooking grains like rice or barley.

Vegetables contain very little acid. Therefore, vegetables *must* be processed in a pressure canner. There is no gray area here, because the failure to do so can put you at risk for botulism (see more on page 329). A water bath canner does not reach and maintain a high enough temperature to kill off the bacteria that causes botulism, but a pressure canner does.

On the next page, there is a quick-reference chart for canning a wide variety of veggies.

Remember, vegetables are a low-acid food and must be processed in a pressure canner with a baseline of 11 PSI, and adjustments for altitude.

VEGETABLE CANNING QUICK REFERENCE

Food	Time for Pints at Sea Level	Time for Quarts at Sea Level
Asparagus	30	40
Beans (green or yellow)	20	25
Beets	30	35
Carrots	25	30
Corn	55	85
Lima Beans	40	50
Okra	25	40
Peas (field)	40	40
Peppers	35	not recommended
Potatoes (white)	35	40
Potatoes (sweet)	65	90
Pumpkin	55	90
Squash (winter)	55	90

Awesome Asparagus

We have found home-canned asparagus to be unpleasantly mushy on its own. With this warning in mind, if you end up with a windfall of asparagus, canned asparagus makes an ultra-delicious, tastes-of-springtime cream of asparagus soup.

Makes approximately 7 (1-quart) jars

15 pounds fresh asparagus

water as needed

salt (optional)

1. Wash your asparagus carefully and gently.

2. Cut the spears into the proper lengths to fit inside your jars, discarding the woody ends.

3. Set a large pot of water to boil.

4. If you are using salt, place the desired amount in the bottom of your sanitized canning jars.

5. Load up the jars with your asparagus spears, packing them in tightly.

6. Ladle or pour boiling water into the jars, allowing 1 inch of headspace.

7. Use a rubber spatula to remove any air pockets, then add more water if needed.

8. Lid the jars and process them in your pressure canner at 10 PSI for 30 minutes if using pint jars and 40 minutes if using quart jars. Remember to adjust for altitude.

Carrots with Honey

Carrots can be jarred in any of a wide variety of shapes: coins, spears, ruffles, large chunks, or even whole, if they fit in the jar! However, don't make them too small or they will be mushy and gross. This year I canned them whole, and they turned out with a far better texture than in previous years, when I cut them into various other shapes. The bigger the pieces are, the better the results are. A drizzle of honey in each jar intensifies the natural sweetness of the carrots. Canned carrots work very nicely as an ingredient in baked goods.

Makes approximately 8 (1-pint) jars

10 pounds carrots

water, as needed

½ teaspoon honey or turbinado sugar per jar (optional)

salt (optional)

1. Wash your carrots, then peel and slice them as desired.

2. Set a large pot of water to boil.

3. If you are using salt, place the desired amount in the bottom of your sanitized canning jars. If you are using honey or sugar, add this to the bottom of the jars. Load up the jars with your carrot pieces, packing them in tightly.

4. Ladle or pour boiling water into the jars, allowing 1 inch of headspace.

5. Use a rubber spatula to remove any air pockets, then add more water if needed.

6. Lid the jars and process them in your pressure canner at 10 PSI for 25 minutes if using pint jars, or 30 minutes if you're using quart jars. Adjust for altitude.

A Cornucopia of Corn

There is no comparison between freshly canned corn and the stuff from grocery store cans. For Southwestern flair, add chopped peppers, onion, and a dash of chili powder to your corn. Approximately three ears of corn will fill a pint jar when the kernels are removed from the cob. Corn expands in the pressure canner, so be sure you leave that inch of headspace!

3 ears makes 1 pint

corn on the cob

water, as needed

salt (optional)

1. Husk the corn and remove the silk with a vegetable brush. This is a messy, back-porch kind of job.

2. Start boiling a big pot of water.

3. Slice the corn off the cob as closely as possible. It will come off in strips.

4. Fill your jars with corn, leaving 1 inch of headspace.

5. Ladle boiling water into the jars, allowing 1 inch of headspace.

6. Use a rubber spatula to remove any air pockets, then add more water if needed.

7. Lid the jars and process them in your pressure canner for 55 minutes at 10 PSI, or 85 minutes if you're using quart jars.

Greenie Beanies

You can also use this process for wax beans or yellow beans, or (our favorite) a colorful combo of the three!

Makes approximately 7 (1-quart) jars

> 14 pounds green beans
>
> water, as needed
>
> salt (optional)

1. Wash your beans carefully, then rinse them well.

2. Snap off the ends of your beans and then snap them into the desired size. Approximately 2-inch-long pieces fit very nicely in the jars.

3. Set a large pot of water to boil.

4. If you are using salt, place the desired amount in the bottom of your sanitized canning jars.

5. Load up the jars with your beans, packing them in tightly.

6. Ladle or pour boiling water into the jars, allowing 1 inch of headspace.

7. Use a rubber utensil to remove any air pockets, then add more water if needed.

8. Lid the jars and process them in your pressure canner at 10 PSI for 20 minutes if using pint jars, 25 minutes if using quart jars.

Peas Please

These instructions are for any type of field peas: green peas, purple hull peas, black-eyed peas, or crowder peas, for example. If you wish to can black-eyed peas with bacon, see the Hoppin' John recipe on page 401.

Makes approximately 9 (1-pint) jars

> 9 pounds peas
>
> water, as needed
>
> salt (optional)

1. Find a comfy place to sit with a couple of bowls, recruit some help, and start shelling peas.

2. Set a large pot of water to boil.

3. If you are using salt, place the desired amount in the bottom of your sanitized canning jars.

4. Load up the jars with your beans, packing them in tightly.

5. Ladle boiling water into the jars, allowing 1 inch of headspace.

6. Use a utensil to remove any air pockets, then add more water if needed.

7. Lid the jars and process them in your pressure canner at 10 PSI for 30 minutes if using pint jars, or 40 minutes if using quart jars.

Sweet and Sassy Coleslaw

Sometimes canned veggies can be sort of bland and a bit of a drag. Not so with this Sweet and Sassy Coleslaw! It has all of the delicious flavor of the slaw you might slave over to fix for a family barbecue, but it sits there patiently on the shelf, awaiting its day on the picnic table. Using red peppers and red onion adds a nice bit of color to the recipe, though you can omit the peppers if you prefer. This recipe is high enough in acid content to safely use a water bath canner, for which instructions are given.

Makes approximately 8 (1-pint) jars

3 heads cabbage	3 cups white vinegar
3 carrots	1 cup water
2 bell peppers (optional)	2 cups sugar
3 small onions	1 tablespoon celery seeds
3 teaspoons canning salt	2 teaspoon dry mustard

1. Shred all of the vegetables in a food processor. Toss them with salt, then put the veggies in a colander to drain.

2. Let the veggies drain for an hour. Then, squeeze them with your hands to get out any remaining liquid.

3. Meanwhile, make your dressing by combining all remaining ingredients in a saucepan and bring mixture to a boil for a minute or two. Remove from heat.

4. In a large bowl, toss together your vegetables and warm dressing.

5. Place the slaw into jars, allowing a ½ inch of headspace.

6. Process in a boiling water bath for 15 minutes for quarts, 20 minutes for pints. Be sure to adjust for your altitude.

Serving suggestion: At serving time, I like to add just a teeny bit of vegetable oil; we prefer sunflower or olive. This gives it more of a "dressed salad" flavor than a "pickled veggie" flavor. This is not the mayo-based coleslaw that a lot of folks think of, but the Southern sweet-and-sour type. However, if your family prefers a creamy slaw, you can drain the liquid at serving time and toss the slaw in a bit of mayo.

Funky Chunky Squash or Pumpkin

It's common canning knowledge that you shouldn't can pumpkin and squash. However, it is actually just pumpkin and squash *purees* that should not be canned. This is because the purees are so thick that they don't heat evenly, leaving them open to the risk of botulism. It's perfectly fine to can your pumpkin or squash in chunks in a pressure canner, and then puree them when you need them.

I leave my pumpkin and squash totally without seasoning so that they can be used flexibly in either sweet or savory dishes. We always save the seeds for roasting.

1 pound squash makes 1 quart

> uncooked pumpkin or winter squash
>
> boiling water, as needed

1. Cut up your pumpkin or squash and remove the rind, seeds, and strings. Cut it into 1-inch chunks.

2. You can raw-pack your pumpkin or squash. Fill your quart jars with cubes, leaving 1 inch of headspace.

3. Fill the jar with hot water, keeping an inch of headspace.

4. Slide a rubber utensil around the sides of the jar to remove air pockets.

5. Lid the jars and process them in your pressure canner 11 PSI for 90 minutes, adjusting for altitude.

Totally Tomatoes

I like to can some of my tomatoes plainly and simply. This way they are a little more versatile and I can use them in any type of recipe with any type of seasoning. Because tomatoes are actually a fruit, not a vegetable, they have a high enough acid content to safely use a water bath canner. Instructions for both water bath canning and pressure canning are given.

Makes approximately 7 (1-quart) jars

> 20 pounds tomatoes
>
> 2 tablespoons lemon juice per jar
>
> water, as needed

1. Prep your tomatoes as per the instructions on page 344.

2. Place your peeled, cored tomatoes in sanitized quart jars. You can cut them up or leave them whole.

3. Add 2 tablespoons of lemon juice to each jar.

4. Fill the jars with boiling water, leaving ½ inch of headspace.

5. Use a rubber utensil to remove any air pockets; failure to do this could cause your jars not to seal.

6. Lid the jars.

7. If you're using a water bath canner, process the tomatoes for 45 minutes, adjusting for altitude. If you're using a pressure canner, process the tomatoes for 15 minutes at 6 PSI, adjusting for altitude.

¡Ole, Ole! Tomatoes and Peppers

This is a homemade version of the store-bought canned Mexican-flavored tomato and pepper goodness, Rotel. It can be added to cheese sauce to make a delicious queso, pureed as a base for chili, or drained and thrown into some taco meat on the stovetop. The sky's the limit!

Use whichever hot peppers you have on hand for this recipe. Lemon juice can be substituted for lime juice, but I like lime juice better.

Makes approximately 7 (1-quart) jars

12 pounds of tomatoes, peeled and cut into chunks

3 bell peppers, diced

1 large onion, diced

2 pounds diced hot peppers

1 cup white vinegar

¼ cup sugar

4 tablespoons chili powder

2 tablespoons canning salt

1 tablespoon lime juice per jar

1. Put all of the ingredients except for the lime juice into a large stockpot and stir to combine everything.

2. Bring the mixture to a simmer and allow it to cook uncovered for 45 minutes to reduce the liquid and meld the delicious flavors.

3. Add a tablespoon of lime juice to each pint jar then ladle in the super-yummy mixture, leaving ½ inch of headspace.

4. Pop the lids on and then process in a water bath canner for 15 minutes, adjusting for altitude.

Tomato-Tomahto Juice

Some say tomato, some say tomahto. This thin puree is as simple as running your tomatoes through the blender, and possibly adding some garlic, onions, and salt to them. It can be used as a base for soup, chili, spaghetti sauce, enchilada sauce, or any other application that requires crushed tomatoes. I like to can this because it's pretty neutral and can be used in so many different recipes throughout the year.

I didn't give measurements with this recipe because this simple sauce can be made from any amount of tomatoes that you happen to lay hands upon. It is also a great way to use up soft or overripe tomatoes quickly.

1½ pounds tomatoes makes approximately 1 quart jar

assorted peeled tomatoes

½ small onion per jar (optional)

1 clove garlic per jar (optional)

sea salt or canning salt, to taste (optional)

1 tablespoon lemon juice per jar (optional if pressure-canning)

1. Peel tomatoes and place them directly into the bowl of your food processor or pitcher of your blender. Approximately 3 cups of unprocessed tomatoes will fill a quart jar. If you're using onions and garlic, add those to the food processor at the same time.

2. Use the pulse option on your processor until the mixture reaches your desired consistency.

3. Pour this into a quart jar.

4. Repeat until you have a canner-load of sauce.

5. Add a dash of salt, if using, to each jar. If you are water bath canning, add 1 tablespoon of lemon juice to each jar. If you are pressure-canning, the lemon juice is not necessary.

6. In a water bath canner, process your sauce for 40 minutes, *or* process using your pressure canner for 25 minutes at 10 PSI, adjusting for altitude.

Snowfall Spaghetti Sauce

Each year I make at least 24 jars of homemade marinara sauce—enough sauce for my family to enjoy spaghetti twice a month. It takes approximately 1.5 pounds of tomatoes to make 1 quart jar of sauce. The following instructions are for a canner-load full of sauce, or 7 quarts. Keep in mind that different types of tomatoes will yield different amounts of sauce, so there will be some variation. *Note:* When it's time to can the sauce, don't worry if the consistency is still a little watery. Over its time on the shelf, it will thicken a little bit. You can cook it down for a bit longer to get it closer to the thickness you desire. If at serving time it is still runnier than you prefer, simply stir in a small tin of tomato paste to thicken it.

Makes approximately 7 (1-quart) jars

20 pounds tomatoes	⅓ cup dried oregano
2 bell peppers	⅓ cup dried basil
2 large onions	1 tablespoon ground cloves
1 to 2 heads garlic	1 tablespoon paprika
⅓ cup sugar	⅔ cup extra virgin olive oil
2½ tablespoons sea salt	black pepper, to taste
2½ tablespoons dried thyme	

SAUCE DIRECTIONS

1. Clean and peel 20 pounds of tomatoes as per instructions on page 344.

2. Using a food processor or blender, puree bell peppers, onions, and garlic.

3. Add the prepped tomatoes and veggies to a large stockpot. Add seasonings and olive oil.

4. With the lid on, bring the sauce to a simmer for about an hour, stirring occasionally. Then, remove the lid, drop the heat, and simmer gently for 3 more hours. Removing the lid will allow the liquid to evaporate so that the sauce can cook down and thicken.

5. To can the sauce, ladle it into quart jars, allowing 1 inch of head space.

6. Wipe the lip of your jars with a cloth dipped in white vinegar and then place the lids on.

7. Process the sauce in your pressure canner for 25 minutes at 7 PSI, adjusting for altitude.

8. Allow the jars to sit undisturbed for 12 hours, or until cooled. Test the seals before putting them away.

You can use this delicious, authentic Italian marinara to make spaghetti and meatballs, chicken Parmesan, as the base of an Italian vegetable soup, or you can thicken it to use as a pizza sauce. See the variations starting on page 414 to turn your marinara into a complete meal.

CHAPTER 10

The Meat of the Matter

The recipes in this chapter are geared toward preparing the meat ingredients of a meal, rather than preparing a complete meal. Having a supply of already prepared basic meats on hand can go a long way toward speeding up mealtimes throughout the year. Canning meat is a great way to take advantage of a good sale or a bulk purchase without having to worry about what will happen if your freezer malfunctions or if you have a power outage.

When you think about canned meat, you probably get the idea of those icky store-bought mystery chunks that you can purchase. Home-canned meat is miles away from that. It can be most closely compared to meat that has been put in the slow cooker to simmer on low all day. Moist, tasty, and so tender that it falls apart when you put a fork to it.

The other benefit to canning your meat is that it will not only be preserved no matter your electricity situation, but it will be immediately ready to eat. Simply warm it up, and if you can't do that, it's safe to eat right out of the jar.

In a disaster situation, having sufficient protein is extremely important. If you perform hard manual labor without adequate protein, your body will begin to catabolize your muscles to provide it with necessary nutrients. This will weaken you physically at a time when you need to be at your peak.

Meats *must* be canned using a pressure canner—remember our talks about botulism? Most meat can be raw-packed, because the heat of the canner will thoroughly cook the meat while it is processed.

About Roast Beast

I use the term "Roast Beast" to apply to any type of non-poultry roast that you might acquire: pork, beef, bison, venison, moose, you name it. When you hit the mother lode, whether it's a great sale, a successful hunt, or a side of beef that's just arrived, take some time to can it right away. Then a great meal is as close as popping the lid off of a jar.

Meat-Canning Prep

I like to plan for a full day of prep, canning, and clean up when I have an abundance of meat in my freezer. This allows me to make the backbone of dozens of meals.

When dealing with a large amount of raw meat, I make it easy for myself by cutting open a cardboard box and laying it out on my counter. Then I use one cookie sheet to hold the meat and place my cutting board in another cookie sheet. This way I don't have to clean up a bloody mess after preparing all that meat for canning. (I'm sure you know this, but be certain to put a few drops of bleach in the wash water afterward in order to kill bacteria left from the raw meat.) A few other meat-canning tips:

- Use wide-mouth jars for canning meat so that it isn't a wrestling match to get it out at serving time. When you pressure-can the meat it becomes fork tender, so you want to be able to remove it from the jar with minimum hassle.

- Even if you like highly seasoned food, don't go too crazy adding seasonings before canning. The flavors will greatly intensify, so use a light hand.

- Take special care when cleaning the rims of the jars, because the fat content in meat can interfere with proper sealing if it gets between the jar and the lid. Try dipping a cloth or paper towel in white vinegar to break down any grease lingering on the lip of the jar.

- Never add thickeners like flour or cornstarch to your liquid. You won't end up with gravy; you'll end up with a nasty, gloppy mess. You can make gravy with the liquid at serving time.

- Slice the roasts into pieces that will fit into your jars. Obviously, if you aren't using wide-mouth jars, those pieces will need to be smaller.

- Some separation of the sauce ingredients and the fat from the meat is perfectly normal. You can either discard the fat or stir it back in, depending upon your preference and dietary requirements.

Raw-Packed Roast Beast

Because the amount of your bounty will vary from batch to batch, this recipe is per jar, and meat measurements are approximate. Use any type of non-poultry hunk of meat for this.

1 pound meat makes 1 quart jar

1 pound roast

1 clove garlic

2 small cooking onions, halved

salt and pepper, to taste

water, as needed

1. Place a hunk of roast in each quart jar, leaving 1½ inches of space for the additional ingredients.

2. Add garlic, onions, salt, and pepper to each jar.

3. Pour water into the jars over the meat and veggies. Using a rubber spatula, run it down the sides of the jar to remove any air pockets, then add more water if needed. Allow 1 inch of headspace.

4. Use a cloth with some vinegar on it to wipe the lip of the jars. Lid the jars.

5. Using your pressure canner, process the jars for 90 minutes at 10 PSI, adjusting for altitude.

Serving suggestion: Use the canning liquid to make gravy when you serve your roast.

Barbecue Canned Beast

You may not want to can your entire beast as a simple roast, so another great way to preserve your meat is in a homemade barbecue sauce. This sweet sauce is especially nice with game, as it softens the flavor that some people find offensive. It can be used either for a full roast or for ground meat.

The result can be removed from the jar, shredded with two forks, and mixed in with the sauce for a tender pulled pork (or pulled whatever).

Feel free to use canned or fresh tomatoes for the sauce. If you're adding hot sauce, Frank's Red Hot is a favorite.

Makes approximately 6 (1-quart) jars

6 pounds beast

water, if needed

INGREDIENTS FOR SAUCE

½ cup fresh bell pepper

6 cloves garlic

3 small cooking onions

6 cups crushed tomatoes

1 cup brown sugar

1 cup honey

½ cup apple cider vinegar

1 teaspoon Worcestershire sauce

1 tablespoon hot sauce (optional)

¼ teaspoon ground cloves

1 tablespoon paprika

1. Using a food processor, puree peppers, garlic, and onion.

2. Mix the puree, along with all other ingredients for sauce, in a saucepan and bring to a boil.

3. Proceed with canning as for regular roast beast (see page 392) but replace the water in the recipe with barbecue sauce. If your jars don't have quite enough barbecue sauce to fill up completely, you can top them off with more water.

Deep South BBQ

This Southern classic can be made with any inexpensive roast, like beef or pork. The smoky flavorful meat only gets better as it sits in the jar. *Note:* Pint jars hold approximately 1 pound of cooked meat

Makes approximately 6 (1-pint) jars

5 to 6 pounds roast

2 large onions, pureed

1 bottle of beer

2 cups ketchup

¼ cup prepared yellow mustard

½ cup brown sugar

¼ cup apple cider vinegar

1 tablespoon garlic powder

1 teaspoon black pepper

1 tablespoon liquid smoke

½ tablespoon Louisiana-style hot sauce

1. Place the roast and onions in a slow cooker, then pour a bottle of beer over them.

2. Cook on low for 10 hours. The meat should be so delightfully tender that it falls apart when you touch it with a fork.

3. Shred the meat with two forks, and return it to the cooking liquid in the slow cooker. Stir to combine.

4. In a saucepan, combine remaining ingredients with a whisk to make your sauce.

5. Stirring frequently, bring the sauce ingredients to a boil.

6. Pour the sauce over the meat in the slow cooker. Stir well. Heat the sauce on low for another 30 minutes.

7. Ladle the hot meat and sauce into sanitized jars.

8. Lid the jars and process them in a pressure canner for 70 minutes at 10 PSI. If you are using quart jars, process at the same pressure for 90 minutes.

Serving suggestion: The meat can be served on a bun or just piled on a plate and paired with Sweet and Sassy Coleslaw (page 386).

Mexi-Meat

For instant gratification of those fiesta cravings, preserve some ground meat that is already seasoned and ready to fill a tortilla. Going with the "use what you've got" principle, you can use ground beef, ground chicken, or ground whatever for these flavorful pints.

Reducing the amount of fat is not only better for your waistline, it's better for the preservation of your food. A high-fat item is more vulnerable to spoilage. After precooking the meat, carefully drain the fat before adding the seasoning. If you really want your product to be lean, you can also rinse the meat under running water, but I usually skip that step.

Makes approximately 6 (1-pint) jars

1 tablespoon olive oil	2 cans tomato paste
2 large onions, finely minced	¼ cup chili powder
6 cloves garlic, finely minced	⅛ cup ground cumin
5 pounds ground meat	

1. Add olive oil to a large stockpot and lightly sauté the onion and garlic.

2. Add your ground meat to the pot, stirring well to combine it with the onion and garlic.

3. Pour in enough water to cover the meat and veggie mixture.

4. Bring the contents of the stockpot to a boil, then reduce heat until the mixture is simmering lightly. Cook for about 20 minutes, stirring occasionally.

5. Using a metal colander, drain your meat mixture carefully.

6. Return the meat and veggie mixture to the stockpot and stir well to combine the tomato paste and spices.

7. Immediately ladle the mixture into prepared pint jars, leaving ½ inch of headspace.

8. Process the jars in a pressure canner for 90 minutes at 10 PSI, adjusting for altitude.

Serving suggestion: Use this meat anywhere you'd use freshly cooked taco filling—on nachos, topping a taco salad, filling a tortilla…the list is endless!

Sloppy Joe Filling

Some things taste better than they look, and this filling is one of those things. It's absolutely delicious, but once it cools in the jars, there is some separation. Use whichever ground meat you have on hand. Don't be deterred by the lengthy prep time, as very little of it is hands-on.

Makes approximately 7 (1-pint) jars

6 pounds prepped tomatoes (page 344)	2 tablespoons paprika
2 cups chopped onions	½ cup apple cider vinegar
2 cups chopped sweet bell peppers	5 pounds lean ground meat
2 cloves garlic, minced	salt and pepper, to taste
1½ cups brown sugar	

1. Using a food processor, puree the tomatoes, onions, bell peppers, and garlic in batches.

2. Pour the vegetable puree into your slow cooker and cook it on low for about 6 to 8 hours with the lid askew. The volume should reduce by half.

3. Stir in the sugar, paprika, vinegar, and salt and pepper and continue to cook on low for 2 to 4 more hours or until the mixture has reached the desired consistency.

4. On a stovetop, lightly brown the ground meat and drain in a metal colander. Rinse if you want to reduce the fat content further.

5. Stir the drained beef into the sauce.

6. Ladle the sauce into sanitized pint jars.

7. Wipe the lips of the jars, then place the lids on.

8. Process in a pressure canner for 90 minutes at 10 PSI.

Serving suggestions: Remember, you may notice a bit of grease separated in your jar of sauce and meat. This is not unusual. You can either drain it off before reheating or stir it in. Once you've reheated your sauce, serve it on a bun for a classic Sloppy Joe, or even on a pita. Add a side of coleslaw! (See the recipe for Sweet and Sassy Coleslaw on page 386.)

Skinless Boneless Chicken

Raw-packing skinless boneless chicken results in a tender poached chicken that is delicious when cut up into chicken salads or when shredded and seasoned to be used in enchiladas or other recipes. For the sake of versatility, this recipe contains only very mild seasoning.

Each quart jar will hold approximately three average-sized chicken breasts or six chicken thighs. The following recipe is per jar, so multiply the ingredients as needed.

Although it can be done safely, I don't recommend canning bone-in chicken. The bones dissolve into gelatinous muck that is neither pretty nor tasty.

Makes 1 quart jar

1 clove crushed garlic

3 skinless boneless chicken breasts, or 6 skinless boneless thighs

½ teaspoon sea salt

½ teaspoon black pepper

water as, needed

1. Place one clove of garlic in the bottom of each sanitized quart jar.

2. Add raw chicken pieces to the jar, pushing them down to pack tightly.

3. Add salt and pepper, and then fill the jar with water, allowing 1 inch of headspace.

4. Carefully slide a rubber spatula utensil down the interior sides of the jars, removing air pockets. Do not skip this step, or your jars may not seal. Wipe the rims of the jars.

5. Lid the jars and process in a pressure canner for 90 minutes at 10 PSI, adjusting for altitude.

Carnitas

This is the most fantastic way to can pork, ever! Carnitas can be used as taco or burrito filling, or you can serve it with refried beans and rice. Or, you can try not to burn your mouth and eat it directly from the skillet. Shoulder roast or stewing beef will work just as well as pork for this recipe. Use either orange juice concentrate or lime juice.

Makes approximately 8 (1-quart) jars

15 pounds of pork

PER QUART JAR

1 clove garlic, minced

⅛ cup minced onion

½ teaspoon ground cumin

½ teaspoon chili powder

½ teaspoon dried oregano

⅛ teaspoon salt

1 bay leaf

1 tablespoon lime juice

1. If necessary, cut pork into bite-sized pieces. Trim the visible fat off the roast.

2. Add pork to quart jars, allowing room for the additional ingredients.

3. Top each jar with the remaining ingredients above in the order listed. Do not add any additional liquid.

4. Wipe the rims of the jars with a paper towel dipped in vinegar, then put the lids on.

5. Process in a pressure canner for 90 minutes at 11 PSI.

Serving suggestions: Carnitas meat should be reheated by draining it and frying it in a cast-iron skillet. You'll end up with lovely, delicious, crispy bits. When the meat is cooked, mix the sauce back in and stir well until it's heated through.

El Pollo Mexicano

In case you can't tell, we're big fans of Mexican food in this house. This is a way to preserve boneless chicken that is immediately ready to fill enchiladas, burritos, and tacos. You can use chicken thighs or breasts for this recipe, and for those of you that don't enjoy cilantro, you can substitute parsley. Lemon juice, lime juice, and white vinegar are all equally effective in this recipe and can be substituted if needed.

Makes approximately 7 (1-quart) jars

10 pounds boneless, skinless chicken	8 cloves garlic, minced
4 pounds peeled, diced tomatoes	3 tablespoons chili powder
4 pounds mixed bell peppers	1 tablespoons ground cumin
¼ pound hot peppers (optional)	⅛ cup chopped fresh cilantro
1 pound diced onion	salt, to taste
½ cup lemon juice	

1. Cut up chicken into bite-sized pieces and fill jars two-thirds of the way.

2. In a large, non-reactive bowl, mix all of the other ingredients together.

3. Ladle the vegetable and spice mixture over the chicken.

4. Use a rubber spatula to remove air pockets.

5. Process the jars in a pressure canner at 11 PSI for 90 minutes, adjusting for altitude.

CHAPTER 11

Beans, Beans, Beans

Beans are a pantry staple for many preppers, but they sure do take a long time to cook! You need to plan ahead, soak them, and let them simmer for a few hours.

For this reason, I always have some jars of home-canned beans on my shelves. There's a lot of room for variety when home canning your beans. You can use whatever beans you have on hand for this: navy beans, white kidney beans, black beans, pinto beans, or even a mix of a few different kinds. And finally, if you need to, feel free to leave out the meat. Some have religious restrictions or follow a vegetarian diet. Just skip the addition of the meat and carry on with the rest of the instructions.

When canning beans, they must be soaked ahead of time, and then the pressure canning process will do the rest of the work. If you don't soak them, they may not get thoroughly cooked. This doesn't mean they're unsafe. However, they will be crunchy and will need to be cooked for an extra hour or so instead of merely being heated up. When canning beans, they must be totally covered with liquid and there must be room for them to expand.

Some question the price efficiency of canning my own beans instead of buying pre-canned beans at the store. This is a valid point—they end up, with the price of the power to can them and the use of a jar lid, to be about the same price as the conventional store-bought canned beans. But if you are using organic beans and comparing the home-canned to store-bought organic beans, doing it yourself is far cheaper.

Basic Pork and Beans

This recipe has worked on any type of bean I've tried it with, including pinto, navy, black, red kidney, white kidney, chickpeas, and black-eyed peas. Adjust the meat you add according to what will blend nicely with your bean of choice, as well as how you intend to use the beans in the future.

Makes approximately 7 (1-quart) jars

5 pounds dried beans	salt (optional)
water or broth, as needed	12 bay leaves
1 to 2 pounds ham, salt pork, or bacon	6 small onions, cut in half

1. Rinse and sort dried beans, then soak them in hot water for at least 2 hours (but overnight is better).

2. Discard the soaking water, then bring the beans to a boil in fresh water or broth.

3. Drain the beans again, this time reserving the cooking water.

4. Distribute the pork evenly across sanitized quart jars.

5. Top the meat with soaked beans, filling each jar no more than three-quarters full.

6. Add to each jar a pinch of salt, if using, 2 bay leaves, and half an onion.

7. In the bean pot, bring 6 cups of the reserved liquid, or broth, to a boil. Add more liquid if necessary.

8. Ladle the hot liquid over the beans, leaving 1½ inches of headspace. The beans must be totally covered with liquid, and there must be room for them to expand.

9. Lid the jars and process in a pressure canner at 10 PSI for 75 minutes for pints or 90 minutes for quarts, adjusting for altitude.

Mexican Pork and Beans

At serving time, these beans can be heated as is, or mashed and lightly fried in a cast iron skillet for refried beans.

Makes approximately 7 (1-quart) jars

5 pounds dried black beans or pinto beans	⅛ teaspoon ground cumin
water or broth, as needed	¼ teaspoon chili powder
1 to 2 pounds salt pork or bacon	1 tablespoon tomato paste
¼ teaspoon garlic powder	½ onion per jar
¼ teaspoon onion powder	salt (optional)

1. Rinse and sort dried beans, then soak them in hot water for at least 2 hours.

2. Discard the soaking water, then bring the beans to a boil in fresh water or broth.

3. Drain the beans again, this time reserving the cooking liquid.

4. Distribute the pork evenly across the jars.

5. Top the meat with soaked beans, filling each jar no more than three-quarters full.

6. Add to each jar a pinch of salt, garlic powder, onion powder, cumin, chili powder, tomato paste, and half an onion.

7. In the bean pot, bring 6 cups of the reserved liquid, or broth, to a boil. Add more liquid if necessary.

8. Ladle the hot liquid over the beans, leaving 1½ inches of headspace. The beans must be totally covered with liquid, and there must be room for them to expand.

9. Lid the jars and process in a pressure canner at 10 PSI for 75 minutes for pints or 90 minutes for quarts, adjusting for altitude.

BBQ Beans

These are your basic Southern picnic beans, delicious served warm, cold, or at room temperature. Use navy, kidney, white kidney, or pinto beans.

Makes approximately 7 (1-quart) jars

5 pounds dried beans

water or broth, as needed

1 to 2 pounds salt pork, ham, or bacon

6 cups tomato juice

½ cup apple cider vinegar or white vinegar

1 tablespoon garlic powder

1 tablespoon onion powder

1 tablespoon chili powder

2 tablespoons dry mustard

1 teaspoon liquid smoke

salt (optional)

2 tablespoons brown sugar or muscovado sugar per jar

½ onion per jar

1. Rinse and sort dried beans, then soak them in hot water for at least 2 hours.

2. Discard the soaking water, then bring beans to a boil in fresh water or broth.

3. Drain the beans again, this time reserving the cooking water.

4. Distribute the pork evenly across your jars.

5. Top the meat with soaked beans, filling each jar no more than three-quarters full.

6. Bring tomato juice, vinegar, spices, and liquid smoke to a boil.

7. Add to each jar a pinch of salt, if using, 2 tablespoons brown sugar, and half an onion.

8. Ladle the hot tomato juice over the beans, leaving 1½ inches of headspace. If necessary, add some of the cooking water. The beans must be totally covered with liquid and there must be room for them to expand.

9. Lid the jars and process in a pressure canner at 10 PSI for 75 minutes for pints or 90 minutes for quarts, adjusting for altitude.

Boston Baked Beans

These beans are tangy and delicious right out of the jar. The liquid is the classic Boston Baked Beans sauce, containing no tomato product. It thickens up beautifully during the canning process.

Makes approximately 7 (1-quart) jars

5 pounds dried beans

water or broth, as needed

1 pound bacon or salt pork

6 tablespoons dark molasses

2 tablespoons white vinegar

2 tablespoons onion powder

1 tablespoon salt

2 teaspoons dry mustard

½ teaspoon ground cloves

1. Rinse and sort dried beans, then soak them in hot water for at least 2 hours.

2. Discard the soaking water, then bring beans to a boil in fresh water.

3. Drain the beans again, this time reserving the cooking water.

4. Distribute the pork evenly across your jars.

5. Top the bacon with soaked beans, filling each jar no more than three-quarters full.

6. In the bean pot, bring 6 cups of the reserved liquid to a boil. Stir in the rest of the ingredients, simmering until they are well combined.

7. Ladle the hot molasses mixture over the beans and pork, leaving 1 inch of headspace. If you didn't make enough molasses mixture so that there is more than 1 inch of headspace, add more liquid as necessary.

8. Lid the jars and process in a pressure canner at 10 PSI for 75 minutes for pints or 90 minutes for quarts, adjusting for altitude.

Hoppin' John

This classic dish is a traditional New Year's Day meal in many parts of the world, said to bring the person who eats it prosperity throughout the coming year. Unlike the other recipes in this section, the black-eyed peas should *not* be soaked ahead of time.

Makes approximately 6 (1-quart) jars

2 pounds chopped salt pork, bacon, or ham	2 cups prepped, diced fresh tomato
3 pounds dried black-eyed peas	2 large onions, finely chopped
6 cloves garlic, crushed	finely diced jalapeño pepper, to taste (optional)
2 cups diced green bell pepper	hot water, as needed

1. Layer the ingredients in each of your jars in the order listed, leaving 1 inch of headspace.

2. Pour hot water over the contents of the jars, allowing 1 inch of headspace for the peas to expand.

3. Use a rubber utensil to slide around the edges of the jar to remove air pockets. Add more liquid if necessary.

4. Lid the jars and process in a pressure canner at 10 PSI for 90 minutes, adjusting for altitude.

CHAPTER 12

Soups & Stews

What could be nicer on a cold winter day than a piping hot bowl of soup? Piping hot soup that came from a jar that you canned a couple of months previously! One of the best things about canning is that you can put dinner on the table in the time it takes to heat something to boiling. I will never forget the first time I popped open a home-canned jar of beef stew. Not only was it delicious, tasting like it had been simmered all day long, but it was an instant-gratification meal.

Canning entire meals is the perfect solution for preppers. Very little fuel will be required to heat a home-cooked meal, each jar is loaded with a variety of protein sources and veggies, and you know that you're getting high-quality ingredients instead of mystery by-products.

When making soup, I recommend layering the ingredients. I don't always precook the soup because the flavors will meld beautifully during the pressure canning process. And as I mentioned before, I'm kind of lazy, so why would I want to make extra work for myself?

The reason for layering is more than just laziness, though. It is so that you get a somewhat equal amount of each item in your soup. Otherwise, you run the risk of having a jar of really chunky, meaty soup and a jar that is mostly broth. The other benefit is that this is a quick and easy method for preparing lots of delicious, healthy meals!

Basically Better Tomato Basil Soup

One of our family favorites is tomato basil soup. For a little variation on the traditional, this soup is delightful with yellow or orange tomatoes. You can use any variety of tomatoes for this soup, but I like to use the juicier tomatoes since there is no need to cook them down for hours to get a thick consistency.

This is a simple, per-jar recipe since tomato harvests vary, and if your garden is anything like mine, they provide you with an ongoing but difficult-to-predict supply for several weeks.

Makes 1 quart jar

INGREDIENTS PER JAR

1 ½ pounds peeled tomatoes	1 teaspoon honey
¼ onion	canning salt, to taste
1 clove garlic	black pepper, to taste
1 teaspoon balsamic vinegar	1 tablespoon dried basil

1. In a blender, puree together all ingredients except for the basil, until it reaches the desired consistency. Some people like it to be very smooth, while others prefer a slightly chunkier soup.

2. Fill your jars with soup straight from the blender, then add your dried basil to the top.

3. Wipe the rim, then put the lid on the jar.

4. Process the soup in a pressure canner at 10 PSI for 20 minutes, adjusting for altitude.

Serving suggestions: If you like creamy tomato soup, heat the contents of your jar, then stir in ¼ cup of milk or cream, heating only long enough to warm it through. Grilled cheese sandwich is optional but delicious!

Bestern Southwestern Chicken Soup

This Mexican-inspired soup is a family favorite. Be sure to soak the beans ahead of time for best results. There is no need to pre-cook them, as they will cook nicely in the pressure canner as long as they have been soaked.

Makes approximately 7 (1-quart) jars

3 cans diced tomatoes, juice reserved

6 cups chicken broth

3 tablespoons chili powder

1 tablespoon cilantro

1 tablespoon ground cumin

3 cups chicken, cooked and shredded

3 cups black beans, rinsed, sorted, and pre-soaked

2 cups corn kernels

1 onion, finely diced

4 cloves garlic, minced

1 bell pepper, diced

salt and pepper

1. In a large stockpot, stir together tomatoes, broth, chili powder, cilantro, cumin, salt, and pepper. Bring this mixture to a boil.

2. Layer the other ingredients evenly in your jars.

3. Top the layered ingredients with your hot broth mixture, leaving 1 inch of headspace. If you run out of broth, it's fine to top up your jars with water, as the flavors will have plenty of time to blend.

4. Lid your jars and process in a pressure canner for 90 minutes at 11 PSI. Be sure to adjust for altitude.

Serving suggestions: Serve your delicious soup topped with a dollop of plain yogurt or sour cream and some crumbled tortilla chips. For heartier fare, you can serve this over brown rice or quinoa.

Splendiferous Split Pea Soup

When you heat this up, you may need to add water or broth to get it to the consistency that you prefer. This soup can't be layered. You'll need to cook up a big pot of it for canning to get the right consistency.

Makes approximately 6 (1-quart) jars

½ pound ham or bacon, diced (about 1 cup)

1 tablespoon olive oil

2 whole onions, finely chopped

6 cloves garlic, finely minced

6 cups split peas, rinsed and sorted

15 quarts of water

3 carrots, peeled and cut into chunks

3 to 4 bay leaves

1 tablespoon dried thyme

1. In a big Dutch oven or stockpot, sauté ham or bacon in olive oil until it is lightly browned.

2. Add in onions and garlic and sauté for about 2 more minutes.

3. Stir in all of the rest of the ingredients and bring to a boil.

4. Reduce heat and simmer, covered, for an hour to an hour and a half, until all ingredients are soft.

5. Even if you prefer a puree, I recommend canning it at this point. It will cook more during processing and most likely be the consistency you desire. If not, you can puree it at the time you heat it up for dinner.

6. Fill quart jars and allow 1 inch of headspace.

7. Process in the pressure canner for 90 minutes at 12 PSI, adjusting for altitude.

Serving suggestions: Go crazy and sauté a little bacon or ham for the top of the soup. Drizzle with sour cream, and serve with fresh crusty bread for dipping.

Great Golumpki Soup

Golumpki is the Polish name for cabbage roll, a fantastic yet time-consuming Eastern European delicacy that I am way too lazy to make. So I turned it into soup because soup is easy, particularly in this layered raw-pack recipe. You can substitute pork for beef.

Makes approximately 6 (1-quart) jars

3 pounds ground beef

6 cups shredded cabbage

1½ cups shredded carrots

2 medium onions, finely chopped

6 cloves garlic, minced

12 cups tomato juice

3 tablespoons brown sugar

1½ cups white vinegar

2 tablespoons dried oregano

2 tablespoons dried basil

salt and pepper, to taste

1. Layer meat, cabbage, carrots, onion, and garlic in equal parts across your jars.

2. In a large stockpot, combine tomato juice, sugar, vinegar, salt, pepper, and herbs. Heat this mixture to a simmer for 10 minutes.

3. Top the ingredients in the jars with your canning liquid. If needed, add more water, leaving 1 inch of headroom.

4. Process in a pressure canner at 11 PSI for 90 minutes. Be sure to adjust for altitude.

Serving suggestions: This soup is great as is, right out of the jar. For a heartier meal, you can add 1 cup of cooked rice, or cook 1 cup of rice into the liquid to give it more of a casserole consistency. Some people like it topped with a drizzle of sour cream.

Autumn Garden Stew

One great way to make use of tasty root veggies in your fall garden is with a hearty stew. Based on what you have available, you can mix and match veggies to your heart's content. Do *not* add flour or any other thickener to your stew until you are ready to eat it. Thickeners do not store well when canned, and they turn your meal into a clumpy mess.

This is a raw-pack recipe, meaning the meat and vegetables will cook in the pressure canner and do not need to be cooked ahead of time.

Use whatever type of beast meat you have on hand. For root vegetables, I suggest potatoes, sweet potatoes, parsnips, turnips, and rutabaga. Feel free to mix and match these veggies, or just pick your favorite and go with that one.

Makes approximately 7 (1-quart) jars

8 cups water or stock	4 to 6 cups cubed root vegetables
1 tablespoon dried thyme	2 cups carrot rounds
½ tablespoon dried marjoram	3 cups finely chopped onion
2 tablespoons dried parsley	6 cloves garlic, crushed and minced
4 pounds cubed beast	

1. In a stockpot, combine water or stock, thyme, marjoram, and parsley, and bring to a boil.

2. Meanwhile, layer meat and vegetables into your jars.

3. Pour the hot liquid over the layered meat and vegetables. Add more water if needed. Leave 1 to 1½-inches of headspace.

4. Lid your jars and process them in your pressure canner for 90 minutes at 10 PSI. Be sure to adjust for altitude.

Serving suggestions: When you are ready to serve your stew, add 1 tablespoon of flour to ½ cup water and whisk into a paste. Stir this into your stew as you heat it up to make a thick, hearty gravy.

Chicken-Needs-Noodles Soup

This soup has everything but the noodles, and the reason for this is that noodles break down and turn into a goopy mess when they are canned. Some people will tell you that they have canned soup with noodles for years and that the noodles are perfect, but I have never had success. When it is soup time, simply pour it into a pot, bring it to a boil, and throw in the amount of pasta that you want. You can make this with any kind of poultry.

Makes 1 quart jar

2 uncooked boneless skinless chicken thighs or 1 chicken breast

½ cup carrot rounds

¼ cup chopped celery

¼ cup finely grated onion

2 cloves fresh garlic, mashed

¼ teaspoon dried oregano

¼ teaspoon dried basil

¼ teaspoon dried thyme

⅛ teaspoon salt

water, as needed

1. Layer your ingredients in the jars.

2. Bring water to a simmer.

3. Ladle hot water into the jars until you have 1 inch of headspace remaining. You will look at this and notice that there is way more liquid than chicken and veggies, but that's important because you need additional liquid for serving time, when you cook the pasta.

4. Lid your jars and pressure-can at 12 PSI for 90 minutes, adjusting for altitude.

Serving suggestion: If you're feeding someone with a tummy ailment, add a little bit of ginger to the soup when re-heating. You can also add some fresh minced garlic at serving time. Add whatever grain works for you at the moment: pasta, rice, orzo, quinoa, and barley are all delicious.

Mexican-Texican Cowboy Chili

Chili is the perfect meal for a snowy winter day. This recipe and the recipe on page 407 provide two very different takes on the traditional chili and are both popular at our house. They are assembled using the layering method and are raw-packed, making it simple to create up to 7 family dinners at one cooking session—or even more, if your canner can hold it!

This recipe is the classic thick, savory chili, loaded with meat and beans. Use whatever meat you have on hand. It's best seasoned with beer, but if you don't have any you can use water instead. Either crushed tomatoes or tomato juice can be used.

Makes approximately 6 (1-quart) jars

10 cups crushed tomatoes

1 can beer

½ cup chili powder

3 tablespoons ground cumin

1 tablespoon salt

1 tablespoon minced parsley

4 pounds ground meat

2 pounds dried pinto beans, pre-soaked

1 cup diced onion

4 cloves garlic, minced

1 cup diced bell pepper

diced jalapeño peppers, to taste (optional)

water, if needed

1. In a stockpot, bring crushed tomatoes, beer, chili powder, cumin, salt, and parsley to a boil.

2. Layer your meat, dried beans, onions, garlic, bell pepper, and jalapeño, if using, evenly across your jars.

3. Pour your hot liquid mixture over the layered ingredients, then top off with water, leaving 1 inch of headspace.

4. Process at 10 PSI for 90 minutes in your pressure canner. Be sure to adjust for altitude.

Sweet and Spicy Chili

This recipe is awesome if you happen to acquire some venison or other game. A lot of people are uncomfortable with the unfamiliar "wild" flavor of the meat, and this extremely well-seasoned chili hides that. Minus the jalapeños, this produces a very kid-friendly flavor.

Ground meat works just as well as stew meat for this recipe. Molasses can be substituted for brown sugar.

Makes approximately 7 (1-quart) jars

8 cups tomato puree

½ cup apple cider vinegar

½ cup brown sugar

½ cup chili powder

1 tablespoon salt

1 teaspoon dry mustard

4 to 6 pounds cubed beast

3 cups dried red kidney beans, pre-soaked

1 slice bacon per jar

2 large onions, diced

6 cloves garlic, minced

1 cup diced bell pepper

finely minced jalapeño pepper, to taste

water, as needed

1. In a stockpot, bring tomato puree, apple cider vinegar, brown sugar, chili powder, salt, and dry mustard to a boil.

2. Layer your raw meat, dried beans, bacon, onions, garlic, and peppers evenly across your prepped jars.

3. Pour your hot liquid mixture over the layered ingredients, then top off with water as needed, leaving 1 inch of headspace.

4. Process at 10 PSI for 90 minutes in your pressure canner. Be sure to adjust for altitude.

Serving suggestions: When serving your chili, shred the bacon with a fork and stir it in.

Tips for Perfect Home-Canned Chili

- Soak the beans ahead of time and they will cook perfectly during the canning process.

- Feel free to take liberties with the ingredients, using whatever you are able to source healthfully. The seasoning is the important part!

- Raw pack all of the ingredients and load the jars using the layering method.

The chili will thicken as it sits on the shelf. You may need to thin it with a small amount of water or tomato juice at serving time.

Chicken Vegetable Chowder Starter

The reason I call this recipe a "starter" is because you'll be adding some dairy at serving time. The USDA strongly cautions against canning anything with dairy products or thickeners, but you can have the basis of this delicious chowder. You can also serve it simply as a chicken and vegetable soup if you don't have access to dairy products. This is a raw-pack, per-jar recipe.

Makes 1 quart jar

2 thighs or 1 breast boneless skinless chicken, cut into bite-sized pieces

½ cup corn

¼ cup green peas

¼ cup diced carrots

½ cup diced potatoes

⅛ cup diced celery

⅛ cup finely minced onion

⅛ cup diced red pepper

1 clove garlic, smashed

salt and pepper, to taste

½ teaspoon dried parsley

¼ teaspoon dried thyme

⅛ teaspoon dried dill weed

water, as needed

1. In clean quart jars, layer the ingredients in the order listed above.

2. Fill each jar with water, leaving ⅛ inch of headspace. Use a rubber spatula to remove any air pockets.

3. Process this in a pressure canner for 90 minutes at 11 PSI, adjusting for altitude.

AT SERVING TIME

1. At serving time, pour half of the liquid out of the jar. Reserve this for thickening your roux.

2. In a saucepan, melt 1 teaspoon of butter, then make a roux by whisking in 2 tablespoons of flour until combined well.

3. Add the liquid and whisk it together with the roux, dropping the heat to low.

4. Meanwhile, in another saucepan, heat the rest of the contents of your jar.

5. When everything is heated through, add ½ cup of milk or cream to your roux, whisking to combine.

6. Combine everything by stirring in the contents of your other saucepan. Serve immediately.

Serving suggestions: Garnish this with some crisp, crumbled bacon and sour cream.

Minestrone

Enjoy some garden goodness with this delicious vegetable soup. This recipe is vegetarian, but if you want to add meat to it, the canning process is the same.

If you drain your tomatoes in a colander before making sauce, you can use the broth that was drained from your tomatoes as the basis of this soup. The USDA recommends that when canning soup, no more than half the jar should be filled with solid ingredients, and the rest should be your broth or other liquid.

These ingredients are suggestions; use any assorted vegetables you have on hand or wish to have in your soup. This recipe is perfect for using up bits of garden odds and ends.

Makes 1 quart jar

SUGGESTED INGREDIENTS

corn	potatoes, diced
carrots	winter squash, cut into cubes
peas	zucchini, diced
green beans	celery, chopped
fresh shelled beans	

SEASONINGS, PER JAR

1 tablespoon minced onion	¼ teaspoon dried thyme
1 clove garlic, minced	½ bay leaf
¼ teaspoon dried basil	salt and pepper, to taste
¼ teaspoon dried oregano	tomato juice or stock, as needed

1. Layer the solid ingredients evenly across your jars, making sure to keep them below the halfway full point.

2. Top each jar with the appropriate seasonings.

3. Ladle tomato juice or stock over your ingredients.

4. Wipe the rims of the jars, put on the lids, and process for 90 minutes at 11 PSI, adjusting for altitude.

CHAPTER 13

Main Dish Meals in Jars

These main dishes require only quick side dishes to allow you to have a great meal on the table faster than you can say "drive-thru." The simple addition of a grain like brown rice, quinoa, or pasta, and depending on availability and season, perhaps a vegetable or salad on the side, will make it seem like you slaved all afternoon over a hot stove as opposed to just opening a jar and boiling some water. (Don't worry. It'll be our little secret.)

A few of these meals, like the Beef Stroganoff on page 411, would be enhanced by stirring in some sour cream at serving time. See the "Serving Suggestions" at the end of each recipe.

All ingredients are uncooked unless the recipe specifically states otherwise. This protects vegetables from getting mushy and overcooked, and allows the meat to get pressure-cooked, which creates a flavorful broth and provides a fork-tender result.

Hungarian Goulash

Goulash is generally served over spaetzle, egg noodles, rice, or mashed potatoes. This is best with *real* Hungarian paprika; without it, you won't get an authentic flavor.

Makes approximately 7 (1-quart) jars

4 tablespoons Hungarian paprika	2 bell peppers, diced
2 teaspoons dry mustard	6 potatoes, diced
1 tablespoon olive oil	6 cups water, plus more as needed
4 onions, quartered	½ cup red wine vinegar
4 cloves garlic, minced	1 (6-ounce) can tomato paste
4 pounds stewing meat	salt and pepper, to taste
4 carrots, sliced into large pieces	

1. In a bowl, mix Hungarian paprika, dry mustard, salt, and pepper.

2. In a large stockpot, heat olive oil and begin to sauté your onions and garlic.

3. Dip your stewing meat in the spice mixture, then place the meat in the stockpot to brown with the garlic and onions. You only need to brown lightly—the meat doesn't need to be cooked.

4. In quart jars, layer your meat and vegetable mixture, carrots, peppers, and potatoes.

5. Add 6 cups of water, vinegar, and tomato paste to the stockpot and mix with any drippings or spices that remain after browning the meat. Bring this mixture to a boil.

6. Ladle hot liquid into jars over the layered contents. Use a table knife or spatula to remove any air pockets in the jars. If necessary, add more water, allowing 1 inch of headspace.

7. Lid the jars and process in your pressure canner for 1 hour and 15 minutes at 10 PSI, adjusting for altitude.

Serving suggestions: When heating your goulash, whisk in 1 tablespoon of flour to thicken the sauce. Once it is hot, stir in ½ cup of sour cream or plain yogurt, and heat only until the sour cream is warmed through.

Beef Stroganoff

Beef stroganoff is delicious served over egg noodles or rice. Use stewing beef or sliced sirloin for best results.

Makes approximately 7 (1-quart) jars

4 to 5 pounds beef, chopped or sliced	1 tablespoon butter
2 onions, finely chopped	2 tablespoons Worcestershire sauce
4 cloves garlic, finely chopped	water, as needed
4 cups sliced mushrooms	salt and pepper, to taste

1. In a large stockpot, sauté beef, onions, garlic, and mushrooms in butter until lightly browned.

2. Stir in Worcestershire sauce, salt, pepper, and enough water to deglaze the stockpot. Use a metal utensil to scrape the bottom of the pot to loosen the flavorful pieces there.

3. Add 2 cups of water and stir well, bringing to a boil.

4. Ladle the stroganoff into sanitized quart jars, distributing the cooking liquid evenly across the jars. Don't worry about adding more liquid—when the meat cooks, it will add flavorful juices.

5. Process in your pressure canner for 90 minutes at 10 PSI, adjusting for altitude.

Serving suggestions: When you are ready to serve the beef stroganoff, heat the sauce then stir in 1 cup of sour cream or plain yogurt. Continue heating the sauce at a low temperature only until the addition is warmed through.

Cajun Jambalaya

The beautiful thing about jambalaya (aside from its incredible blend of Cajun flavors) is that it's one of those use-what-you've-got kinds of recipes: ham, chicken, sausage, or even all three. At serving time, you can toss in some fresh shrimp, too.

This recipe won't look like the other "meal" recipes; it will look more like a soup. You need to cook rice in the flavorful broth at serving time. Use quart jars, and make sure each one contains at least 2 cups of liquid to cook the rice.

Andouille sausage is the traditional sausage choice for this dish, but any smoked sausage will work. Use green or red pepper bell, or a combination of both. Tabasco is a good option for the hot pepper sauce, but you can use your favorite.

Makes approximately 7 (1-quart) jars

1 tablespoon olive oil

3 to 4 pounds boneless, skinless chicken thighs and breasts, cut into bite-sized pieces

2 cups smoked sausage, cut into chunks

2 cups chopped onion

2 cups chopped bell pepper

2 ribs celery, chopped

6 cloves garlic, minced

2 tablespoons smoked paprika

2 tablespoons dried thyme

cayenne pepper, to taste

2 tablespoons Cajun spice blend

6 cups peeled tomatoes with juice, divided

¼ teaspoon hot pepper sauce

4 cups chicken broth

4 cups water

salt and pepper, to taste

1. In a large stockpot, warm the olive oil and lightly brown the first 6 ingredients.

2. In a small bowl, mix paprika, salt, pepper, thyme, cayenne, and Cajun spice blend.

3. Sprinkle the vegetable and meat mixture with spice mixture, then add tomatoes and hot sauce, and stir well to combine.

4. Ladle the ingredients into sanitized quart jars, filling them no more than halfway.

5. Meanwhile, place the broth, tomato juice, and water in the stockpot and bring it to a boil, deglazing the bottom of the pot.

6. Ladle 2 cups of hot liquid into each jar, allowing 1 inch of headspace. You can top up with water if you need to.

7. Lid the jars and process in a pressure canner for 90 minutes at 10 PSI, adjusting for altitude.

Serving suggestions: When it's jambalaya time, add 1 cup of rice to the contents of your jar. Bring it to a boil, reduce heat, put the lid on, and simmer until your rice is cooked and most or all of the liquid has been absorbed. Remove from heat and fluff rice. Allow the dish to sit for 5 minutes covered, then enjoy the rich Cajun flavor!

Chicken Cacciatore

The rich herbed tomato sauce and the tender chicken will not last long on the pantry shelves, because as soon as you serve one jar of it, your family will beg you to make it again!

To make life simple, this is a raw-pack recipe. A mix of chicken breasts and thighs provides a good flavor, but you can choose just one or the other if you'd like.

Makes approximately 7 (1-quart) jars

4 pounds boneless, skinless chicken breasts and thighs, cut into bite-sized pieces

2 cups red and green bell peppers, cut into chunks

3 medium onions, cut into eighths

2 cups sliced mushrooms

8 cloves garlic, smashed

1 bottle red wine

4 cups diced tomatoes with juice, divided

2 tablespoons dried oregano

2 tablespoons dried basil

2 tablespoons dried thyme

salt and pepper, to taste

1. Layer chicken, peppers, onions, mushrooms, and garlic in quart jars. Season with salt and pepper.

2. In a large stockpot, bring wine, tomatoes, and herbs to a boil. Season with salt and pepper.

3. Ladle hot liquid over the layered ingredients in your jars.

4. Lid the jars and process them in your pressure canner for 90 minutes at 11 PSI, adjusting for altitude.

Serving suggestions: When heating the cacciatore, stir in a small can of tomato paste to thicken the sauce. Serve over pasta or rice, with a side of garlic bread.

Pot Roast Dinner

This is basically like canning roast beast, except it is a complete meal. Each jar will provide a hearty dinner for two. Use whatever type of meat you have on hand.

Makes 1 (1-quart) jar

1 pound roast

1 clove garlic

1 small cooking onion, quartered

1 large carrot, cut into chunks

1 potato, cut into bite-sized pieces

salt and pepper, to taste

water, as needed

1. Place a hunk of roast in each quart jar, leaving enough space to layer the additional ingredients.

2. Add potatoes, carrots, garlic, onions, salt, and pepper to each jar.

3. Pour water into the jars over the meat and veggies. Using a rubber spatula, run it down the sides of the jars to remove any air pockets, then add more water if needed. Allow 1 inch of headspace.

4. Use a cloth with some vinegar on it to wipe the lips of the jars.

5. Lid the jars.

6. Using your pressure canner, process the jars for 90 minutes at 10 PSI, adjusting for altitude.

Serving suggestions: When you are ready to serve your roast, use the canning liquid to make gravy.

Marinara Sauce and Meatballs

Meatballs go through the canning process very nicely. I have always made them eggless because my youngest daughter was allergic to eggs when she was little. It seems as though these slightly dry meatballs hold together better during the canning process than the ones that contain egg. You can use whatever type of ground meat you have on hand.

I usually freeze bread to make breadcrumbs; to actually make the crumbs, I use a food processor. Always account for the amount of salt in your breadcrumbs and adjust the salt in your recipe accordingly.

Makes approximately 7 (1-quart) jars

5 pounds ground meat	1 tablespoon garlic powder
2 cups very fine crumbs	1 tablespoon onion powder
2 tablespoons salt	½ batch Snowfall Spaghetti Sauce (page 390)
2 tablespoons dried parsley	

1. Combine the meat, breadcrumbs, salt, parsley flakes, garlic powder, and onion powder in a large bowl, using your hands to mix well.

2. Form very firm meatballs. They should fit nicely in the palm of your hand.

3. Place 8 to 10 meatballs into each sanitized quart jar. Don't overfill the jars with meatballs, because you want to leave room for sauce.

4. Heat marinara sauce until it is simmering, about 10 minutes.

5. Cover the meatballs with hot marinara sauce.

6. Very gently use a rubber spatula to remove air pockets so that the sauce completely fills the jar, allowing 1 inch of headspace at the top.

7. Process for 90 minutes in a pressure canner at 10 PSI, adjusting for altitude.

Meat Sauce Marinara

Use any type of ground meat for this recipe. For a lower-fat recipe, rinse the meat after browning and add the seasonings after you rinse it instead of during the cooking process.

Makes approximately 7 (1-quart) jars

3 to 4 pounds ground meat

1 tablespoon onion powder

salt and pepper, to taste

½ batch Snowfall Spaghetti Sauce (page 390)

1. Brown the ground meat in a large skillet over medium heat, stirring in seasonings.

2. Drain the meat and blot it with a paper towel to remove some of the fat.

3. Fill quart jars halfway with meat, then ladle hot spaghetti sauce over the meat. Use a rubber spatula to remove air pockets and add more sauce, if needed.

4. Wipe the lip of the jar carefully, and put the lids on.

5. Process the meat sauce in your pressure canner for 90 minutes at 10 PSI, adjusting for altitude.

Marinara with Sausage and Peppers

The flavor of the sausage gives a whole new spin to your basic (yet incredibly delicious) marinara sauce. This goes nicely with a chunkier pasta like rigatoni or fusilli.

Makes approximately 7 (1-quart) jars

6 pounds lean Italian sausages

3 tablespoons olive oil

3 cups of red bell peppers, cut into long spears

2 large onions, diced

3 cups halved button mushrooms

½ cup brown sugar

½ batch Snowfall Spaghetti Sauce (page 390)

1. Slice Italian sausages into chunks.

2. Heat olive oil in a large skillet over medium heat. Sauté Italian sausage until it is lightly browned.

3. Remove sausage and add peppers, onions, and mushrooms. Sauté veggies until caramelized.

4. Layer sausage and veggies evenly across your quart jars.

5. Add brown sugar to marinara. Mix well.

6. Add marinara sauce to jars, leaving ½ inch of headspace.

7. Wipe the lips of the jars carefully, and put the lids on.

8. Process the meat sauce in your pressure canner for 90 minutes at 10 PSI, adjusting for altitude.

Apple-Spiced Pork Chops

For the flavor of pork chops and applesauce, try this tasty meal in a jar. Wide-mouth jars work best in this recipe.

You can thicken the liquid from the jar to make an apple-flavored gravy, and you can serve this with rice, quinoa, or mashed potatoes. Thick-sliced lean roast works just as well as pork chops in this recipe.

Makes approximately 6 (1-quart) jars

3 small cooking onions, cut into quarters	6 pounds boneless pork chops
6 cloves garlic	3 to 4 tart apples, cut into eighths
1 tablespoon brown sugar per jar	salt and pepper, to taste
⅛ teaspoon ground cloves per jar	

1. In each jar, layer half a cooking onion, a clove of crushed garlic, sugar, ground cloves, salt, and pepper.

2. Trim the visible excess fat off your pork and cut it into pieces that will easily fit in the jars.

3. Fill the each jar halfway with pork, then layer 4 slices of apple in each.

4. Add more pork, then top off the jars with the rest of the apples. Do not add any cooking liquid.

5. Wipe the rims of the jars with a vinegar-dampened cloth, then cap the jars.

6. Pressure-can at 11 PSI for 90 minutes, adjusting for altitude.

Sweet and Sour Chicken

Enjoy some Asian flair with this recipe that is sure to become a family favorite. At serving time, you can thicken the canning liquid and serve this dish over rice or noodles with some steamed veggies on the side. Optionally, you can use pork for this recipe. Red or yellow bell peppers are best for this recipe, but you can use whichever you like best. If no whole pineapples are available near you, you can substitute three cans of pineapple chunks and reserve the juice. Coconut aminos can be substituted for soy sauce.

Makes approximately 7 (1-quart) jars

3 cups pineapple juice	5 pounds boneless skinless chicken, cut into bite-sized pieces
¾ cup brown sugar	2 medium onions, diced
1¼ cups apple cider vinegar	3 bell peppers, diced
6 tablespoons soy sauce	1 whole pineapple, cleaned and diced
4 tablespoons tomato paste	crushed chili pepper, to taste (optional)
1 teaspoon ground ginger	
4 cloves garlic, minced	

1. In a large saucepan, bring to a boil pineapple juice, sugar, vinegar, soy sauce, tomato paste, ginger, and garlic, stirring frequently. Simmer until the sugar is dissolved and the mixture is smooth.

2. In your jars, layer chicken, onions, peppers, and pineapple. If you're using crushed chilis, add them now.

3. Ladle the sauce over the contents of the jars.

4. Wipe the rims of the jars, put the lids on, and process in a pressure canner at 11 PSI for 90 minutes, adjusting for altitude.

Irish Brisket and Potatoes

This jar makes a hearty meal with the versatility to be used for either breakfast or dinner. Be very, very careful to use a light hand with the spices and if your brisket is already spiced, leave them out altogether, especially the pickling spice. You will also want to omit adding any extra salt in this recipe.

Makes approximately 7 (1-quart) jars

6 pounds corned beef brisket	5 cups diced potato
10 cups water	2 cups carrots, cut into chunks
2 tablespoons pickling spice (optional)	2 onions, diced

1. Trim your brisket to remove as much fat as possible, then cut it into bite-sized pieces.

2. Put water and pickling spice, if using, into a stockpot and bring it to a boil.

3. Layer potatoes, carrots, and onion in the bottom third of your wide-mouth quart jars.

4. Layer brisket on top of the potatoes and allow 1 inch of headspace.

5. Ladle spiced water into the jars, maintaining the inch of headspace. I strain the spices out, because they greatly intensify while this sits on the shelf.

6. Using a rubber spatula, remove any air pockets.

7. Wipe the rims of the jars with a paper towel dipped in vinegar, then put the lids on.

8. Process in a pressure canner at 11 PSI for 90 minutes, adjusting for altitude.

Serving suggestions: You can serve this with boiled cabbage for a classic Irish dinner. You can also drain the liquid and dump the contents of the jar onto a cutting board. Dice the meat, potatoes, and carrots, then fry it up in a hot cast-iron skillet for a tasty corned beef hash. Top it with a fried egg for a hearty breakfast.

Beef Burgundy

This is a family favorite that can be served over mashed potatoes or egg noodles. Even better, you can thicken the sauce and, for extra French flair, serve over a toasted sourdough baguette. Any red meat roast will go well with this recipe.

Makes approximately 7 (1-quart) jars

6 slices bacon, diced

3 pounds halved mushrooms

6 cloves garlic, minced

6 onions, quartered

2 bottles red wine

1 tablespoon dried thyme

4 cups of carrots, cut in large chunks

6 pounds roast beef, cut into bite-sized pieces

salt and pepper, to taste

1. In a large stockpot, lightly brown the bacon. Then, reserve the fat and lightly sauté mushrooms, garlic, and onion.

2. Drain bacon and sautéed veggies on a plate lined with a paper towel.

3. Add red wine, salt, pepper, and thyme to the stockpot and bring it to a boil. Reduce heat and allow it to simmer.

4. Divide your sautéed vegetables, bacon, and the carrots across your wide-mouth quart jars. Top with your roast.

5. Ladle the red wine mixture into the jars, maintaining 1 inch of headspace.

6. Wipe the rims of the jars, then put the lids on.

7. Process in a pressure canner for 90 minutes at 10 PSI, adjusting for altitude.

PART 4

Dehydrating

Introduction

We do not know the name of the first master dehydrator, that innovator who recognized that apples left outside in intense sunshine could be saved and eaten later. Their story is old, perhaps as old as Egyptian civilization, and lost in time. However, it is safe to say that drying food as a preservation method has been around for as long as people have been keeping records.

During the Middle Ages, people in Europe built rooms as an extension of distilleries that were specifically designed to dehydrate food by the heat of an indoor fire. Food was strung across the room, smoked, and dried. The lack of sunlight and dry days made it impossible to dry food outside, and these specialty houses solved the problem for people living in a cool, wet climate.

By the mid-1800s, a process was developed so vegetables could be dried at 105°F and compressed into cakes. These dried vegetables were a welcome source of nutrition for sailors who suffered through long voyages without fresh food. During World War II, soldiers used dehydrated food as lightweight rations while serving on the battlefield. We know these today as "meals ready to eat" (MREs). After the war, housewives did not rush to add this compact, but often tasteless, food into their daily cooking routines, and dehydrated food fell out of favor.

We probably have the backpacking community to thank for the modern resurgence of dehydrated food. Their demand for simple, lightweight, and nutritious meals has created a need for prepackaged fruit, vegetables, side dishes, and full-course meals, along with a renewed interest in dehydrating machines and other means of drying foods. These new convenience foods can be found at any grocery and outdoor store and are known for their easy preparation and quick cooking time. The taste has improved so much that you would consider it a fine dinner. Modern preppers have taken this challenge a step further by learning to produce, store, and rotate a year's worth of food in their own prepared pantry.

This book teaches you the basics of dehydrating fruit, vegetables, and protein; gives detailed information about drying 50 types of fruits and vegetables; and shares some time-tested and family-loved recipes for everyday use. Everything you need to learn to stock your own healthy, shelf-stable pantry is included.

As a prepper who is also a gardener, I wish to take my pantry preparations beyond beans, rice, wheat, and powdered eggs. Dehydrating my garden bounty fills the gap left by food that can't be canned and a freezer susceptible to power outages. A clean water source and fire are the only things that stand between my family and a hot meal prepared with dehydrated ingredients.

This book is not just for experienced gardeners, conscientious preppers, and expert preservers. It is for anyone who loves fresh food and wants to have a hand in how it is preserved. To accommodate the active lifestyles of today, dehydrating needs to fit easily into your daily routine, take as little time as possible, and require a minimum amount of preparation time. By combining bulk buying with batched preserving sessions, as well as an efficient dehydrator, you can be drying food to use every day.

Anyone can use this book, including:

- **Preppers** who want to create a healthy year's supply of food that is tailor-made for their family's dietary needs.
- **Homesteaders** who have the land to plant additional crops and want to create their own extended pantry supply.
- **Busy families** who want to purchase in bulk and have ingredients for quick, healthy meals at their fingertips.
- **Suburban and urban gardeners** who are trying to grow and preserve their harvest in an efficient way.
- **Parents** who want to replace their children's consumption of sugary and empty-calorie snacks with healthy alternatives.

My dream is that after you learn how to dehydrate, you will see the possibilities for quick, healthy meals and begin to use these techniques every day. May you never waste another orange peel, wilted celery stick, or bag of spinach again!

CHAPTER 1

Why Dehydrate?

Years ago, when I was just beginning to get serious about putting together a food storage plan, my husband and I decided to purchase a side of beef from a local farmer. Our extra chest freezer was in a detached garage about 20 feet from the house, and we loaded it up with all the wonderful cuts we had asked the processor to wrap for us. That chest freezer was full of frozen meat, vegetables, and fruit with enough to last for months and months of homemade meals. It was fantastic—and stupid.

One day I went out to get a roast and found that the kids had rummaged through the freezer several days earlier and the lid had not closed properly. Yep—all the food inside had thawed, and all our hard work and money went down the drain, gone, ruined.

I learned a valuable food storage lesson that day. The rule of three in food preservation is to make sure that you do not put all your eggs in one basket; that is to say, you need to have your food stored in at least three separate ways. Of course, you'll still want to have food in the freezer, but learning to process food in canning jars using a water bath and pressure canner is important too. Dehydrating fills the gap and allows you to have another avenue of properly stored food that has a short- or long-term shelf life.

Benefits of Dehydrating

One of the reasons I like dehydrating so much is because it is easy, and there is only a small learning curve to get started. Basically, if you can chop food, blanch vegetables, and know what specific food should look like when it is completely dry, you can be successful in adding dehydrated food to your pantry.

Freezer space can be in short supply when you are trying to store a year's reserve of food. Why use that precious space when you can dehydrate the food and maintain the same quality? Dehydrating saves freezer space for more important things in your food storage plan.

Compared to canned food, dehydrated food has a long shelf life. This food, when stored with the oxygen removed, will be edible for at least five years. While home pressure–canned food may lose its color and texture after one or two years, dehydrated food retains its quality. Commercially purchased dehydrated food has an even longer shelf life, sometimes up to 20 years.

Also unlike canning, dehydrating has minimal processing watch time. I can do other things while my food is dehydrating, while I'm pretty much tied to the stove while I'm canning. The chopping time remains the same, but there is no additional time required for watching the pot boil. Once you have the food cut and placed on the dehydrator trays, you can walk away and return hours later to check on the process.

Dehydrated food is portable and weighs less than any other kind of stored food. During processing, 70 to 95 percent of the water is removed from the food. It is the best choice for packing in emergency kits and taking on hiking or backpacking trips.

Additionally, dehydrated food tastes great, and the drying process actually intensifies the flavor of the food you produce. Food reconstitutes beautifully with water, juice, or broth, and it will often look and taste like it is freshly cooked. You can easily make your own instant meal packages with dehydrated food. Combine the ingredients into two- to four-person meal portions and store it in Mylar bags with oxygen absorbers. It's easy to reach into the pantry shelves and have a quick meal ready in minutes.

Bulk purchases of food items are less expensive, so when you buy in bulk and dehydrate your own food, you'll save money in the grocery budget over the long term. The cost of food in the United States increased 1.9 percent in 2019 and is projected to reach 2 to 3 percent by the year 2021.[1] Bulk purchases and dehydrating give you an edge against food inflation. Have a bag of spinach or lettuce that will not be used before it expires? Just pop it onto a dehydrator tray and preserve it for later. You'll find dozens of ways to preserve food that would otherwise go to waste, saving even more money.

The Prepared Pantry

To get a prepared pantry, you must purposefully plan your pantry to create an extended supply of food. For some, that will be a three-month food supply; others will want a supply to last a year. This extended stash of food, purchased at the best price or grown yourself, will stave off hardship during an economic downturn just as much as your savings account will. It's best to preserve these items when they are at peak season and when they are at the best price. It's like setting the lowest price on your food to ward off inflation. I've found that if I can save even 20 cents per pound on an item that we eat regularly, it is worth it. What are 20 cents of savings for something you use every day, like yogurt? For a family of four that uses a cup of yogurt every weekday, it adds up to $208 a year. That's $208 that could pay off a debt or purchase other food items.

Begin to fill out your stocked pantry by storing things that you use all the time. For some families that might be pancake mix, and for others it could be applesauce. My family always has spicy mustard, a variety of sauces, and salad dressings in our food supply.

In order for this to be cost-effective, you should only dehydrate and store what you regularly eat. It isn't a good purchase if it sits on your shelf and goes bad. That can of jellied cranberries that's been sitting in your pantry for the last year is reaching its useful shelf life and will be wasted money. What could you do with it? You could add to its shelf life by adding applesauce and spices to make fruit leather.

---

1 https://www.ers.usda.gov/data-products/food-price-outlook.

For the most prepared pantry, store a combination of frozen food and shelf-stable foods. Use this book and take the time to learn the basics of dehydrating, along with how to freeze fruits and vegetables. Master the art of water bath and pressure canning (see Part 3).

Ultimately, making a daily trip to the grocery to get supplies defeats the purpose of a fully stocked pantry, which is to have healthy food at all times and to save money. See the chart below for pantry items that will get you started on your ultimate prepared pantry.

PANTRY ESSENTIALS

Staples	Baking Ingredients	Spices/ Seasoning	Oils and Fats	Protein
Cornmeal Noodles Powdered eggs Powdered milk Salt Stock (chicken, beef, vegetable, bouillon cubes) Sugar Tomato paste, sauce, or powder Wheat or spelt, in grain form White flour White rice Yeast	Baking chocolate, unsweetened Baking powder Baking soda Condensed milk Cornstarch Cream of tartar Evaporated milk Honey Maple extract Molasses Nuts Powdered sugar Vanilla extract	Allspice Apple cider vinegar Balsamic vinegar Cayenne pepper Cinnamon Dill Garlic (fresh and dried) Lemon juice Lemon zest or dried lemon peel Mustard (prepared or seeds) Nutmeg Onion (powder and diced) Oregano Paprika Pepper Rosemary Soy sauce Thyme Worcestershire sauce	Butter Olive oil Shortening Vegetable oil	Beans, dried or canned Beef, frozen or canned Chicken, frozen or canned Jerky Tuna, canned

In addition to the basic staples, you should stock a variety of canned, dehydrated, and frozen fruits and vegetables that you can use to make quick meals and that your family will eat.

Do you have a variety of spices? Our spice cabinet is huge, and I think it's the secret to our pantry. If you have a variety of herbs and spices to use in different combinations, you can create a host of individualized meals. Ground beef can be served several times a week when you have the seasonings to mix up the menu and make unique meals. We purchase our spices in bulk once or twice a year from The San Francisco Herb Company (https://sfherb.com). They have spice blends and individual herbs and spices that I cannot grow at home.

Shopping Tips

Don't overlook buying canned goods from the store. Most grocery stores have a twice-yearly canned goods sale that allows you to stock up on items you may not be able to purchase or grow yourself.

Purchase meat when it's on sale and wrap it into family portion sizes, or invest in a FoodSaver machine to remove excess oxygen.

One Year of Food Storage for a Family of Four

My pantry is stocked and rotated on the "store what you eat" philosophy, so we preserve and store the food that we like the most. This also helps with meal preparation, and we can reach into the pantry and pull out the ingredients for a home-cooked meal at any time. Dehydrating is not our only preservation method, but it is the one that we lean on the most for food that has a long shelf-stable life. We have well-balanced and nutritious meals available at any time. You can use our basic formula to put together a food storage plan for your family for up to a year.

Start by tracking what you eat for two weeks. Not just the meals, but the actual ingredients used to make each one. Most families have a set of about 14 basic recipes that they rotate through on a regular basis. Keeping a two-week meal rotation will help to cut out food fatigue (are we having *that* again?) and make rotating your food easier.

Here's an example. Take your favorite spaghetti meal, break it down by ingredients, and put the recipe in a spreadsheet or write on an index card. Note each of the ingredients.

- 1 (16-ounce) box spaghetti
- 1 (15-ounce) can tomato sauce (or 15 ounces homemade sauce)
- 1 pound ground meat or premade frozen meatballs
- 1 tablespoon Italian seasoning
- 1 teaspoon garlic
- ½ cup cheese, shredded
- 1 (8-ounce) box biscuit mix
- 16 ounces fresh fruit
- 16 ounces fresh vegetables

Now, buy enough of each of those shelf-stable items to stock your pantry for a year of that meal (calculating that you will eat the meal twice a month):

- 24 (16-ounce) boxes spaghetti
- 24 (15-ounce) cans tomato sauce (or dehydrated tomato powder equivalent)
- 24 pounds frozen or canned ground beef (or 2 #10 cans freeze-dried beef)
- 24 tablespoons Italian seasoning
- 24 teaspoons garlic

- 12 cups cheese, shredded
- 24 (8-ounce) boxes biscuit mix

- 24 servings dehydrated fruits x the number of people in your family
- 24 servings dehydrated vegetables x the number of people in your family

Does stocking one meal at a time seem daunting? After you have identified the 14 meals your family eats, begin by slowly purchasing individual items during each weekly grocery shopping trip. Start with one month's worth of meals (two times each recipe), two months, or three months, depending on what will fit into your grocery budget.

FOOD STORAGE GUIDELINES FOR 1 ADULT FOR 1 YEAR

Commodity	Amount
Grains (cereal, corn, oats, pasta, rice, wheat)	400 pounds
Dairy products (cheese, powdered milk)	30 pounds
Legumes (dried beans, lentils, nuts, peas)	60 pounds
Sweeteners (brown sugar, honey, molasses, sugar, syrup)	60 pounds
Leavening agents (applesauce, baking powder, baking soda, powdered eggs, yeast)	6 pounds
Salt (bouillon cubes, sea salt, soy sauce, table salt)	6 pounds
Fats (butter, shortening, vegetable oil)	30 pounds
Fruit (before processing)	200 pounds
Vegetables (before processing)	200 pounds
Meat (beef, chicken, fish, pork, turkey, etc.)	100 pounds

Do this for each of the meals that you have identified over that two-week period. Every breakfast, lunch, dinner, and snack should be accounted for. This method allows you to track what you already eat, helps you to break it down by ingredients, and allows you to plan out the specific number of months you want your pantry to serve. It also helps to know how many pounds of fresh fruit and vegetables will need to be dehydrated each year in order to supply the meals you eat. It is highly customizable, so you can modify it specifically for your exact needs.

You may find that breakfast and lunch do not need to be rotated as frequently as dinners. Most of us are fine with eating yogurt, cereal, eggs, or toast and jam several times a week. Start with five to seven of these recipes, but keep dinners on a longer rotation schedule.

You can get basic recommendations for the amounts of protein, carbs, fruit, vegetables, grains, and calories to store by visiting the food storage calculator at ProvidentLiving.com, which has been adapted into a reference chart above.[2] Don't let the chart be that last word on what to

---

2 Provident Living, "Food Storage Calculator," accessed November 13, 2017, http://providentliving.com/preparedness/food-storage/foodcalc.

store, however; you know what your family likes to eat, and you may find that your family eats more fruits and vegetables than is suggested. Note: One serving of fresh fruits or vegetables is about 4 ounces. However, each fresh fruit or vegetable dehydrates differently. Reference Chapter 9 to see how fresh fruits and vegetables convert to their dehydrated forms to get a more accurate idea of serving sizes.

CHAPTER 2

Dehydrating Methods

Harness the Sun

Drying food by sunlight has been practiced for hundreds of years and works best for those living in a hot, dry climate. It is not recommended for those living in colder, damp, northern climates. Even those living in the South have too much humidity for success. The optimal temperature is between 90°F and 100°F, with less than 60 percent humidity.

If those conditions fit your climate, create a series of drying racks from old picture frames by covering them with window screening or cotton sheeting. Tack the screens to the bottom of the frames with staples. Think about the food safety of the materials you are using and plan accordingly. The screens should be safe for contact with food, so avoid hardware cloth or other materials that are coated with galvanized metal and can be found at the home improvement store. Choose, instead, stainless steel, Teflon-coated fiberglass, or plastic. These materials will clean nicely and not oxidize when they are exposed to the sun.

Place the food you are drying on the screens and set the prepared frames in full sunlight for several days until the food is dry. Airflow is important for success. The trays can be stacked with wooden blocks between them to aid the process. Cover the food with cheesecloth to keep pests away during the drying time. Bring the racks in at night before the dew falls, or if there is excessive wind or it looks like it might rain. You don't want all your hard work to be undone.

For those that are living off-grid, solar drying may be your only option. Several plans can be found online for creating an enclosed solar box dehydrator. The enclosed-box drying method is less susceptible to humidity than regular solar methods and, compared with sun drying on racks, the temperature is higher and drying time is shorter. These appear to be relatively easy to make using salvaged materials around your home. Search "solar dehydrator box" or "solar dehydrator plans" in your favorite search engine for ideas.

In the Oven

Dehydrating in the oven is perhaps the most inefficient way to preserve your food because you need to keep your oven door open during the process. Oven drying takes two or three times longer than drying in a dehydrator and has a higher energy cost. While it does produce a safe and tasty product, the quality is different from food prepared in an electric dehydrator. Oven-dried food is more brittle and usually darker and less flavorful than food dried in a dehydrator.

Don't let this deter you; an oven will work in a pinch if it is all you have. It requires little or no investment in equipment.

Test your oven temperature with a thermometer before you use it to dry food. Set the oven to the lowest temperature setting and prop open the door for one hour. The oven should maintain a temperature of between 130° to 150°F. If the oven does not maintain the temperature range, your finished product will begin to cook instead of dry. Conversely, if the temperature is too cool, you run the risk of food spoilage.

Here are some tips for oven drying:

- Use your oven to dry small amounts of food at a time. If you overload the oven, the drying time will be extended.
- Position the oven rack at its lowest setting.
- Prepare the food as recommended (see meat recommendations in Chapter 7, and fruit and vegetable recommendations in Chapter 9) and place it on a cookie sheet, or place cotton sheeting directly on the wire rack.
- Prop the door open with a wooden spoon or block of wood; you'll need airflow for this to be successful.
- Set a timer for one hour, check for dryness, and turn the food.
- Repeat every hour until the food is dry.

Using a Dehydrator

Years ago I purchased an old Ronco dehydrator at a garage sale for just a few bucks. It has 10 trays, no motor, and uses radiant bottom heat to dry the food. I thought I was in heaven. This machine is considered a dinosaur by today's fancy dehydrator standards, but I still have it and use it every year when I'm drying herbs. I love how quiet it is.

My next garage sale treasure was a Harvest Maid Dehydrator with a box of four extra trays. I have used that machine for years, creating all the things you read about in this book. It has an electric motor and blower at the base of the unit. Seriously, I've used these second-hand machines for at least 15 years. They are workhorses and prove that you don't need a fancy machine to have a prepared pantry.

Today's electric dehydrators make your pantry preservation even easier, and they run more efficiently than those old machines. In addition, many new machines have a timer to allow you to start and stop drying when it suits your schedule, and their 1,000-watt heaters get the job done in record time. There are three basic dehydrator designs on the market today.

Types of Dehydrators

Dehydrators need to circulate air in order to do their job. This is accomplished by pushing air vertically through the machine, either from the bottom or the top, or by circulating air from the side horizontally.

Older model vertical airflow dehydrators have a heating element and fan located at the base of the unit, and the trays are stacked on top. This was the golden standard for years, and with a moving motor, it's a step up from my old Ronco machine. The one drawback to these old airflow machines is that the food does not dry evenly on the trays. The trays always need to be rotated from the top of the stack to the bottom to ensure each tray gets equal airflow. That can be a problem if you were hoping to load the machine and walk away until the food is dry.

In modern dehydrators, vertical airflow is accomplished by having a powerful motor at the top of the stack. This allows for a cleaner heating element and forces heated, pressurized air downward through the outer ring of the food trays. These machines are very efficient. At the same time, the circulating air moves horizontally across each tray and out through the bottom, and the air converges at the center for fast, even drying. I've found that with my Nesco Gardenmaster machine, there's no need to rotate trays—all the food dehydrates at the same time and it can handle up to 20 trays. You can efficiently dry a lot of food at one time.

Excalibur is the gold standard of horizontal airflow dehydrator units; it is also the most expensive. The heating element and fan are located in the back of the machine and provide horizontal airflow, which is said to reduce flavor mixing when you are dehydrating several different foods at one time. All trays receive equal heat distribution, and because cool air is drawn in, heated, and distributed evenly over each tray, the food dries faster and retains more nutrients, without tray rotation. If you are going to dry a lot of jerky, soup, or fruit leather, a dehydrator with horizontal airflow may be the best choice.

I now own five different dehydrators, including a Nesco Gardenmaster and an Excalibur 9-tray model. Each one, old and new, is regularly used for different drying purposes. You don't need a dehydrator to dry food, but it sure does make it easier and more efficient.

When you are drying large batches, it's helpful to have more than one dehydrator. The machine with bottom heat dries my herbs; it is the least precise of the machines and the one that needs tray rotation. It works well for herbs because they are not prone to spoiling, like some fruit or vegetables that need constant airflow. The Nesco Gardenmaster top-heat machine makes terrific work of fruit and vegetables, and I've found that there is very little tray rotation that needs to take place. It has digital time and heat instruments so I can schedule time in half-hour stages and adjust the temperature in 5°F increments. The Excalibur machine is square and is perhaps a more efficient use of tray space. With horizontal heating from the back, it makes excellent jerky and leathers.

The one you choose is a personal preference. All the machines on the market today will dry food. Start with one that fits your budget then expand to a large-capacity machine if you need to.

Dehydrator Basics

As a general rule, food should not be touching as it dries on dehydrator trays. This additional space aids with airflow and will help to dry your product fast and evenly. Also, juicy fruits like strawberries, mango, or watermelon will stick together when drying if they touch on the trays. The exception to this rule is leafy vegetables like cabbage, lettuce, spinach, or cilantro. They can be added to trays up to ½-inch thick, although you will need to reach in every few hours and stir the leaves.

If you have a machine with bottom heat, it is often necessary to aid your machine with air circulation by rotating the trays from top to bottom. Set a timer for halfway through the drying process and move the top tray to the bottom, shuffling each tray as you go. When finished, the original tray on the top will now be on the bottom of the stack. If you have a machine with horizontal airflow, rotate the trays 90 degrees halfway through the process. As you use your machine more often, you'll get to know its ins and outs and how much help it needs with airflow.

There are many variables in food dehydration. Humidity, methods of food handling, and different kinds of produce will change the quality of your dried food each time you make a batch. The only way to become an expert is to keep experimenting until you understand how each of the items you wish to store in your pantry will behave. Fortunately, dehydrating is a forgiving preservation method.

Tips for Dehydrator Drying

Try different methods. Don't be afraid to experiment with different dehydration methods. Vary the way you make cuts and the thickness of the foods you use. Julienne a potato at least one time to see how it turns out.

Set aside a small portion of a product to test pretreatment recommendations. Pretreatments can be a hassle and are not always necessary. Experiment with using a pretreatment dip or blanch and compare that to not using a pretreatment process at all so you can see how the finished product meets your needs and preferences. Keep records so you remember which is preferred.

Spread food evenly, in single layers, on trays. Unless you're drying leafy greens, overlapping items will take longer to dry and might stick together.

Separate foods by their thicknesses on dehydrator trays. Take green onions, for instance. Each stalk has a dark green and a white portion, which dry at different rates. If you keep them all mixed together on a tray, you'll need to pick out the dry green portions after a few hours. If you separate pieces by the thickness at the beginning, you can just remove the finished tray of greens when they are done. It will save you a lot of energy if you plan ahead.

Do not mix fresh items in with those in the process of dehydrating. Don't add fresh food to a partially dried batch; it will slow the drying time on all the trays.

Consolidate partially dried foods onto fewer trays. Halfway through the process, combine partially dried foods onto fewer trays. Keep in mind that modern machines are most efficient if they operate with at least four trays. If you don't have four trays of food to dry, be sure to add empty trays to the stack to help with airflow.

Do not start and stop the dehydration process. Dehydrating works by continually moving heated air over your food, which helps prevent spoiling and off flavors. Each item needs to dry continually for the recommended time. You don't want the heat to stop on a partially dried batch, so make sure timers are set to continue the process overnight while you sleep.

Microwave Drying

Microwave drying is not recommended for fruit, vegetables, and meat because of the uneven way they cook. All microwaves are designed to retain the moisture content in foods, not as a method of drying them. Also, fruits have high sugar content and will have a tendency to burn if they are overcooked in the microwave.

If you are determined to use your microwave for dehydrating, follow these rules:

1. Cut food no more than ¼ inch thick.

2. Lay the product directly on the turnstile.

3. Dry in small batches.

4. Do not overlap food.

5. Use the defrost setting (reduced power) to minimize the hardening effect that can happen when food is dried too quickly.

6. Turn the food every 15 minutes until it has dried to the consistency you are looking for.

Microwave drying is not a process where you can push the button and step away, unlike drying with an electric dehydrator. You must constantly monitor the batch to make sure the food does not get too dry, burn, and catch fire. And it *will* catch fire if you do not watch it continually!

For the best success, skip the fruit, and use the microwave to dehydrate only herbs or leafy greens. These contain a very minimal amount of moisture and are best suited for microwave drying. Place washed and towel-dried herbs on a paper towel or napkin and dry in 30-second increments until they reach the consistency you are looking for. See Chapter 8 about drying herbs for more information.

CHAPTER 3

Basic Dehydrating Instructions

Learning to dehydrate gives you a tremendous variety of food that can be stored in your prepared pantry. Fortunately, there is room for creativity in the process. There is more than one way to prepare food for processing, but each fruit and vegetable is treated differently. This chapter will discuss small- and large-batch processing, how to pretreat food using blanching and oxidizing techniques, and how to store the food once you have it dried.

Keep these tips, applicable to all methods of dehydrating, in mind as you begin:

- **Clean your produce:** Thoroughly clean each piece of produce. This is especially important if you are not buying or growing organic.
- **Use fresh, ripe produce:** Choose fruit and vegetables at their peak freshness. Items that are underripe will not have a good flavor. Overripe fruit can still be used when making fruit leather.
- **Cut pieces evenly:** Use a mandoline or salad chopper to achieve evenly cut pieces; this helps with faster drying times.
- **Group similarly sized pieces on the same tray:** The size of the piece to be dehydrated is important; for even drying, keep all like sizes and thicknesses together on the trays.

Supplies

Basic Supplies

One of the best things about dehydrating food is how simple it is. Only a few basic supplies are needed for success, and most of them are already in your kitchen.

- Cutting board
- Drying racks
- Heat source (dehydrator, the sun, an oven)
- Jars, for storage
- Plastic fruit leather trays or plastic wrap
- Pot, for blanching
- Sharp knife
- Slotted spoon
- Strainer to wash produce

Additional Supplies

Once you become proficient at dehydrating, you'll find ways to incorporate dry food into all of your food preparations. After a while, I looked for time-saving items to help the process along and have added several other supplies to my food drying "kit."

Here are some other tools that make quick work of cutting, chopping, and pureeing. You might want to purchase them as budget allows:

- 100cc oxygen absorbers
- apple peeler/corer—once you use one, you'll never process an apple by hand again!
- blender or food processor
- canning funnels—handy for transferring dried items into jars
- food-grade buckets for long-term storage of all supplies
- mandoline slicer, to quickly give you uniform and specialty cuts for soft and hard vegetables
- Paraflexx trays
- salad shooter, for soft vegetables like zucchini and tomatoes
- vacuum sealer and bags
- vegetable brush, to scrub root vegetables clean
- vegetable peelers, to save your fingers from sharp knives

None of these extended supplies are necessary, but they are handy to have if you are doing large batches of food processing and if you want to extend the shelf life. Having them around can make a long job go quickly and allow you to process more food. Start with the least expensive items and purchase others as you increase your skills.

Dehydrating in Small Batches

Today's dehydrators are so economical to use that you can afford to have one running on the counter at all times. They are terrific for preserving the last of the spinach bag or apples that will not get eaten before they start to turn. Anything can be dehydrated in small batches. Recently, I purchased several bundles of cilantro for homemade salsa and found that there were two large handfuls left over. Rather than making another batch of salsa or putting the cilantro in the compost pile, I cleaned the leaves, trimmed the stems, and processed two trays. This was ground into powder and will later be used to flavor sauces and dip. Use these tips to dehydrate small batches of food.

- Most dehydrators need proper airflow to do their job and work best with at least four trays. If you don't have four trays of food, alternate full and blank trays to make the required number.
- Cut the food into uniform sizes to aid with uniform drying times.
- It's alright to have trays with different food items, but steer clear of mixing onion or garlic with other types of food; their flavors will taint the food on the other trays.

Dehydrating in Large Batches

When I can't grow enough of my own, I like to purchase large quantities of in-season fruit and vegetables from the local farmers produce stand. This lets me quickly stock my pantry. Large-batch dehydrating can be an all-day task and requires some stamina to get the job done.

Produce growers have standardized the way they package their product, so if you want to purchase fruit or veggies in bulk from the local market, they will sell it to you (often at a discount) in 40-pound boxes. That is a lot of produce to wash, cut, treat for oxidizing, and place on dehydrating trays, so it's good to do so efficiently. Here are some tips for processing larger batches of dehydrated food.

- Processing is easier if you break it into stations. Set up a cleaning station, cutting station, and blanching or oxidizing station to make the best use of your space.
- Consider purchasing tools to speed up the processing. Using a mandoline slicer or food processor will make the cutting job go faster and give you uniform pieces.
- Plan ahead and know which cuts you will be making. A 40-pound box of apples can be made into chips, diced for baking, or turned into applesauce and dried.
- Make sure you have enough dehydrators to hold the produce. Borrow from friends if necessary.
- Set up a conditioning and packaging area, so dried food can get stored as soon as possible.
- Get help from friends and family. Teach the next generation how fun it is as they learn to dry their own food.

Blanching Vegetables for Dehydrating

Each vegetable has its own rule to follow before being placed in the freezer or dehydrator, and you should know the rules before you decide if you want to break them. Some vegetables need to be blanched, others might need to be blanched, and some should be left alone.

When you blanch vegetables, you boil or steam them for a few minutes, then quickly cool them in ice water. Each vegetable has a different time requirement for blanching, usually from 2 to 5 minutes. This process stops the enzyme activity that causes plants to lose nutrients and change texture once they are frozen.

Blanched vegetables can be placed directly onto dehydrator trays and processed for the proper time.

No-blanch vegetables. Several vegetable crops freeze or dry well and do not require blanching at all. These are my favorites, because they are so easy to get into the pantry! They can be washed and halved, quartered, or chopped, then towel dried and placed directly in the dehydrator for processing. Do not wash mushrooms; it will cause them to discolor. Instead, wipe the mushrooms clean with a towel. For herbs and leafy greens (such as parsley, cilantro, and spinach), cut leaves with stems several inches long. Tie in bunches and swish in cold water to wash, then towel dry.

BLANCHING FRUIT AND VEGETABLES

Never	Maybe	Always
Apples	Asparagus (½-inch pieces or smaller)	Asparagus (larger than ½-inch pieces; whole)
Apricots	Carrots (diced)	Beets
Bananas	Cauliflower	Broccoli
Berries	Celery	Chickpeas
Cabbage	Cherries	Carrots (sliced; whole)
Citrus	Eggplant	Corn
Coconuts	Figs	Grapes
Cucumbers	Ginger	Green beans (whole)
Garlic	Green beans (French sliced; 1-inch pieces)	Green peas (in pod)
Herbs	Green peas (no pod)	Parsnips (larger pieces)
Horseradish	Onions	Plums
Kiwis	Peaches	Peanuts
Leafy greens	Nectarines	Potatoes
Leeks	Parsnips (diced)	Rhubarb
Mangoes	Pears	Tomatoes, fresh
Melons		Yams
Mushrooms		Winter squash
Papayas		
Peppers		
Pineapples		
Summer squash		
Tomatoes, frozen		

Maybe-blanch vegetables. Some crops *may* require blanching. These usually call for minimal blanching time in boiling water, and you may find that you'll have great success skipping it all together. The texture of these foods when they are rehydrated remains good for soups, stews, and casseroles. These have a storage life up to one year, so it is best only to prepare what you will use in that time frame and continually rotate your supplies.

The key to being able to skip the blanching on these vegetables is the way you cut them before processing. If the pieces are small enough, that you can usually skip the step. These vegetables should be thoroughly cleaned, chopped, and towel dried to get out any excess moisture.

The process for dehydrating is simple. Place the vegetables in a single layer on dehydrator sheets and process according to individual temperatures and times. After drying, store in canning jars in a cool dark place.

Always-blanch vegetables. Some vegetables will always require blanching before you store them in your freezer or process them in the dehydrator. You should only use vegetables that are in excellent condition.

Set Up a Blanching Station

If you find blanching vegetables as distasteful as I do, consider creating a blanching station to make the process go faster. Begin by making an assembly line from your stovetop to your sink.

You'll need a stockpot, several clean towels, cold water, a bag of ice, and a sieve for removing the vegetables from the pot.

1. Bring a stockpot filled with water to a rolling boil.
2. Fill your kitchen sink or a tub insert with cold water and ice.
3. Place a small batch of vegetables in the boiling water for the recommended time and promptly remove it to the cold water bath using the sieve.
4. Once the blanched vegetables are cooled, remove from the water and place on a kitchen towel to pat dry.
5. Process for drying on dehydrator trays.

You will find that the water in the stockpot will need to be replenished a few times during the process and that you will need to add ice to keep the cool water cold.

Fruit Pretreatments to Prevent Oxidization

Certain fruits turn brown when they are exposed to the air for too long. You can probably name a few, including apples, bananas, pears, and peaches. Pretreating the fruit before drying will keep it from turning color, and may help retain nutrients and texture. This process is not necessary, and if you decide to skip it, you will still have a tasty finished product. Keep in mind that if you skip pretreatments, the fruit may not look the way your family expects it to look, and they may be less inclined to eat it. Two types of pretreatments may be used on fruit: dipping in a solution and steam blanching.

Fruit Dipping

Dehydrating is not an exact science, and there is room for your own interpretation when dehydrating fruit. Which should you choose, honey dip, lemon juice, or ascorbic acid? I would recommend trying fruit using each type of dip and then make a batch with none at all. You may find that the whole process is not important for your family.

Ascorbic acid or citric acid (vitamin C) dip. Vitamin C and ascorbic acid can be found in the pharmacy or in the canning aisle of your local grocery store. This method does not leave an aftertaste on the fruit.

To make the solution: Mix 2 tablespoons of powder with 1 quart water. Soak the fruit in small batches for 2 to 3 minutes. Remove with a slotted spoon and let dry before placing on dehydrator trays.

Fruit juice dip. Pineapple, lemon, and lime have naturally occurring citric acid, and the juice makes a fine pretreatment, but it is less effective than using ascorbic acid. Dipping in juice may add a slight flavor to the fruit.

To make the solution: Stir 1 cup juice into 1 quart warm water and soak fruit in small batches for 10 minutes. Remove with a slotted spoon and let dry before placing on dehydrator trays.

Honey dip. A honey dip will make the fruit sweeter and add extra calories. This will give you the consistency of store-bought dehydrated fruit, which your children may prefer.

To make the solution: Dissolve 1 cup sugar in 3 cups hot water. Let it cool until it is barely warm and stir in 1 cup honey. Dip fruit in small batches, remove with a slotted spoon, and drain thoroughly before placing on dehydrator sheets. This fruit will stick to your trays, so consider using parchment paper or non-stick dehydrator tray covers.

Blanching

Steam blanching. Most fruits are too delicate to be boiled and still retain their shape. Instead, to prevent oxidation, steam the cut fruit pieces in batches for 1 minute, then remove to an ice water dip and drain thoroughly before placing on trays.

Boil blanching. Some fruits need to be fully blanched first to prepare the outside skin for drying, which improves the texture and drying time of the finished product. These include apricots, blueberries, cranberries, gooseberries, currants, grapes (raisins), and plums (prunes). These fruits simply have to be placed in a colander, dipped in boiling water for 30 seconds, then cooled in ice water and drained.

There is one important thing to remember with these pretreatment dips: Your fruit must be as dry as possible before beginning the dehydrating process. If you add wet fruit to the trays, you will significantly increase the drying time of each batch.

Food Touching on Trays

There is a significant difference between drying herbs, vegetables, and fruit. You may wonder if fresh items can touch on the tray as they are drying. Follow these general rules:

Herbs and leafy greens. Herbs and leafy greens can be placed in piles on the drying trays. Their low water content will keep them from sticking together, and they will dry fast. Pick out the dried leaves every hour, mix up the remaining leaves, and continue processing until all are finished.

Vegetables. Most vegetables can be placed close together on drying trays and can touch each other. If you are using the proper drying temperature of 125° to 135°F, they will reduce in size fairly quickly and still have enough room for airflow. They will not stick together when drying. Again, pick out dried pieces every few hours and allow the rest to continue drying.

Fruits. Due to the high sugar content of most fruits, fruits should be placed on drying trays in a single layer without any pieces touching. Any pieces that touch will dry together in one piece and perhaps even stick to the tray while they dry. Use tray covers or parchment paper to reduce the amount of sticking, and turn pieces every few hours as needed.

Conditioning the Finished Product

Properly dried fruit will have a moisture content of 20 percent. Since those doing home food production do not have a way to measure the moisture content, we use a conditioning process to equalize the moisture in the finished product. Conditioning ensures that all the pieces of fruit have dried evenly, and it helps to prevent mold and bacteria from growing during storage. This should be done before packaging for long-term storage.

1. Take the cooled, dried fruit and pack it loosely in glass canning jars. Make sure there is enough room for movement when the jar is shaken.

2. Cap the jar tightly and shake it daily for seven days.

3. Check for moisture condensation. Return any pieces showing moisture to the dehydrator to continue drying.

4. Once the process is complete, proceed with regular packaging. Instructions can be found in Chapter 5.

If you find that pieces have begun to grow mold, they must be thrown away; there is no way to save them.

General Rehydrating Techniques

Dehydrated food is often hard, brittle, and looks somewhat unappealing. Once you introduce water back into it, you'll be surprised how quickly and thoroughly the food returns to its original shape. Not all pieces of dehydrated food can be rehydrated using these methods. Most fruits make great snacks and are eaten dried. Some vegetables are eaten as chips or used in powdered spice mixes instead of rehydrated.

Soak

Soaking is the easiest, and also the slowest, way to rehydrate food. Place a measured amount of dried food in a bowl and soak it in an equal amount of water until it reaches the desired plumpness, usually 10 to 30 minutes. Pour off any water that is not incorporated back into the food.

Fruit should be soaked in cool water. Vegetables can be soaked in cool, warm, or even boiling water. For a taste variation, consider soaking in juice or broth and then, instead of pouring off the additional liquid, add it directly to the recipe.

Be sure to follow the individual rehydrating requirements for each item found in Chapter 9.

As a general rule, if you will be soaking food for up to an hour, you can do it on the kitchen counter. If you are getting things ready early in the day and plan to use the food during dinner, place the bowl in the refrigerator while it is soaking. It will only absorb as much liquid as it needs and you can pour off any remaining. Refrigeration will prevent spoilage and contamination. Food should never be on the counter for longer than two hours without being refrigerated.

Spray

Sometimes delicate fruit only needs to be sprayed with water in order to start plumping back to its original shape. Place the food in a shallow bowl or on a plate and spray until water droplets form on the food. Allow the water to soak in, and keep spraying until the fruit returns to its original shape. Keep a spray bottle handy in the kitchen and give this a try.

Simmer or Cook

I like to add dehydrated vegetables to my morning scrambled eggs. Rather than taking the time to rehydrate everything before using it, I place it all in a skillet with just enough water to cover and simmer for 5 minutes. Once the water has evaporated, they are plumped up, and I'm ready to add the eggs. Some food does not need to rehydrate before being added to a recipe. When making soup, you can add dried corn, beans, broccoli, cauliflower, or peas directly to the pot and then add additional broth or water to keep your soup at the desired thickness.

Record Keeping

When you are learning to dehydrate different kinds of food for the first time, or when you haven't done it in a while, it is helpful to be able to look back on the process you used before. Record keeping is the key. It will improve your dehydrating techniques and save you a lot of trial and error the next time you want to dry an item. This can be accomplished with a card file or in a spreadsheet on your computer. Here are some things that you might want to track:

- Date dried
- Quantity dried (e.g., 12 apples)
- Weight of produce before drying (e.g., 6 pounds)
- Weight of produce after drying (e.g., 2 pounds)
- Humidity percent on day of drying
- Drying temperature
- Drying time
- Packaging used
- Special conditioning

- Use-by date
- Preparation method, including:
  » Cut used (julienne, fry cut, crinkle cut, waffle cut, diced, etc.)
  » Cut thickness
  » Quantity and type of spices used
  » Blanching or oxidizing process used
- Additional notes: how it turned out, what you would change next time

CHAPTER 4

Food Purchasing & Safety Information

The process of dehydrating is rather simple, and you might be tempted to jump right in and get started without taking safety considerations into account. After all, how difficult can it be to dehydrate an apple? That's the beauty of dehydrating your own food. It's not difficult at all, so it's easy to make that extra effort to make sure your food is safe to eat. If you choose the best produce, clean it properly, make sure it is conditioned for storage, and steer clear of a few trouble items, you will have a fully stocked pantry before you know it.

Select the Best Produce

Fresh fruit and vegetables will produce the best final results. If you can purchase from a farmers market or grow your own fruits and vegetables, even better.

Fruit. Begin by choosing firm fruit that is at the peak of ripeness and flavor. Handle it gently to reduce the possibility of bruising, and process it as soon as possible after you bring it home. If you find some of the fruit has become bruised or is overripe by the time you get to it, process it as fruit leather.

Vegetables. Vegetables will be ready for dehydrating when they are fresh, tender, and mature. Process them as soon as possible after harvest. Immature vegetables will have poor color and flavor and after they are rehydrated, they will not have the fresh taste you are seeking. Avoid overly mature vegetables, which can get fibrous. As with fruit, overripe vegetables can be turned into leather, which can be used in soup as a flavoring and thickening agent.

Clean Fruit and Vegetables

Every mother would strive to feed her family only the freshest, organic produce available because no one wants to introduce chemicals and pesticides into their children's daily meals. Unfortunately, purchasing organic produce is not always easy on your budget. You may also find that you have access to large quantities of fresh produce, but it is not organic. Fortunately, there is an option for cleaning fruit and vegetables that do get sprayed with chemicals. You can clean off more than 95 percent of pesticides if you are diligent in this process.

See Best Practices for Cleaning Fruits and Vegetables on page 331 for detailed information on how to clean fruit and vegetables. Use this process for cleaning all of your fruit and vegetables before processing them for dehydrating. Not only does it remove pesticides and traces of fertilizer, but it also removes plain old dirt. It may add an extra step, but it's worth it. The best part of all is that you already have these items in your pantry.

Leafy Greens Wash

Leafy greens like lettuce, spinach, and cilantro can be a problem to clean thoroughly, and according to the CDC, they are more likely to be contaminated with E. coli bacteria. This natural wash was found to kill 98 percent of bacteria on produce. It's simple to do, and uses materials straight from your pantry.

Mix 3 cups cool water and 1 cup distilled white vinegar in a bowl or shallow tub. Allow your greens to soak in the bowl for about 2 minutes, and then rinse them well.

What Not to Dehydrate

Dehydrating is so easy that you might be tempted to throw everything that you like to eat into your machine. However, for safety reasons, there are a few items that are not recommended. Others take so long to process that it is better to purchase them from professionals instead of trying it yourself. Overall, it is better to err on the side of caution when you are dealing with these items.

Eggs. You can find plenty of instructions online for dehydrating eggs. However, raw eggs need to be stored at a temperature under 45°F to prevent salmonella poisoning, so in my mind, that means you shouldn't let raw eggs sit on a dehydrator tray for 10 to 12 hours as they are processing.

Some people cook their eggs first, process them for drying, and then powder them. I've heard that there is a consistency issue with these eggs and that you will never get them to rehydrate properly without being grainy. In my opinion, your best bet is to purchase powdered eggs from the professionals. A #10 size container will cost around $35 and will be well worth the investment. Those eggs will provide you with a whole year of eggs for use in baking, plus you'll never have to wonder if you are going to make your family sick.

Foods high in fat. These are not good candidates for dehydrating. High-fat foods don't tend to dry well and are prone to spoilage. Just like eggs, these items are dehydrated or freeze-dried by professionals and are readily available for purchase online. Don't take the risk of doing it yourself. High-fat items to steer clear of include butter, cheese, and avocado.

Meat and fish. Always use extra care when dehydrating any meat products. It's best to store dried meats (even jerky) in the refrigerator or freezer, so why take up the precious storage space? You'll have better success with meat and fish if you store them using the pressure canning method. They will be good for a year, completely shelf stable, and you can pour them right out of the jar for a quick meal.

Jerky is the only exception. Choose a lean cut of raw meat, as free from fat as possible, and dry or brine cure the batch for 6 to 12 hours. The finished product can be stored in vacuum-sealed bags for added shelf life. We'll discuss the details of making your own jerky in Chapter 7.

Milk. It's hard to keep milk inside dehydrator trays, and the whole process tends to be messy. Really, the amount of time it takes to get a small amount of powdered milk is not worth it in the long run. After all, it's mostly water. Purchase whole powdered milk from the professionals; it's a better use of your money and time.

The bottom line is this: Even though food may show up on a do-not-dehydrate list, it doesn't mean that it can't be dehydrated; rather, the time, effort, potential risk, and long-term storage options make it not worth doing. If you're looking to build a long-term pantry, focus on the quick success of dehydrating fruit and vegetables and learn to make jerky. They will build your pantry fast.

Light, Oxygen, Heat, and Humidity

If you live in the South, humidity can be an issue for months on end. The humid time of the year also tends to coincide with harvest time, so there are special considerations for dehydrating food in a humid climate. According to the article "Drying Food" published by the University of Illinois, College of Agriculture, "The higher the temperature and the lower the humidity, the more rapid the rate of dehydration will be. Humid air slows down evaporation. Keep this in mind if you plan to dry food on hot, muggy summer days."[3]

The process of dehydrating helps moisture escape food through evaporation. Without proper ventilation, humid air trapped in a dehydrator soon takes on as much moisture as it can hold, and then drying can no longer take place. For this reason, be sure there is plenty of ventilation around your food dryer. The food will dry faster and use less energy when there is sufficient airflow.

If you live in a humid climate, you will also need to package your dried produce as quickly as possible. If you leave your dried tomatoes on the counter overnight in a humid house, they will need to be reprocessed a second time the next day. Dehydrated food is like a moisture sponge; it loves to absorb liquid and humidity. It can easily absorb moisture from the atmosphere and become less dry and susceptible to mold. We'll talk all about how to avoid this with packaging and storage in Chapter 5.

Light, heat, and oxygen are the three elements most likely to reduce the shelf life of dehydrated foods. Here are a few general rules:

- Displaying canning jars full of processed food on an open shelf looks pretty, but it is a surefire way to undermine all the hard work you've done. Always keep your food in a cool, dark, dry cabinet to ensure the longest shelf life.

---

3 Judy Troftgruben, "Drying Food," University of Illinois at Urbana-Champaign College of Agriculture, April 1984, https://archive.org/details/dryingfoods1227trof/page/n3/mode/2up.

- Storage temperature helps determine the length of storage. With proper packaging, most dried food can be stored for one year at 60°F and six months at 80°F.

- Pack foods in amounts that can be used all at once. Every time you open a package, you introduce moisture and air that can lower the quality of the food.

- Check dried foods regularly during storage to see if they are still dry. Glass containers work well for this; moisture that collects on the sides is easy to see.

- Discard all food that has developed an off smell or shows signs of mold.

- If the dehydrated food shows signs of moisture and the food has not spoiled, you can use it immediately, or reprocess and repackage it.

There is one final thing to be aware of as you are drying food. It's called "case hardening." You may be tempted to turn up the heat on the dehydrator, quickly remove the moisture, and get the job done. After all, it stands to reason that taking moisture out of the food more quickly will use less energy, right? Unfortunately, it doesn't work that way. If drying takes place too fast, the cells on the outside of the food will give up moisture faster than the cells on the inside. The surface will become hard, preventing the escape of moisture from the inside, and it will take even longer for food to dry. And if you turn up the heat too much, you'll cook your food instead of dehydrating it.

Using Frozen Vegetables

If you do not have access to a large garden or farmers market, consider purchasing frozen vegetables for dehydrating. These vegetables can often be purchased in large bags, and I find them to be an economical choice. Be on the lookout for grocery coupons for even bigger savings.

There is no need to blanch frozen vegetables; this was done by the processor before freezing. That's a quick win for your pantry, because all frozen vegetables can be placed right on the food dehydrator trays with no additional preparation. You don't even need to thaw them. Just throw the bag on the countertop a few times to break up any frozen clumps. If you find that there is residual ice in spots, place those clumps in a kitchen or paper towel and give them a good rubbing. The ice crystals will be absorbed by the towel, and the product is ready for dehydrating. Processing times range from 6 to 16 hours. Follow the suggested dehydrating times found in the description for each vegetable in Chapter 9.

These vegetables dehydrate well from a frozen state:

- Broccoli
- Carrots
- Cauliflower
- Corn
- Okra
- Peas
- Vegetable mix (baby lima beans, carrots, corn, green beans, peas)

A word of caution: Look for vegetables that have been frozen in their most natural state. Any bags that have added sauce or oil are not suitable for dehydrating and should not be used. You'll also find that some manufacturers add sugar to their vegetables. Look closely at the ingredients, and decide if this fits your food storage plans.

Using Frozen Fruit

Another great way to save freezer space and have almost-fresh fruit is to purchase large bags of frozen fruit to dehydrate. This is a sound way to store fruit that you cannot grow yourself. You will often find these bags on sale at the local grocery store.

There is no need to pretreat the fruit; the commercial packaging has already subjected the food to the blanching and oxidizing treatment. All you have to do is start with a bag of frozen fruit, spread it evenly onto your dehydrator trays, and set the heat to 125° to 130°F. Dry for 6 to 8 hours. If you can get it set up before bed, they will be completely dry in the morning when you wake up.

Frozen fruit has a tendency to drip inside of the dehydrator as it dries, so if you are dehydrating more than one kind of fruit, it's best to place an extra Paraflexx sheet or plastic fruit leather tray under each type of fruit. That way, strawberry juice will not drip on the pineapple chunks below.

These fruits dehydrate well from a frozen state:

- Blueberries
- Mangoes
- Peaches
- Pineapple
- Strawberries

Buying Large Quantities of Produce

My food storage plan is based on bulk purchases. What that really means is that I look for items on sale and purchase them in quantity. I also wait until the right time to make those purchases.

Take fresh fruits and vegetables, for example. I know that blueberries are in season from June to August. I also know that when blueberries come to the grocery store or farmers market in June, they'll be expensive. Everyone wants fresh blueberries for their recipes, and the seller knows they can charge top dollar—and that we'll most likely pay—because they're fresh blueberries, after all!

By mid-August, the market will have been saturated, and fresh blueberries will not be such a hot off-the-shelf item. That's when the bulk purchaser gets their reward for waiting. The market will be flooded with berries that the farmers are trying to get out of their fields, and guess what—they will lower their prices to entice you to purchase. Now the price is so low that you can buy blueberries in bulk and preserve enough for the rest of the year. If you live near a blueberry farm and are willing to go to a u-pick event, you'll get an even better deal.

Don't overlook the local independent fruit stand businesses for making bulk purchases. They will often sell to you in bulk and give you a discount. Buying by the case or tray is usually cheaper anyway. You can also look at a big box store, like Costco or Sam's Club, or ask the local grocery store if they will sell to you at a discount if you purchase by the box.

There is always power in numbers, and bulk buying groups may be your answer. If you can join with other like-minded people to make your purchases together, you will get an even better deal. Here are some examples:

- Join a CSA and support a local farmer.
- Look for local food co-ops and see what they have to offer. These might be the best places to purchase dry goods like flour, grains, and beans. http://www.coopdirectory.org
- See if there is a Meetup group in your area that purchases in bulk. https://www.meetup.com

Still stumped? Create your own group. You must have like-minded friends! Do a Facebook poll and see which of your friends within a 20-mile radius are interested in saving money on their food storage. Once you have the basic group, brainstorm items that need to be purchased and put the group to work finding deals.

Purchase a Bushel, Bag, Box, or Flat

Not all people have the time, space, or inclination for growing their own large garden and realistically, no one can grow everything that their family wants to eat. For example, bananas are hard to grow in most parts of the world. There is a whole grassroots movement around eating locally, but we will not delve into the benefits of it in this book. In most parts of the world, we are blessed to be able to purchase any fruit or vegetable from a local farmer, grocery, or big box store.

When I lived outside of Portland, Oregon, I would frequent a local produce stand called Justy's Produce and Flowers. I love that place and miss their helpful service and the ability to purchase fresh food in large quantities. So far, I have not found anything that compares here in Central Texas. I believe every town should have a helpful produce guy (or gal) that will find you a box of pickling cucumbers, or Roma tomatoes, at a terrific price. If you understand which produce is in season each month and the standard box size for purchasing in bulk, you, too, can save money and have enough to put into storage.

Packaging standards. Individual crops have specific industry packaging size and weight standards for sale in the wholesale market. This is done so everyone in the industry speaks that same packaging language, and everyone understands what they are buying and selling. Each crop has a different requirement for handling, so different size boxes, cartons, lugs, crates, flats, bags, sacks, and bulk bins are used as industry standards. Two common measurements are bushels and pecks. A bushel holds 8 gallons (32 quarts) of produce, which is equal to 4 pecks and 2,150 cubic inches. Here are some of the other common packaging standards that you should know.[4]

- *Bags* are paper and polyethylene, often with handles, and hold ¼ peck to ½ bushel

---

4 Karen Gast, "Containers and Packaging for Fruits and Vegetables," *Postharvest Management of Commercial Horticultural Crops*, March 1991.

- *Baskets* are made of wood, and hold anywhere between ¼ peck and 1 bushel

- *Boxes, cartons, or hampers* hold anywhere from ½ peck to 1 bushel

- *Flats* hold 12 (1-pint) boxes

- *Lugs* are shallow containers, usually wood, that vary in size

- *Sacks* are 50 or 100 pounds of dry vegetables or commodities like potato, onion, beans, and rice

- *Trays* are used for berries and are made of corrugated paper. They hold either 6 to 8 quarts or 10 to 15 pounds

Grade and size standards. In addition, each produce crop is packaged in a uniform grade and size set by the U.S. Department of Agriculture or by individual states. Most of the fresh produce available for purchase in the grocery store is U.S. Grade No. 1 or better. The difference between No. 1 and lower grades is often small and has to do with how the product looks, not how it tastes. These products lower than No. 1, are often sold to institutions and companies who will turn them into a finished product.

I first learned about the grading system from Justy at his produce stand when I wanted a box of pickling cucumbers, and he asked me if U.S. No. 2 pickles were okay with me. He explained that they would be firm, fresh, and free from disease but irregular in diameter and color. Cucumber diameter and color are not important for my pickle making, so I went ahead and ordered. The price was significantly less.

The USDA publishes grade standards for each fruit[5] and vegetable[6] sold in the U.S. (visit the links in the footnotes to see the standards for individual fruit and vegetables). For example, apples are sold in five different grades: 1) U.S. Extra Fancy, 2) U.S. Fancy, 3) U.S. No. 1, 4) U.S. No. 1 Hail, and 5) U.S. Utility.

Why do you, the home preserver, need to know these grade standards? Because you are also turning these apples into a finished product, and now that you know the language, you can purchase these lesser grades at a greatly reduced price. The difference between U.S. No. 1 and U.S. No. 1 Hail will not affect your applesauce in the slightest: "U.S. No. 1 Hail" consists of apples which meet the requirements of U.S. No. 1 grade except that hail marks where the skin has not been broken and well-healed hail marks where the skin has been broken, are permitted, provided the apples are fairly well formed.[7]

You only need to ask your grocer or produce guy for these different grades. You can save significant money if you purchase this way.

---

5 United States Department of Agriculture, "Fruits," Agricultural Marketing Service, accessed September 23, 2020, https://www.ams.usda.gov/grades-standards/fruits.

6 United States Department of Agriculture, "Vegetables," Agricultural Marketing Service, accessed September 23, 2020, https://www.ams.usda.gov/grades-standards/vegetables.

7 United States Department of Agriculture, "Apple Grades & Standards," Agricultural Marketing Service, accessed September 23, 2020, https://www.ams.usda.gov/grades-standards/apple-grades-standards.

CHAPTER 5

Storing Your Dehydrated Food

The prepared pantry concept is at the core of my preparedness plan, and dehydrated foods play a big part. Once you've mastered drying your own food, you'll need to learn to store it properly so all your hard work will be edible for years to come.

Necessary Equipment

These basic supplies will keep dried food in a shelf-stable condition for a longer period of time. We use canning jars for most of our pantry storage. They are easy to find, easy to store, and can be used for all the food preservation processes you will be doing.

Storage containers naturally create a sealed environment for your food. To extend the shelf life, remove the oxygen from the storage container. This is done with oxygen absorbers. By removing the oxygen and creating a nitrogen environment, you will protect your food from insect damage and help preserve the quality. Oxygen-absorbing packets contain iron powder and work by reacting with the oxygen in your container, causing the powder to rust. They are not dangerous to your food.

You can purchase different sizes of oxygen absorbers depending on the container you are using for storage. You need one 100cc oxygen absorber per quart canning jar, and one 300cc oxygen absorber (or three 100cc absorbers) for each gallon of product. For storing 5- or 6-gallon buckets, you can purchase larger, 2,000cc oxygen absorbers. You can find them at Discount Mylar Bags (http://www.discountmylarbags.com) or on Amazon.com.

You can also consider getting a vacuum sealer with a jar attachment. I use a FoodSaver vacuum sealer. These are handy to have and can be used instead of the 100cc oxygen absorbers when using canning jars. A vacuum sealer is helpful, but not necessary.

We use food-grade buckets for all of our long-term storage, including both edible and nonedible supplies. Look for plastic that has ♳ PETE or ♴ HDPE stamped on them. Find these at ULine.com, Wal-Mart, Amazon.com, or befriend a local bakery or ice cream shop.

Plastic freezer bags with zip tops are recommended for long- and short-term storage. They are sturdy and will keep out more air than regular storage bags.

Finally, plastic-coated foil Mylar pouches can be used instead of plastic freezer bags but this is the most expensive way to set up your storage. These sturdy bags are used in conjunction with oxygen absorbers to remove air and light from your dried food.

Short-Term Vs. Long-Term Pantry

We keep two types of pantry items in our house: short-term and long-term.

Short-term items. Our short-term pantry contains items that will be used in the next six months. Because these pantry items will have repeated exposure to light, heat, and humidity, they will have a shorter shelf life.

A short-term pantry might include bread and pancake mixes, along with other items with leavening; crackers; bars with dried fruit and nuts; quart-size containers of the most common dehydrated fruits and vegetables; and canned food and spices.

When we package our own food items, we store these small quantities in glass mason jars, food-grade plastic jars, or plastic zip-top bags. It's important to keep your short-term pantry clear of clutter, so you always know what is in there.

Linda Loosli at *Food Storage Moms* has a creative way to add extra space to a small pantry. She recommends that by taking the time to add "a few extra shelves to your small pantry, you gain almost 50 percent more cupboard space depending on how your cabinets are built." Her system also includes large and small buckets with flour and sugar for everyday baking, which she refills when needed. Find out more at https://www.foodstoragemoms.com/2013/10/small-pantry.

Long-term items. It is possible to keep home-processed food for two to five years if you remove the oxygen component. I do this by packaging dry food with a FoodSaver vacuum pack machine and placing these packages inside of plastic buckets with oxygen absorbers.

Here's the process. Once you have completely dried your fruits or vegetables and they have been properly conditioned (see page 439), it's time to package them for storage. Divide the food into smaller portion sizes (perhaps six meals) and package them using a FoodSaver Bag, which removes all the oxygen. If you don't have a FoodSaver, use 1-gallon zip-top freezer bags, remove as much air as you can, and add one 300cc oxygen absorber per gallon bag. If the item has sharp edges (like dried carrots), I also wrap it in a layer of plastic wrap to soften the edges. Be sure to label each of these smaller packages with the name of the product and the date it was dried, so you can rotate it properly.

Next, I place a 2,000cc oxygen absorber in the bottom of a 5-gallon bucket and start layering in the smaller packaged items. You should be fairly quick about this. An oxygen absorber can only be exposed to air for 5 to 10 minutes before it begins to lose its potency. Once it's sealed, label the outside of the plastic bucket with the contents and the date it was sealed.

The smaller packages of items are stored in our extended pantry area and moved to the short-term pantry as needed. It is safe to open the 5-gallon buckets to remove packages, as long as the buckets are promptly re-sealed.

In addition to storing the food we dehydrate, we also purchase dehydrated vegetables, milk, and beans sealed in #10 cans from ProvidentLiving.org. Most dried food that is processed by professionals has a 20- to 30-year shelf life. At the time of this writing, a 2.4-pound can of diced onions is $9. It would take me almost 10 pounds of onions, untold hours, and I will have cried many tears to dry that many. The prices are very reasonable, so this is where I purchase my onions and carrots instead of drying them myself.

Keeping Inventory

It's hard to remember what you have on hand without an inventory system of some kind. It becomes even more difficult if you live in a small house and are storing items in nontraditional areas, like under beds or in closets. Keeping track of every item and where it's stored is essential, so you don't waste food.

This tracking system can be as simple as a yellow pad, an in-depth Excel spreadsheet, or even an online food storage tracker like Home Food Storage by Long Term Glass Wares, LLC.

I can honestly say that I have tried just about every inventory-keeping tactic on the market today and it's tough to keep my inventory list updated. The problem is that you have to get your family sold on keeping track of the food too, or they will remove food and mess up your system. Eventually, you may find that you will be the only person allowed to "check out" the food from the long-term areas in order to keep the inventory correct.

Rotating Your Food

Basic pantry protocols call for rotating your food. First-in-first-out (FIFO) is the best way to keep a rotation of fresh food. Rotating food FIFO means that each package of food has been dated, and you always have the oldest item stored at the front of the cabinet so you can use it first. When new items are added to storage, they are placed at the back of the cabinet.

There are several fancy ways to set up your shelves for FIFO storage, and making a rotating storage shelf may be the answer you are looking for. Search online for DIY building plans. Ultimately, the most important thing to remember when rotating food is to cook what you have in your pantry on a regular basis. If you are making soups, stews, and chili using dehydrated rather than fresh ingredients, you will always be using your current stock.

By labeling short-term and long-term storage containers with the contents inside and the date they were dried, you can keep track of your supply, rotate as needed, and avoid wasting the food that you put so much time and money into preparing.

CHAPTER 6

Fruit & Vegetable Leathers

Fruit leathers or fruit roll-ups are a favorite among kids and grownups alike. They are a wonderful way to use small quantities of fruit when they become too ripe for other drying methods. It's a treat that no one can pass up. You can use any kind of fruit that you have on hand. There are two basic preparation methods: uncooked and cooked fruit leather.

Sugar and honey are interchangeable in fruit leather recipes. Honey will produce a slightly tackier roll and a deeper flavor. Consider substituting pure maple syrup for a different taste. If you're using sugar, it's best to create simple syrup first, so you can be sure there are no granules in the finished product. Sugar will create a slightly more brittle finished product.

Dehydrator Tray Liners for Making Leather

A regular dehydrator tray is not going to trap the pureed food used in a fruit leather. Most commercial dehydrators come with one or two plastic fruit roll sheets specifically for this process. These are made from a rigid plastic with a slight outer lip that traps the food and keeps it from coming off the tray. Even if you purchased your machine used, it is easy to find additional trays online. If you make a lot of fruit leather, you may want to purchase enough liners to fit each tray.

Using a round machine is not the most efficient way to make leather, so I prefer to make mine in the square Excalibur machine. Their non-stick dehydrator sheets work terrifically for this, and they are easy to clean.

It's not necessary to go out and purchase something expensive as a liner for your leather; you can easily use parchment paper or plastic wrap and cut it to the size of your dehydrator trays. If you are going to be making leather on round trays, be sure to leave the middle section uncovered, as this is where the airflow takes place during the drying process. Foil and wax paper are not suitable for this project.

Tip: If you have trouble keeping your puree on the trays, create a bowl with your tray liners by pinching each corner together and securing them with 1-inch office binder clips.

General Instructions for Uncooked Fruit Leather

1. Thoroughly wash the fruit. If using nonorganic fruit, use the cleaning method found on page 331 to remove as much dirt and pesticide as possible.

2. Remove stones and large seeds. For fruit with small seeds, like strawberries, blackberries, and raspberries, seed removal is a personal preference. This is best accomplished by blending the berries into a pulp and then pushing the pulp through a fine mesh strainer. The pulp will flow through, and the seeds will be caught.

3. Peel the fruit and remove rough skins that are not usually eaten (melon, citrus). I tend to leave skins on my fruit if at all possible; there are many nutrients to be gained from leaving on the skin.

4. Cut the fruit into medium pieces and place them into a blender or food processor. Add citrus or ascorbic acid if you are worried about oxidation of the fruit (see page 437). Blend the fruit to a thick puree.

5. If the puree is too juicy, drain it through a fine mesh strainer until it has a thick pudding-like consistency. This is all a matter of preference, so don't be afraid to experiment. You will learn the consistency that is right for your machine and the fruit being used. If the batch is too thick, add water in 1-teaspoon increments until you reach the desired consistency.

6. Taste the mix and add honey or sugar, to taste. Add any spices at the quantity of ½ teaspoon per 4 cups of pureed fruit.

7. Prepare your drying trays and add the fruit puree to within an inch of the edge. Using a ladle, scoop and spread the puree evenly on the tray. It should be no more than ¼ inch thick or the drying time will be affected. The outside areas of the tray dry faster, so they should be thicker than the center. Swirl the puree around with a ladle to redistribute it the way you want.

8. Dry at 125°F for 6 to 8 hours until the leather is sticky. Once it is dry, it will be translucent and slightly tacky to the touch. It will easily peel away from the plastic wrap or dehydrator sheet. It is best removed when warm.

General Instructions for Cooked Fruit Leather

Sometimes it is best to cook fruit before making a puree. Simmering the fruit before placing it in the dehydrator helps to cook down watery produce and concentrates the flavor. Some fruits, like rhubarb or cranberries, are always cooked before being eaten and would not taste good in a puree if you skipped this step. Other fruits, like apples, pears, coconuts, cherries, and blueberries, need to be softened before they will come to a smooth puree consistency.

1. Wash and prepare the fruit as described in steps 1, 2, and 3 above.

2. Cook the fruit in a saucepan. Help the fruit break down as it cooks by mashing it with a fork.

3. Add honey or sugar, to taste, and ascorbic acid to prevent oxidization, if you'd like.

4. Blend the fruit to a thick puree.

5. Continue with steps 5 to 8 from the instructions on page 452.

Get creative with your finished fruit leathers. They can be rolled and eaten as is, or rehydrated and used in pie fillings and dessert toppings. Make them into a beverage by combining five parts water with one part leather in a food blender.

How to Store Fruit Leather

Fruit leather is easiest to work with when it is still slightly warm. If you let it completely cool, take 5 minutes to warm it up in the dehydrator. After the leather is dry and there are no sticky parts, there are several ways to store it.

1. Lay a sheet of leather out on a piece of parchment paper or plastic wrap and roll it up like a scroll. Using kitchen shears, cut the scroll into 1-inch sections. If you want to create bite-size pieces, cut 1-inch squares from the sections. If you wish to skip the paper, it's still possible to roll the fruit leather, but it may need to be coated so it won't stick together. Dusting it with cornstarch or arrowroot powder is an option. Neither of these will change the flavor of the finished product.

2. Store your cut rolls in plastic freezer bags or a tightly sealed canning jar in a cool, dry place. For long-term storage, big batches can be stored in the freezer or refrigerator. We keep a batch in a jar in the pantry and include a 100cc oxygen absorber.

What Can Go Wrong

Properly dried fruit leather will be translucent and slightly tacky to the touch. It will easily peel away from the plastic wrap or dehydrator sheet. However, if the finished product is too brittle, there is a way to rehydrate it slightly.

1. Place the leather sheet back in the dehydrator on a tray.

2. Wet a paper or cloth towel and add it to a separate dehydrator tray.

3. Place the tray with the towel under the tray with the brittle sheet.

4. Place the cover on the machine and let the machine sit. Do not turn on the heat.

5. Check back after several hours or even overnight. The leather will have absorbed some of the moisture from the air.

6. If the finished product is too sticky, return the tray to the dehydrator and dry in 15-minute increments until the center is no longer sticky.

Vegetable Leather

Vegetable leathers are easy to make and can be used as veggie wraps when you roll them up with your favorite spreads. These leathers will keep for 6 to 12 months if stored in plastic bags or canning jars in the freezer. Break them up and make a powder, or stir bits into soups or casseroles.

Dry pureed, cooked vegetables on trays in the dehydrator at 135° to 140°F using the instructions below. The process is the same as for fruit leather, except you will always use the cooked method.

1. Select, wash, and prepare the vegetables in small pieces.
2. Cook the vegetables in a skillet or saucepan until soft.
3. Drain off any excess liquid.
4. Add spices, to taste.
5. Blend the mixture to a thick puree.
6. Prepare your drying trays and add the vegetable puree within an inch of edge. Using a ladle, scoop and spread the puree evenly on the tray. It should be no more than ¼ inch thick or the drying time will be affected. The outside areas of the tray dry faster, so they should be thicker than the center. Swirl the puree around with a ladle to redistribute it the way you want.
7. Dry at 135° to 140°F for 8 to 12 hours until the leather is finished. Once it is dry, it will be translucent and slightly tacky to the touch. It will easily peel away from the plastic wrap or dehydrator sheet. It is best removed when warm.

Vegetable leather can be used several ways:

- A savory, portable snack
- Paste for spaghetti sauce or pizza
- Reconstituted in soups

Highly Concentrated Food

Dehydrated fruit and vegetables lose between 80 percent and 90 percent of their moisture during drying. That makes the food highly concentrated, smaller, and lighter, so when you are eating it, the serving sizes can be deceiving. A cup of dehydrated apple chunks doesn't look like much, but it took two to three medium apples to make it. Would you really eat that many apples in one sitting? How about tomatoes—it takes nine medium tomatoes to make 1 cup of tomato dices!

If you are limiting the amount of sugar in your diet, a large portion of dried fruit will have concentrated fructose levels, potentially causing tooth decay in kids.

Finally, there's more fiber in dehydrated food, and while fiber is actually good for you in small doses, the high levels found in dried fruit could quickly lead to intestinal problems like gas, bloating, cramping, and diarrhea. It's best to be aware and take note of portion sizes, and extra calories, so you can adjust your snack sizes accordingly.

CHAPTER 7

Making Jerky

Once you've learned the art of making jerky, you have the ability to raise your food storage plan to a higher level. Not only are you producing fruit and vegetables, but now you're also making a protein that is all-natural and free of additives, food colorings, and preservatives.

Homemade jerky can be made from any lean meat. Choose beef round, flank and chuck steak, rump roast, and brisket. Most cuts of pork, venison, turkey, or chicken work well. Stay away from highly marbled and fatty cuts.

Safe Jerky

The temperature of raw meat while processing jerky is of particular concern. You must use a dehydrator that reaches a temperature of 160°F so it will kill harmful microorganisms that may be present on meat. If your dehydrator does not have a blowing fan and the ability to reach 160°F, it is not suitable for making homemade jerky.

Safe meat handling procedures should be followed at all times. Wash your hands with soap and water and use clean utensils. Never cross-contaminate different batches of meat by using the same cutting board, knife, or tongs.

Thaw meat in the refrigerator, never on the countertop. Leaving food out too long at room temperature can cause bacteria (such as *Staphylococcus aureus*, *Salmonella enteritidis*, *Escherichia coli O157:H7*, and *Campylobacter*) to grow to dangerous levels that can cause illness. Bacteria grow rapidly in the range of temperatures between 40°F and 140°F, doubling in number in as little as 20 minutes. This range of temperatures is often called the "Danger Zone."[8]

Prepare the Meat

First, remove any visible fat and connective tissue from the meat. Fat becomes rancid and quickly takes on an off flavor. Using a fatty meat will greatly reduce the shelf life of your finished product.

Meat is easier to cut when it is partially frozen, especially if you do not have an electric meat slicer. Cut it into strips no thicker than ¼ inch, 1 to 1½ inches wide, and 4 to 8 inches long. The bigger the piece of meat, the longer it will take to dry. For chewy jerky, cut with the grain of the meat; for brittle jerky, slice across the grain.

---

8 United States Department of Agriculture, "Danger Zone," USDA Food Safety and Inspection Service, accessed September 23, 2020, https://www.fsis.usda.gov/shared/PDF/Danger_Zone.pdf.

Pretreating the Meat

To reduce spoilage, you need to reduce the amount of bacteria on the meat. This can be done by using one of three methods to treat the meat before drying: presoaking in vinegar, marinating and precooking the meat, or freezing the meat before cooking. If the meat has been frozen for 60 days, all bacteria are destroyed and soaking or precooking is not necessary.

Vinegar presoak. Slice the meat, add it to a large bowl, cover with a 5 percent vinegar solution, and soak for 10 minutes. Drain the meat from the vinegar presoak and place it in a plastic zip-top bag to get ready for marinating.

Add any brine ingredients to the marinating bag, making sure that all pieces of meat are completely covered. Add additional water if necessary. Refrigerate 1 to 4 hours or overnight. Drain before dehydrating.

Marinate and precook. Slice the meat. Add the brine ingredients to the marinating bag, making sure that all pieces of meat are completely covered. Add additional water if necessary. Refrigerate 1 to 4 hours or overnight.

Precook the meat to reduce chances of food-borne illness. Add the strips of meat and marinating sauce to a large pot and boil, uncovered, for 5 minutes, or until the meat reaches an internal temperature of 160°F. Drain.

Dehydrating the Jerky

Place the strips in a single layer on dehydrator sheets, pat each piece dry with a paper towel so they are not dripping marinade, and make sure they don't touch or overlap. There is no need to rinse. Dehydrate at 160°F. After four hours, check the batch and remove any small pieces that are dry. Depending on slice size, the whole batch will take approximately 4 to 6 hours to complete. Remove dried strips from the trays and cool. Jerky is done when you can take a piece and bend it. It should crack and leave strands, but not break.

If the meat strips were not pretreated in marinade prior to drying, you might want to take an extra drying step in an oven after dehydrating. Place the dried strips on a baking sheet and cook at 275°F for 10 minutes, or until the jerky reaches an internal temperature of 160°F. Remove any visible fat beads before packaging for storage.

Creating Specialty Jerky Brines

There are many ideas online for creating jerky. Ultimately, flavorful brine sets the stage for your success. Once you learn the basics of making brine, you are free to experiment and create a one-of-a-kind creation that your family will love. Your specialty jerky brine needs at least three of these four elements: salt, acid, sweetness, and spice. Even a savory marinade benefits from a little sweetness, so most brine incorporates all four elements.

Salt helps to preserve and provides flavor. Try kosher salt, canning salt, sea salt, and table salt. Soy sauce is another option, but you should still add some traditional salt too.

Acids include apple cider vinegar, balsamic vinegar, lemon juice, lime juice, soy sauce, white vinegar, and wine.

Sweeteners are optional and include sugar, brown sugar, corn syrup, fruit juice, honey, and molasses.

Spices and seasonings are optional but encouraged, and include dill seed, garlic, mustard seed, onion, paprika, pepper, red pepper, and just about anything that you can think of.

Try some of these combinations, look at commercially prepared products for ideas, and try our favorite recipes from this book.

- Classic Beef (page 508)
- Beef Steak (page 508)
- Spicy Cajun (page 508)
- Teriyaki (page 508)
- Chile Lime
- Garlic Chili
- Hatch Chili and Onion
- Orange Chipotle
- Pineapple Orange

Storing Jerky

Jerky is not a long-term storage item. It can be stored in sealed bags at room temperature for up to two weeks. For the longest shelf life and flavor, homemade jerky can be stored in containers in the refrigerator for up to one month, or in the freezer for up to six months.

Rehydrating Jerky in Meals

We often think of jerky as a tasty snack for quick days or to take on hiking trips, but the meat can be rehydrated and successfully used in soup and stew. In a large saucepan, combine 3 cups water, 1 cup jerky chunks, and any dehydrated vegetables you will be using. They should be completely covered with the water. Suggested vegetables include tomato, potato, bell pepper, onion, carrot, or garlic. Add any additional water as the meat and vegetables expand, if needed. Allow the mix to sit for 30 minutes to rehydrate. Once rehydrated, place the pan over medium heat and bring to a boil. Add any fresh ingredients and spices, then simmer for an additional 30 minutes to an hour, until jerky is tender and fresh vegetables are cooked.

CHAPTER 8

Soups, Powders, & Herbs

You may often find yourself with leftover fruit, vegetables, and herbs that could be put to good use. In this chapter we'll discuss the pros and cons of dehydrating soup, how to make your own specialized powders, and how to dry herbs for tea and crafts.

Soups

Similar to making fruit and vegetable leather, soup becomes a quick precooked meal that just needs hot water to bring it back to life. Unlike leather, soup is first cooked on the stove and dried until it is crisp. The vegetables must be cooked for this to be an instant meal. Otherwise, vegetables that were only blanched during processing will still be in their partially uncooked form. This technique works best with a thick soup recipe, like split pea, carrot, or winter squash, because they will stay on the trays instead of running off. Soup with a broth base is not a good choice.

Is it worth it?

That depends on the kind of meals you want to prepare. I tend to be the sort of cook that takes several dry ingredients from the pantry, drops them into a pot of bouillon, broth, or water, and makes a tasty meal from the things we have on hand. This method assumes that you have the time to cook from scratch at home. If you find that you need a homemade soup meal for busy days, traveling, or backpacking trips, a make-ahead soup might be just the thing. With one day of hard work and a bit of preplanning, you can make a large batch of healthy soup that is easily prepared, dried, and stored for when you need it. Store single serving portions in jars in a dark, cool pantry for up to six months.

Tips for Success

   1. This technique should only be used for soup without meat or dairy, and that has very little fat. Such ingredients will shorten the shelf life of the dry soup. Do not choose a recipe that uses milk as the base unless you are willing to cook with water and add powdered milk when packaging.

   2. Thoroughly cook the ingredients of the soup on the stovetop to the desired thickness. Remember, the boiling water used during serving will not cook the food, only rehydrate it, so everything must be thoroughly cooked.

3. Consider using an immersion blender to get the vegetables into smaller, uniform pieces before drying.

4. Typically, one dehydrator tray of soup equals one serving. For quick drying, spread one or two ladles of soup on Paraflexx or plastic tray covers no more than ¼ inch thick.

5. Dry on dehydrator trays for 4 to 8 hours until the soup is brittle. You may need to peel the soup off the tray and flip it halfway through the drying cycle.

6. Run one tray of dry soup through a blender until it reaches a powder consistency and measure it. This will help you know how much is required for one serving.

7. Determine the amount of boiling water needed to reconstitute one tray (one serving) of soup to the thickness you like. Typically, 1 to 1½ cups of water will do.

8. Package the soup in canning jars in single serving portions. Make sure there is enough space left in the jars to add the boiling water. These jars can handle the heat and will not break or melt.

9. Make a recipe card with the name of the soup and the directions to use when serving. Place it inside of each jar, listing the amount of water needed and any other ingredients that will complete the recipe.

Powders

Pulverized fruit powder can be bought commercially, but it can be hard to find and somewhat expensive—especially for the home cook. However, powdering your own fruit, vegetables, and spices is an economical way to add nutrients to your food storage on a budget.

To start, follow the dehydrating directions found in Chapter 9 for your favorite fruit or vegetable. Food should be dried until moisture-free so if you try to squeeze two pieces of produce together, they will not stick. To get the desired texture, it is best if you dry the fruits or vegetables in small pieces. Aim for the light texture of copy paper. If the produce still feels moist, continue drying in 2-hour increments until it dries throughout.

The dried product needs to be conditioned for one week to remove any remaining moisture. Place the dried fruit into a plastic bag or canning jar, filling the container no more than three-fourths full. Let the fruit sit, or condition, and shake the bag or jar once every day or two.

Some dehydrated fruits are inherently sticky due to their sugar content, like raisins, figs, plums, and apricots. These should be dried in very small pieces if you wish to powder them. Even when you are using a well-dried batch of fruit, stickiness is simply an innate quality of fruit powder. If you find that the finished product clumps, add ½ to 1 teaspoon of arrowroot powder to the fruit before blending; this will help to even out the clumps.

You can process small batches of fruit or vegetables in a food processor, blender, or coffee grinder until they are powdered. This is a cumbersome process that may take several tries, but is worth it.

Once you reach the grind you are looking for, transfer the powder to an airtight container and store it at room temperature for three months or in the refrigerator for six months. Be aware, homemade fruit and vegetable powder is not a long-term storage item, so only process as much powder as you think you will need for the next few months and leave the dried produce whole until you need another batch.

Here are some tasty suggestions for using homemade fruit or vegetable powder in your daily meals:

- Add it to hot or cold cereal
- Add it to the batter of doughs for muffins, cakes, or quick bread. In any recipe, replace ½ cup flour with ½ cup fruit powder
- Add powder to smoothies. Make a fruit smoothie milkshake by adding ¼ cup fruit powder, 1 cup milk, 1 tablespoon honey, and ice cubes to a blender
- Use it when making homemade ice cream, frozen yogurt, or sorbet
- Add it to meringue as a flavor enhancer and coloring agent
- Add fruit powder to your fermented beverages for a zingy second ferment
- Use it as a spice rub for meats
- Use it in glazes and frosting
- Rehydrate it for a fruit puree, like applesauce, at a later date
  See the Tomato Powder recipe on page 499 for a more detailed example.

Herbs

Herbs have been dried and used for home health and hearth for thousands of years, and they are a big part of any preparedness garden. You probably have all the usual suspects already in attendance: rosemary, chives, oregano, and mint, just to name a few.

Dried herbs can be used to make herbal tea blends for protection against seasonal colds and flu, and as an addition to your prepared pantry as you create your own rubs and spice blends for cooking. They have many self-reliant uses:

- Candles
- Cleaners
- Flavored vinegar
- Herb-flavored oils
- Potpourri

- Seasonings
- Shampoo
- Soap
- Tea blends

You can dry herbs in small batches throughout the growing season as time allows. In the long run, it costs less to purchase individual plants and dehydrate your own than it does to purchase dried herbs from the store. Your plants will respond to regular cuttings by growing thicker. Pruning keeps them compact and prevents plants from flowering and setting seed, so you can have several harvests.

Look for fragrant herbs with large leaves. Everyone has their favorites, but these 10 herbs are easy to grow and versatile for cooking, tea, and healing.

- Basil
- Bee balm
- Chamomile
- Ginger
- Lemon balm
- Lemon verbena
- Mint
- Plantain
- Rosemary
- Stevia

There are only a few rules for harvesting and drying herbs.

1. Pick flowers at the peak of freshness. New leaves at the tips will have the most concentrated flavor.

2. Harvest flowers and leaves on a sunny day, just before the flowers open. The leaves should be completely dry, so harvest during a dry, sunny day in the mid-morning, after the dew has evaporated, or in the evening before the dew forms.

3. Use scissors to cut off your harvest. Leave 4 to 6 inches of stem on the plant for later growth.

4. Once harvested, keep the picked herbs out of direct sunlight until you can begin the drying process. Consider bringing a basket with a towel to cover the cuttings while you harvest.

Drying Herbs

Begin drying freshly cut herbs as soon as possible, before they begin to wilt. Remove any bruised or imperfect leaves and stems. Inspect the harvest for seeds and insects. Discard these to the compost pile.

To preserve the volatile oils in your herbs, try to rinse and handle the leaves as little as possible. Rinse the stems in cool water and gently shake off excess moisture, then pat dry with a towel. Remove leaves from the stems and run them through a salad spinner, if you have one. Another easy way to remove excess water is to use a large muslin towel as a spinner. Just place the wet leaves inside the large towel, gather the corners, and head outside to swing it around a few times. The water will exit as you spin the towel.

The point of this spinning is to get the leaves as dry as possible before you begin the dehydrating process, in order to keep drying time way down. If you are growing organic herbs, there is no need to wash your herbs unless they are very muddy or buggy.

Microwave drying. This method is only safe for herbs and is the fastest way to dry if you only have a small harvest each day. It is done in small batches of 1 or 2 cups at a time. Spread a clean cup of leaves in a single layer between two sheets of paper towels, and microwave in 30-second intervals. If you have an oven with the wattage of 1,000 or higher, special attention is needed to make sure the leaves and paper do not catch fire. Trust me; I know this from experience!

After 30 seconds, check the leaves, turn them over, and heat for another 30 seconds. Remove small leaves as they are finished and repeat the process in 30-second increments until the herbs are crackly dry. This will only take two or three minutes.

Hanging. Hanging herbs in the kitchen can add a homey touch, but this is not the most efficient way to dry your herbs. Leaving them exposed to the air and sunlight for an extended period of time means they will lose their flavor.

To prevent this, you should lay cut stems out and sort them by size. Bunch six to ten stalks together in bundles and fasten them tightly with a rubber band or twist tie. The rubber band will not come loose as the herbs dry. It's best to hang the bundles out of direct sunlight and in a room that will not get too much moisture but has good air circulation. Bathrooms are not a good place to do this.

If you must hang them to dry in the sun, it should be done on a day with little humidity. Place the herb bundles in a paper bag that has several holes cut for circulation. Attach the bag to a string or clothesline using clothespins. These bags must be brought inside at night, so dew does not affect them. Depending on the humidity in your home, the drying time will be one to three days.

Screen drying. The goal with screen drying is to allow air circulation all around the screen. Keep the drying screens elevated by placing blocks underneath. Drying screens should not be placed in direct sunlight while drying.

The herbs can touch each other on the screens because they will shrink as they dry. Screen drying is a slower process than the other methods. Due to lack of airflow, the drying process will take from two to four days.

Dehydrator drying. Drying herbs in a dehydrator can be quite easy. Wash as directed on page 461, separate the leaves from the stems, and lay them out in a single layer up to ¼ inch thick. It's okay to have them touch; herbs will not stick together while they dry.

Herbs are dried at cooler temperatures than fruits and vegetables to help reduce the evaporation of the essential oils during the drying process. For the best results, dry in the 90° to 100°F range. Strong herb flavors, like garlic, ginger, and rosemary, should be dried separately from mild herbs that might pick up their flavors. Drying times range from two hours for leafy herbs to six hours for woody stems or roots.

Storing Herbs

As soon as you've dried your herbs to a stage where they can easily be powdered between your fingers, they are ready for storage. Remove the leaves from the stalks (if you didn't do it before) and keep the leaves whole. Crumbling the leaves releases the aromatic oils that you want for your teas, tonics, and lotions, so do not crush the leaves until you are ready to add them to recipes. To use the herbs, crush the leaves in your hands or powder them in a mortar and pestle or with a rolling pin, then measure as directed by your recipe. Use sparingly; you'll want about one third of the amount of dried herbs as you would use fresh herbs in your recipes.

Keep the leaves in airtight containers. Mason jars work well, but any reclaimed lidded glass container will fit the bill. Glass works best because metal and plastic can affect the flavor of some herbs and after a while, the flavor will transfer to the container. I saved chopped peppermint in a 1-gallon plastic jug. It's been in there for a few years. The herbs are still fragrant, but I will never be able to store anything else in the jar; the scent has completely permeated the container. From now on, it is peppermint or nothing!

The recommended storage time for herbs is one year. It is best practice to grow enough fresh herbs to last from harvest to harvest. After one year, the herbs will still be good, just not as aromatic. I use my older herbs for soaps and craft projects. No matter what, your herbs should be stored in a cool, dark place, away from heat.

If you have a bumper crop of your favorite herb, you can remove the oxygen from the jar and freeze herbs in FoodSaver containers. As long as you keep moisture out of a storage container, you can get up to 18 months of storage in the freezer.

CHAPTER 9

Dehydrating 50 Common Fruits & Vegetables

In this chapter, we'll take the guesswork out of dehydrating your favorite fruit and vegetables. You may even find food that you did not know you could dry for home storage. Each entry lists the best way to clean, cut, dry, and rehydrate individual items for future use.

Apples

Apples are first on the list and are possibly the easiest fruit to start dehydrating. Once you have them clean, they require only a little preparation. We like to leave the skin on our apples for extra fiber and nutrition. They make a healthy snack all on their own.

Clean: For nonorganic apples, follow the cleaning tips on page 331. Wash organic applies with warm water. Dry apples with a cloth.

How to prepare: Use an apple peeler/corer for consistently sized cuts. Otherwise, core and slice into eight equal-size pieces, or use a mandoline slicer.

Suggested thickness: ⅛ inch for chips; small chop for baking

Drying time: 6 to 12 hours, depending on thickness

Temperature: 125°F

Consistency when dry: Leathery to crisp, with no moisture in the middle

Blanching requirements: N/A

Oxidizing treatment: Treat cut pieces with ascorbic acid or lemon juice.

How to rehydrate: Pour boiling water over the dried apples until just covered and let pieces soak for 30 minutes, or until they rehydrate to the consistency you are looking for.

Consistency when rehydrated: Like cooked apples (soft)

Yield: 2 to 3 medium apples = 1 cup dried apples = 1¼ cups rehydrated apples

Apricots

Apricots are worth waiting for, even with their extended drying time. Use rehydrated in pies and other desserts, and dried as a healthy snack.

Clean: For nonorganic apricots, follow the cleaning tips on page 331. Wash organic apricots with warm water, then dry.

How to prepare: Remove pit. No need to remove skins.

Suggested thickness: Cut in half or in quarters for quicker drying time.

Drying time: 8 to 12 hours for quarters; 12 to 24 hours for halves.

Temperature: 125°F

Consistency when dry: Leathery

Blanching requirements: N/A

Oxidizing treatment: Use lemon juice or ascorbic acid, if you want them to retain their light color.

How to rehydrate: Soak in hot water or warmed juice for 15 to 20 minutes, or simmer on the stovetop, until the fruit is plump and has absorbed the water.

Consistency when rehydrated: Soft and plump

Yield: 2 pounds fresh apricots = 6 ounces dried apricots = 2 cups rehydrated apricots

Asparagus

Asparagus is a beloved vegetable at our house, and we can eat it every day for weeks. The growing season is short, and when asparagus is out of season, it is expensive. In order to save money on our favorite veggie and keep it on the table, we dehydrate it as much as possible. Process dried pieces into powder and add it to soup.

Clean: For nonorganic asparagus, follow the cleaning tips on page 331. For organic asparagus, wash with warm water and pat dry well.

How to prepare: Cut off tough ends first.

Suggested thickness: 1-inch pieces

Drying time: 8 to 12 hours

Temperature: 125°F

Consistency when dry: Brittle

Blanching requirements: 3 to 4 minutes

Oxidizing treatment: N/A

How to rehydrate: Cover 1 cup asparagus with 2¼ cups of boiling water and soak for 30 minutes, or add dried pieces directly to soup.

Consistency when rehydrated: Soft, like cooked

Yield: 2 cups fresh asparagus = 1 cup dried asparagus = 1½ cups rehydrated asparagus

Tip: If you sort your cut asparagus pieces onto dehydrator trays by thickness, you will save time and additional work. The spear tips dry quite a bit faster than the fibrous stalks, so keeping them on separate trays saves you the time and effort of fishing them out from many pieces that have not finished drying.

Bananas

Achieving the texture of store-bought banana chips is almost impossible for the home food processor that does not want unnecessary additives on their fruit. Did you know that in order to achieve that extra sweetness and crispness, they actually dip the bananas in sugar syrup and deep fry it? I'm assuming that you want to get away from the extra additives and calories as you are dehydrating fresh bananas for your food storage.

Used rehydrated banana in smoothies and in cereals, or chill the pieces and serve them on their own. Or, just enjoy as chips!

Clean: Wash and dry, then peel. There is no special treatment for organic versus nonorganic.

How to prepare: The best tasting bananas are slightly green at the top and have a few brown spots on the peel. Use overripe bananas in leather.

Suggested thickness: ⅛-inch rounds for chips

Drying time: 8 to 12 hours

Temperature: 125°F

Consistency when dry: Brittle, snaps easily

Blanching requirements: N/A

Oxidizing treatment: Dip or spray with lemon juice to prevent browning.

How to rehydrate: Mix 1 part water to 1 part chips, then simmer at a low temperature for 5 minutes.

Consistency when rehydrated: Like fresh

Yield: 5 large bananas = 2 cups dried bananas = 4 cups rehydrated bananas

Tip: Save the peels and dehydrate them too. They are a terrific potassium boost for your garden. Get instructions at http://preparednessmama.com/dry-banana-peels.

Beans (Green, Yellow, Snap)

If you are looking for a pantry-stable vegetable that is easy to dry and good for you, the green bean is it. While we do like to eat fresh beans from the garden, I prefer to purchase beans in large frozen bags from the grocery store to use for dehydrating. This is because I do not enjoy the process of cutting and blanching that is required for fresh beans. Thankfully, the local store has an excellent selection of organic beans, so my processing time is reduced to practically nothing. The peak season for green beans is from April to October, and you will get about 3 cups of beans per pound.

Clean: For nonorganic beans, follow the cleaning tips on page 331. For organic beans, wash with warm water and pat dry.

How to prepare: Remove strings if necessary. Cut before blanching. You do not need to prepare if dehydrating from the frozen state.

Suggested thickness: 1½-inch pieces, or cut lengthwise into 4-inch-long thin strips

Drying time: 8 to 14 hours

Temperature: 125°F

Consistency when dry: Hard, brittle

Blanching requirements: Boil or steam blanch for 2 to 3 minutes.

Oxidizing treatment: N/A

How to rehydrate: Cover 1 cup green beans in 2¼ cups warm water and soak for 30 minutes until plump. Or, add directly to soup without rehydrating.

Consistency when rehydrated: Like fresh

Yield: 2 cups fresh beans = 1 cup dried beans = 2 cups rehydrated beans

Beets

Harvest beets for storage late in the fall before the ground freezes. They have the best flavor when they are 2 inches in diameter. Except for gold varieties, beets will "bleed" away their color when cut.

Clean: For organic and nonorganic beets, scrub clean with a vegetable brush and warm water.

How to prepare: Cover with water and cook in a large saucepan until tender, about 45 minutes. Place the pot under running cold water and rinse until beets can be handled.

Suggested thickness: Peel, then cut into ⅛-inch strips.

Drying time: 8 to 12 hours; stir at 4-hour mark.

Temperature: 125°F

Consistency when dry: Hard

Blanching requirements: N/A

Oxidizing treatment: N/A

How to rehydrate: Cover 1 cup dry beets in 2¾ cups warm water for 1½ hours.

Consistency when rehydrated: Like cooked

Yield: 2 cups fresh beets = 1 cup dried beets = 1½ cups rehydrated beets

Tip: Add 2 tablespoons of lemon juice or vinegar to the cooking water. This will help to keep the beets from bleeding.

Blueberries

If you are lucky enough to be able to grow blueberries in your own home garden, you're in for a treat. Dehydrated blueberries are fairly easy to make and will keep for over a year if stored properly in a cool, dry part of your pantry. Skip the processing time and use frozen berries.

Just as with processing cranberries (page 438), the outer shell of the blueberry needs to be pierced to make sure the heat reaches the inside and allows the berry to dry completely. This is accomplished by piercing each berry individually, which is time-consuming, or adding them whole to a metal strainer and submerging in boiling water for 30 seconds. If using frozen berries, it is not necessary to do the additional water bath processing or piercing.

Add rehydrated blueberries to muffins and pancakes or use the recipe on page 494 to make Blueberry Basil Syrup.

Clean: For nonorganic blueberries, follow the cleaning tips on page 331. Rinse delicately. Rinse organic berries with warm water and dry delicately.

How to prepare: Remove stems. Pierce each berry with a skewer or pin, blanch for 30 seconds, or freeze until solid.

Suggested thickness: Leave whole

Drying time: 10 to 18 hours

Temperature: 125 to 135°F

Consistency when dry: Hard, will not stick together when squeezed

Blanching requirements: See notes above.

Oxidizing treatment: N/A

How to rehydrate: Submerge in cool water for 10 to 15 minutes.

Consistency when rehydrated: Not as plump or juicy as fresh. In baked goods, use without rehydrating to keep moisture content down.

Yield: 2 pints fresh blueberries = 1 cup dried blueberries = 2 cups rehydrated blueberries

Tip: Berries will drip during dehydrating. Add an extra tray with a fruit leather insert below them to catch the juice and protect other items from getting juiced.

Broccoli

Broccoli is wonderful to have in the pantry. I like to powder broccoli stalks to use when making broccoli soup. Dried florets can be rehydrated for soup, stew, or even for cooking as a side dish. Look for a head with deep color and closed flowers.

Clean: For nonorganic broccoli, follow the cleaning tips on page 331. For organic broccoli, wash with warm water and pat dry.

How to prepare: Cut the head from the stalk. Separate the florets into equal-size pieces. Chop the stalk into equal-size chunks.

Suggested thickness: Equal-size pieces

Drying time: 8 to 12 hours; stalks may take longer.

Temperature: 125°F

Consistency when dry: Crisp

Blanching requirements: For florets, water blanch for 2 minutes or steam blanch for 3 minutes. For stalks, cook in boiling water for 5 minutes until tender, then drain.

Oxidizing treatment: N/A

How to rehydrate: Soak 1 cup broccoli in 2 cups water. Soak until liquid stops absorbing, for 30 to 60 minutes. There's no need to soak if you're adding the broccoli to a recipe that has water and requires cooking.

Consistency when rehydrated: Tastes fresh, although not crunchy

Yield: 2 cups fresh broccoli = 1 cup dried broccoli = 2 cups rehydrated broccoli.

Cabbage and Brussels Sprouts

Cabbage may not be the first vegetable on your dehydrating list, but it should be right up in the top 10. Its nutritional advantages make it a recommended addition to your pantry. The peak season for cabbage falls between October and January, and for each pound of cabbage, you can process 6 cups of freshly shredded leaves. When fresh, a tightly wrapped head will last 14 days in the refrigerator, but if you take the time to dehydrate, you can have "like fresh" leaves for an entire year. This process works for all varieties of cabbage, and it's not even smelly as it dries! To try your dried cabbage in a recipe, check out Slow Cooker Stuffed Cabbage Rolls on page 511.

Clean: For nonorganic cabbage, follow the cleaning tips on page 331. For organic cabbage, wash with cool water, and pat dry.

How to prepare: Remove the outer leaves and stem, and core the head. Slice into thin strips.

Suggested thickness: ⅛-inch shreds or whole leaves

Drying time: 8 to 12 hours

Temperature: 125°F

Consistency when dry: Flexible and dry, like paper

Blanching requirements: N/A

Oxidizing treatment: N/A

How to rehydrate: Soak one part dried cabbage in 3 parts cool water for 3 minutes, or add pieces directly to soup.

Consistency when rehydrated: Like fresh, but not as crisp

Yield: 3 cups fresh cabbage = 1 cup dried cabbage = 3 cups rehydrated cabbage

Tip: Some people swear by blanching cabbage and others don't think it's necessary at all. Try dehydrating your cabbage both ways and see which you prefer. Me? I'll skip the extra step every time! However, you can dehydrate whole cabbage leaves for use in a poultice for healing. To make a poultice, rehydrate the leaves in cool water and lay them flat between two sheets of plastic wrap. Use a rolling pin to bruise them; it gets the healing juice flowing. Next, place the leaves directly on your skin, cover with plastic wrap, and secure with a cloth wrap overnight.

Carrots

Carrots are a staple in my pantry. We use them several times a week in stir-fry meals and soups. They lose over 80 percent of their water during the dehydrating process and will shrink down to practically nothing when they are dry. Take this into account and use tray inserts when you are drying them, or you may find that they have fallen through to the bottom of your dehydrator.

Clean: For nonorganic carrots, follow the cleaning tips on page 331 and scrub with a vegetable brush. For organic carrots, place in a colander and scrub with a vegetable brush and warm water. No need to peel.

How to prepare: Slice off the top and bottom ⅛ inch, slice into rounds or cubes.

Suggested thickness: ⅛-inch rounds; ¼-inch cubes; shredded

Drying time: 10 to 12 hours

Temperature: 125°F

Consistency when dry: Hard, brittle

Blanching requirements: Blanch for 3 to 4 minutes in boiling water, until they are bright orange.

Oxidizing treatment: N/A

How to rehydrate: To get a like-raw texture, soak in cool water for 15 to 30 minutes. For cooked carrots, combine carrots and water in a one to one ratio, bring to a boil, cover, and reduce heat to low for 10 minutes. Add directly to soup or stew without rehydrating.

Consistency when rehydrated: Anywhere from crunchy to just-cooked, depending on rehydrating method

Yield: 2 cups fresh carrots = 1 cup dried carrots = 1¼ cups rehydrated carrots

Tip: Be sure to add extra water to your recipe if you are adding carrots directly from a dehydrated state. They will take up a lot of liquid as they plump back to their original shape.

Cauliflower

There are many ways to use cauliflower besides as a side dish. We puree it and use it as a thickener in soup and stew. If you grate it into small pieces (ricing), you can rehydrate and use it to make pizza crust or a mashed potato substitute. Try Cauliflower Soup (page 509) or Riced Cauliflower Pizza Crust (page 514).

The peak season for cauliflower is September to November, and the average size of a head is 2 pounds. Each pound of fresh cauliflower will lose 75 percent of its water and become ¼ pound when dried, so dehydrating is a nice way to extend the shelf life of this healthy vegetable.

Clean: Wash organic and nonorganic cauliflower with warm water and dry. If the heads are fresh from the garden, soak in salt water for 10 minutes to dislodge any bugs.

How to prepare: Remove large stalks and outer leaves.

Suggested thickness: Cut into small, 1- to 2-inch, uniform-size florets, or rice the cauliflower and set it to dry on fruit leather trays.

Drying time: 8 to 12 hours

Temperature: 125°F

Consistency when dry: Crisp

Blanching requirements: To keep the florets white, steam 4 to 5 minutes. Skip this step if you will be using it as an ingredient and the color isn't important. Cook large stalks until soft, cut, and add to trays.

Oxidizing treatment: N/A

How to rehydrate: Soak 1 cup cauliflower in 1 cup water for 15 to 20 minutes.

Consistency when rehydrated: Like cooked

Yield: 4 cups fresh cauliflower = 1 cup dried cauliflower = 4 cups rehydrated cauliflower

Celery

Celery is such a versatile vegetable, but most people rarely use the whole stalk before it goes bad. We dehydrate ours, so there is always a supply on hand for soup and stew. Don't forget to grind it and make celery salt for adding a savory flavor to salads and spice blends.

One head of celery fills two trays of my Nesco Gardenmaster dehydrator. The pieces will dry to half their size, so consider adding a catch tray so the smaller pieces won't slip through.

Clean: For nonorganic celery, follow the cleaning tips on page 331. For organic celery, wash with warm water and pat dry.

How to prepare: Cut off the ends and separate the stalks. If you are making celery powder, keep the leaves.

Suggested thickness: ½-inch chunks

Drying time: 4 hours for leaves; 8 to 12 hours for stalk pieces

Temperature: 125°F

Consistency when dry: Crisp

Blanching requirements: Steam for 1 minute if planning to rehydrate into whole pieces. Skip if you're planning to make powder.

Oxidizing treatment: N/A

How to rehydrate: Place whole pieces in warm water for 10 to 15 minutes, or add directly to soup or stew.

Consistency when rehydrated: Soft, like cooked

Yield: 3 cups fresh celery = 1 cup dried celery = 2 cups rehydrated celery

Tip: Place celery leaves and small pieces on a separate tray from the larger stalks. These will dry in half the time, and you won't have to fish them out from the rest of the batch.

Cherries

Some people prefer to dip their cherries in boiling water for 30 seconds before they dehydrate them. I find that it is an unnecessary step that does not improve the quality of the dried fruit. However, if you are using a lighter cherry like Rainier or Emperor Francis, you may want to use an oxidizing treatment to preserve the color of the dried fruit.

Clean: For nonorganic cherries, follow the cleaning tips on page 331. Wash organic cherries with warm water, then dry.

How to prepare: Stem the fruit, cut in half, and remove the pit.

Suggested thickness: Whole or half

Drying time: 12 to 24 hours

Temperature: 125°F

Consistency when dry: Should not stick together; dried cherry will click when dropped on a countertop.

Blanching requirements: Your preference

Oxidizing treatment: Your preference

How to rehydrate: Simmer on stovetop until rehydrated. Use in desserts and syrup.

Consistency when rehydrated: Chewy

Yield: 10 ounces fresh cherries = 1 cup dried cherries = 1½ cups rehydrated cherries

Tip: Use a skewer and water bottles as a cherry pitter.

Citrus

Purchase thin-skinned citrus for the best flavor and juice. The peels can be used whole or made into powder for various recipes. Dried pieces can be steeped in vinegar to aid in cleaning, added to water for a tasty drink, or made into candied rinds. The pith can be used to make natural pectin. Powder the dried peels and mix with sugar, make lemon pepper spice, or add to scones and baked goods. Use in place of extract or zest. All store-bought citrus must be washed to remove the wax coating before dehydrating.

Clean: For nonorganic citrus fruits, follow the cleaning tips on page 331. For organic fruits, wash with warm water then dry.

How to prepare: Use a mandoline for even cuts. Save the ends to dry for use in vinegar-based cleaner. Remove the pith and cut into strips.

Suggested thickness: ⅛-inch sliced rounds

Drying time: 4 to 8 hours

Temperature: 125°F

Consistency when dry: Crisp

Blanching requirements: N/A

Oxidizing treatment: N/A

How to rehydrate: Cover with cool water for 10 to 15 minutes.

Consistency when rehydrated: Like fresh

Yield: 1 medium orange or 2 to 3 lemons = 1 cup dehydrated citrus rounds = 1 tablespoon citrus powder = ¾ cup rehydrated citrus rounds

Tip: Dry the citrus ends with the rest of the batch and save them for making infused vinegar for cleaning. To use, add dried citrus ends to a canning jar and cover with white vinegar. Allow the mixture to steep for one to two weeks. Strain the citrus peels and discard to the compost pile. The vinegar can be diluted one to one with water and will retain the fresh scent.

Coconut

The fresh taste of your own dried coconut is worth the effort. It also makes healthy milk for drinking and flour for baking. For ideas on how to use your dehydrated coconut, see Shredded Coconut (page 501), Coconut Flour (page 502), and Sweet Potato Coconut Flour Pancakes (page 511).

Clean: Wash and dry, then process using instructions below. There is no special treatment for organic versus nonorganic.

How to prepare: Poke a hole in the top of the nut and drain the water. Cut in half. Remove the outer bark and skin and shred or slice the meat into equal-size pieces.

Suggested thickness: Shredded, or cut into ⅜-inch pieces

Drying time: 4 to 8 hours

Temperature: 125°F

Consistency when dry: Leathery to crisp

Blanching requirements: N/A

Oxidizing treatment: N/A

How to rehydrate: Add twice as much hot water as coconut and soak for 30 minutes.

Consistency when rehydrated: Like fresh

Yield: 1 small coconut = 1 cup dehydrated coconut = 1½ cups coconut flour = ¾ cup rehydrated coconut

Corn

We eat a lot of corn but do not grow it ourselves because of where we live. Central Texas is corn country, and there are acres and acres of GMO corn growing in the field right next door. Corn is a wind-pollinated crop, and it is likely that there would be cross-pollination between the GMO corn and the open pollinated crops I would be growing. Instead, I purchase frozen organic corn from Costco. This saves us a ton of prep time, because there is no cutting or blanching required.

Clean: For nonorganic corn, follow the cleaning tips on page 331. For organic corn, wash with warm water and pat dry. No need to clean if using frozen corn.

How to prepare: Shuck the ears and clean each corn cob, removing all tassels. Place whole cobs in boiling water and cook until tender, 6 to 8 minutes. Transfer to a bowl of ice water and allow the corn to cool. Use a de-cobber or sharp knife to remove the kernels from the cob. Pour kernels evenly onto dehydrator trays.

Suggested thickness: Individual kernels

Drying time: 6 to 8 hours for fresh; 8 to 10 hours for frozen

Temperature: 125°F

Consistency when dry: Brittle

Blanching requirements: See above.

Oxidizing treatment: N/A

How to rehydrate: Soak 1 cup corn in 2¼ cups water for half an hour. Or, add directly to soup, stew, and skillet meals.

Consistency when rehydrated: Like fresh cooked

Yield: 2 cups fresh corn kernels = 1 cup dried corn kernels = 1½ cups rehydrated corn

Cucumbers

While we often think of making pickles when we want to preserve cucumbers, putting them into the dehydrator can bring another dimension to your soups and sauces. You can take dried cucumber chips, process them into a powder, and add them to homemade salad dressing (see Creamy Cucumber Salad Dressing on page 498). Or you can include them in morning smoothies, or spice the chips up using the recipe for Zucchini Chips on page 506.

Clean: For nonorganic cucumbers, follow the cleaning tips on page 331. For organic cucumbers, wash with warm water, then dry.

How to prepare: Slice into rounds.

Suggested thickness: ¼ inch thick

Drying time: 4 to 6 hours

Temperature: 135°F

Consistency when dry: Brittle; should snap when bent.

Blanching requirements: N/A

Oxidizing treatment: N/A

How to rehydrate: Soak in cool water for 30 to 60 minutes.

Consistency when rehydrated: Fresh tasting, limp texture

Yield: 1 cup fresh cucumber = ¼ cup dehydrated cucumber = ¾ cup rehydrated cucumber

Tip: You can make a pickle brine to rehydrate your cucumber slices. (See the Dehydrated Refrigerator Pickles recipe on page 507.) They'll turn out just as crunchy as fresh homemade refrigerator pickles. Or, you can dehydrate a jar of store-bought pickle spears or chips. Your family will love the change in texture, and it beats carrying a messy pickle in your lunch box. Be cautious though: These pickle chips are very salty when finished, and it is easy to eat a whole jar in one sitting.

Eggplant

Useful for Italian eggplant and tomato casseroles, eggplant will darken if not blanched before processing for storage. Oriental eggplant is long and thin and has a milder flavor than standard grocery store eggplant. It makes an excellent garden crop for USDA Plant Hardiness Zones 4 to 11.

Clean: For nonorganic eggplant, follow the cleaning tips on page 331. For organic eggplant, wash with warm water and pat dry.

How to prepare: Dice, slice, or cube. Prepare as you would use in recipes.

Suggested thickness: ¼ inch thick

Drying time: 6 to 12 hours

Temperature: 125°F

Consistency when dry: Leathery

Blanching requirements: Blanch for 15 seconds in boiling water.

Oxidizing treatment: N/A

How to rehydrate: Combine eggplant and cool water in even ratio, and then soak for 30 minutes.

Consistency when rehydrated: A bit leathery, but the flavor is excellent, like cooked eggplant.

Yield: 2 cups fresh eggplant = 1 cup dried eggplant = 1¼ cups rehydrated eggplant

Figs

Figs are extremely sticky as they dry. Be sure that they do not overlap or they will stick together. Consider using parchment paper on the trays for easy cleanup. Be sure to use only ripe fruit for this project. Before storage, lightly toss your figs with sugar if they stick together.

For any recipe calling for peaches, pears, prunes, or dates, you can successfully substitute figs. Try out these fruits by making Oatmeal Fig Cookies on page 522.

Clean: For nonorganic figs, follow the cleaning tips on page 331. Wash organic figs with warm water and pat dry.

How to prepare: For fresh figs, remove stems and cut out blemishes. Pierce the skin if drying whole small figs.

Suggested thickness: Cut in half or quarter. Place figs on the tray skin-side down.

Drying time: Time varies. Start checking at eight hours; could take up to 24 hours to finish. Turning the fruit may speed up the process.

Temperature: 125°F

Consistency when dry: Leathery and flexible

Blanching requirements: If drying figs whole, plunge in boiling water for 30 seconds.

Oxidizing treatment: N/A

How to rehydrate: Pour enough boiling water to cover, then let sit for 30 minutes.

Consistency when rehydrated: Not typically rehydrated. Used dried as snacks and in recipes.

Yield: 2 cups fresh fig pieces = 1 cup dried figs

Tip: Extend the shelf life of store-purchased dried figs by running them through the dehydrator for a few hours.

Garlic

Garlic seasoning is a pantry staple at our home; we use it with almost every meal. Garlic is planted in the fall after the first frost, and there are over 50 different varieties of soft-neck and hard-neck garlic adapted to every growing region. If possible, try to grow your own garlic and preserve it; the fresh taste will be worth it. You can purchase garlic cloves for planting at TheGarlicStore.com, SeedSavers.org, or TerritorialSeed.com. Using the square-foot gardening spacing method, you can grow nine cloves per square foot.

If you are not the gardening type, purchase large jars of organic garlic from a big box store and save yourself a lot of chopping time. A 32-ounce container will run you around $14 and make approximately 8 ounces of garlic powder when it's dried.

Clean: For organic and nonorganic garlic, separate and peel cloves, then remove root ends.

How to prepare: Slice with a mandoline or chop in a food processor.

Suggested thickness: See above.

Drying time: 6 to 12 hours

Temperature: 125°F

Consistency when dry: Crisp

Blanching requirements: N/A

Oxidizing treatment: N/A

How to rehydrate: Use as powder or break into bits for soup or stir-fry.

Consistency when rehydrated: Like cooked

Yield: 1 cup fresh garlic = ¼ cup dehydrated garlic = ¾ cup rehydrated garlic

Tip: Store the dried garlic in an airtight container in the freezer and grind it as you are using it in recipes. It will keep its freshness for over a year if stored this way.

Ginger

Candied ginger is expensive, so we make our own. The cooking process also makes ginger syrup, which can be bottled and used for ginger ale, on pancakes, or drizzled over your favorite oatmeal. See page 521 for our Candied Ginger recipe!

Clean: For organic and nonorganic ginger, wash with warm water and dry.

How to prepare: Peel if making candied ginger.

Suggested thickness: ⅛-inch slices

Drying time: 4 to 6 hours

Temperature: 135°F

Consistency when dry: Pliable

Blanching requirements: No need to cook if chopping for ground ginger. If making candied ginger, see instructions on page 521.

Oxidizing treatment: N/A

How to rehydrate: Not usually rehydrated. Instead, chop and use in salads, cookies, gingerbread, or in herbal tea.

Consistency when rehydrated: N/A

Yield: 1 cup fresh ginger = ½ cup dried ginger = ¾ cup rehydrated ginger

Grapes

If you are lucky enough to grow your own grapes, you have an advantage. Commercially grown grapes are notorious for pesticide residue and are consistently in the top 10 of the Environmental Working Group (EWG) list of "Dirty Dozen."[9] Pay special attention to cleaning your nonorganic grapes before dehydrating.

Clean: For nonorganic grapes, follow the cleaning tips on page 331. Wash organic grapes with warm water, then dry.

How to prepare: Remove from stems after blanching.

Suggested thickness: Leave whole

Drying time: 15 to 30 hours, depending on size

Temperature: 135°F

Consistency when dry: Pliable

Blanching requirements: Dip in boiling water for 30 seconds, then into ice water to cool. This makes the skins ready for processing and reduces the drying time by half.

Oxidizing treatment: N/A

How to rehydrate: N/A

---

9 "DIRTY DOZEN: EWG's 2017 Shopper's Guide to Pesticides in Produce," EWG, Accessed November 13, 2017, https://www.ewg.org/foodnews/dirty_dozen_list.php#.We5VcGiPKUk.

Consistency when rehydrated: Dried grapes are raisins and cannot be reconstituted. Use dried in recipes or for snacks.

Yield: 1 cup fresh grapes = ¼ cup raisins

Tip: Dried and powdered grape leaves make a nice tea. Wash the leaves and pat dry. Pile the grapes on dehydrator trays, no more than ½ inch thick, then stir after three hours. Dry at 90°F for approximately 6 hours, or until crisp.

Green Onions and Leeks

Green onions and leeks dehydrate extremely well with minimal effort. Look for them to go on sale during their peak season, August to December, and stock up.

Clean: Prepare organic and nonorganic onions by washing with cool water, and pat to dry.

How to prepare: Cut off root ends, cut off ¼ inch from tops, remove any limp leaves.

Suggested thickness: Slice into ½-inch-thick rings.

Drying time: 8 to 12 hours

Temperature: 125°F

Consistency when dry: Papery

Blanching requirements: N/A

Oxidizing treatment: N/A

How to rehydrate: Add directly to soup, or spritz with cool water.

Consistency when rehydrated: Like fresh

Yield: 2 cups fresh green onions = 1 cup dried green onions = 1¼ cups rehydrated green onions

Tip: Separate green stalks from white ends on dehydrator trays. The tops will dry at a different rate, and this will keep you from picking out the dried parts while waiting for the rest to finish.

Horseradish

Horseradish is an old-fashioned crop enjoying a comeback in the garden. Harvest the roots each fall and leave enough roots in the ground for next year's crop. Make your own sauce in a blender with ¼ cup grated root, 1 tablespoon mustard, 1 teaspoon vinegar, 1 cup sour cream, and salt and pepper to taste.

Clean: Wash organic and nonorganic horseradish with warm water and a vegetable brush, then dry.

How to prepare: Remove small rootlets and stubs. Peel and scrape the root.

Suggested thickness: Grate and spread in a single thickness on dehydrator trays.

Drying time: 4 to 8 hours

Temperature: 125°F

Consistency when dry: Brittle

Blanching requirements: N/A

Oxidizing treatment: N/A

How to rehydrate: Soak 1 cup horseradish in 1 cup warm water for 30 minutes; rehydrating not necessary if using horseradish in cooking.

Consistency when rehydrated: Like fresh

Yield: 1 cup fresh horseradish = ½ cup dehydrated horseradish = ¾ cup rehydrated horseradish

Tip: Store the horseradish pieces in a vacuum-sealed jar until you need to use it. Break off a piece and run it through a coffee grinder that you set aside just for pungent herbs and spices.

Kale

Kale is enjoying a health food craze right now. It is high in iron, vitamin K, and vitamin A, and is filled with powerful antioxidants. Dehydrate with the purpose of making powder for smoothies (see powdering instructions on page 459), or experiment with making your own seasoned Kale Chips (page 506).

Clean: For nonorganic kale, follow the cleaning tips on page 331 and page 442. For organic kale, wash with cool water and pat dry.

How to prepare: Discard the stems by pinching or slicing.

Suggested thickness: 2- to 3-inch-wide pieces

Drying time: 2 to 6 hours

Temperature: 135°F

Consistency when dry: Crisp and papery

Blanching requirements: N/A

Oxidizing treatment: N/A

How to rehydrate: Use in smoothies or soup, eat dry as a chip.

Consistency when rehydrated: Like cooked

Yield: 2 cups fresh kale = 1 cup dried kale = 2 cups rehydrated kale

Kiwi

Kiwi grows on a vine in fairly acidic soil and can grow prolifically if you have the right conditions. It needs one male plant for every eight female plants, sturdy support, and temperatures with at least 240 frost-free days. Dried kiwi is best used as snacks and in a fresh salad.

Clean: Wash organic and nonorganic kiwi with warm water, then dry.

How to prepare: Remove peel.

Suggested thickness: Cut into ⅜- to ½-inch slices. Pieces should not touch on the trays, or they will stick together.

Drying time: 6 to 12 hours

Temperature: 125°F

Consistency when dry: Flexible, not sticky

Blanching requirements: N/A

Oxidizing treatment: Use lemon juice dip if you wish to keep the bright color.

How to rehydrate: Spray until plump, or eat dry as snacks.

Consistency when rehydrated: Like fresh

Yield: 2 cups fresh kiwi = 1 cup dried kiwi = 1½ cups rehydrated kiwi

Lettuce

We often have excess lettuce during the growing season, and it seems a shame to relegate it all to the compost bin. Some of the specialty spring mixes can become quite bitter once dried, so experiment to find the type of lettuce that suits your needs. Also, skip drying iceberg lettuce. It has very little nutritional value and is not worth the dehydrator space used to dry it. Lettuce is not typically rehydrated.

Clean: For nonorganic lettuce, follow the cleaning tips on page 331 and page 442. For organic lettuce, wash with cool water and pat dry.

How to prepare: Separate leaves from the head and remove thick stems or thick veins; they will slow the drying time.

Suggested thickness: Single leaves or half leaves

Drying time: 4 to 6 hours

Temperature: 110°F

Consistency when dry: Papery

Blanching requirements: N/A

Oxidizing treatment: N/A

How to rehydrate: Use as powder for smoothies or in green powder blend.

Consistency when rehydrated: N/A

Yield: 1 cup fresh lettuce = ¼ cup dehydrated lettuce leaf = approximately 1 tablespoon powdered lettuce leaf

Mangoes or Papayas

These flavorful treats have become a staple for morning yogurt toppings. Rehydrated mango and papaya can be used in smoothies or made into syrup.

Clean: For nonorganic mangoes or papaya, follow the cleaning tips on page 331. Wash organic fruits with warm water, then dry.

How to prepare: Remove skin with a vegetable peeler, then cut flesh into large flat sections from top to bottom. A mandoline works well for this because the fruit is slippery.

Suggested thickness: ⅜-inch slices or wedges. Use parchment paper to reduce sticking. Pieces will stick to dehydrator trays if sliced too thin.

Drying time: 6 to 12 hours

Temperature: 125°F

Consistency when dry: Flexible and papery, not sticky

Blanching requirements: N/A

Oxidizing treatment: If preferred, spray with lemon juice as you are adding to trays.

How to rehydrate: Place in a bowl and cover with boiling water for 15 minutes.

Consistency when rehydrated: Like fresh

Yield: 2 cups fresh mango = 1 cup dried mango = 1½ cups rehydrated mango

Melons

We never can grow enough melons to keep the kids happy, so we purchase them during peak season and then dehydrate them. You'll find that a few long slices of dry honeydew or cantaloupe are perfect for an afternoon snack.

Clean: Wash the outside of organic and nonorganic melon with dish soap and warm water and pat dry.

How to prepare: For melon dices, remove flesh from the rind and cut into even pieces. For slices, cut the melon in half and remove seeds. Cut the melon into eight sections, remove the rind, and slice each eighth into five pieces.

Suggested thickness: ¼- to ½-inch-thick slices, 1½-inch dices

Drying time: 8 to 10 hours

Temperature: 125°F

Consistency when dry: Pliable, with dry centers

Blanching requirements: N/A

Oxidizing treatment: N/A

How to rehydrate: Not usually rehydrated; eaten dried as snacks or as a garnish in oatmeal or yogurt.

Consistency when rehydrated: Soft

Yield: 2 cups fresh melon = 1 cup dried melon = 1½ cups rehydrated melon

Mushrooms

Some cooks would never think of preserving food in their kitchen without first washing it. Mushrooms may be the exception. Wet mushrooms will turn black and not dry well. But mushrooms are grown commercially in a soilless medium of sterilized hardwood sawdust or straw, so they are sanitary to eat without washing. For those that have a texture aversion to mushrooms, you can dry and process them to a powder.

The flavor released by mushrooms is called umami and adds depth to soups, stews, meatloaf, burger patties, and omelets.

Clean: Wash with cool water and air dry for 1 hour before processing. Or, skip the washing and remove any growing medium with a towel or soft brush.

How to prepare: Remove woody stems and set aside to make mushroom powder.

Suggested thickness: Small mushrooms can be dried whole; large ones should be cut into ⅜-inch slices. Purchase them pre-sliced when they're on sale, and save yourself time.

Drying time: 4 to 8 hours

Temperature: 125°F

Consistency when dry: Brittle

Blanching requirements: N/A

Oxidizing treatment: N/A

How to rehydrate: Use as powder or add directly to your dish during cooking.

Consistency when rehydrated: Like cooked

Yield: 1 cup sliced, fresh mushrooms = ½ cup dehydrated mushrooms = 1 teaspoon of mushroom powder

Onions (Yellow, White, Red, Sweet)

Onions are a staple in many home-cooked meals. You can store them in a pantry for a few months by hanging fresh onions in a mesh bag or pantyhose. For long-term storage, dehydrating is the only option. Buy them in bulk during peak season, August through December, and be sure to give them their own dehydrator time, as their unique flavor can taint other foods.

Clean: Treat organic and nonorganic onions the same. Wash with cool water, and dry.

How to prepare: Remove papery outer layer and cut into rings.

Suggested thickness: ½-inch pieces, sliced, chopped, or minced, depending on how it will be used.

Drying time: 10 to 14 hours

Temperature: 125°F

Consistency when dry: Brittle

Blanching requirements: Blanch 15 to 30 seconds in boiling water to speed up drying time. Skip blanching if you are making onion powder.

Oxidizing treatment: None, although sweet onions may turn yellow or pink. The color goes away once rehydrated.

How to rehydrate: Add onion directly to pot when cooking meals, or grind to make powder.

Consistency when rehydrated: Like fresh

Yield: 2 cups fresh onion = 1 cup dried onion = 1¼ cups rehydrated onion

Tip: Diced onions will easily fall through dehydrator tray holes. Dry them in 2- to 3-inch-long slices or rings and easily mince them in a food processor once they are completely dry.

Peaches or Nectarines

Use dried fruit as a healthy snack alternative. I prefer drying nectarines, mostly because I do not enjoy the process of removing the skin from peaches. Peach cobbler is mighty tasty, though, and might get me to reconsider. They are also great when cooked, pureed, and added to fruit leather. For another twist, try the Honey Peach BBQ Sauce (page 497).

Clean: For nonorganic peaches or nectarines, follow the cleaning tips on page 331. Wash organic fruits with warm water, then dry.

How to prepare: Peel if desired. Remove pit.

Suggested thickness: Cut into quarters or eighths. Lay on dehydrator sheets, not touching.

Drying time: 10 to 15 hours

Temperature: 125°F

Consistency when dry: Leathery

Blanching requirements: If removing skin from peaches, blanch for one minute in boiling water until the skin blisters.

Oxidizing treatment: Use lemon juice or ascorbic acid.

How to rehydrate: Pour boiling water over the dried fruits until just covered and let soak for 30 minutes, or until they rehydrate to the consistency you are seeking.

Consistency when rehydrated: Firm, like fresh

Yield: 2 cups fresh peaches or nectarines = 1 cup dried peaches or nectarines = 1¼ cups rehydrated peaches or nectarines

Pears

Interchangeable with apples at our house, pears can be rehydrated and made into a tasty spiced butter (try Slow Cooker Spiced Pear Butter on page 497) or used fresh to make fruit leather.

Clean: For nonorganic pears, follow the cleaning tips on page 331. Wash organic peaches with cool water, then dry.

How to prepare: Remove stems, and peel if desired. Slice and remove tough center and seeds.

Suggested thickness: Halves, quarters, or eighths

Drying time: 12 to 24 hours, depending on slice thickness

Temperature: 125°F

Consistency when dry: Leathery

Blanching requirements: Blanch for 2 minutes in place of oxidizing treatment.

Oxidizing treatment: Use ascorbic dip to keep from browning, if not blanching.

How to rehydrate: Pour boiling water over the dried pears until just covered and let soak for 30 minutes. Add more water if necessary.

Consistency when rehydrated: Like fresh cooked

Yield: 2 cups fresh pears = 1 cup dried pears = 1½ cups rehydrated pears

Peas and Chickpeas

Peas are a fantastic addition to your food storage plan. Each cup has very little fat and 8 grams of protein. If you purchase frozen peas, you can add them directly to the dehydrator trays and skip all the processing time. Canned peas are also a quick option, if you don't mind the taste.

Clean: Shell organic and nonorganic fresh peas and wash with warm water; drain and rinse canned peas; add frozen peas directly to trays.

How to prepare: Remove fresh peas from the pod.

Suggested thickness: N/A

Drying time: 8 to 12 hours

Temperature: 125°F

Consistency when dry: Hard

Blanching requirements: Steam or boil fresh peas for 4 minutes.

Oxidizing treatment: N/A

How to rehydrate: Add directly to soup or stew, or cover and soak in cool water for 1 hour.

Consistency when rehydrated: Like fresh

Yield: 3 cups fresh peas = 1 cup dried peas = 3 cups rehydrated peas

Peanut (Raw)

Unshelled raw peanuts that have been properly cured can be stored in airtight containers and will keep for up to a year. Follow the instructions below to get them ready for drying. Once you have prepared the peanuts for dehydrating, you can make roasted peanuts and Homemade Roasted Peanut Butter (page 498).

How to clean and prepare: Shell and soak 4 cups of raw peanuts in warm water with 1 tablespoon of kosher or sea salt for 12 to 24 hours. Drain and rinse. Place on dehydrator sheets in a single layer. Turn nuts at least once during the processing.

Suggested thickness: N/A

Drying time: 12 to 24 hours

Temperature: 155°F

Consistency when dry: Brittle

Blanching requirements: N/A

Oxidizing treatment: N/A

How to rehydrate: N/A, roast for snacking and making nut butter.

Consistency when rehydrated: N/A

Yield: 4 cups raw peanuts = 4 cups dehydrated peanuts = 4 cups rehydrated peanuts

Peppers (Hot, Sweet)

We grow as many of these as we can each year. They dehydrate wonderfully and keep in the pantry for long-term storage. We add diced peppers to our morning eggs: To a 10-inch skillet, add a handful of peppers and cover with water. Simmer until the water evaporates and then cook your eggs as usual.

Clean: For nonorganic peppers, follow the cleaning tips on page 331. For organic peppers, wash with warm water and pat dry.

How to prepare: Wash, stem, and core. Remove the pith and seeds. Protect eyes and hands if cutting hot peppers.

Suggested thickness: ⅜-inch disks or ½-inch dices

Drying time: 8 to 12 hours

Temperature: 125°F

Consistency when dry: Leathery to brittle

Blanching requirements: N/A

Oxidizing treatment: N/A

How to rehydrate: Soak 1 cup dried pepper in 2 cups water for 1 hour then drain, or simmer peppers in water for 10 to 15 minutes.

Consistency when rehydrated: Like fresh cooked

Yield: 2 cups fresh peppers = 1 cup dried peppers = 1½ cups rehydrated peppers

Pineapple

We use a lot of pineapple in our morning smoothies, and fresh pineapple is a treat when it is in season and a good price. If you can't find fresh pineapple, look for frozen or canned fruit packed in its own juice when it goes on sale. You control the sugar content when you make it yourself. Add pineapple powder to smoothies, eat it dry as a snack, or rehydrate for a fresh-tasting treat. For a delicious dessert, try Steve's Low-Fat Pineapple Cake on page 520.

Clean: Fresh organic or nonorganic pineapple should be washed with warm water and dried.

How to prepare: Remove top and bottom, quarter the flesh, and remove core and tough skin.

Suggested thickness: ½-inch cubes, ¼-inch slices, or crushed. Strive for uniformity on the trays, keeping like sizes together.

Drying time: 8 to 16 hours, depending on size of cuts

Temperature: 125° to 135°F

Consistency when dry: Brittle

Blanching requirements: N/A

Oxidizing treatment: N/A

How to rehydrate: Soak in cool water until plump.

Consistency when rehydrated: Like fresh

Yield: 2 cups fresh pineapple = 1 cup dehydrated pineapple = 1½ cups rehydrated pineapple = ¼ cup pineapple powder

Plums

Years ago, we had a plum tree that was completely unappreciated by our family. It continued to put out fruit each year without fail, and we did not see its potential until years after we had it removed. Think of all the jam we missed, what a waste! Use very ripe plums for the sweetest finished product: prunes.

Clean: For nonorganic plums, follow the cleaning tips on page 331. Wash organic plums with warm water, then dry.

How to prepare: Half or quarter the plum and remove the pit. Lay plums on trays skin side down, not touching.

Suggested thickness: Use quarters, which will dry faster than halves.

Drying time: 24+ hours

Temperature: 125°F

Consistency when dry: Leathery, pliable

Blanching requirements: Place in boiling water for 30 seconds to soften the skin.

Oxidizing treatment: Use lemon juice or ascorbic acid, if you'd like, for lighter colored fruit.

How to rehydrate: Place dried plums and water in a saucepan; bring to a boil. Cover, reduce heat, and simmer for 10 minutes, or until very tender.

Consistency when rehydrated: Like cooked

Yield: 2 cups fresh plums = 1 cup dried plums = 1½ cups rehydrated plums

Tip: Make prune powder. Cut the pieces into smaller sizes if you plan to powder the plums, and use the powder in smoothies.

Potatoes

Another staple of the prepared pantry, potatoes are so versatile that you don't want to be without them. The lowly potato keeps for four to six months in a properly ventilated root cellar; however, most of us don't have the luxury of an on-site cellar. For long-term storage of up to five years, dehydrate the potatoes. I find that it's best to have a use in mind before I dehydrate: Does the finished recipe need slices, shreds, or cubes? Shredded potatoes can be used in most recipes; try Hash Brown Mix in a Jar on page 515.

Any type of potato can be dehydrated. However, you may find that those with waxy skin, like yellow, white, and red potatoes will dry and rehydrate the best. If you are using frozen potatoes, it is not necessary to do the blanching process before dehydrating.

You might find that the center of the potato turns black after dehydrating. This happens when the outside dries quicker than the center. These potatoes are still OK to eat, but should not be stored long term.

Clean: For organic and nonorganic potatoes, scrub clean with hot water and a vegetable brush.

How to prepare: Keep peel for added nutrients. After cooking, process into slices, cubes, or shreds.

Suggested thickness: ⅛-inch round slices, ⅓-inch cubes, shreds

Drying time: 8 to 16 hours

Temperature: 125° to 135°F

Consistency when dry: Brittle, transparent

Blanching requirements: Boil for 5 to 6 minutes so a knife can be inserted partway through the potato.

Oxidizing treatment: Dip white potatoes in lemon juice or ascorbic acid.

How to rehydrate: Add directly to soup or stew, along with additional water; alternatively, soak in hot water for 30 minutes.

Consistency when rehydrated: Like fresh

Yield: 2 cups fresh diced potatoes = 1 cup dried potatoes = 1¼ cups rehydrated potatoes

Raspberries and Blackberries

I grew up in the Pacific Northwest, where the berries of summer have names like loganberry, blackberry, salmonberry, boysenberry, and marionberry. If you happen to live in berry country, you know these are the tastiest when purchased right from the farmer. Now that I live in Texas, these berries are expensive, and the quality does not compare. I rarely purchase them at the store and instead choose to purchase frozen berries. Next time I go back to Oregon in July, I'm going to dehydrate batches and batches of berries and FedEx them home!

Clean: For nonorganic berries, follow the cleaning tips on page 331. If possible, do not wash, because these berries are fragile. Completely air dry before dehydrating, because wet berries will not retain their shape during the drying process.

How to prepare: Stand berries on their flat end to dry all sides. Use dehydrator sheets; they will drip as they dry and you'll have juice on the trays below.

Suggested thickness: Dry whole

Drying time: 15 to 20 hours, depending on size

Temperature: 125°F

Consistency when dry: Brittle, or crushed to a powder

Blanching requirements: N/A

Oxidizing treatment: N/A

How to rehydrate: Mist with a spray bottle to retain shape; simmer in juice or water for pie filling. Make berry powder for smoothies.

Consistency when rehydrated: Like fresh cooked

Yield: 2 cups fresh berries = 1 cup dried berries = 1¼ cups rehydrated berries

Rhubarb

An old favorite once found in every kitchen garden, rhubarb is enjoying a boost in popularity as a home garden crop. It thrives in cold climates, where the ground freezes in the winter. The roots and leaves are poisonous and should not be eaten. The tender stalks are used for jam, pies, and as a condiment sauce, often combined with berries.

Clean: For nonorganic rhubarb, follow the cleaning tips on page 331. For organic rhubarb, wash with warm water and pat dry well.

How to prepare: Discard leaves, then cut stem into equal-size pieces.

Suggested thickness: ½-inch to 1-inch pieces

Drying time: 8 to 12 hours

Temperature: 135°F

Consistency when dry: Brittle

Blanching requirements: Steam 5 minutes or boil 1 minute until slightly tender. Dip in ice water to cool.

Oxidizing treatment: N/A

How to rehydrate: Soak in hot water until plump.

Consistency when rehydrated: Like fresh

Yield: 2½ cups fresh rhubarb = 1 cup dried rhubarb = 1½ cups rehydrated rhubarb

Spinach

Just like preserving lettuce, drying spinach leaves may seem like a strange thing to do. After all, the yield for 1 cup of spinach leaves is only 1 tablespoon of spinach powder. However, the health benefits of adding powdered spinach to smoothies, soups, and baked goods make it well worth your time. We purchase large bags of organic spinach at the local big box store, eat as much as we can, and then dehydrate the rest. This method makes spinach cost-effective, and nothing goes to waste.

Clean: For nonorganic spinach, follow the cleaning tips on page 331 and page 442. For organic spinach, wash with cool water and pat dry.

How to prepare: If using for cooking, remove stems. If powdering, leave whole.

Suggested thickness: Whole leaves

Drying time: 4 to 6 hours

Temperature: 110°F

Consistency when dry: Brittle

Blanching requirements: N/A

Oxidizing treatment: N/A

How to rehydrate: Add 1 cup dried spinach to 1 cup water and soak for half an hour. Alternatively, add directly to a recipe, or powder for baking.

Consistency when rehydrated: Like cooked

Yield: 2 cups fresh spinach = 1 cup dried spinach = 1½ cups rehydrated spinach = 1 tablespoon spinach powder

Strawberries

Strawberries are at the top of the EWG's "Dirty Dozen" list of fruit with the most pesticides. Unless you are purchasing organic or growing your own crop, it will be especially important to clean them thoroughly before drying them. If you don't have a source for fresh berries, frozen strawberries dry exceptionally well, but they will not hold their shape like fresh berries do after drying.

Clean: For nonorganic strawberries, follow the cleaning tips on page 331. For organic berries, wash with warm water and pat dry lightly.

How to prepare: Remove tops and soft spots.

Suggested thickness: Cut small to medium berries in half. Cut large berries into quarters.

Drying time: 8 to 16 hours

Temperature: 125°F

Consistency when dry: Pliable, dry in center

Blanching requirements: N/A

Oxidizing treatment: Use lemon juice or ascorbic acid, if you'd like, for lighter colored fruit.

How to rehydrate: Soak in hot water or warmed juice for 15 to 20 minutes, or simmer in water on the stovetop until the fruit is plump and has absorbed the water.

Consistency when rehydrated: Plump, but mushy. Best for sauces or shortcake.

Yield: 2½ cups fresh strawberries = 1 cup dried strawberries = 1 cup rehydrated strawberries

Summer Squash

An end-of-season garden often has an abundance of summer squash. We grow traditional zucchini, yellow crookneck, and pattypan each year, and then we cut them into cubes or shredded pieces for soup. They also make healthy chips. The Zucchini Chips recipe on page 506 is so popular that it's hard to keep them around the house. We change up the spices to fit the mood, and they are made with no oil, so the calories are minimal.

Clean: For both organic and nonorganic squash, wash using natural soap and warm water, then towel dry.

How to prepare: Cut off the ends, then use a mandoline to cut uniform slices.

Suggested thickness: ⅛- to ¼-inch rounds for chips, or ½-inch cubes

Drying time: 10 to 12 hours for chips, 12 to 18 hours for cubes

Temperature: 125°F

Consistency when dry: Crisp

Blanching requirements: N/A

Oxidizing treatment: N/A

How to rehydrate: Soak in warm water 15 minutes, drop whole into soup, or eat as chips.

Consistency when rehydrated: Like cooked

Yield: 2 cups fresh summer squash = 1 cup dried summer squash = 1½ cups rehydrated summer squash

Sweet Potatoes and Yams

Sweet potatoes are high in beta carotene, magnesium, calcium, potassium, and iron, as well as vitamins E and C. Just the things you'd like to have in a shelf-stable food storage plan! They will last three to five weeks in a dark, cool pantry and two to three months in the refrigerator. Dehydrating brings their storage time to as much as five years. For more ways to enjoy these tubers, try Sweet Potato Chips (page 505), Sweet Potato Powder (page 499), and mashed sweet potatoes (page 500), all of which can be made with yams too.

Clean: Scrub organic and nonorganic sweet potatoes clean with a vegetable brush and warm water, then pat dry.

How to prepare: Leave the skins on for added fiber, or peel and grate, slice, or cube.

Suggested thickness: ⅛-inch round slices; ⅓-inch cubes; shreds. Cut when cold.

Drying time: 8 to 16 hours

Temperature: 125°F

Consistency when dry: Brittle

Blanching requirements: Steam or boil until completely cooked. Cool in refrigerator overnight.

Oxidizing treatment: N/A

How to rehydrate: Add 1 cup dried sweet potatoes to 2 cups boiling water, soak for an hour. Alternatively, add cubes directly to a soup, or eat chips dried.

Consistency when rehydrated: Like freshly cooked

Yield: 2 cups fresh sweet potatoes = 1 cup dried sweet potatoes = 1½ cups rehydrated sweet potatoes

Tomatoes

Everyone wants to have tomatoes in their prepper food storage. It is the most versatile fruit you can store. We dry tomato pieces with the skin on and use them to make powder. The powder is then rehydrated to make paste and sauce. I find it quicker to dry them than to go through the whole process of blanching and skin peeling (something I heartily dislike), which is needed when you process them in a water bath canner.

Clean: For nonorganic tomatoes, follow the cleaning tips on page 331. For organic tomatoes, wash with warm water and pat dry.

How to prepare: Optionally, remove the skins by blanching. Core tomatoes and remove tomato ends.

Suggested thickness: Cut stewing or slicing tomatoes into quarters; cut cherry tomatoes in half.

Drying time: 8 to 12 hours

Temperature: 135°F

Consistency when dry: Leathery to brittle

Blanching requirements: With a knife, cut an X on the bottom of the tomato, just deep enough to penetrate the skin. Drop tomato into boiling water. Blanch for 20 to 30 seconds. Use a slotted spoon to remove tomato from boiling water. Immerse tomato in ice water. Use a knife to remove the tomato core. Skin will slip off.

Oxidizing treatment: N/A

How to rehydrate: Place tomatoes in a bowl and cover with cool water for 30 to 60 minutes, then drain. Alternatively, add a small amount of cool water to individual tomato pieces with a spray bottle. Continue this every 15 minutes or so until the fruit has plumped up.

Consistency when rehydrated: Soft, like cooked

Yield: 2 cups fresh tomatoes = 1 cup dried tomatoes = 1½ cups rehydrated tomatoes = ⅔ cup tomato powder

Tip: You can use shelf-stable tomato powder to make these common tomato products:

- Tomato paste = Equal amounts tomato powder + water
- Tomato sauce = 1 part tomato powder + 3 parts water
- Tomato soup = 1 part tomato powder + 1 part water + 2 parts cream
- Tomato juice = 1 teaspoon tomato powder + ½ cup water

Watermelon

Dehydrating a watermelon is not something that readily comes to mind, but if you are looking for a tasty snack that brings a bit of summer into your winter diet, this is it. You can store this long-term for more than a year (if you can keep it around that long) by first putting your dehydrated fruit in the freezer for two weeks to pasteurize it, and then by vacuum packing it in serving-size packages, with oxygen absorbers in each bag. Place the vacuum-packed bags in a storage container out of direct light.

Clean: Wash the rind of organic or nonorganic watermelon with soap and warm water, and dry.

How to prepare: Slice the melon into ½-inch-thick rounds. Cut meat away from the rinds and cut into 2- to 3-inch pieces. Discard seeds.

Suggested thickness: ½-inch rounds

Drying time: 8 to 12 hours

Temperature: 125°F

Consistency when dry: Like fruit leather

Blanching requirements: N/A

Oxidizing treatment: N/A

How to rehydrate: Not typically rehydrated; eaten as a dry snack.

Consistency when rehydrated: N/A

Yield: 2 cups fresh watermelon = ½ cup dehydrated watermelon = 1½ cups rehydrated watermelon

Tip: Black watermelon seeds can be made into a tasty snack similar to sunflower seeds. Rinse seeds to remove watermelon pulp and place on a dehydrator tray for 2 hours at 140°F, until completely dry. Place the dry seeds in a frying pan over medium heat and continually turn until roasted. Add 1 cup water and 1 tablespoon salt, then stir until evaporated. Allow them to cool completely before shelling and eating.

Winter Squash (Pumpkin, Acorn, Butternut, Delicata)

Winter squash is shelf stable for many months in the root cellar or in a cold, dark area of your pantry, but it will rapidly deteriorate if stored below 50°F. If you grow more than you can store, dehydrating is a viable option. The advantages of using a dehydrator to preserve your winter squash are threefold: The finished product is lightweight, it requires little storage space, and it will keep for many years if stored away from direct light and heat.

Winter squash varieties include acorn, buttercup, butternut, banana, golden delicious, Hubbard, and sweet meat. Dehydrated pumpkin and other winter squash cubes work well for soups and sautés (Sautéed Winter Squash with Apples on page 512). Dried and rehydrated cubes do not work well for pies and other recipes, like leathers (try Pumpkin Pie Leather on page 503); it is hard to get the correct consistency because of case hardening, so purees work better. Shredded squash dries well in small bird-nest serving sizes; try making Garlic Creole Spiced Squash Nests (page 513).

Clean: Wash the outside of organic or nonorganic winter squash with soap and warm water, then towel dry.

How to prepare: Peel and seed the squash, then puree or cut into pieces. To puree, cut the squash in half and cook, cut side down, at 400°F until completely soft, 30 to 45 minutes. Scoop the pulp into a bowl and use an immersion blender to puree. Flatten the pulp onto Paraflexx sheets no more than ¼ inch thick.

Suggested thickness: Cut into ¼-inch cubes or ¼-inch-thick strips, 1 to 2 inches long. Alternatively, puree or shred.

Drying time: 8 to 12 hours

Temperature: 140°F for 2 to 3 hours, then reduce temperature to 130°F and continue drying until squash is tough and brittle, 3 to 6 hours.

Consistency when dry: Brittle

Blanching requirements: Boil for 3 minutes.

Oxidizing treatment: N/A

How to rehydrate: Pour boiling water over the dehydrated squash pieces and let soak for 30 minutes before draining and proceeding with your recipe. Save the soaking liquid to use in soups. Drop bird-nest shreds into boiling water. Or, for fruit leather, pour boiling water over pieces cut into 1-inch squares, then mix until it reaches the consistency you are looking for.

Consistency when rehydrated: Like freshly blanched

Yield: 2½ cups fresh winter squash = 1 cup dried winter squash = 2 cups rehydrated winter squash

CHAPTER 10

Recipes

Blueberry Basil Syrup

Making a syrup from dehydrated fruit is a great way to extend the usefulness of your pantry. Plus, who doesn't like warm blueberries on their Sunday morning pancakes? You can swap blueberries for any fruit, omit or replace the herbs in this recipe, or substitute store-bought juice instead of processing fresh fruit into juice. It's that versatile!

Yield: 3 cups   Prep time: 10 minutes   Cook time: 10 minutes

2 cups dehydrated blueberries	¼ cup dried basil leaves
2 cups sugar	⅛ teaspoon ascorbic acid (optional)

1. To make blueberry juice, cook the dehydrated blueberries in 2½ cups water in a nonreactive pan. Bring to a boil and simmer for 10 minutes, stirring and mashing the fruit as it cooks. Strain through a colander to remove the berries. Set aside berries.

2. Combine the blueberry juice, sugar, and basil leaves in a saucepan, and bring to a full boil. Reduce the heat and simmer for 5 minutes. Skim off any foam.

3. Remove saucepan from the heat and strain out the basil leaves.

4. Optionally, if you like blueberry pieces in your syrup, return the strained syrup to the saucepan and add back the berries. Simmer for 2 minutes.

5. Remove saucepan from heat and add ascorbic acid. Stir to combine.

6. Pour the finished syrup into sterilized jars, seal, and label. This syrup can be used immediately or stored in swing-top bottles for up to a year with ascorbic acid added, or 6 months without it. Reducing the sugar content will reduce the shelf life. You can store any opened bottles in the refrigerator for up to 2 weeks.

Pectin with Citrus Pith

Dehydrating citrus can leave you with a lot of pith (that white, bitter substance under the flavorful rind), which is high in pectin. Most food preservation techniques call for composting the pith, but you can turn it into homemade pectin for thickening jam and jelly. Any citrus works for this recipe, and you can freeze small amounts of pith until you have enough for a batch. Looking for citrus with a lot of pith? It's all about the skin thickness. Thick-skinned citrus fruits will have a lot of pith inside.

Yield: 2 cups   Prep time: 5 minutes   Cook time: 20 minutes, plus rest time

½ pound citrus pith and seeds

¼ cup citrus juice, such as lemon

1. Use a vegetable peeler to remove the skin from the fruit. Save the skin for dehydrating.

2. Use a vegetable peeler to remove the pith. Chop the pith and set it aside, along with the seeds.

3. Add pith, seeds, and citrus juice to a medium, nonreactive pot. Let pot stand for an hour.

4. Add 2 cups water and let it stand another hour.

5. Bring the ingredients of the pot to a boil over high heat. Reduce heat, and simmer for 15 minutes. Cool to room temperature.

6. Place mixture in a jelly bag and allow it to drain. Press to remove juice.

7. Store extra pectin in the freezer.

The Pectin Test

Pour 1 teaspoon of homemade pectin into a glass cup. Add 1 teaspoon of rubbing alcohol and shake gently. If the pectin forms a solid jelly clot, it is ready to use in a recipe in a one-to-one ratio with sugar.

Pink Grapefruit Jelly

Yield: 2 cups   Prep time: 15 minutes   Cook time: 30 minutes

 4 handfuls dehydrated pink grapefruit peels
 or rounds

 2 cups cool water

 1½ cups sugar

1. Place grapefruit peels or rounds in a large bowl and cover with cool water until plump, about 15 minutes. Drain and reserve the grapefruit liquid.

2. Chop the rehydrated grapefruit into small pieces.

3. Measure ½ pound of the chopped grapefruit pieces, and add to a nonreactive pot along with the reserved water and sugar. Add enough water to cover the grapefruit pieces, if needed. Boil until thoroughly cooked, 30 minutes.

4. Drain through a jelly bag. Allow to slightly cool and press out all liquid.

Ginger and Lemon Infused Honey

It's best to use dried herbs for this recipe. To reduce the risk of adding bacteria to the infused honey, you must wash and completely dry off any fresh herbs or spices you plan on using. Use this recipe when you feel a cold coming on, as it is very soothing.

Yield: 1 cup   Prep time: 5 minutes, plus 2-week wait time

 1 tablespoon dried ginger

 1 teaspoon dried citrus peel

 1 cup raw, unfiltered, unpasteurized honey,
 slightly warmed

1. Place the dried ginger and citrus into a coffee grinder and chop to release the aromatic flavors.

2. Place the ginger and citrus in a tea bag or square of cheesecloth and tie with string so the bag/cheesecloth will remain closed. (It is almost impossible to pick dried herbs out of honey.)

3. In a pint jar, pour three quarters of the slightly warmed honey over the top of the herb bag. Use a chopstick or skewer to stir the honey, remove air bubbles, and make sure the herb bag is completely moistened.

4. Top off the jar with the remaining honey. Screw the lid on tightly. Place the jar out of direct sunlight, in an area where you will be able to monitor the process.

5. Allow the flavors to infuse for 2 weeks. If you have a problem with the spice bag floating to the surface, turn the jar upside down.

6. After 2 weeks, remove the tea bag and store the honey in the pantry for up to a year.

Honey Peach BBQ Sauce

Brush this sweet, spicy sauce over chicken or pork in the last few minutes of grilling. It thickens as it cools. Use less chipotle for a milder sauce.

Yield: 1 cup   Prep time: 30 minutes   Cook time: 20 minutes

16 slices dehydrated peaches or 1 cup fresh sliced peaches

2 teaspoons olive oil

1 cup chopped onion

1 teaspoon salt

1 teaspoon chipotle powder

¼ teaspoon ground cumin

pinch of allspice

¼ cup honey

4 teaspoons apple cider vinegar

1. Place peaches in a large bowl, cover with warm water, and soak for 30 minutes. Drain and discard soaking liquid. Roughly chop the rehydrated peaches and set aside.

2. Coat the bottom of a medium saucepan with olive oil. Over medium heat, add onions and cook until softened and starting to brown, 5 minutes.

3. Add salt, chipotle, cumin, and allspice and cook until the spices smell fragrant, about 30 seconds.

4. Add rehydrated peaches, honey, and vinegar, and stir to coat.

5. Cover saucepan, increase heat to medium-high, and cook until the peaches are completely soft and breaking down, 15 minutes.

6. Transfer to a blender to puree, or use an immersion blender. Add additional apple cider vinegar for thinner sauce.

Slow Cooker Spiced Pear Butter

As an alternative, you can make the recipe with fresh pears and dehydrate the finished recipe. To reconstitute, add small amounts of boiling water until the butter reaches the consistency you want.

Yield: 3 cups   Prep time: 1 hour   Cook time: 4 to 8 hours

1 pound dehydrated pear sections (approximately 10 fresh pears)

¼ cup brown sugar

1 tablespoon cinnamon

1 teaspoon ground ginger

½ teaspoon ground nutmeg

1. Add the dehydrated pears to a slow cooker and add enough water to cover the fruit. With the lid off, cook on low for 1 hour until the pears rehydrate.

2. Add the remaining ingredients to the slow cooker, stir to combine, and cover.

3. Cook for 4 hours on high or 6 to 8 hours on low.

4. Use an immersion blender to puree the mixture, or transfer to a blender and blend in small batches.

5. Store in the refrigerator for up to 3 weeks.

Homemade Roasted Peanut Butter

Enjoy this peanut butter as is, or experiment by adding dark chocolate powder, banana chips, white chocolate chips, maple, or coconut during the blending process. Did you know that raw peanuts taste like beans? For the best flavor, raw peanuts must be soaked and dehydrated before they are roasted for peanut butter.

Yield: ½ cup   Prep time: 20 minutes   Cook time: 5 minutes

    2 cups dehydrated peanuts

    honey, to taste

1. Preheat oven to 300°F.

2. Spread peanuts no more than ½ inch thick on a baking sheet. Roast for 20 minutes. When properly roasted, they will be slightly browned and have the taste of peanuts, nutty and pleasant, not like a bean.

3. In a food processor, grind the roasted peanuts until butter forms, approximately 5 minutes. Scrape the sides and add honey to taste, processing another minute until it reaches the consistency you want. Additional vegetable or peanut oil can be added if you want thinner peanut butter.

Creamy Cucumber Salad Dressing

Yield: 2 cups   Prep time: 15 minutes

    1 cup dehydrated cucumber chips

    ½ cup dehydrated green onions

    ½ teaspoon dried garlic

    ¾ cup light sour cream

    1 tablespoon light mayonnaise

    1 tablespoon lemon juice

    1 teaspoon dried dill weed, basil, or parsley

1. Place cucumber chips and onions in a large bowl, cover with cool water, and soak for 15 minutes. Drain and discard soaking liquid.

2. Blend the rehydrated vegetables and remaining ingredients in a blender or small food processor until smooth.

3. Add a splash of milk if the dressing needs to be thinned.

Tomato Powder

The drier your tomatoes, the easier they will be to powder. So if you intend to turn your dried tomatoes into a powder, you may want to dehydrate them for an extra hour or two than is recommended in the Tomatoes section on page 491. The entire process can take quite a bit of time and is entirely dependent on the quality of the grinder you use; I've found that a coffee grinder works best. It's worth it, however, to have a few cups of tomato powder on hand for quick cooking needs.

Yield: ⅔ cup   Prep time: 5 minutes

1 cup dehydrated tomatoes, divided

1. In ¼-cup batches, grind dehydrated tomatoes in a food processor, blender, or coffee grinder until tomatoes reach powder form.

2. Transfer to a mesh strainer and, using a spatula, move the pieces around until the powder falls through the mesh.

Sweet Potato Powder

Sweet potato powder rehydrates quickly using boiling water to create "instant" mashed sweet potatoes. It's great if you are making baby food, or want to serve a healthy side dish. Store the sweet potato powder in a jar and refrigerate for up to 1 month. For additional storage time, include a 100cc oxygen absorber in the jar, or vacuum-seal the jar with a FoodSaver jar attachment. Refrigerate for up to 3 months.

Yield: 2 cups mash, ½ cup powder   Prep time: 60 minutes   Cook time: 5 to 8 hours

2 pounds sweet potatoes

1. Peel sweet potatoes, or leave skins on for an added nutritional benefit. Cut into thin strips. Boil for 10 to 15 minutes, until the sweet potatoes are soft, then drain and reserve cooking liquid. Alternatively, bake whole and cut strips when cooked.

2. Mash the sweet potatoes to a smooth consistency. Thin with water, preferably cooking liquid, if necessary.

3. Spread ½ cup of potato mash on each Paraflexx sheet, plastic wrap–lined tray, or on fruit leather sheets. Spread VERY thin.

4. Dry at 135°F for 4 to 6 hours. When the top is dry, turn the sheets of sweet potatoes over, remove the tray wrap, and dry the underside for another 1 to 2 hours if necessary.

5. Stop drying when the sweet potato sheets are crispy, and the product crumbles.

6. Process into a powder by adding the dehydrated sweet potato bark into a blender or food processor and blending.

Other Uses for Sweet Potato Powder

- Make instant mashed sweet potatoes by slowly adding hot water to powdered sweet potatoes until you reach a thick mashed-potato consistency. Add sugar and spices as needed.

- Make sweet potato biscuits by replacing ½ cup white flour with sweet potato flour.

- Add sweet potato powder to morning smoothies.

- Make morning porridge by combining 1 tablespoon sweet potato powder, dried fruit, and ½ cup quick oats with 1 cup boiling water.

Green Powder Blend

If you find yourself with extra greens in the crisper drawer, don't let them go to waste. Any greens will do. It's easy to make a green powder blend that uses these leftovers, and it will be every bit as healthy as eating fresh greens. You can use the powder in smoothies to add more greens to your diet. Store vegetables as individual powders or create a blend of your favorites.

Yield: 2 cups powder   Prep time: 5 minutes   Cook time: 4 to 8 hours

> 6 cups fresh spinach leaves
> 6 cups fresh kale leaves

1. It is not necessary to trim the vegetable leaves before dehydrating; however, you may want to remove tough ribs, stems, and seeds.

2. Dry vegetables at 100°F and begin checking for dryness at 4 hours. Depending on the size of the leaves and their thickness, this may take up to 8 hours.

3. Once dry, rub the leaves between your hands to break them into smaller pieces. Grind the pieces in a food processor, blender, or coffee grinder until greens reach powder form. Strain powder through a sieve. Re-blend any large pieces until it is all powdered.

Leftover Vegetables You Can Powder

- beet and turnip tops
- bell peppers
- herb cuttings
- kale
- leeks and green onions
- lettuce greens
- spinach
- bok choi

Celery Salt

Use this salt for everyday cooking, canning, and even fermenting projects. Be sure to adjust your recipe for the salt content. Store celery salt in a canning jar; it will last for at least 1 year under normal pantry conditions.

Yield: 1 cup   Prep time: 5 minutes

> ½ cup dried celery stalks and leaves
>
> ½ cup kosher salt, plus more as needed

1. Grind the celery in a coffee grinder or food processor until finely ground.

2. Add the kosher salt and process in short bursts for a minute, until the mixture reaches the consistency you are looking for. Play around with the ratio of salt and celery to fit your taste.

Shredded Coconut

You really have to love fresh coconut to go through all the trouble of cracking, peeling, and shredding them! Use a small-holed or medium-holed grater for fine or regular shreds, a slicer for coconut chips, or a vegetable peeler for thicker chips.

Yield: 2 to 3 cups   Prep time: 20 minutes   Cook time: 6 to 10 hours

> 1 small fresh coconut, husked

1. Poke a hole in the top of the coconut and drain the milk.

2. Using a hammer, break the coconut in half along the center mark. Remove the hard outer shell.

3. Remove the soft outer membrane with a vegetable peeler or sharp knife.

4. Grate the fresh coconut meat in several ways.

5. Dry small and medium shreds on a dehydrator tray at 110°F for 6 to 8 hours. Thick coconut shreds may take up to 10 hours to finish.

Coconut Flour

Sometimes it will be necessary to increase the amount of liquid used in a recipe that has coconut flour. Since coconut flour loves moisture, it will absorb additional liquid in a recipe. Store flour for up to 6 months in an airtight container, in a dark, cool cabinet until ready to use.

Yield: ½ cup   Prep time: 5 minutes   Cook time: 2 to 4 hours

> 1 cup Shredded Coconut (page 501)
>
> 2 cups water

1. Place the shredded coconut in a blender with 2 cups water. Process on high until the coconut is finely chopped.

2. Strain the milk through a jelly bag; save to drink.

3. Take the pulp, spread it on a dehydrator Paraflexx sheet, and dry it at 110°F for 2 to 4 hours.

4. Once dried, process the dehydrated pulp into a fine powder. This coconut flour will have less fat and also require more water or egg when used in recipes.

Variation: You can omit the water and process the shredded coconut in small batches in a blender until it is the consistency of a fine powder. This flour has a higher fat content and won't be as drying in recipes.

Strawberry Banana Rolls

Most often used as snacks, fruit leather can also be rehydrated and used in pie fillings and dessert toppings, or made into a soup base with vegetables, bouillon, and spices. Use these for backpacking or emergency kit snacks.

Yield: 3 large trays, 24 rolls   Prep time: 10 minutes   Cook time: 6 to 8 hours

> 2 pounds strawberries, hulled
>
> 3 medium-size ripe bananas
>
> honey (optional)
>
> water or fruit juice, as needed

1. Cut the strawberries into quarters, then add to a blender.

2. Break bananas up into 2-inch pieces, then add to the blender.

3. Add honey to taste, if desired.

4. Following the no-cook directions for fruit leather on page 451, blend the fruit until smooth. Add water or juice in 1-tablespoon increments, as needed, to thin the mixture.

5. Cover dehydrator trays with a plastic fruit leather tray or plastic wrap. Spoon the mixture in equal amounts onto dehydrator trays. Cover with tray covers or plastic wrap. Dry at 125°F for 6 to 8 hours.

Cinnamon Apple Leather

Yield: 4 large trays, 36 rolls   Prep time: 40 minutes   Cook time: 6 to 10 hours

8 sweet apples, peeled and cored

1 cup water

ground cinnamon, to taste

2 tablespoons lemon juice

sugar, to taste (optional)

1. Roughly chop the apples. Add apples and water to a large pot. Cover and simmer over medium-low heat for 15 minutes.

2. Mash the apples in the pot, then add cinnamon, lemon juice, and sugar, if using. Simmer for 10 minutes.

3. Allow mixture to cool, then run small batches of apples through a blender or food mill until a consistent puree forms.

4. Cover dehydrator trays with a plastic fruit leather tray or plastic wrap. Spread the puree onto dehydrator trays to form a ¼-inch-thick layer. Cover with tray covers or plastic wrap. Dry at 125°F for 6 to 10 hours.

Pumpkin Pie Leather

Yield: 3 large trays, 24 rolls   Prep time: 5 to 20 minutes if using canned pumpkin; 40 to 60 minutes for fresh pumpkin   Cook time: 8 to 10 hours

1 (29-ounce) can pumpkin or 3 cups fresh pumpkin, cooked and pureed

¼ cup honey

¼ cup applesauce

2 teaspoons ground cinnamon

½ teaspoon ground nutmeg

½ teaspoon powdered cloves

½ teaspoon ground ginger

1. Mix all the ingredients in a large bowl until puree forms.

2. Cover dehydrator trays with a plastic fruit leather tray or plastic wrap. Spread the puree onto dehydrator trays to form a ¼-inch-thick layer. Cover with tray covers or plastic wrap. Dry at 130°F for 8 to 10 hours.

Pizza Blend Tomato Leather

This tomato leather can be made plain and rehydrated to make sauce, or you can use the Pizza Seasoning Blend, below, to add flavor.

Yield: 2 large trays, 16 rolls   Prep time: 40 minutes   Cook time: 8 to 12 hours

1 pound tomatoes, cored and quartered

½ tablespoon Pizza Seasoning Blend (optional)

1. Cook the tomatoes in a covered medium saucepan over low heat for 15 to 20 minutes. Remove from heat and let cool for a few minutes.

2. Puree the cooked tomatoes in a blender or food processor until smooth. Add seasoning, if using, and blend.

3. Return the puree to the saucepan and heat until the water has evaporated and the sauce has thickened.

4. Cover dehydrator trays with a plastic fruit leather tray or plastic wrap. Spread the tomato puree onto dehydrator trays to form a ¼-inch-thick layer. Cover with tray covers or plastic wrap. Dry at 135°F for 8 to 12 hours.

PIZZA SEASONING BLEND

1½ teaspoons dried basil	½ teaspoon dried thyme
1½ teaspoons dried oregano	½ teaspoon garlic powder
1½ teaspoons dried onion	½ teaspoon salt
1½ teaspoons dried rosemary	½ teaspoon red pepper flakes

Mix together and run through a spice mill or coffee grinder to get a powder. Use ½ tablespoon per pound of tomatoes.

Mixed Vegetable Leather

Yield: 1 large tray, 8 rolls   Prep time: 40 minutes   Cook time: 4 to 8 hours

2 cups tomatoes, cored and cut into chunks	1 sprig basil
1 small onion, chopped	salt, to taste
¼ cup chopped celery	

1. Cook all the ingredients in a covered medium saucepan over low heat for 15 to 20 minutes. Remove from heat and let cool for a few minutes.

2. Add to a blender and puree until smooth.

3. Return the puree to the saucepan and heat until the water has evaporated and the sauce has thickened.

4. Cover dehydrator trays with a plastic fruit leather tray or plastic wrap. Spread the puree onto dehydrator trays to form a ¼-inch-thick layer. Cover with tray covers or plastic wrap. Dry at 135°F, until it is pliable (for a wrap), about 4 hours, or until crisp (to use in soups and casseroles), 6 to 8 hours.

Tomato Wraps

This vegetable leather does not require cooking. Use as a wrap for snacks, or around meat and cheese. Try this method with other vegetables, like cucumber, spinach, zucchini, yellow squash, eggplant, or carrot. Experiment with adding spices, peppers, onions, garlic, ground flax, or chia seed.

Yield: 2 large trays, 6 wraps   Prep time: 5 minutes   Cook time: 4 hours

    2 pounds tomatoes, cored and chopped

    seasonings, to taste

1. Puree the fresh tomatoes in a blender or food processor until smooth.

2. Add seasoning as desired.

3. Cover dehydrator trays with a plastic fruit leather tray or plastic wrap. Spread the puree onto dehydrator trays to form a ¼-inch-thick layer. Cover with tray covers or plastic wrap. Dry at 125°F until pliable and able to remove from the trays, but not crisp, about 4 hours.

Sweet Potato Chips

My family enjoys sweet potato chips, a healthy alternative to store-bought potato chips. Some people recommend making these chips without cooking the potatoes, but I don't. Without precooking, the chips will be hard as a rock, and impossible to eat. Season chips with your favorite flavors. Try sugar, cinnamon, and nutmeg; salt, pepper, and onion powder; or salt and smoked paprika. Alternatively, you can leave the chips "naked" and rehydrate them to use in soups and stews.

Yield: 6 cups   Prep time: 15 minutes   Cook time: 4 to 8 hours

    4 large sweet potatoes

1. Peel potatoes, or leave skins on for an added nutritional benefit.

2. Using a mandoline, slice each potato into ⅛-inch-thick rounds.

3. Add the rounds to a large pot of boiling water and cook until just soft, about 10 minutes. Drain and discard liquid. Do not overcook; they should retain their shape when handled.

4. Lay wet sweet potato rounds on dehydrator trays. They should not touch.

5. Sprinkle salt and seasoning on chip rounds (optional).

6. Dry at 125°F for 4 to 8 hours until the chips are crispy and the centers are done.

Kale Chips

Flavor kale chips with your favorite seasoning blend, or eat them "naked." Consider these blends: lemon pepper, salt and pepper (simple but very tasty, especially tossed with apple cider vinegar), or Cajun seasoning blend.

Yield: 2 cups   Prep time: 5 minutes   Cook time: 4 to 6 hours

> 1 bunch kale, stems removed
>
> 1 tablespoon olive oil or apple cider vinegar
>
> seasoning, as desired

1. Cut the kale leaves into 2- to 3-inch strips.

2. Brush the kale lightly with olive oil or use apple cider vinegar as a low-fat alternative to oil. This gives the seasoning something to adhere to.

3. Sprinkle the kale with your choice of seasoning.

4. Lay the seasoned kale onto dehydrator trays and dry at 125°F for 4 to 6 hours, until they are crisp.

Zucchini Chips

The spice measurements below are just suggestions. Start with these spice measurements; you'll know how to adjust to your taste after the first batch. Use 1 teaspoon chili powder for mild, 2 teaspoons for medium, and 3 teaspoons for a spicy chip.

Yield: 5 cups   Prep time: 15 minutes   Cook time: 10 to 12 hours

> 4 medium zucchini squash
>
> ¼ cup apple cider vinegar
>
> salt, to taste
>
> pepper, to taste
>
> chili powder, to taste

1. Slice the zucchini into ¼-inch-thick rounds. It's best to keep the thickness the same for even drying. Experiment with using a crinkle cut slicing blade that makes ridges in the chips; the ridges tend to give spices more area to grab onto.

2. Add apple cider vinegar, salt, pepper, and chili powder to a wide bottomed, nonreactive bowl. Stir until incorporated.

3. Add a handful of raw chips to the bowl and toss until they are just coated with the vinegar and spice mix. Separate any pieces that stick together and make sure that all the zucchini slices are coated with the spices.

4. Arrange the chips on dehydrator trays. They can touch but should not overlap.

5. Dry at 135°F for 10 to 12 hours. If you have a bottom-heating dehydrator, you may need to rearrange the trays halfway through the drying cycle. After 5 hours, move the top trays to the bottom so the chips will be evenly dried.

CAJUN SEASONING BLEND

This is a versatile blend that we use when making kale or zucchini chips. We also add it to soup and skillet meals. Store seasoning blends in an airtight container in the pantry, for up to a year.

Yield: 1½ cups

¼ cup garlic powder

¼ cup kosher or sea salt

½ cup paprika

2 tablespoons pepper

2 tablespoons onion powder

2 tablespoons dried oregano

1 tablespoon dried thyme

1 tablespoon cayenne powder (optional)

Mix all the ingredients into a jar with enough room to shake the ingredients.

Dehydrated Refrigerator Pickles

Many other dehydrated vegetables can be pickled following this method, such as green beans, okra, zucchini, carrots, garlic scrapes, etc. Swap out the dill seed for turmeric, black peppercorns, or mustard seeds. Pick your favorite vinegar: apple cider, white, balsamic, or red or white wine. Experiment to find your family's favorite recipe.

Yield: 1 pint   Prep time: 5 minutes   Cook time: At least 24-hour wait time

1 cup vinegar

1 cup water

1½ tablespoons pickling salt or kosher salt

1 garlic clove, smashed

¼ teaspoon dill seed

⅛ teaspoon red pepper flakes

1½ cups dehydrated cucumber slices or spears

1. To prepare the brine, combine vinegar, water, and salt in a small saucepan over high heat. Bring to a rolling boil, then remove immediately and allow to cool.

2. Add the garlic, dill seed, red pepper flakes, and dehydrated cucumber slices to a pint-size canning jar.

3. Pour the cooled brine over the cucumbers, filling the jar to within ½ inch of the top. You might not use all the brine.

4. Refrigerate for at least 24 hours before eating. The cucumbers will plump and magically become pickles overnight.

My Classic Beef Jerky

Use a lean cut of beef, like eye round roast, top round roast, or bottom round roast.

Yield: ¾ pound   Prep time: 15 minutes, plus overnight   Cook time: 5 to 8 hours

1½ pounds lean beef

2 cups white vinegar

CLASSIC BEEF BRINE

¼ cup soy sauce

⅓ cup Worcestershire sauce

1 tablespoon barbecue sauce

½ teaspoon pepper

½ teaspoon salt

½ teaspoon onion

½ teaspoon garlic

1. Cut beef into ¼-inch slices.

2. In a medium bowl, pretreat the beef slices with the white vinegar for 10 minutes. Drain and discard the white vinegar.

3. Add the drained beef slices and brine ingredients to a 1-gallon zip-top bag. Add water, if necessary, to completely cover the meat. Soak overnight in the refrigerator.

4. The next day, drain the brine, lay out the meat so the pieces do not touch, and dehydrate at 160°F for 5 to 8 hours until crisp but pliable.

Teriyaki Brine: For an Asian twist, use these ingredients for the brine: ⅔ cup teriyaki sauce, 1 tablespoon soy sauce, ½ cup water or pineapple juice, ½ teaspoon onion powder, ½ teaspoon fresh garlic, ½ teaspoon salt, and ½ teaspoon pepper.

Spicy Cajun Brine: If you like spicy, try a Cajun brine: ½ cup balsamic vinegar, ⅓ cup Worcestershire sauce, ⅓ cup water, 1 tablespoon molasses, 1 tablespoon Cajun spice, 1 teaspoon smoked paprika, ½ teaspoon salt, ½ teaspoon pepper, and ¼ teaspoon cayenne powder.

Beef Steak Jerky

Use a lean cut of beef, like eye round roast, top round roast, or bottom round roast.

Yield: ¾ pound   Prep time: 15 minutes, plus overnight   Cook time: 5 to 8 hours

1½ pounds lean beef

2 cups white vinegar

BEEF STEAK BRINE

¼ cup balsamic vinegar

⅓ cup Worcestershire sauce

1 tablespoon molasses

1 tablespoon Steak Seasoning Blend (see recipe below)

1 teaspoon fresh garlic

1 teaspoon onion powder

1. Cut beef into ¼-inch slices.

2. In a medium bowl, pretreat the beef slices with the white vinegar for 10 minutes. Drain and discard the white vinegar.

3. Add the drained beef slices and brine ingredients to a 1-gallon zip-top bag. Add water, if necessary, to completely cover the meat. Soak overnight in the refrigerator.

4. The next day, drain the brine, lay out the meat so the pieces do not touch, and dehydrate at 160°F for 5 to 8 hours until crisp but pliable.

STEAK SEASONING BLEND

2 tablespoons coarse salt	1 tablespoon mustard seed
1 tablespoon pepper	½ tablespoon dill seed
1 tablespoon coriander	½ tablespoon red pepper flakes

Mix together and run through a spice mill or coffee grinder to get a powder. Use ½ tablespoon per 1½ pounds of meat.

Cauliflower Soup

Make this soup your own by adding your choice of seasonings: cumin, parsley, and basil all work well. Serve with an added pinch of cheese for garnish.

Yield: 6 cups   Prep time: 40 minutes   Cook time: 15 minutes

2 cups dehydrated cauliflower	⅛ cup quinoa
⅛ cup dehydrated onion	4 cups vegetable stock
⅛ cup dehydrated celery	pepper, to taste
2 slices dehydrated garlic	salt, to taste
2½ cups water	seasoning, to taste

1. Place cauliflower, onion, celery, and garlic in a large bowl and cover with 2½ cups boiling water. Soak until vegetables are almost rehydrated, about 30 minutes. Drain and discard soaking liquid.

2. In a large saucepan, add the vegetables, quinoa, vegetable stock, salt, pepper, and seasoning, to taste. Cook over medium heat for 15 minutes, until the cauliflower and quinoa are soft and fully cooked.

3. Remove from heat and pour small batches into a blender to mix. Be careful—it will be very hot. Blend until smooth, 45 to 60 seconds.

Asparagus Soup

Yield: 6 cups   Prep time: 10 minutes   Cook time: 20 minutes

2 cups dehydrated asparagus

1 cup water

2 tablespoons butter or extra virgin olive oil

½ teaspoon dried basil or 10 fresh basil leaves, chopped

4 cups chicken broth or stock

salt and pepper, to taste

1. Place the asparagus and water in a saucepan and simmer over medium heat for 5 to 10 minutes until the asparagus pieces are plump. Drain and reserve asparagus liquid.

2. Add the asparagus, butter, and basil to a stockpot at medium heat until the butter is melted, about 1 minute.

3. Add the chicken stock and asparagus water to the stockpot and bring heat up to high until the mixture comes to a boil. Reduce heat and simmer for 10 minutes. Remove from heat and cool about 5 minutes.

4. In small batches, pour the warm soup into a blender and puree to desired texture. After pureeing, transfer small batches to a large bowl to keep them separate. I like to keep a few blender batches with larger pieces, so the soup has texture.

5. Return mixture to the stockpot and add salt and pepper to taste.

Thermos Vegetable Soup

Make this in the morning, and it will be ready to eat by lunchtime. Combine any dried vegetables for this soup, including peas, tomatoes, broccoli, onion, zucchini, celery, and carrots. This works best if your vegetables are all approximately the same size.

Yield: 2 cups   Prep time: 5 minutes   Cook time: 4 hours

⅓ cup dried vegetables

¼ teaspoon dried parsley

¼ teaspoon dried sweet basil

pinch garlic powder

pinch onion powder

salt and pepper, to taste

1 tablespoon spaghetti, broken into small sections

2 cups boiling chicken or beef broth

1. Fill an empty Thermos with boiling water. Just before you pack the ingredients in the Thermos, pour out the hot water.

2. Add the dried vegetables, parsley, basil, garlic powder, onion powder, salt, pepper, and pasta to the Thermos.

3. Bring the chicken or beef broth to a rolling boil and pour over dry ingredients. Quickly cover the Thermos and close securely. If possible, shake or turn over the Thermos every hour until ready to eat.

Sweet Potato Coconut Flour Pancakes

Yield: 6 medium pancakes   Prep time: 5 minutes   Cook time: 2 to 4 minutes

5 eggs

¼ cup milk

½ teaspoon vanilla extract

½ cup unsweetened applesauce

¼ cup Coconut Flour (page 502)

¼ cup Sweet Potato Powder (page 499)

1 tablespoon granulated sugar or honey

¼ teaspoon baking powder

ground cinnamon, to taste

¼ teaspoon salt

1. Preheat a griddle or large skillet over medium heat.

2. In a large bowl, whisk eggs, milk, vanilla, and applesauce until combined.

3. In a medium bowl, whisk coconut flour, sweet potato flour, sugar or honey, baking powder, cinnamon, and salt until well blended.

4. Add dry ingredients to wet ingredients. Stir with a fork until ingredients are well combined and no lumps remain.

5. Drop batter by the ladleful, approximately ¼ cup at a time, onto the hot griddle. Cook 2 to 4 minutes per side until small bubbles begin to form on top, then flip.

6. Serve warm with your favorite pancake toppings.

Slow Cooker Stuffed Cabbage Rolls

Yield: 8 to 12 rolls   Prep time: 20 minutes   Cook time: 8 to 10 hours

8 to 12 dehydrated cabbage leaves

¼ cup dehydrated diced onion

⅔ cup tomato powder

1 tablespoon brown sugar (optional)

1 teaspoon Worcestershire sauce (optional)

1 cup cooked white rice

1 egg, beaten

1 pound extra-lean ground beef

1 teaspoon salt, plus more to taste

1 teaspoon pepper, plus more to taste

1. Bring a large pot of water to a boil. Add dehydrated cabbage leaves and boil for 2 to 3 minutes, until soft. Drain and set aside.

2. In a small bowl, cover diced onion with hot water to rehydrate, about 15 minutes.

3. To make tomato sauce, put the tomato powder in a medium bowl. Slowly pour in 2 cups of boiling water and whisk well to reduce chunks. Whisk in brown sugar and Worcestershire sauce, if using. Set aside.

4. In a large bowl, combine cooked rice, egg, ground beef, onion, 2 tablespoons tomato sauce, salt, and pepper. Stir with a spoon, or dig in and mush with clean hands.

5. Place about ¼ cup of the mixture in each cabbage leaf, roll up, and tuck ends in. Place rolls in slow cooker.

6. Pour remaining tomato sauce over cabbage rolls. Cover and cook on low 8 to 10 hours.

Sautéed Winter Squash with Apples

Yield: 2 cups   Prep time: 1 hour   Cook time: 10 minutes

1 cup dehydrated winter squash cubes	½ teaspoon celery salt
½ cup dehydrated onion	½ teaspoon garlic powder
½ cup dehydrated apple	½ teaspoon thyme
2 tablespoons butter	salt and pepper, to taste

1. Place dehydrated squash cubes and onion in a large bowl and cover with 2 cups of warm water. Soak for 1 hour. Drain any remaining water.

2. Rehydrate the apple by placing it in a separate bowl and covering with cool water for 1 hour.

3. Melt the butter in a large saucepan over medium heat.

4. Add the squash, onion, and celery salt to the saucepan, stirring occasionally until the squash begins to brown, about 5 minutes.

5. Add the garlic powder and apple, cooking until the apples are tender, about 2 minutes.

6. Add thyme, salt, and pepper to taste.

Dehydrated Winter Squash Nests

These squash nests will be cooked before eating, so it is not necessary to blanch them. However, you may find that peeling and spiralizing is easier if the squash is microwaved for 3 minutes after seeding. Delicata and butternut squash work well for this recipe.

Yield: 10 to 15 squash nests   Prep time: 30 minutes   Cook time: 4 to 6 hours

1 large winter squash, peeled and deseeded

1. If using a spiralizer, cut the squash into manageable pieces and shred the squash into long strands. If you don't have a spiralizer, draw a vegetable peeler down over the squash, making thin, broad, noodle-like slices, or use a julienne peeler to get spaghetti-like strands.

2. Not all the pieces will spiral in one long section, so separate the parts that do by removing them from the pile.

3. Add the long strands to dehydrator trays and arrange them in a nest by piling each piece on top of itself. Add the smaller pieces to dehydrator trays in small handfuls to form nests, 5 or 6 piles to a tray.

4. Dry at 140°F for 2 hours, turn heat down to 130°F and dry an additional 2 to 4 hours until the pieces are brittle.

Garlic Creole Spiced Squash Nests

Yield: 10 nests   Prep time: 35 minutes   Cook time: 5 minutes

10 Dehydrated Winter Squash Nests (page 512), or 2 cups dried squash shreds

⅓ cup all-purpose flour

2 cloves garlic, minced

2 large eggs, beaten

1 tablespoon Creole Spice Blend (below)

2 tablespoons olive oil

10 teaspoons cheddar cheese

1. Partially rehydrate the squash nests by soaking in hot water for 30 minutes. Drain and discard soaking liquid.

2. In a large bowl, combine flour, garlic, eggs, and Creole seasoning. Dip the butternut squash nests in the egg mixture, taking care not to break apart the nests.

3. Heat olive oil in a large skillet over medium-high heat.

4. Scoop out 1 nest for each serving. Place in the skillet and flatten the squash with a spatula, then cook until the underside is golden brown, about 2 minutes.

5. Flip and cook on the other side, about 2 minutes longer.

6. Top each nest with 1 teaspoon of cheddar cheese and serve immediately.

CREOLE SPICE BLEND

Yield: about ½ cup

1 tablespoon onion powder

1 tablespoon garlic powder

1 tablespoon dried basil

½ tablespoon dried thyme

½ tablespoon black pepper

½ tablespoon white pepper

½ tablespoon cayenne pepper

2½ tablespoons paprika

1½ tablespoons salt

Combine onion powder, garlic powder, dried basil, dried thyme, pepper, paprika, and salt in a small bowl. Mix thoroughly.

Riced Cauliflower Pizza Crust

This cauliflower crust is a healthy alternative to traditional pizza crusts. Substitute one quarter of the cheese with a low-fat alternative to reduce calories.

Yield: 2 (8-inch) crusts   Prep time: 40 minutes   Cook time: 15 to 20 minutes

1 cup dehydrated cauliflower	2 eggs
4 cups water	2 cups grated Parmesan cheese

1. Preheat oven to 400°F.

2. Place cauliflower in a large bowl, cover with 4 cups hot water, and soak for 20 minutes. Drain and discard soaking liquid.

3. Chop the rehydrated cauliflower by hand, or with a food processor, until the pieces are small and uniform in size.

4. Cook the riced cauliflower in a skillet over medium heat. Stir until cauliflower is dry and the moisture is removed.

5. Set the cauliflower aside and allow it to cool. It may cool faster if it is removed from the skillet.

6. In a separate bowl, whisk the eggs. Mix in Parmesan cheese.

7. Add cooled cauliflower to the bowl, and stir until completely mixed.

8. Working on parchment paper, split the mixture into 2 equal portions. Work each piece into an 8-inch circle, about ¼ inch thick. Keep more of the mixture on the edges so the rounds will cook evenly and the edges will not burn.

9. Slide the parchment paper onto a baking sheet and cook at 400°F until the rounds are browned and firm, about 15 to 20 minutes.

Ideas for Serving Cauliflower Crust

- Spread with tomato sauce, spices, cheese, and pizza toppings. Bake like a pizza for 10 to 15 minutes until the cheese melts and the toppings are cooked.

- Spread with tomato sauce, spices, and toppings. Roll into a log and bake on parchment paper for 15 minutes. Top with cheese, green onions, and sour cream. Cut into 1-inch sections to serve.

- After the crust has cooled, section the crust into 16 equal strips. Sprinkle with your favorite spices (see Cajun Seasoning Blend on page 507), then reheat at 400°F for 10 minutes. The strips will be a tasty, crisp snack.

Fajita Beans and Rice

This is a spicy blend; omit cayenne pepper for a mild version.

Yield: 1 pint jar dry; 6 cups cooked   Prep time: 35 minutes   Cook time: 20 to 25 minutes

1 cup Quick Brown Rice (page 516)

2 cups Quick Cook Beans (page 516)

¼ cup dehydrated sweet bell pepper

¼ cup dehydrated onion

¼ cup dehydrated carrot

¼ cup tomato powder

¼ teaspoon dried garlic

1 teaspoon chili powder

½ teaspoon salt

½ teaspoon paprika

½ teaspoon brown sugar

¼ teaspoon black pepper

¼ teaspoon oregano

¼ teaspoon cumin

⅛ teaspoon cayenne pepper

1. Place all ingredients in a 1-pint wide-mouth jar or Mylar bag. Add a 100cc oxygen absorber and seal tightly. Store for up to 5 years.

2. To serve, remove the oxygen packet and empty the contents of the jar into a large skillet. Cover with 6 cups water and bring to a boil over high heat. Reduce heat to medium, cover, and simmer for 15 to 20 minutes, occasionally stirring until the beans are done.

3. Garnish with grated cheese, to taste.

Hash Brown Mix in a Jar

Dry the ingredients separately and combine. This recipe makes 1 jar, with 2 meals.

Yield: 1 pint jar dry; 2 cups cooked   Prep time: 10 to 15 minutes   Cook time: 10 to 15 minutes

2 cups dehydrated potato shreds

½ cup dried onion

½ cup dried sweet pepper

¼ cup dried minced garlic

1 teaspoon vegetable oil

1. Mix the potato shreds, dried onion, dried sweet pepper, and dried minced garlic in a large bowl. Place in a canning jar or Mylar bag. Add a 100cc oxygen absorber and seal tightly. Store for up to 5 years.

2. To prepare, empty 1 cup of the jar's contents into a bowl and cover with boiling water for 10 to 15 minutes until plump. Strain and squeeze to remove excess water.

3. Heat oil in a skillet over medium heat.

4. Add potato mixture to the skillet, gently pressing into a thin, even layer as it cooks.

5. Cook until very crispy and brown each side for approximately 3 minutes.

Quick Brown Rice

Store dehydrated rice in canning jars with 100cc oxygen absorbers, or remove oxygen with a FoodSaver attachment. Due to the high fat content of brown rice, Quick Brown Rice should be used within 6 months.

Yield: 2 cups dehydrated rice; 3½ cups cooked rice   Prep time: 5 to 7 hours   Cook time: 17 minutes

   2 cups uncooked brown rice

1. Cook 2 cups of regular brown rice according to package directions; make sure all liquid is absorbed.

2. Cover your dehydrator trays with parchment paper or Paraflexx liners and spread the cooked rice in a single layer. Dehydrate at 125°F for 5 to 7 hours. Midway through the drying process, break up any rice that is stuck together and rotate trays. When fully dry, the rice should click when dropped on a tabletop.

3. To rehydrate, measure 1 cup of dried rice, place in a saucepan, and cover with ¾ cup water. Soak for 5 minutes to begin rehydration, then bring to boil and boil for 2 minutes. Remove from heat, cover, and let sit 10 minutes. Fluff with a fork.

Quick Cook Beans

Yield: 3 cups   Prep time: 10 minutes, plus 8 hours   Cook time: 8 to 10 hours

   4 cups dry beans

1. Soak dried beans overnight. Discard water.

2. After at least 8 hours of soaking, add the beans to a large pot, cover with water, and bring to a boil. Reduce heat and simmer for 10 minutes. Drain.

3. Spread the partially cooked beans in a single layer on dehydrator trays and process between 95°F and 100°F for 8 to 10 hours. They will be hard when dry.

4. Store in canning jars with 100cc oxygen absorbers or remove oxygen with a FoodSaver attachment. The shelf life is 5 years.

To rehydrate: Soak 1 cup dehydrated beans and 2 cups water in a saucepan for 5 minutes. Bring to a rolling boil for 10 minutes. Do not cover.

Mrs. B's Stovetop Baked Beans

Yield: 3 cups   Prep time: 15 minutes   Cook time: 10 minutes

1 cup Quick Cook Beans (page 516)	2 teaspoons mustard
2 cups water	⅛ cup packed brown sugar, or to taste
¼ cup dehydrated chopped onion	1 teaspoon Worcestershire sauce

1. Rehydrate the Quick Cook Beans by soaking the beans with 2 cups water in a saucepan for 5 minutes. Bring to a rolling boil for 10 minutes. Do not cover.

2. Add the remaining ingredients. Stir until brown sugar is dissolved.

3. Reduce the heat to medium and simmer for an additional 5 minutes until beans are soft and sauce forms. Add additional water in 1-teaspoon increments, if needed.

Mexican Fiesta Bake

Yield: 1 (2½-quart) baking dish   Prep time: 45 minutes   Cook time: 15 minutes

1 cup dehydrated tomatoes	2 cups ground beef
1 cup fresh or dehydrated cilantro leaves	1 teaspoon garlic
½ cup dehydrated, diced green pepper	1 lime, juiced
½ cup dehydrated corn kernels	6 corn tortillas, cut into 1-inch squares
¼ cup tomato powder	1 cup cheddar cheese
2 fresh jalapeño peppers	

1. Preheat oven to 350°F.

2. Place the dehydrated tomatoes in a small bowl and cover with 2 cups of cool water for 30 minutes, or until plump and tender. Drain and dice into bite-sized pieces.

3. Place the cilantro leaves, diced green pepper, and corn in a small bowl and add enough cool water to cover. Let soak for 10 to 15 minutes or until peppers plump. Drain.

4. To make tomato sauce, slowly add 12 ounces of hot water to ¼ cup tomato powder. Mix until smooth. Set aside.

5. Clean, seed, and dice 2 fresh jalapeño peppers.

6. Cook the ground beef in a large skillet until completely browned.

7. Add the tomato sauce, garlic, lime juice, tomato, cilantro, green pepper, corn, tortillas, and jalapeño to the ground beef. Stir, and heat throughout.

8. Transfer to a 2½-quart baking dish and top with cheese.

9. Bake for 15 minutes until the cheese is bubbly.

Rose Hip Mint Tea

Rose hips have more vitamin C than most citrus fruits. They are sweet and could be used on their own to make a tea, but the addition of mint makes this drink even more refreshing. This recipe is also a great help with stomach ailments and flatulence.

Don't throw out the rose hips once they've been used to make tea. Eat them, instead. They retain their nutritional value, so after you're done drinking the tea, add the rose hips to soups or serve them as a side at the supper table.

Yield: 1 cup   Prep time: 0 minutes   Steep time: 10 to 15 minutes

- 1 teaspoon dried rose hips
- 1 teaspoon dried spearmint or peppermint
- 1 cup water

1. Add the mint and rose hips to a French press or teapot and pour in 1 cup of hot water. Some tea makers grind their rose hips before using them, but it really is not necessary.

2. Cover and steep for 10 to 15 minutes. The longer you steep, the deeper the flavor and color will be.

Orange Mint Tea Blend

Yield: 1 cup   Prep time: 5 minutes, plus rest time   Steep time: 10 minutes

- 2 tablespoons dried, chopped mint
- 2 tablespoons dried orange
- 3 or 4 whole cloves (optional)

1. Measure the dry ingredients into a coffee grinder or mortar and pestle and process until they are mixed into uniform pieces. Place in a jar with a tight lid and allow the flavor to develop for a few days.

2. Add 1 teaspoon of Orange Mint Tea Blend to a tea ball infuser, teapot, or French press. Cover and steep for 10 minutes. This also makes a refreshing iced tea.

Lemon Verbena Sun Tea

Lemon verbena is medicinally known as a digestive herb. It helps soothe indigestion, flatulence, and colic. It is mildly astringent, and using it to create a rinse for your mouth can help ward off candida.

Yield. 1 quart   Prep time: 0 minutes   Steep time: several hours

- 1 handful dried lemon verbena leaves
- 1 quart water

1. Crush a handful of dried leaves and add them to a large glass jar.

2. Cover leaves with 1 quart water and let the jar sit out in the sun for several hours.

3. Strain the leaves and add ice to enjoy a refreshing drink.

Lemonade with Dehydrated Citrus

Yield: 5 quarts   Prep time: 0 minutes   Cook time: 3 hours rest time

   1 cup sugar

   5 quarts water

   15 pieces dehydrated citrus rounds

1. Add the sugar to 5 quarts water and stir until dissolved.

2. Add citrus pieces and stir.

3. Add ice to help keep the rinds submerged. Let it sit for at least 3 hours.

4. Stir and pour into glasses with some of the rehydrated citrus rounds as a garnish.

Apple Crisp with Oat Topping

Yield: 1 (8 x 8-inch) glass pan   Prep time: 35 minutes   Cook time: 30 minutes

3 cups dehydrated apple slices	½ cup flour
¾ cup sugar, divided	½ cup oats
⅛ teaspoon ground cinnamon, plus more, to taste	pinch salt
2 tablespoons cornstarch	½ stick cold butter

1. Preheat oven to 375°F. Prepare an 8 x 8-inch glass pan with cooking spray.

2. Place the apple slices in a bowl and add just enough hot water to cover. Let it sit for 30 minutes. Drain and reserve the liquid.

3. Toss the rehydrated apples with ½ cup sugar and cinnamon, to taste.

4. In a measuring cup, mix cornstarch and 2 tablespoons cold water until completely incorporated and no lumps remain.

5. Place the apples and reserved liquid into a medium saucepan and simmer for 5 minutes. Add the cornstarch slurry and heat until the mixture thickens. If the apples look too dry, add more liquid, 1 tablespoon at a time, until you reach the consistency you want.

6. Spoon the apples into the prepared pan, pushing down, so the apples are covered in the sauce.

7. To create the topping, add the flour, oats, remaining sugar, salt, and ⅛ teaspoon cinnamon to a small bowl. Using a pastry blender or food processor, cut the cold butter into the dry ingredients until the mixture resembles coarse crumbs.

8. Pour the topping over the apple filling and spread evenly until it reaches all corners. Bake for 30 minutes until the topping is golden brown and the filling is bubbling.

Steve's Low-Fat Pineapple Cake

This recipe is a family favorite that has been adapted for low-fat diets. It is not overly sweet, but it satisfies your cravings.

Yield: 1 (8 x 8-inch) cake   Prep time: 25 minutes   Cook time: 25 to 30 minutes

4 cups dehydrated pineapple

2 cups water

2¼ cups all-purpose flour

1 cup granulated sugar

2 teaspoons baking soda

pinch salt

2 teaspoons vanilla extract

2 eggs

1 (3.5-ounce) package sugar-free vanilla instant pudding

1½ cups fat-free whipped cream

1. Preheat oven to 350°F. Grease and flour an 8 x 8-inch baking dish.

2. Crush the dehydrated pineapple in a plastic zip-top bag with a rolling pin, or pulse in a food processor. Pineapple should be in pieces, not powdered. Reserve 2 cups.

3. Put the rest of the crushed pineapple in a small bowl and completely cover with 2 cups cool tap water for 15 to 20 minutes. Add more water if needed. Drain and reserve the pineapple liquid.

4. In a medium bowl, whisk together the flour, sugar, baking soda, and salt.

5. Add the vanilla extract and eggs to the small bowl with rehydrated pineapple, and mix.

6. Add the wet ingredients to the dry and stir until batter forms.

7. Pour the batter into the prepared baking dish.

8. Bake for 25 to 30 minutes until the cake is golden brown and a toothpick comes out clean. Let cool before adding topping.

9. Whisk the 2 cups crushed pineapple, pineapple liquid, and sugar-free pudding mix together until combined. Add extra water in 1-teaspoon increments, if needed. Gently fold in the whipping cream until incorporated.

10. Spread topping over the cake. Refrigerate until ready to serve.

Candied Ginger

You can save and store the ginger syrup from step 5 in your refrigerator for up to 2 months. If you find that you've run out of syrup, you can use the candied ginger to make more.

Yield: 8 ounces candied ginger   Prep time: 40 minutes, plus 1 hour conditioning time   Cook time: 4 to 6 hours

   1 large (8-ounce) ginger root

   4 cups water

   2¼ cups sugar, divided

1. Wash and peel the ginger root. Using a mandoline, cut the root into ⅛-inch slices.

2. Add 4 cups water and 2 cups sugar to the saucepan, and stir until sugar is dissolved.

3. Add the ginger pieces to the saucepan, and bring to a boil.

4. Reduce the heat to a simmer and cook for 30 minutes, keeping the saucepan partially uncovered so steam can escape.

5. Strain the ginger mixture and save the syrup in a canning jar.

6. Place the ginger pieces on a rack or dehydrating tray for 1 hour to condition, until they are sticky but not wet.

7. Toss the pieces in the remaining ¼ cup sugar until they are lightly coated. You can skip this part and cut down on the sugar content; they will still taste sweet from the simple syrup.

8. Place ginger slices on the dehydrator tray and dry at 135°F for 4 to 6 hours or until the pieces are pliable but not sticky inside.

Ginger Syrup

You can create a ginger syrup 3 times, with the same ginger root, without changing the taste of the ginger. Once you save the syrup, return the ginger root to the pan, add another 4 cups water and 2 cups sugar and simmer for another 30 minutes. Here are 5 ways you can use ginger simple syrup:

1. Add to warm tea in place of sweetener

2. Pour over pancakes or waffles

3. Top your ice cream

4. Use in salad dressing

5. Bake with winter squash

Oatmeal Fig Cookies

Fig and oatmeal just naturally go together. Use your favorite recipe and add fruit or use this timeless classic.

Yield: 2 dozen cookies   Prep time: 10 minutes, plus 1 hour chill time   Cook time: 12 to 14 minutes

1½ cups all-purpose flour

1 teaspoon baking powder

½ teaspoon salt

3 cups old-fashioned rolled oats (for a softer cookie, process half the oats in a blender until finely ground)

1 cup butter, softened to room temperature

1 cup packed brown sugar

½ cup granulated sugar

2 eggs

1 teaspoon vanilla extract

1 cup rehydrated figs, cut into pieces

1. Preheat oven to 350°F. Line baking sheets with parchment paper.

2. In a large bowl, whisk the flour, baking powder, and salt. Stir in the oats.

3. In another large bowl, cream the butter and sugars with a hand mixer. Add the eggs and vanilla, then cream again.

4. Add the flour mixture to the liquid, then stir until combined. Stir in the rehydrated fig pieces.

5. Chill the dough for 1 hour or overnight.

6. Place tablespoon-sized scoops onto the baking sheets, spacing cookies 2 inches apart. Bake for 12 to 14 minutes, until cookies are lightly browned.

Conversions

COMMON CONVERSIONS

1 gallon = 4 quarts = 8 pints = 16 cups = 128 fluid ounces = 3.8 liters
1 quart = 2 pints = 4 cups = 32 ounces = .95 liter
1 pint = 2 cups = 16 ounces = 480 ml
1 cup = 8 ounces = 240 ml
¼ cup = 4 tablespoons = 12 teaspoons = 2 ounces = 60 ml
1 tablespoon = 3 teaspoons = ½ fluid ounce = 15 ml

VOLUME

US	US equivalent	Metric
1 tablespoon (3 teaspoons)	½ fluid ounce	15 milliliters
¼ cup	2 fluid ounces	60 milliliters
⅓ cup	3 fluid ounces	90 milliliters
½ cup	4 fluid ounces	120 milliliters
⅔ cup	5 fluid ounces	150 milliliters
¾ cup	6 fluid ounces	180 milliliters
1 cup	8 fluid ounces	240 milliliters
2 cups	16 fluid ounces	480 milliliters

WEIGHT

US	Metric
½ ounce	15 grams
1 ounce	30 grams
2 ounces	60 grams
¼ pound	115 grams
⅓ pound	150 grams
½ pound	225 grams
¾ pound	350 grams
1 pound	450 grams

TEMPERATURE

Fahrenheit (°F)	Celsius (°C)
100°F	38°C
110°F	43°C
125°F	52°C
130°F	55°C
135°F	57°C
140°F	60°C
150°F	65°C
175°F	80°C
200°F	95°C
225°F	110°C
250°F	120°C
275°F	135°C
300°F	150°C
325°F	160°C
350°F	175°C
375°F	190°C
400°F	205°C
425°F	220°C
450°F	235°C
475°F	245°C
500°F	260°C